ANTHROPOLOGICAL PAPERS OF
THE UNIVERSITY OF ARIZONA
NUMBER 31

FORT BOWIE
MATERIAL CULTURE

ROBERT M. HERSKOVITZ

THE UNIVERSITY OF ARIZONA PRESS
TUCSON, ARIZONA
1978

About the Author...

ROBERT M. HERSKOVITZ completed his undergraduate work at Hofstra University and received his M.A. in anthropology from the University of Arizona. He has done archaeological fieldwork in Arizona, California, and New Mexico, and he prepared the Fort Bowie report while serving as Archaeologist with the Arizona State Museum. In 1975 he assumed the position of Preservator at the Arizona Historical Society, Tucson.

THE UNIVERSITY OF ARIZONA PRESS

I.S.B.N. 0-8165-0563-2
L.C. No. 78-6607

Library of Congress Cataloging in Publication Data

Herskovitz, Robert M
    Fort Bowie material culture.
    (Anthropological papers of the University of
Arizona; no. 31)
    Bibliography: p.
    Includes index.
    1. Fort Bowie National Historic Site. I. Title.
II. Series: Arizona. University. Anthropological
papers; no. 31.
F819.F6H47 979.1'53 78-6607
ISBN 0-8165-0563-2

CONTENTS

FIGURES

TABLES

ACKNOWLEDGMENTS

As with all projects of such size and scope, the Fort Bowie artifact analysis and final report reflect the contributions not only of the author, but of many helpful people. While space does not permit me to thank every individual who assisted, I wish to acknowledge a number of people to whom I am particularly indebted.

I want to express special thanks to James E. Ayres, Arizona State Museum, who, as Principal Investigator, organized and directed the project and assisted in the preparation of this report. I also appreciate the support of Raymond H. Thompson, who, as Director of the Arizona State Museum, helped guide the report through to publication.

The artifact analysis was carried out under Contract 494P20999 with the National Park Service, which also contributed funds toward the publication of this report. I would like to thank several individuals within the Park Service for their cooperation and interest. These include Keith Anderson, Don P. Morris, Bill Hoy, Gordon Chappell, and John Bancroft, as well as John B. Clonts, who provided the faunal and butchering analysis that is incorporated into Chapter 7. I would further like to thank Gordon Chappell for taking the time to read and critically review the manuscript.

Thanks are due to Alan Ferg, who prepared the analysis of the bird bone. In connection with the analysis, Kenneth Neveln provided access to the National Park Service comparative faunal collection at the Western Archeological Center, Tucson; Charmion McKusick identified and commented on the domestic turkey bones; and Amadeo M. Rea helped with the use of his collection and by commenting on a draft of the analysis report.

I am grateful to several individuals for the illustrations that accompany the report. Helga Teiwes produced the majority of the photographs, while A. Clifford Pollack produced the illustrations of the glass, the line work reproductions, and Figures 47, 52, 66, and 67. Jeannette Ruth Schloss drew the map of Fort Bowie, and the line drawings in Figures 2, 3, 16, 47, 52, and 56 are the work of Marc Severson.

I would like to thank several individuals who made available private libraries that were invaluable to the research undertaken. They are Arthur Woodward of Patagonia, Arizona, and Gordon Cox of W. C. Cox and Company, Tucson. John Gilchriese of Americana Unlimited, Tucson, also assisted in the use of Mr. Cox's library. I also want to thank James E. Ayres for making available his collection of trade catalogs and other pertinent material.

I would like to thank Barbara Kranichfeld for her efforts, especially during the period when she served as my assistant on the project. I am also very grateful to William Liesenbein, whose expertise immeasurably enhanced the completeness of the information and identifications in the chapter on ceramics. John Olsen and Jeffrey Riegel provided the translations of Chinese that are included in the report, and Lisa Washbon Huckell performed the shell identifications. Walter Birkby performed the analysis of the hair samples that were recovered and provided the X-ray that made possible the identification of the 1865 Spencer firearm action. Stanley J. Olsen contributed helpful comments on the chapter on faunal analysis.

I am grateful to the following individuals, most of them students at the University of Arizona, who collectively volunteered several hundred hours of their time to work on this project: Elaine Freed, Carl Halbirt, Bruce Huckell, Paula Kavanaugh, Nancy Kays, W. Bruce Masse, David McLeod, and Kerry Tiller. Kay Devner and Norman Tessman provided needed assistance with their knowledge of historic bottles, and Gerald Kelso assisted in the identification of the early ammunition and weapons parts.

I would also like to acknowledge the cooperation and interest of the staff of the Arizona Historical Society. Sidney Brinckerhoff and Jay Van Orden were of great assistance, particularly in the identification of the military artifacts.

Special thanks are also due to Barbara Fregoso, who typed this manuscript in several draft versions; to Gail Hershberger, who painstakingly edited the manuscript; and to the University of Arizona Press, which has undertaken its publication.

Finally, I want to thank my wife, Lana, for her constant support and encouragement. Her efforts and understanding were greatly appreciated throughout.

ROBERT M. HERSKOVITZ

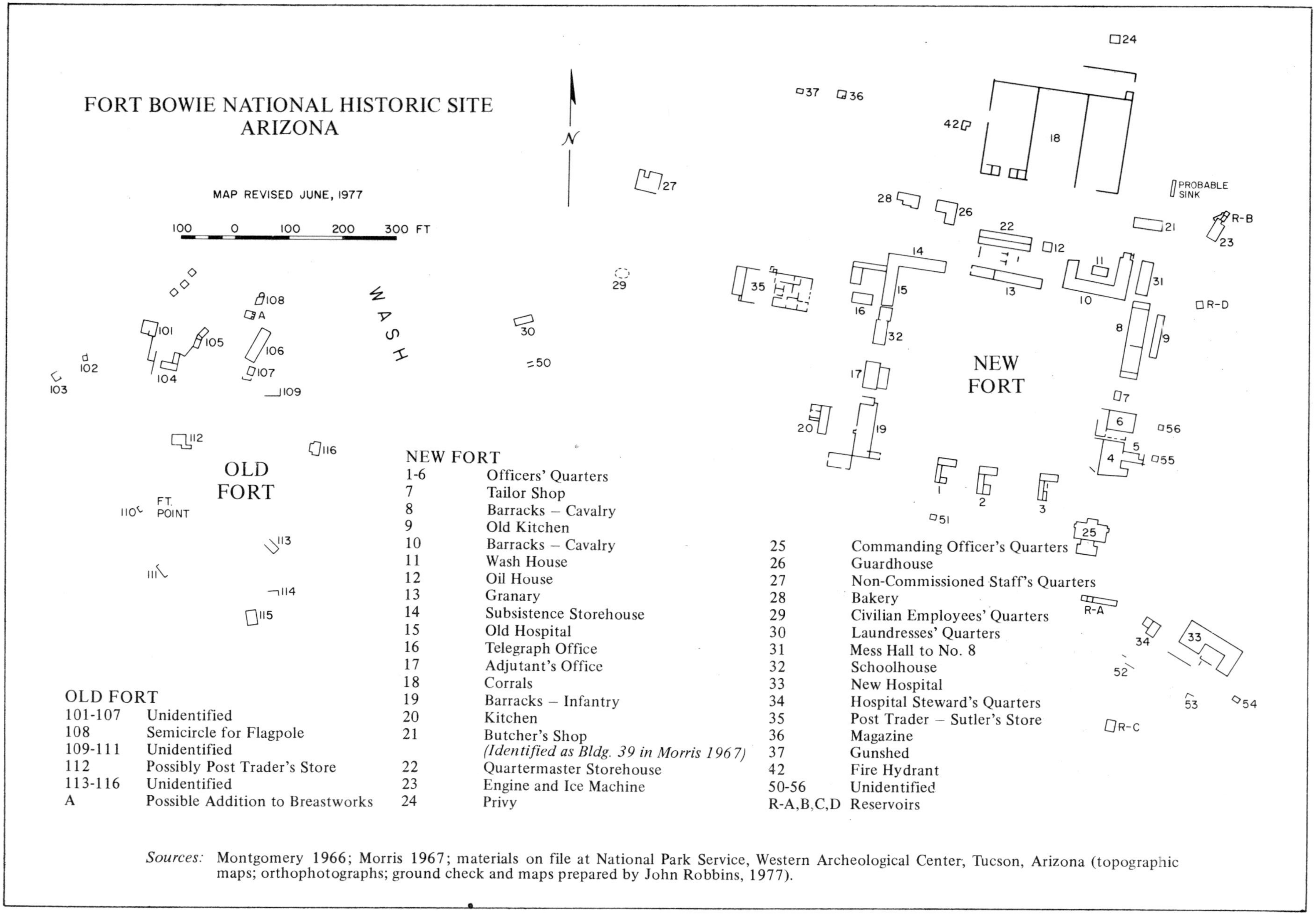

FORT BOWIE NATIONAL HISTORIC SITE ARIZONA

MAP REVISED JUNE, 1977

100 0 100 200 300 FT

WASH

N

OLD FORT

NEW FORT

FT. POINT

PROBABLE SINK

NEW FORT

1-6	Officers' Quarters
7	Tailor Shop
8	Barracks – Cavalry
9	Old Kitchen
10	Barracks – Cavalry
11	Wash House
12	Oil House
13	Granary
14	Subsistence Storehouse
15	Old Hospital
16	Telegraph Office
17	Adjutant's Office
18	Corrals
19	Barracks – Infantry
20	Kitchen
21	Butcher's Shop *(Identified as Bldg. 39 in Morris 1967)*
22	Quartermaster Storehouse
23	Engine and Ice Machine
24	Privy
25	Commanding Officer's Quarters
26	Guardhouse
27	Non-Commissioned Staff's Quarters
28	Bakery
29	Civilian Employees' Quarters
30	Laundresses' Quarters
31	Mess Hall to No. 8
32	Schoolhouse
33	New Hospital
34	Hospital Steward's Quarters
35	Post Trader – Sutler's Store
36	Magazine
37	Gunshed
42	Quartermaster Storehouse
50-56	Engine and Ice Machine
R-A,B,C,D	Privy

OLD FORT

101-107	Unidentified
108	Semicircle for Flagpole
109-111	Unidentified
112	Possibly Post Trader's Store
113-116	Unidentified
A	Possible Addition to Breastworks

Sources: Montgomery 1966; Morris 1967; materials on file at National Park Service, Western Archeological Center, Tucson, Arizona (topographic maps; orthophotographs; ground check and maps prepared by John Robbins, 1977).

Fig. 1a. Map of Fort Bowie.

Fig. 1b. View of the old fort in 1867–68, facing west. Running left to right in the foreground is the wash separating the old fort from the new fort.

Fig. 1c. View of the new fort in 1894, facing southeast. In the left foreground are the corrals (see Fig. 1a, Bldg. 18). The two-story building in the center background is the commanding officer's quarters (Bldg. 25). Under construction in the foreground is the bakery (Bldg. 28). Note cattle in the corral, tents on the parade ground, and soldiers at the flagpole.

1. INTRODUCTION

Fort Bowie, a 19th-century U.S. Army post in Apache Pass, the dividing point between the Dos Cabezas and Chiricahua mountains in Arizona, played a distinctive role in the settlement of southern Arizona. It served as one of the major command posts from which the Army conducted its campaigns against Cochise, Geronimo, and the Chiricahua Apache tribe from the 1860s through the 1880s.

The prominence of the post is attributable primarily to its strategic location. Apache Pass was convenient and frequently was used by travelers on their way to California. More important, the presence of several springs in and around the pass made it one of the few reliable watering holes for many miles. For these reasons, Apache Pass was also the location of one of the way-stations for the Butterfield Overland Mail route from 1858 to 1861. The popularity of the pass was appreciated by the Apache, and it was dreaded by travelers as the site of numerous ambushes and depradations.

One event that occurred in Apache Pass prior to the founding of Fort Bowie, but had great significance later, was the so-called Bascom Affair of February 1861. This incident involved Lieutenant George Bascom's futile attempt to obtain the release of a stepson and some livestock of rancher Johnny Ward, captured by the Apache in a raid on Ward's ranch in October 1860. Bascom's first move was to arrest Cochise and several Apaches who were with him. Some question has arisen as to Cochise's involvement in the kidnapping; it has been suggested that the Coyotero rather than the Chiricahua Apaches were responsible. Many of the specifics of the incidents that followed are confused, but the ultimate result was the escape of Cochise, the hanging of six Apaches, and failure to obtain the release of Mickey Free, Ward's stepson. This incident so enraged and embittered Cochise that it started a war between the Apaches and the Anglo community that lasted until 1872.

Fort Bowie was officially founded on July 28, 1862, following the Battle of Apache Pass, July 15-16, 1861, when the Chiricahua Apache ambushed a contingent of the California Volunteers who were engaged in maneuvers against Confederate forces in Arizona. Under orders of Brigadier General James Carleton, commander of the California Volunteers, 100 men of the 5th California Volunteer Infantry occupied Apache Pass on July 28 and immediately began construction of Camp Bowie. What began as a series of stone breastworks enclosing a number of tents eventually developed into a post comprising 16 stone and adobe buildings, including a sutler's store.

The first fort proved inadequate for a variety of reasons, and in February 1868 construction of a new, second fort was initiated just east of the first location. It was during the occupation of this second fort that most of the major events of the later Apache campaigns occurred. It was in 1872 that the peace with Cochise was negotiated and the Chiricahua Reservation established, with its agency located in Apache Pass next to Fort Bowie. The fort served as the main base from which Brigadier General George Crook's campaigns against the Apache were conducted during the period 1881 through 1886. It was also the headquarters for Brigadier General Nelson A. Miles' campaign after he relieved Crook in April 1886, and it was to Fort Bowie that Geronimo and the remnants of his band were brought following his final surrender on September 4, 1886. On September 8, the prisoners were moved from the fort to the railroad at Bowie Station, where they began their journey to captivity in Florida.

With Geronimo's surrender, the major hostilities between the Apache and the Army came to an end. However, occasional small raids and skirmishes went on for several years, and the continuing wariness of settlers in the area, together with successful lobbying by local civilian suppliers to the Army, kept the fort open. Finally, on October 17, 1894, the last troops were withdrawn and Fort Bowie ceased to be an active military post.

Much has been written about Fort Bowie and its history. The preceding historical sketch is intended merely to provide some perspective within which the artifactual material collected may be viewed. For more detailed accounts, the reader is referred to Richard Murray's thesis, *The History of Fort Bowie* (1951), Robert Utley's *Historical Report on Fort Bowie, Arizona* (1962), and Richard Mulligan's article, "Apache Pass and Old Fort Bowie" (1965).

Fort Bowie was designated a National Historic Site on August 31, 1964. Prior to opening the site to the public, the National Park Service undertook stabilization activities in 1967 and 1968. Under the supervision of Don P. Morris, the surface of both the old and new forts (Fig. 1) was cleared of vegetation, debris, and artifactual material. The remains of 43 adobe and masonry structures at the new fort, 16 at the old fort, and what was believed to be the Butterfield Stage Station were stabilized to prevent further deterioration. (The identification of the latter building, which is about 1/8 mile from the new fort, beyond the area shown in Figure 1, has since been questioned.) This work entailed installation of drainage systems within structures, as well as reinforcement and capping of standing walls. A detailed description of that work is presented in the stabilization reports (Morris 1967, 1968).

Other work undertaken at the site included the excavation of four test trenches in the trash dump of the second fort, located north of the northeast corner of the fort. This action was an emergency salvage measure instituted to obtain a sample of material from the dump. At the time, the trash dump was the location proposed for an entrance road and a visitor center parking area, construction of which was understood to be imminent.

It was within this context of stabilization and emergency salvage that 17,000 artifacts were recovered. Although sizable, this collection is only a partial, unsystematic sample, and it is not exhaustive either for the entire site or for any specific location that was examined. Provenience control was not maintained with the same accuracy or precision that would have been utilized had the project been conceived as an archaeological excavation, proceeding after the development of a detailed and deductive research design. While the provenience of some material was recorded in terms of both building and room, much of it was marked only by building or was merely designated "surface."

These factors placed certain restraints upon the analysis of the artifacts, which was undertaken some four years after the fieldwork was completed. Neither a spatial nor a provenience analysis could profitably be carried out. However, the artifact collection has great value and importance because of its size and diversity and the time period that it represents. The collection includes more than 12,000 specimens of glass, metal, ceramic, leather, rubber, wood, shell, and bone, as well as more than 4,700 faunal specimens, mainly the remains of butchered domesticated animals. This material, more than 95 percent of which was identified, reflects both the military and the civilian aspects of late 19th century life at a U.S. Army outpost.

Identification of the material was a difficult and time-consuming task, owing to the fact that there have been very few published comprehensive reports dealing with material culture of this time period. Consequently, the primary objectives of this work have been: (1) to identify and describe the material culture, and (2) to present the data in such a manner that they can serve as an aid and guide for the identification of historic artifacts from sites of a similar time period. It is also hoped that this descriptive analysis will be of value in further archaeological research at the post, by making it possible for investigators to devote more research time to interpretation than to identification and description.

In order to accomplish these goals, a combination of two systems of classification has been utilized to organize the material for this report. The initial categorization of the collection is made in terms of material – glass, metal, ceramic, and so on. Within these major categories, whenever practical, the subdivisions are made along functional or cultural lines, such as "alcoholic beverage bottles," "arms and ammunition," and "kitchen and table wares." While function was used as the primary classification scheme by Clonts (1971) in his excellent preliminary report on a portion of the collection, it proved to be too cumbersome as the primary organizational approach for an identification guide encompassing the entire collection. It is hoped, however, that the use of the functional classifications as a secondary system will help to provide the reader with some perspective on the life of a 19th century frontier military post. Included in the comprehensive index are entries for specific objects, such as buttons and marbles, that were made from more than one type of material and are thus described in more than one location.

Because many of the Fort Bowie artifacts are illustrated or described in published catalogs of the 19th century (now becoming increasingly available in reprint editions), measurements in this report are generally given in standard U.S. units (inches, ounces, pints, and so on) rather than in the metric units ordinarily used in archaeological reports. Decimal fractions and metric measurements are used when finer distinctions are required.

The legible portions of embossed, molded, and incised legends and inscriptions on the artifacts are enclosed within single quotation marks. A dash denotes the presence of an illegible portion. Missing and illegible portions that can be supplied are enclosed in brackets. A slash mark indicates a break in an inscription that appears on more than one line. The capitalization of letters follows the form of the original legend.

2. GLASS

As a category, the 2,501 whole and fragmentary glass artifacts are the third largest group of materials recovered. Bottles alone constitute 86.5 percent of this number; however, the remainder include a variety of other glass items: stoppers, jar lids, pressed and cut glass objects, lamp shades and chimneys, window panes, a small mirror, buttons, beads, marbles, an artificial gem, insulators, medicine droppers, syringe parts, and glass tubing and rod.

An attempt has been made to standardize the terminology used to describe color. Flint is the term used in the catalogs of the period to describe clear glass, and this term has been retained. Sun-colored amethyst (SCA) is merely flint glass that has been discolored to a shade of amethyst as a result of the sun's action upon the manganese in the glass. Four other shades of blue, three of brown, and four of green are used. Table 1 gives their approximate equivalent from a standard reference, *Munsell Book of Color* (Munsell 1965).

TABLE 1

Glass Color Names and Munsell Equivalents

Color Name	Hue	Value/Chroma
Light blue	7.5 BG	8/2
Medium blue	7.5 BG	4/8 - 4/10
Dark blue	5 PB	3/6
Deep blue-green	5 BG	4/4
Light brown	5 YR	5/8
Medium brown	10 R	4/8
Dark brown	7.5 R	2/2
Light green	10 GY	9/2
Medium green	7.5 GY	6/10
Dark green	2.5 GY	4/4
Very dark green	2.5 G	2/2

Source: Hue and Value/Chroma determinations based on
Munsell 1965.

BOTTLES

The bottles reported in this chapter number 2,164, but this figure does not include every fragment recovered. Rather, it is the minimum number of individual bottles in the collection. This total was derived by counting whole and partial bottles as well as those fragments discernible as representing a single, discrete bottle. Primarily these fragments are bases, although in some cases body fragments were counted. Body fragments with no embossing, label, or neck finish were not counted, since it would have been virtually impossible to avoid counting the same bottle more than once. Bases rather than neck finishes were chosen for establishing the minimum number of bottles because they are more numerous – an indication of their greater durability.

The bottles have been divided into eight categories: Non-Alcoholic Beverages, Alcoholic Beverages, Proprietary Medicines, Chemicals and Medicinals, Household and Personal, Foodstuffs, Fruit Jars, and Bottles of Undetermined Contents. These categories are mostly self-explanatory and attempt to make divisions on the basis of the intended use of the contents. It was the contents, after all, that were the original criteria used by the consumer in making his selection. Occasionally, an item or group of items could have been included in more than one category – bitters and Jamaica ginger, for example, are included with proprietary medicines because they were sold as such, although not infrequently they served as alcoholic beverages. The fruit jars are not included with Foodstuffs and are a separate subcategory as a matter of convention.

The terminology for bottle shapes and neck finishes has been derived from several sources. The catalogs for Whitall, Tatum and Company (Pyne Press 1971) and the Illinois Glass Company (Century House 1965) were prime resources. Nelson and Hurley (1967) were consulted for ink bottle shapes and terminology. Figure 2 shows the most commonly mentioned shapes.

"Neck finish," or more commonly, "finish," refers to "the addition of a collar or band of glass to the neck of a bottle at or near the lip of the orifice, or, the manipulation of the molten glass at the neck terminus of a bottle to produce a finished effect" (Switzer 1974: 7). Fourteen bottle finishes and their variants are illustrated in Figure 3, in slightly idealized form. Most of the bottles recorded at Fort Bowie were hand or tool finished; the club sauce, screw, and crown finishes found were produced in molds.

All measurements for bottles are reported in terms of volume. A customer in a store presumably made a selection between two or more quantities of a given product on the basis of volume, not the height, width, or diameter of a bottle. Volume, therefore, is considered the most relevant dimensional statistic when discussing bottles.

Fig. 2. Bottle Shapes

Not to scale

a. Beer	*k.* Fluted prescription	*u.* Plain oval	*ee.* Square ring peppersauce
b. Champagne	*l.* Pomade/morphine	*v.* Vial	*ff.* French barrel mustard
c. Case	*m.* Panel	*w.* Oval castor oil	*gg.* Round horseradish
d. Jo Jo flask	*n.* Ball neck panel	*x.* Club sauce	*hh.* Florida water
e. Shoofly flask	*o.* Baltimore oval	*y.* Olive oil	*ii.* Oval polish
f. Union oval flask	*p.* Union oval	*z.* Olive bottle	*jj.* Snuff jar
g. Picnic flask	*q.* Philadelphia oval	*aa.* Eclipse olive oil	*kk.* Carmine ink
h. Soda water	*r.* Blake	*bb.* American square pickle	*ll.* Conical ink
i. Packing	*s.* Oblong tooth powder	*cc.* Octagonal peppersauce/spice	*mm.* Round ink
j. Round prescription	*t.* French square	*dd.* Gothic peppersauce	*nn.* Igloo ink

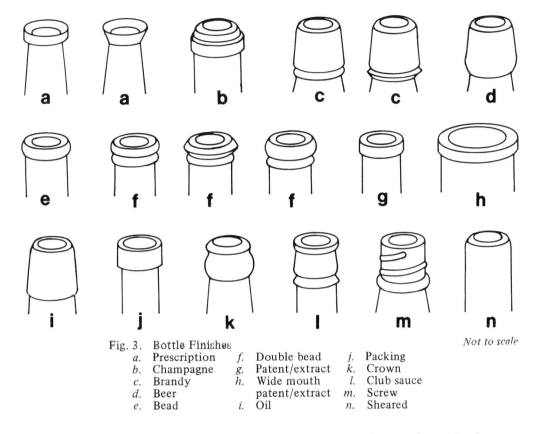

Fig. 3. Bottle Finishes

a.	Prescription	*f.*	Double bead	*j.*	Packing
b.	Champagne	*g.*	Patent/extract	*k.*	Crown
c.	Brandy	*h.*	Wide mouth	*l.*	Club sauce
d.	Beer		patent/extract	*m.*	Screw
e.	Bead	*i.*	Oil	*n.*	Sheared

Not to scale

There are a number of sources dealing with the history of bottles and their manufacture in greater detail than is possible here. Toulouse (1969a) has written a two-part article entitled "A Primer on Mold Seams," which is quite informative. *American Glass* (McKearin and McKearin 1941) is a standard reference, and *A Close-up of Closures* (Lief n.d.) is a brief, but good, starting place for that subject. Lorrain (1968) has also written an informative article on 19th-century American glass.

Non-Alcoholic Beverages

Forty-three bottles are identifiable as having contained a non-alcoholic beverage. The largest number of these are round-bottomed bottles (Fig. 2 *h*) bearing the embossed lettering 'Ross's Belfast.' This product was soda water imported from Ireland. There were 28 of these bottles, and although they all held 10 oz., are light green, and have an applied beer finish (Fig. 3 *d*), they are not identical. Five of them have numerical basemarks: '1,' '2,' '103,' and '933.' Additional distinctions can be made from the manner of the embossing. There are three styles of apostrophes used in spelling the name 'Ross's': one is a triangle, another is a curved line similar to a reversed letter *c*, and the third is the sign commonly used to denote the planet Venus or the female sex: ♀. It was not possible to determine whether the differences observed in the apostrophes indicate anything other than that more than one mold was used to produce the bottles.

Domestically manufactured soda or pop was also present at Fort Bowie. There are eight bottles that bear the remnants of paper labels belonging to an unidentified Lordsburg, New Mexico, company. The legend 'Chas. App– and Co.' is all that can be discerned of the firm's name. It was possible to distinguish four of the firm's products: strawberry soda (Fig. 4 *a*), sarsaparilla, sarsaparilla with iron (Fig. 4 *b*), and orange cider (Fig. 4 *c*). Of the eight bottles, seven are beer type with a capacity of 24 to 26 oz. (Fig. 2 *a*), and the eighth is a dark green champagne type that held 24 oz. (Fig. 2 *b*). Basemarks on four of the bottles indicate manufacture by at least two firms – Streator Bottle and Glass Company, and one as yet unidentified, 'B.G. Co.' The four other bottles have no basemark. The bottling of soda in these containers, rather than in the more usual soda bottles of the period, almost certainly indicates reutilization of the bottles.

In addition to soda pop, root beer was present, in the form of a concentrate. It is represented at Fort Bowie by one light green base and body fragment of what may have been a French square shape (Fig. 2 *t*). The body bears the legend 'Improved/Root Beer.' This is part of a trademark, "Hires Improved Root Beer," registered on April 1, 1879, by Charles E. Hires of Philadelphia (USPO 1879b: 466). The exact date for the inception of the sale of this concentrate was not determined, although it was obviously before March 7, 1879, the date on which the patent application was filed. The concentrate began to be replaced around 1900 by the liquid carbonated form with which we are familiar today (Devner 1968: 45).

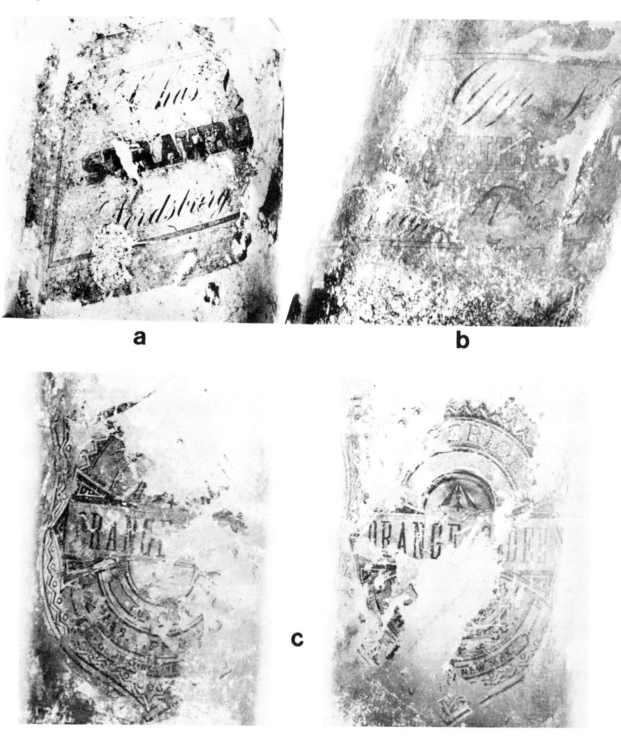

Fig. 4. Soda Pop Labels
  a. Strawberry pop
  b. Sarsaparilla with iron
  c. Orange cider

Width of *a:* 3 in.

A third non-alcoholic beverage consumed at Fort Bowie was mineral water. This is evidenced by the fragments of seven medium green colored bottles of the Congress Spring Company, Saratoga, New York. An illustration in Munsey (1970: 107) is quite similar to at least some of these bottles, and is dated around 1870-1880. It shows a large 'C' on the side of the bottle, encircled by the firm's name and location. A full-page advertisement in the Van Schaack, Stevenson and Reid catalog (1874: 275) notes that "Every genuine Bottle of Congress Water has a large 'C' raised on the glass"; the name of the firm, however, is given as the Congress Empire Spring Company. For those who may be unfamiliar with the product, the ad states quite succinctly that it is "... the best of all the Saratoga Waters for the use of persons of Constipated Habit."

Alcoholic Beverages

Bottles that originally contained some sort of alcoholic beverage outnumbered those in every other category. Such beverages included beer, stout, champagne, wine, and liquor (whiskey and kümmel). Products like bitters and Jamaica ginger are not considered alcoholic beverages per se, although their alcoholic content by volume might warrant such a categorization. They were sold ostensibly as proprietary medicines and therefore have been included in that category.

Beer

Within the category of alcoholic beverages, beer bottles, totaling 1,634, are by far the most numerous. This figure does not include the beer-type bottles with soda labels discussed in the previous section. The beer bottles in this section are predominantly brown, although some are light blue or light green. The finishes are either what has been termed beer type (Fig. 3 *d*), frequently called "blob-top" by bottle collectors, or brandy type (Fig. 3 *c*). These finishes each have a ridge or bulge designed so that the wire holding a cork stopper in place could be fastened securely. The manner in which the wire was fastened is illustrated in Figure 5 *a*. The capacity of all of these bottles is what has been referred to as a "short quart," or approximately 24 to 26 oz. No pint beer bottles were recovered at Fort Bowie.

The beer bottles recovered are summarized in Table 2. It is organized with the basemarks in alphabetical order, followed by numerical and abstract-symbol basemarks, and finally plain bases. Discounting the plain bases, those with single dots, and those with either a single circle or multiple concentric circles, 95 different basemarks were recorded. Of these, 32 have been attributed tentatively or positively to 29 manufacturers.

The dates given are generally the years during which the company was in existence, not just the years in which the basemark was used, although in many cases these dates are identical. It should be kept in mind that prior to 1873, beer was distributed exclusively in barrels and kegs. Beginning in that year, the use of pasteurization made the bottling of beer

possible. Anheuser, the first company to apply the process, began its bottling operation at this time (Krebs 1953: 24-5).

The 'BG C̲O̲' basemark is not identified by Toulouse (1971). Jones, however, offers two possibilities. One, the Bushwick Glass Company, apparently dates to about 1860. An 1892 listing in the National Bottlers Gazette notes: "Bushwick Glass Works, William Brookfield, 83 Fulton Street, New York, Manufacturer of Bottles, carboys, battery jars, insulators . . ." (Jones 1968: 10). The second possibility, the Belleville Glass Company, was incorporated February 3, 1882, and officially opened for business September 1, 1882, with general offices in St. Louis. The company apparently went into receivership on June 25, 1886, and seven days later it was purchased by Adolphus Busch (Jones 1968: 11).

The mark 'FHGW' is the subject of some speculation. It has been identified by Toulouse (1971: 20) as Frederick Hampson Glass Works, Lancastershire, England. He has dated the specimens he has seen to about 1880-1900, certainly not earlier than 1870, on the basis of the manufacturing technology that they exhibit. Jones (1968: 17) attributes the mark to F. Hitchins Glass Works, the successor to the Lockport Glass Works, New York. Hitchins bought out the other three original partners of Lockport sometime between 1850 and 1860 and ran the company until 1872, when it was purchased by Alonzo J. Mansfield (McKearin and McKearin 1941: 194).

Holt Glass Works, West Berkeley, California, is tentatively identified as the firm responsible for three beers with 'H' on the base. Toulouse (1971: 231-2) indicates that a number is usually present beneath the 'H' on these bottles, which were produced between 1893 and 1906.

'IG C̲O̲' is a mark that may belong to one of two firms. Ihmsen Glass Company's use of this mark may date from either 1855 or 1879 (Toulouse 1971: 263-4). The other possibility is the Illinois Glass Company, Alton, Illinois, which operated from 1873 until 1929. Toulouse (1971: 264) dates this mark about 1880-1900. Jones (1968: 17) prefers the former of these two possibilities.

In the case of 'L.G. Co.,' Toulouse and Jones again differ in their opinions as to the companies represented. Toulouse (1971: 23) believes that this is the mark of the Louisville Kentucky Glass Company. It was used around 1880 on hand-finished beer bottles. Jones is less positive, stating that the mark might have represented any of several glass companies: Leathe, Louisville, Libby, Lancaster, or Lockport (Jones 1968: 18).

Missouri Glass Company, St. Louis, is Jones' identification for 'MG Co.' This firm, not listed by Toulouse, existed continuously from 1859 to 1911, according to Jones (1968: 19). Toulouse attributes this mark to the Modes Glass Company, Cicero, Indiana (Toulouse 1971: 360-1), an identification unlikely for the Fort Bowie specimens because the Modes Company was in existence only between 1895 and 1904; the fort had been abandoned one year before the firm was established.

TABLE 2

Glass Beer Bottles

Basemark	Quantity	Mold Designations	Bottle Manufacturer	Dates
A	6			
ABG Co.	12	1,2,3,6,7,10		
A&DHC	21	2,3,4,6,7,8,9	Alexander & David H. Chambers, Pittsburgh	Post-1865-1866+
A G W L	9	1,2	American Glass Works, Pittsburgh	1865-ca. 1880
B	2			
BG Cº	25	1,3,4,H,I,T,X,1 dot, 2 dots	Belleville Glass Co., Belleville, Ill., or Bushwick Glass Co., Brooklyn, N.Y.	
BiXby	1			
C & Cº	1	12	Cunninghams & Co., Pittsburgh	1879-1907
C & Co LIM	40	0,1,2,3,4,6,7,8,11,13		
C B	5	2,K1263,K4175		Ca. 1870-1880
cCcº	69	1,A,D,E,H,I,K,L; 2 dots	Carl Conrad Co., St. Louis	1876-1883
CCG Co	22	3,5,7,8,10,11,13,14,21	Cream City Glass Co., Milwaukee	1888-1894
C & I	5		Cunningham & Ihmsen, Pittsburgh	1865-1879
C/MILW	7	1,2,3	Chase Valley Glass Co., Milwaukee	1880
C.S. & Cº	1	408	Cannington Shaw & Co., Lancaster, England	1875-1913
C.V.Cº / Nº 2/MILW	25	1,4,5,6,Γ,8,T	Chase Valley Glass Co., No. 2, Milwaukee	1880-1881
D	6			
D.Cº	1			
DOC	49	2,3,4,5,6,7,10,11,12,17,18, 21,23,A,G,S	Dominec O. Cunningham, Pittsburgh	1882-1937
D.S.G. Co	49	8,19,39,G,H,J	DeSteiger Glass Co., La Salle, Ill.	Ca. 1879-1896
E	3			
F	1			
F.B.C.	5	5,6		
F.B. Cº	9	1,2,3		
F.G.G. Co	1			
F G Mfg Cº	1			
FHGW	129	1-8,10,12-19,21,22,24,29,31, 33,35-38,40,43,44,55,89	Frederick Hampson Glass Works, Lancastershire, England, or F. Hitchins Glass Works, Lockport, N.Y.	
G	4			
◇G◇	1			
GW	1			
H	3		Holt Glass Works, W. Berkeley, Cal.	1893-1906
HH	2			
H. Heye	129		H. Heye, Bremen and Hamburg, Germany	
I	1			
IGC	6	B,H,3+	Ihmsen Glass Co., Pittsburgh,	Ca. 1870-1895
IG Cº	3		or Illinois Glass Co., Alton, Ill.	1873-1929
I.G.CO. L.	4	11,12,13		
IGO	1	1		
JN	1			
K	1			
KYGW CO	2		Kentucky Glass Works Co., Louisville	1849-1855+
L	1			
L.G. Co.	75	2-6,10,15-19,21,23-28, 1 dot, 2 dots, A-C	Louisville Kentucky Glass Co.	
M	80	1-8		
M/Pat 85	2	7		Patented 1885?
M+	4			

TABLE 2

(continued)

Basemark	Quantity	Mold Designations	Bottle Manufacturer	Dates
MA	11			
MB	5			
MC	3			
McG	1	1		
MD	4			
A MG	2			
MG Co	26	1,2,4-9,11,12	Missouri Glass Co., St. Louis, or Modes Glass Co., Cicero, Ind.	
A MG Co	11	2,4,6,8	Missouri Glass Co., St. Louis	
+ MG C$\underline{o}$	17	2,4,5,6,12		
MGW	22	2-4,6-8		
MGW/PAT 85	1		Same as M/Pat 85?	Patented 1885?
M.J.H. Co.	1			
NB	2			
P	1			
R & Co R & Co.	176	1,3,10 13,18,22 23,35-46, 52-55,57,58,A,B,C,E,L	Ripley & Co., Birmingham, Pa.	
R&Co/PAT 85	7	14,15,17,18	Ripley & Co., Birmingham, Pa.	Patented 1885?
R Ⓒ B	2	3795		
S.K & Co	1			
S. McKee & Co	15	1,2,3,5,7,8	S. McKee & Co., Pittsburgh	1836-1886+
S. McKee & Co. Pitts. PA	1			
SB&G C$\underline{o}$	86	1,3,5-13,16,19,20,25,26, 28-35,D-F,H,J,O	Streator Bottle & Glass Co., Streator, Ill.	1881-1905
T	2			
W	1			
Whitney Glass Works/ Glassboro, N.J.	1		Whitney Glass Works, Glassboro, N.J.	1887-1918
W.M^c & Co.	1		William McCulley & Co., Pittsburgh	1841-ca. 1886
WG C$\underline{o}$/MILW	16	Q,R,S,U,V		
WIS G Co/MILW	69	A,D-H,K-S,9,11,14,16, 19-21,23,27	Wisconsin Glass Co., Milwaukee	1881-1885
WIS Glass C$\underline{o}$/MILW	24	11,18,19,33-35,37,38,40,M		
X	6			

Basemark	Quantity	Basemark	Quantity	Basemark	Quantity
1	10	7	6	25	1
2	6	8	8	44	1
3	5	9	6	48	2
4	6	10	4	933	1
⨆	1	11	1	...	1
5	6	12	6	⋈	2
6	4	12oZ	2	plain	251

Ripley and Company is the firm Jones (1968: 24) believes used the mark 'R & Co.' Daniel C. Ripley established a factory in 1866 with three other partners. In 1872 he left that firm and opened a company of his own. The firm functioned at least as late as 1892, as evidenced by an 'R & Co.'

bottle with a crown finish – an innovation made that year. While many collectors apparently believe that the 'R & Co.' mark on beer bottles indicates Roth and Company of San Francisco, Toulouse (1971: 439) disagrees. He feels that the shape of the beer bottles is wrong for Roth, a whiskey and

Fig. 5. Glass Bottles
    a. Beer bottle finishes
    b. Hartt's Herbal Rock Rye and Barley
    c. Gilka
    d. Chesebrough Pomade
    e. Chesebrough Vaseline

    f. Valentine's Meat Juice
    g. St. Jakobs Oel
    h. 'U.S.A. HOSP DEPT'
    i. Chinese pill

Height of *i:* 2-5/8 in.

liquor dealer from 1879 to 1888. He lists the mark as "Maker and User Unknown."

Considering the number of bottles recovered and the 32 basemarks either definitely or tentatively identified, it is something of a surprise to find that only three brewers of the beer that went into these bottles are identifiable.

The firm of Mayle and Gamm is represented in the collection by a single bottle. It has the basemark 'A & D H C,' and has the following legend embossed on its side: 'MAYLE & GAMM/ NIAGRA [*sic*] FALLS N.Y./ "EXPORT BEER"/ BOTTLING WORKS.' Information regarding this company's history could not be found. The bottle was manufactured between 1873 and about 1886 by Alexander and David H. Chambers, Pittsburgh (Toulouse 1971: 37-8).

The Joseph Schlitz Brewing Company is identifiable from four bottles bearing the remnants of its paper labels. Two of these have the 'R & Co.' basemark, one has 'MC' on its base, and one is plain. The firm was founded in 1849 by August Krug (Baron 1962: 211). Schlitz assumed control in 1856 upon the death of Krug. "The bottling department established by the Schlitz Company in 1877 was conducted through an exclusive arrangement by Voechting, Shape & Co." (Baron 1962: 211). The date on which this agreement terminated is not known. From 1872 to 1892, Schlitz was one of the four most important western shippers of beer (Cochran 1948: 71).

Anheuser-Busch is represented at the fort by more bottles than any other brewery. Seven bottles were recovered with fragments of paper labels identifying the contents as Anheuser-Busch beer. Three of these bottles have no basemark, and each of the remaining bottles has one of the following marks: 'ABG Co.'; 'FHGW'; 'L.G. Co.'; 'MG.' In addition, there were 69 bottles with the 'CCCO' monogram of Carl Conrad Company, a firm that produced and bottled beer for Anheuser. The Anheuser-Busch company had its origin in the Bavarian Brewery of Urban and Hammer, which went bankrupt in 1857 after two years of operation. Eberhard Anheuser was the major creditor and became sole owner through purchase of the remaining interests. Anheuser brought his son-in-law into the business in 1865, and by 1873 Busch was a full partner. The name of the company was changed to E. Anheuser Company's Brewing Association; the firm was incorporated in Missouri under this name on July 7, 1875. On April 29, 1879, the name was changed once again, this time to Anheuser-Busch Brewing Association. This name lasted for 30 years, until November 27, 1919, when Anheuser-Busch, Incorporated, was adopted. This sequence of company names and dates is given by Krebs (1953: 17-20, 427).

Liquor

In addition to beer bottles, there were 108 other glass alcoholic beverage bottles recovered. Essentially they fall into four subcategories, as shown in Table 3: liquor, champagne, wine, and stout. The term "liquor" has been used for bottles of undetermined specific contents, which are grouped on the basis of their shape, volume, and color.

One bottle that held bourbon was identified on the basis of the embossing on the recovered body fragment. A published drawing (Silva and Silva 1967: 11), clearly shows the Fort Bowie specimen to have been Choice Old Cabinet Kentucky Bourbon. It was handled by Crane, Hastings and Company, San Francisco, sole agent. Wilson and Wilson (1968: 47) report that the firm, established in 1875 by Byron G. Crane and Everett L. Hastings, was in operation until 1895. They were also the agents for Copper Distilled Cedar Valley Kentucky Bourbon.

J. A. Gilka, Berlin, was the manufacturer of a liqueur called kümmel (Ferraro and Ferraro 1964: 45-6). Part of one bottle was recovered (Fig. 5 *c*). It has the name '—A. Gilka.' embossed on one of its eight sides. On another is the crest, which has been noted in the recessed base of some of these bottles. Jensen and Jensen (1967: [52]) report that these bottles held one quart.

One nearly complete picnic flask was recovered; it bears the following embossing: 'HARTT'S/HERBAL/ROCK. RYE/AND/BARLEY./IXL/HK&FBT&CO' (Fig. 5 *b*). This is apparently the product of H. K. and F. B. Thurber and Company, New York, who also manufactured some of the extracts and Jamaica ginger recovered at Fort Bowie. No information pertaining to Hartt's was located, and it is conceivable that it was something other than whiskey, since Thurber and Company was not known as a distiller.

Champagne

The 49 specimens identified as champagne bottles present a problem. While they all have the traditional champagne kickup (concavity in the base), champagne finish, and general shape (Figs. 2 *b*, 3 *b*), all but one lack a legible label. This fragmentary bottle has the remnants of a blue and white paper label with part of a word, 'DEDO–.' The identification of champagne as the contents has been made on the basis of form, disregarding the possibility that these bottles may have been refilled with other products. R. Wilson (In press) has noted the presence of champagne bottles in quantity at other military posts of the period, specifically Fort Union, New Mexico, and Fort Laramie, Wyoming.

Wine

The wine bottles have been identified on the basis of size, shape, and color (Table 3), since none of these specimens bore labels.

Stout

Guinness's stout was distributed in bottles as early as 1870, according to Jones (1963b: [10]). Six round, dark green Guinness bottles were recovered, one of which has part of a paper label remaining. It appears to be very similar, if not identical, to a label illustrated in Colcleaser (1967: 89) that reads in part: 'Guinness's Extra Stout/E. & J. Bourke/

TABLE 3

Glass Alcoholic Beverage Bottles (Excluding Beer)

Contents	Shape	Volume (Ounces)	Color	Finish	Quantity
Bourbon	Beer		Light brown		1
Kümmel	Octagonal		Medium brown		1
Liquor	Flask	12	Light brown	Double ring	1
Liquor	Flask		Light brown	Double ring	1
Liquor	Jo-Jo flask		Flint	Double ring	2
Liquor	Picnic flask	5	Flint	Double ring	1
Liquor	Picnic flask		Flint	Double ring	1
Liquor	Shoofly flask	5	SCA	Double ring	1
Liquor	Shoofly flask	14	Light brown	Double ring	2
Liquor	Union oval flask	12	Light brown	Double ring	2
Liquor	Union oval flask	14½	Light brown	Double ring	6
Liquor	Union oval flask	14½	Medium brown	Double ring	3
Liquor	Union oval flask	31	Light brown	Double ring	1
Liquor	Union oval flask		Light brown	Double ring	5
Rye	Picnic flask	12	Flint	Double ring	1
Champagne	Champagne	12	Dark green	Champagne	20
Champagne	Champagne	28	Dark green	Champagne	6
Champagne	Champagne		Dark green	Champagne	23
Wine	Round wine	24	Light blue	Beer	4
Wine	Round wine	24	Dark green	Packer	1
Wine	Round wine	25	Light green	Deep ring	1
Wine	Round wine	25	Dark green		1
Wine	Round wine	35	Dark green	Packer	3
Wine	Round wine		Dark green		8
Stout		12	Dark green	Beer	6
Unknown	Round	24	Very dark green	Brandy	2
Unknown	Round	25?	Medium brown		1
Unknown	Round	25?	Very dark green		3

Dublin.' Bourke was but one of 24 companies that bottled Guinness and Bass stout for export (Jones 1963b: [9]). Guinness's Dublin Stout, Barclay's, and Byass's stout in the 1874 price list and catalog of Van Schaack, Stevenson and Reid (1874: 75) all sold in pints for $2.75 per dozen.

Unknown

The bottles listed in Table 3 with contents "Unknown" are believed to have contained an alcoholic beverage, again on the basis of form. Two of the very dark green bottles thought to have contained 25 oz. have the basemark 'AB & CO,' and a third has 'S & LC.' Little else can be said about them.

Proprietary Medicines

Those bottles that originally contained proprietary medicines are quite informative. They provide a fascinating insight into 19th-century notions of health and of sickness, both real and imagined. More than 20 manufacturers and nearly as many different products are represented in the Fort

Bowie materials. These 43 bottles are listed with summary descriptions in Table 4.

The ingredients of these preparations frequently included extracts, gums, and tinctures derived from plants with narcotic properties. While certain products may have been recommended by medical doctors in some cases, most purchases were evidently prompted by self-diagnosis and treatment. This practice was encouraged by heavy advertising on the part of the manufacturers, whose extravagant claims for cures were as yet unrestrained by any governmental regulations. The alcoholic and narcotic content of these preparations was often incredibly high by today's standards (Young 1961, 1967), and it has been noted that proprietary medicines and bitters were also used as substitutes for more orthodox alcoholic beverages. This led, not infrequently, to alcoholism and drug addiction on the part of the imbibers, who had little or no awareness of what was transpiring. Arthur J. Cramp, who wrote exposés of quackery and nostrums in the early part of this century, is cited by Holbrook (1959:

TABLE 4

Glass Proprietary Medicine Bottles

Manufacturer	Product	Volume (Ounces)	Shape	Finish	Color	Quantity
J. C. Ayer Co.	Cherry Pectoral				Light blue	1
J. C. Ayer Co.	Sarsaparilla				Light blue	3
F. Brown	Jamaica Ginger	4	Oval castor oil	Patent/extract	Light blue	1
Butler & Claridge	Rheumatic Remedy	5 drams	Panel, 3 sides	Prescription	Flint	1
Callan	Brazilian Gum		French square		Light blue	1
Chamberlain Medicine Co.	Cure for Consumption(?)	4½(?)			Light blue	1
Chamberlain Medicine Co.	Curacoa Bitters		Panel, 3 sides		Medium brown	1
Chesebrough Mfg. Co.	Vaseline	¾	Ointment box		White ("opal")	2
Chesebrough Mfg. Co.	Vaseline	2½	Ointment box		White ("opal")	1
Chesebrough Mfg. Co.	Vaseline	2½	Pomade	Ring	Flint	1
Perry Davis	Vegetable Pain Killer	1	Panel, 4 sides		Light green	1
Evans Chemical Co.	Big G	5	Philadelphia oval	Prescription	Flint	1
J. Folger & Co.	Jamaica Ginger	3	Oval castor oil	Oil	Light green	1
Lewis Hess	Damiana Bitters	11			Light green	1
C. I. Hood Co.	Sarsaparilla		Panel(?)		Light blue	2
Jonathan Kidd	American Worm Specific	½	Vial		Light green	1
Dr. J. G. B. Siegert & Son	Angostura Bitters	8	Modified beer	Brandy	Very dark green	4
Thurber	Jamaica Ginger	1¾	Oval castor oil		Light green	1
D. Dodge Tomlinson	H.H.H. Horse Medicine	6	Panel, 4 sides		Light green	1
Valentine Meat Juice Co.	Valentine's Meat Juice	2	Pear shaped	Prescription	Light brown	3
Vogeler & Co.	St. Jakobs Oel	3½	Vial	Double bead	Light blue	1
Wm. R. Warner		2(?)			Medium green	1
Wm. R. Warner		3	French square	Patent/extract	Flint	1
Weeks & Potter	Cuticura System	14	French square	Oil	Light blue	3
'–ud's/druggist'			Blake	Prescription	Flint	1
Unknown	Jamaica Ginger(?)	2	Oval castor oil		Light green	4
Unknown	Jamaica Ginger(?)	4	Oval castor oil		Light green	3

50) as having praised the J. C. Ayer Company for printing on the label of its sarsaparilla the percentage of heroin that it contained (this information is not given on the company's trade cards, however). Perry Davis Vegetable Painkiller contained both alcohol and opium as major ingredients (Holbrook 1959: 153). St. Jacobs Oil also contained tincture of opium. Tomlinson's H. H. H. Horse Medicine, on the other hand, contained no narcotics, but was 52.3 percent alcohol (Cramp 1912: 559). Hood's Sarsaparilla was mild by comparison, with only 18 percent alcohol, according to Adams (1906: 21).

The J. C. Ayer Company of Lowell, Massachusetts, is represented by bottles from its two top products. Ayer's Cherry Pectoral was the company's first product; it appeared in bottles around 1847, but it was apparently first sold some four years earlier (Wilson and Wilson 1971: 105). An advertisement for Cherry Pectoral states that it "cures colds, coughs, and all diseases of the throat and lungs" (Fike 1966: 22). These claims are extremely modest when compared to those made for Ayer's Sarsaparilla. A trade card in the collections of the Arizona State Museum, Tucson, claims that

. . . Ayer's Sarsaparilla produces rapid and complete cures of Scrofula, Erysipelas, Salt Rheum, Tetter, Scald Head, Ring Worm, Sores, Boils, Humors, Pimples, Ulcers, Tumors, Eruptions, and all scrofulous diseases and conditions.

. . . always relieves and often cures Liver Complaints, Female weaknesses and Irregularities, Rheumatism, Neuralgia, Jaundice, Dyspepsia, Emaciation and General Debility.

Holbrook (1959: 49) states that the "alleged formula of Ayer's Sarsaparilla" consisted of fluid extract of the following: sarsaparilla (3 oz.), stillingia (3 oz.), yellow dock (2 oz.), may apple (2 oz.); also, sugar (1 oz.), iodide of potassium (90 gm), and iodide of iron (10 gm). Adams (1906: 21) states, however, that Ayer's Sarsaparilla was 26 percent alcohol "according to an official state analysis." Cramp (1912:

617), in a book published by the American Medical Association, stated that another product, Ayer's Compound Concentrated Extract of Sarsaparilla, consisted of 53.3 percent glycerin, no alcohol, and 3.4 gm potassium iodide per fluid ounce. The price for both of these Ayer preparations was the same. The 1874 catalog of Van Schaack, Stevenson and Reid lists both products as costing $1.00 per bottle retail and $7.85 per dozen wholesale. A portion of a catalog of the same company published in 1882 gives the same retail price, but a wholesale price of $7.75 (Fike 1965: 35).

F. Brown's Essence of Jamaica Ginger is one of several brands of Jamaica ginger found at Fort Bowie. Like bitters, Jamaica ginger had a high alcoholic content and was apparently used as a beverage as much as for any medicinal value. Whatever the brand, it was sold in virtually the same shape bottle. The Illinois Glass Company catalog (Century House 1965) lists the oval castor oil bottle (Fig. 2 w) in five sizes: 2, 2½, 3, 4, and 6 oz. An advertisement for Fred Brown's Jamaica Ginger (Colcleaser 1967: 82) claimed that the firm was established in 1822 and that the product was useful in cases of cramps and colic. Frederick Brown, Sr., of Philadelphia, patented his product in 1858, and, according to the Wilsons, "it is believed that the brand outsold all others combined for at least 30 years before 1900" (Wilson and Wilson 1971: 108).

Butler and Claridge, pharmacists of Washington, D.C., produced a medicine called Rheumatic Remedy. The label on the one specimen found claims that it treats "rheumatic, gout and neural" and gives the dosage as "15 to 20 drops four times a day in a wine glass." Since this bottle held but 5 drams, it was almost certainly a sample distributed by the manufacturer, a common practice with proprietary medicine firms of the late 19th century. The only information found concerning this firm is that James A. Butler and James A. Claridge were listed as druggists in *Boyd's Directory of the District of Columbia* (Boyd 1889, 1894) from 1889 through at least 1894, the year in which Fort Bowie was abandoned.

Even less was discovered about Callan's World Renowned Brazilian Gum. Only a portion of this French square bottle was found, but enough remained of the product name for it to be located in a list from Thompson's *Bitters Bottles* (1947: 83). No other reference to this product has been located, and no bottle manufacturer could be identified for the basemark, a 'G' within a diamond.

The Chamberlain Medicine Company of Des Moines, Iowa, is represented by fragments from the bottles of two of their products. The first was not positively identified but is probably their Cure for Consumption. This bottle, which Wilson and Wilson (1971: 28) date to about 1890, appears to be the only one of Chamberlain's that had the company name and location on the larger panel, rather than on the smaller side panel. The company, which started in Marion, Iowa, in 1879 and moved to Des Moines about one year later, also produced Von Hopf's Curacoa Bitters, of which there is one partial specimen from Fort Bowie (Thompson 1947:

63; Devner 1968: 97). Wilson and Wilson (1971: 110) date the inception of this product to about 1882.

Vaseline, or petroleum jelly, was marketed by the Chesebrough Manufacturing Company in at least two different types of containers. The flint colored pomade jar with a ring finish (Fig. 5 d) held 2½ oz., a popular size. The ointment boxes (Fig. 5 e) are of "opal glass" (a period term for white glass) and were made in several sizes. The Whitall, Tatum catalog for 1880 (Pyne Press 1971: 25), for example, lists ½, 1, and 2 oz. sizes. The earliest possible date for these containers is 1859. This is the year in which Robert A. Chesebrough discovered the medicinal properties of the jelly and introduced it to the public, according to Jones (1963a: [13]). Wilson and Wilson (1971: 110) give approximately 1887 as the date for the earliest retail sales in bottles and tin cans, previous sales having been wholesale in large-volume containers. Although the term "Vaseline" undoubtedly was used much earlier, it was not until 1878 that it was registered as a trademark (USPO 1878b: 871). Trademark patent #6,041 was granted for "the arbitrarily selected word 'Vaseline'" to the Chesebrough Manufacturing Company as a trademark for an "Emollient and Remedial Preparation of Petroleum" (USPO 1878b: 811). In any case, by 1892 retail sales were apparently large and the products quite varied. A Marshall Field and Company catalog (1892-3) lists nine distinct Vaseline preparations sold variously in 1, 2, and 5 oz. bottles as well as ½, 1, and 5 lb. cans.

Perry Davis Vegetable Pain Killer was invented in 1840 and first registered in 1843 (Devner 1964: 42). An advertisement in Van Schaack, Stevenson and Reid (1874: 349) advised that "Pain Killer" was an effective remedy for ". . . Bruises, Cuts, Burns . . . Dysentery or Cholera or any sort of Bowel Complaint . . . Coughs, Colds, Canker, Asthma and Rheumatic difficulties." Two trade cards in the collections of the Arizona State Museum advise that Pain Killer could be used either internally or externally. One of the cards, written entirely in Spanish, gives a lengthy list of ailments for which Pain Killer was allegedly effective, along with dosages and instructions. It was sold in three sizes – small, medium, and large, at $.25, $.50, and $1.00 retail. Pain Killer contained both of the "active" ingredients frequently used in proprietary medicines of the time – alcohol and opium. Holbrook (1959: 153) gives the formula as follows: gum myrrh 2¼ lb., capsicum 10 oz., gum opium 8 oz., gum benzoin 6 oz., gum fuiaic 3 oz., and alcohol 5 gal. When Perry Davis died in 1862, his son assumed control of the highly successful business and continued to run it until his death in 1880. The firm was finally sold and remained in Providence, Rhode Island, for another 15 years before it was moved to New York (Munsey 1970: 67-8).

The Evans Chemical Company of Cincinnati, Ohio, produced a product called Big G. At one dollar per bottle, Big G was guaranteed to cure several diseases in one to five days (Fike 1966: 17). Fike quotes another ad claiming that "Big G [is] a non-poisonous remedy for gonorrhoea, Gleet,

Spermatorrhoea and Whites." All of this was accomplished with the following ingredients, according to *The Peoples Home Medical Book* (Ritter n.d.: 288): zinc acetate 15 grains, berberine hydrochlorate 15 grains, glycerin 4 drams, and water sufficient to make 8 ounces. The dosage was three injections a day. It is interesting to note that the ad in Fike specifically states "not astringent," although *Dorland's Illustrated Medical Dictionary* lists zinc acetate as an astringent used in treating gonorrhea (Arey and others 1957: 1556).

J. A. Folger Company, San Francisco, marketed at least one proprietary medicine, as well as coffee, spices, and other foodstuffs. A single bottle that originally contained Essence of Jamaica Ginger was found at Fort Bowie; according to Newhall (n.d.: 31), it postdates 1865 – the year in which Marden and Folger went bankrupt and Jim Folger assumed all debts and started on his own as J. A. Folger Company.

According to embossing on the bottles, Lewis Hess was the manufacturer of Baja California Damiana Bitters. Wilson and Wilson (1969: 24) state that "Henry Weyl sold Damiana Bitters for three years before Hess bought the brand in 1876." Another element is introduced by the *Official Gazette of the United States Patent Office* for 1876. On May 16, 1876, William A. Winder and Melville M. Shearer, San Francisco, California, obtained label patent #718 for the title "Baja California Damiana Bitters" (USPO 1876b: 925). One week later, the same two individuals were granted trademark patent #3,713 for Bitters with the "words and letters 'Baja California Damiana Bitters'" (USPO 1876b: 966). On the same day they also obtained another trademark patent, #3,712, which granted them a patent for a bitters with "a picture or representation of an American eagle, perched or standing upon a cactus plant, with a serpent held in its beak" (USPO 1876b: 966). All of these patent dates are clearly evident in the illustration of a Damiana Bitters bottle in *Western Bitters* (Wilson and Wilson 1969: 25). This photograph also shows a patent date of August 1, 1876, printed on the label. On this date Winder and Shearer, their address now given as San Diego, California, were granted patent #180,692 entitled "Composition Beverage" (USPO 1877a: 200). The entry reads as follows: "A composition beverage, consisting of the following ingredients, viz: tincture or fluid extract orange-peel, tincture or fluid extract cardomon-seed, tincture or fluid extract damiana, whiskey or proof spirits and water, substantially as described." As to the product itself, Adams (1906: 21) placed Damiana Bitters in the category of "bracers." These were products that sold largely over the bar, according to Adams, and were equivalent to whiskey and gin.

Although only fragments of two bottles of Hood's Sarsaparilla were identified, it was quite a popular product of the time. An 1894 article in the *Lowell Daily Citizen,* Lowell, Massachusetts, noted that the Hood lab built in 1883 had been enlarged three times by 1893 (Kalbach 1971). According to Coburn (1920: 22), in 1876, "shortly after becoming sole owner, Mr. Hood began the manufacture of his famous Hood's Sarsaparilla."

An undated advertisement claims that Hood's Sarsaparilla "will cure, when in the power of medicine, scrofula, salt rheum, boils, pimples, dyspepsia, headache, biliousness, catarrh, rheumatism, neuralgia," in addition to "that tired feeling, pains in the back, weakness, languor, dyspepsia distress and scrofula" (Fike 1966: 34). All of this was apparently accomplished on the basis of 16 to 21 percent alcoholic content. An analysis by federal chemists reported that Hood's was 16½ percent alcohol mixed with water containing sugar, potassium iodide, and 6.5 percent vegetable extracts that ". . . bore indications of the presence of sarsaparilla, licorice and a laxative drug resembling senna" (Cramp 1921: 596).

A product called Doctor McLane's American Worm Specific is represented at Fort Bowie by just one fairly complete vial. It presents an interesting problem, for it apparently predates 1860 and thus the founding of Fort Bowie itself, in 1862. According to the Wilsons' research, Jonathan Kidd became sole owner of a firm in 1844, "and it's believed that he had bottles embossed for the medicine" a few years later. John and Cochran Fleming "evidently acquired sole rights to McLane's worm medicine in 1860 [and] they renamed it Vermifuge" (Wilson and Wilson 1971: 127). This is at least partially verified by an 1874 listing of Dr. McLane's Celebrated Vermifuge at $.25 and $1.00 (Van Schaack, Stevenson and Reid 1874: 63). There are perhaps two reasonable explanations for the presence of this bottle. Either the vial may have remained on a supplier's shelf for several years before it was actually sold, or someone at Fort Bowie kept the vial long after its initial utilization and reused it as a container for some other substance. What actually transpired will never be known.

The Rumford Chemical Works, East Providence, Rhode Island, were the manufacturers of Horsford's Acid Phosphate. While the product name did not appear in the embossing on the bottle, a patent date of March 10, 1868, did. The *Annual Report of the Commissioner of Patents* shows that two patents were issued to Eben N. Horsford on that date. One of them is entitled "Manufacture of Acid Phosphate to be Used in Food," while the other deals with the "Preparation of Acid Phosphate of Lime" (USPO 1869a: 678). Later patents register the trademark (USPO 1877b: 643) and label (USPO 1878a: 718) of Horsford's Acid Phosphate. The title is quite apt, for the formula in the patent records is 14 parts triassic phosphate of lime to 10 parts sulphuric acid (USPO 1869b: 678). The medication dates some 13 years earlier than the first patents, according to Dennis (1973: 25), and was but one of 19 different products listed on an 1870 company letterhead. A trade card in the collection of the Arizona State Museum proclaims that Horsford's Acid Phosphate when combined in "a delicious drink with water and sugar only" is beneficial in the treatment of "dyspepsia, indigestion, headache, mental and physical exhaustion, nervousness, hysteria, night sweats of consumption, etc."

Johann Gotthes Benjamin Siegert began producing the bitters bearing his name as early as 1842 in Trinidad.

Dr. J. G. B. Siegert and Sons produced an Angostura Bitter that was advertised in an 1883 newspaper not only as an appetizing tonic, "to impart a delicious flavor to a glass of champagne, and all summer drinks," but also as a cure for dyspepsia, diarrhea, fever, ague, and all the disorders of the digestive organs (R. Wilson, In press). Siegert's was considered to be one of the eight main bar bitters, according to one author (Devner 1968: 8).

The firm of H. K. and F. B. Thurber and Company, wholesale druggists and merchants of New York, appears to be the manufacturer of 'Thurbers Pure Ess. Jamaica Ginger,' as the embossing on the bottle identifies it. This was just one of many products the firm either manufactured itself or for which it was an agent. The firm existed at least as early as April 16, 1878, the date on which it received a patent for the "Eureka" trademark (USPO 1878b: 678).

Daniel Dodge Tomlinson's H. H. H. Horse Medicine, a liniment for sprains and bruises, was also recommended for headache, toothache, rheumatism, neuralgia, cramps, and cholera (Devner 1968: 44). Like almost all of the patent medicines of this era, the product had alcohol as its base ingredient – in this case, 52.3 percent. Other ingredients included ammonia, camphor, soap, and salicylic acid (Cramp 1912: 559). H. H. H. Horse Medicine was handled by Williams and Moore of Stockton, California, from 1868 to 1880. In 1880 the partnership was dissolved, with Henry Moore retaining the rights to the product until his retirement in 1898 (Wilson and Wilson 1971: 119). An 1874 advertisement in the Van Schaack, Stevenson and Reid catalog (1874: 307), however, introduces some questions as to the completeness and accuracy of the above account. It announces that Francis and Eldridge of Philadelphia have appointed Van Schaack, Stevenson and Reid as sole western agents for H. H. H. Horse Medicine. The addenda to the price list (Van Schaack, Stevenson and Reid 1874: 73) lists H. H. H. Horse Medicine in two sizes at $1.00 and $.50 retail, with wholesale prices of $7.75 and $4.00 per dozen bottles.

A product with a uniquely shaped bottle was Valentine's Meat Juice (Fig. 5 f). Produced in Richmond, Virginia, beginning in 1871, this preparation was advertised as being beneficial "In all forms of Fever, Extreme Exhaustion, Critical Conditions before and after operations, when other Food Fails to be retained..." (Hill Directory Co. 1925: 204). Although no documentation can be presented here, it has been suggested that prior to the turn of the century, Meat Juice was one of the many cures for "social diseases." Valentine's Preparation Meat Juice is listed in Van Schaack, Stevenson and Reid (1874: 70), selling for $1.25 retail and $10.00 per dozen wholesale. Two years later, trademark patent #3,903 was granted to Mann S. Valentine. It was for "the letter 'V' and the bird's nest resting thereon containing eggs" and was applicable to "Meat-Juice and Compound of Meat-Juice and Glycerine" (USPO 1877a: 167).

Charles A. Vogeler Company, Baltimore, was the manufacturer of St. Jacobs Oil (or St. Jakobs Oel) (Fig. 5 g) from

1882 until after 1900. The original owner was Wilmer Keller, who originated the mixture in 1877, according to Wilson and Wilson (1971: 136). An 1888 newspaper ad modestly proclaims:

> St. Jacobs Oil. The Great German Remedy for Rheumatism, Neuralgia, Sciatica, Lumbago, Backache, Soreness of the Chest, Gout, Quinsy, Sore Throat, Swellings and Sprains, Burns and Scalds, General Bodily Pains, Tooth, Ear and Headache, Frosted Feet and Ears, and all other Pains and Aches. [R. Wilson, In press]

The Pure Food and Drug Act of 1906 obviously had a major effect on the ingredients of St. Jacobs Oil, as it did for so many proprietary medicines. Wilson and Wilson (1971: 136) give Keller's approximate formula as including gum camphor, chloral hydrate, chloroform, sulphate ether, tincture of opium, oils of origanum, sassafras, and alcohol. By 1914, however, an analysis by the Michigan Dairy and Food Department identified the ingredients as consisting of turpentine 81 percent, alcohol 10 percent, and ether 9 percent (Cramp 1936: 185).

The firm of William R. Warner and Company, Philadelphia, is represented by a 3-oz. French square bottle and a fragment of a green base with the Warner name embossed on it. This company dates to 1856 (Devner 1970: 144). It was not possible to determine what the precise content of either bottle had been, but it may have been one of their "Safe" cures.

A large French square bottle of the firm of Andrew G. Weeks and Warren B. Potter, Boston, Massachusetts (later the Potter Drug and Chemical Company) originally held 14 oz. of their Cuticura System of Curing Constitutional Humors. The Cuticura trade mark was registered in 1878 and was applicable simply to "Medicinal Preparation" (USPO 1878b: 774). The manufacturers claimed that their product would cure skin and blood humors, scurvy, ulcers, glandular swellings, and contagious humors with concurrent loss of hair, and would rid one of birthmarks. According to Cramp this was accomplished mostly with water, sugar, and glucose, with a little potassium iodide, alcohol, and extractive (Cramp 1912: 595).

One fragment of a medium brown colored case bottle that was recovered bore the embossed letters '-ied-.' These were found to be part of the word "Schiedam," the name of a town in Holland. Comparison of this fragment with whole bottles indicates that it is probably a part of an Udolpho Wolfe's Aromatic Schnapps bottle. In addition to this bitters, other products originating in or using the name of Schiedam are Vollmers bitters and several brands of gin. For gin, Ferraro and Ferraro (1964: 27-30) mention the firm of J. J. Meder and Zoon, and Blumenstein (1966: 56-7) illustrates a case bottle of Herman Jensen/Schiedam. Schiedam gin is also listed in an 1874 price list of Van Schaack, Stevenson and Reid (1874: 75) at $3.75 per gallon.

Several other bottles believed to have held proprietary medicines are listed as "Unknown" in Table 4. Two oval castor oils, although not marked or embossed, were most likely containers for Essence of Jamaica Ginger. In addition, there is a fragment of one Blake (Fig. 2 *r*) with '–ud's/druggist/ –tal' embossed on it. This probably refers to the manufacturer of the proprietary medicine, perhaps some sort of dental preparation.

Chemicals and Medicinals

The bottles that are known or presumed to have contained chemicals or nonproprietary medicines are listed in Table 5. While the entries are mainly self-explanatory, a number of the specimens do deserve comment. For the most part these are plain, unembossed bottles that were ordered in bulk by pharmacists and hospitals and were used to dispense prescriptions.

One bottle, a packing shape (Fig. 2 *i*) with a patent/ extract finish (Fig. 3 *g*), has the following embossed vertically on its side: 'Mallinckrodt Chemical Works, St. Louis.' The firm was established in 1867 and specialized in substances used by chemists and in medicine, photography, and the arts (Devner 1970: 14). It is not clear what its original name was, but by 1873 it was called G. Mallinckrodt and Company. In 1883 the name was changed to Mallinckrodt Chemical Works, with Edward Mallinckrodt listed as president (Gould 1883). As of 1977 the firm was still doing business under that name.

The other chemical company identified was McKesson and Robbins. It is represented by four identical bottles that have 'McKesson & Robbins New York' embossed in their bases. The embossing is negative or impressed and runs around the circumference of the base. This firm had its origin in 1833 when John McKesson opened a drugstore on Maiden Lane in Manhattan, New York. Six years later he took Daniel Robbins in as a partner (Fortune 1940: 73). In 1862, the year Fort Bowie was founded, the company was listed in the New York City Directory as "McKesson & Robbins, drugs, 91 Fulton and 82 Ann" (Trow 1862: 548).

The one Philadelphia oval included in this section has been so categorized because of a partial label present on two of the pieces of this fragmentary specimen. The label reads in part: 'No..../Direc–.' Across the width of the label below the word 'Direc[tions]' are four dotted lines with space for writing out the instructions. The label had a heading that is almost completely illegible, but it is apparent that this was a pharmacy label. The basemark 'T' is not known to be the specific mark of any one company.

Three 1-quart bottles have 'U.S.A. Med.l Dept. molded on their sides. Four other bottles have 'USA HOSP DEPT' molded within a raised oval-shaped outline. Three of the 'USA HOSP DEPT' bottles are oval shape bottles (Fig. 5 *h*), while the fourth is a prescription shape (Fig. 2 *j*). Chappell (1975: personal communication) has suggested that the distinction between the terms "Hospital Department" and "Medical Department" has temporal significance, with the former dating to the 1860s and 1870s and the latter to the 1880s and 1890s. This hypothesis is based on observations of specimens in private collections and is not yet supported by primary source documentation, either archaeological or bibliographic.

One Chinese pill bottle recovered (Fig. 5 *i*) is similar in size and shape to many examples recovered by the Tucson Urban Renewal Archaeological Project. The specimens recovered in Tucson invariably held a medicinal product of some type, generally in pill form.

Basemarks are present on seven of the round prescription bottles. There are six different makes, as noted under *Embossing* in Table 5. One mark has the letters 'IGCO' within a diamond; Toulouse (1971: 264) identifies it as belonging to the Illinois Glass Company of Alton, Illinois, and dates it to about 1900–1916. This specimen was recovered from Building 3, and if it is not a post-occupation deposit, it would move the initial date for this mark back to at least 1894. A second mark, 'A. G. Co,' is tentatively identified by Toulouse (1971: 39) as belonging to the Arsenal Glass Company, Pittsburgh, which operated from about 1865 to 1868. These dates are possible, although they seem a little early for the level of technology represented by the specimen. The other four basemarks, including the formée cross, are not attributable to any specific company.

Household and Personal

There are 51 bottles and fragments categorized as "Household and Personal" (Table 6), the terms being used in a broad sense. Products such as ink, for example, were not restricted to use in the household. The products used on leather were probably applied to uniform accoutrements, harness, and saddles, so that a narrow use of "household" would again be inadequate. The intent has been to create and use categories that are consistent and that make sense in terms of life at Fort Bowie.

An advertisement in the *American Druggist* (1884) provides the basis for identifying a fragmentary 4-oz. bottle as having contained No. 4 Genuine Eau de Cologne. According to the ad, this product of Johann Maria Farina, Julich Platz No. 4, Cologne-on-the-Rhine, Germany, was imported by Park and Tilford, New York, in their capacity as "sole wholesale agents for the United States"; it was distributed in 2, 4, and 8 oz. bottles, as well as ½ and 1 pt. wicker-covered containers. Other advertisements in the same journal document the fact that at least three firms in Cologne with nearly identical names were manufacturing and marketing colognes having very similar names. Two of these, including the type represented at Fort Bowie, were apparently imitations that were named in order to capitalize on the popularity of the original product, No. 4711 Eau de Cologne.

E. W. Hoyt and Company of Lowell, Massachusetts, were the producers of Hoyt's German Cologne. Developed around 1859, it was initially sold over the counter in Hoyt's drugstore in Lowell (Hill 1884: 61). An increase in the demand for the cologne resulted in part from the distribution

TABLE 5

Glass Chemical and Medicinal Bottles

Shape	Volume (Ounces)	Finish	Color	Embossing	Quantity
Chinese pill			Light green		1
Fluted prescription	4	Patent/extract	Flint		1
Packing	16	Patent/extract	Dark blue		1
Packing	17	Patent/extract	Light blue		2
Packing	17	Patent/extract	Light green	Mallinckrodt Chemical Works, St. Louis	1
Packing	17½	Prescription	Light green		4
Packing	18	Patent/extract	Deep blue-green		2
Packing	19½	Prescription	Medium brown	McKesson & Robbins New York	4
Packing	31½	Double bead	Dark green		1
Packing	32	Patent/extract	Light green	U.S.A. Med.l Dept.	3
Packing	33	Patent/extract	Light green		2
Packing	34½	Patent/extract	Light green		1
Philadelphia oval	4		Flint	Basemark: 'T'	1
Plain oval	½	Wide mouth prescription	Dark blue	USA HOSP DEPT	3
Pomade/morphine	1	Wide mouth patent/extract	Flint		1
Pomade/morphine	1-1/3	Wide mouth patent/extract	Flint		2
Pomade/morphine	1½	Patent/extract	Flint	Reversed '1'	1
Prescription		Patent/extract	Dark blue	USA HOSP DEPT	1
Prescription		Prescription	Flint		1
Round prescription	1 dram	Patent/extract	Light green		1
Round prescription	¼	Patent/extract	Flint		1
Round prescription	1/3	Patent/extract	Light green		2
Round prescription	½	Patent/extract	Light green		1
Round prescription	¾		SCA		1
Round prescription	1	Patent/extract	Flint		1
Round prescription	1	Prescription	Light green		1
Round prescription	1¼	Prescription	SCA		1
Round prescription	1½	Prescription	Flint		3
Round prescription	1½	Ring? Bead?	Flint		1
Round prescription	1½	Wide mouth patent/extract	Flint	1 with basemark: ◇IGCO◇	3
Round prescription	1¾	Prescription	Flint		1
Round prescription	2	Prescription	Flint		1
Round prescription	2	Wide mouth patent/extract	Flint		1
Round prescription	2½	Patent/extract	Flint	Basemark: 'McM'	1
Round prescription	3	Prescription	Flint		1
Round prescription	3	Wide mouth patent/extract	Flint		1
Round prescription	3½	Prescription	Light blue		1
Round prescription	4	Bead	Dark blue		1
Round prescription	4	Wide mouth patent/extract	Light green	Basemark: '2'	1
Round prescription	4½	Prescription	Light blue		1
Round prescription	5	Patent/extract	Flint	Basemark: 'GW'	1
Round prescription	5	Prescription	Light green		1
Round prescription	5½	Wide mouth patent/extract	Light green	Basemark: 'A.G. Co'	1
Round prescription	6	Wide mouth patent/extract	Flint	2 with basemark: ✠	3
Round prescription	7	Wide mouth patent/extract	Light blue		1
Round prescription	12	Patent/extract	Medium brown		1
Round prescription	10	Patent/extract	Deep blue-green		1
Round prescription	16	Patent/extract	Light green		1
Round prescription	18	Wide mouth patent/extract	Flint		1
Round prescription		Prescription	Flint		4
Round prescription		Wide mouth patent/extract	Flint		1
Round prescription			Medium green; light blue		24

TABLE 6

Glass Household and Personal Bottles

Contents	Manufacturer	Volume (Ounces)	Shape	Finish	Color	Quantity
Cologne	Farina	4	Cylindrical panel		Flint	1
Cologne	E. W. Hoyt & Co.	1	Cylindrical panel		Flint	1
Crown dressing	Frank Miller & Son	4	French square	Wide mouth patent/extract	Light green	3
Florida water	Murray & Lanman	2	Florida water	Oil	Light blue	1
Florida water	Murray & Lanman	7	Florida water		Light green	1
Ink	Carter	8	Cylindrical	Patent/extract	Flint	1
Ink	Carter	2½	Cylindrical	Prescription	Flint	2
Ink	Carter	2	Conical ink	Double bead	Light green	1
Ink	Carter	?	Igloo ink	Patent/extract	Flint	1
Ink	Carter	?			Light blue; "straw"	2
Ink	Stafford's	16	Cylindrical	Oil with pour spout	Medium green	1
Ink		2	Conical ink	Bead	Light green; light blue	2
Ink		2	Conical ink	Sheared	Light green	2
Ink		1¼	Carmine ink	Patent/extract	Flint	1
Ink		?	Cylindrical; conical	Double ring; sheared	Light green; flint	6
Japanese Blacking		3	Oval polish	Patent/extract	Light green	1
Mucilage		2½		Sheared	Light green	1
Perfume	Colgate	?	Cylindrical(?)		Flint	1
Perfume	Pinaud	2	Cylindrical	Patent/extract	Flint	1
Perfume		2(?)		Patent/extract	Flint	3
Perfume (?)		2	Cylindrical	Patent/extract	Flint	1
Perfume (?)			Oval panel		SCA	1
Perfume (?)			Oval		SCA	1
Sewing machine oil	Excelsior	4½	Triangular panel		Flint	1
Sewing machine oil		2	Ball neck panel	Prescription	Flint	1
Shoe blacking	Wolff & Randolph		French square	Wide mouth patent/extract	Light green	3
Shoe polish	Whittemore	5	Oval polish	Prescription	Light blue	1
Snuff		7½	Snuff jar	Applied ring	Medium brown	1
Tooth cleanser	Riker		Panel		SCA	1
Tooth cleanser	Hall & Ruckel	2½	Ball neck panel	Patent/extract	Flint	5
Tooth powder		1½	Oblong tooth powder	Wide mouth patent/extract	Flint	1
Unknown cosmetic	Cutex	¾	Rectangular	Patent/extract	Flint	1

of sample vials, which began in the fall of 1867. In January 1872 Hoyt, together with F. B. Shedd, established the firm of E. W. Hoyt and Company. Devner (1970: 55-6) says that the firm manufactured Hoyt's German Cologne until about 1915. German cologne was sold in three sizes – small, medium, and large, at $.25, $.50, and $1.00 – according to excerpts from the 1882 price list of Van Schaack, Stevenson and Company (Fike 1965: 37).

"Crown dressing for ladies shoes, etc." (Trow 1884: 4) was imported by Frank Miller and Sons, New York (Trow 1884: 4); according to their advertisement, the firm was established in 1838. A complete bottle found at Fort Bowie (Fig. 6 *a*) has 'Frank Miller's/Crown/Dressing/New York USA' embossed on one side, with a crown depicted between the words 'Crown' and 'Dressing.' A paper label covers two other sides; the text on one side appears to be in English, and that on the other side is in French and reads in part: 'POU[R] DAMES ET ENFANTS/[B] OTTES ET SOULIERS/S[A] CS DE VOYA[G] E/& – – /PREP– – PAR/FRANK MILLER– / NEW YORK' ("for women and children/boots and shoes/ traveling bags/ . . .").

"Murray & Lanman of No. 69 Water Street, New York, sent their Florida Water to help sweeten the air and hair in the barracks and post boudoirs," according to Woodward (1958: 164) in reference to Fort Union, New Mexico. Florida Water was apparently an all-purpose preparation – an 1892 newspaper advertisement claimed that it was "a most refreshing lotion after exposure to the sun" (R. Wilson, In press). It is interesting to note that the smaller of the two Fort Bowie specimens bears embossing in Spanish, as follows: 'Agua de Florida/Murray Y Lanman/Drougistas/New York.' The same is embossed in English on the 7 oz. specimen.

Fig. 6. Glass Bottles and Stoppers   Diameter of *l*: 1¼ in.

   a. Frank Miller's Crown Dressing   *f.* Van Buskirk's Sozodont
   b. Stafford's Ink   *g.* Durkee's extract
   c. Perfume   *h.* Heinz Horseradish
   d. Perfume   *i.* Glass stopper (peg type)
   e. Excelsior Sewing Machine Oil   *j-l.* Glass stoppers (ground shaft type)

Carter's Inks account for 7 of the 19 ink bottles. The shapes include cylindrical, conical, and igloo type, after the terminology used by Nelson and Hurley (1967), while volumes range from 2 to 8 oz. The company was established in 1858, and in 1869 it was first advertised in the Boston City Directory, listing additional plants in New York and Chicago. From 1872 until 1901 the firm was officially Carter, Dinsmore and Company, and the name was then changed to Carter's Ink Company in 1902 (Nelson and Hurley 1967: 72). Precise dating of these bottles has not been possible, since the embossing, on the side or base, merely reads 'Carter's,' in one case above the number '23.'

Of the remaining 12 ink bottles, only one is identifiable as to company – a 16-oz. Stafford's Ink (Fig. 6 *b*). Background and company history data for the Stafford firm were not located.

A 3-oz. oval polish shaped bottle (Fig. 2 *ii*) was embossed with the words 'Japanese Blacking' on two opposing sides of the bottle. The substance is quite possibly that used in the process referred to as "japanning" or "black japanning." Luscomb (1967: 109) defines the process as a high grade of varnishing in which heat is used for drying between successive coats. It was developed as a substitute for Oriental lacquering and was used on papier-mâché, pewter, wood, brass, and tin buttons. It was also used extensively on cast-iron rim lock cases (see Fig. 22 *a, c*). The possibility also exists that Japanese Blacking was boot or leather blacking and not a varnish. Since no reference has been found to "Japanese blacking" in the literature, no definite conclusion can be made.

One bottle was identified as a mucilage container, on the basis of shape, the bottle being conical with ten sides. It should be noted, however, that ink was sometimes bottled in a container of this size and form.

Perfume is known or strongly suspected as the contents of eight bottles found at Fort Bowie. Colgate and Company, established in 1806 as a soap and candle manufacturer (Devner 1970: 51), is represented by one bottle body fragment. It was identified through comparison with whole specimens recovered during Tucson Urban Renewal excavations and now in the collections of the Arizona State Museum. The precise date when the firm expanded into perfumes is not known, but advertisements for perfume and toilet water date from at least 1877 (Devner 1964: 10).

The firm of Ed. Pinaud, Paris, France, was established in 1812 as a manufacturer of perfumes, and its products were introduced into the United States in 1870 (Devner 1970: 61). Pinaud is represented at Fort Bowie by a single 2-oz. cylindrical bottle with the name embossed on the side.

Several other bottles have been classified as perfume bottles, primarily on the basis of their size and shape. One of these is illustrated in Figure 6 *c*. It is still corked and contains an estimated ½ oz. of an amber-colored liquid. There is a partial label on the neck of this bottle that appears to read 'BEA–'S.' This bottle and the fragments of two other identical specimens bear the basemark 'B37.' Figure 6 *d* illus-

trates another bottle holding 2 oz. that has been classified as a probable perfume bottle.

Sewing machine oil is represented in the artifact collection by two bottles. One is a triangular bottle (Fig. 6 *e*) that bears the embossed legend 'Excelsior/Sewing Machine Oil/New Bedford, Mass.' A bottle listed in Fike (1965: 41) is similar to this specimen, but the location of the firm is given as Chicago, Illinois. 'Sperm Sewing Machine Oil' is embossed on the other bottle in this category. Like the triangular Excelsior bottle, it has an 'N' as its basemark. The ball neck panel is similar in size, shape, and embossing to that of the bottle listed in Fike (1965: 40). The entry in Fike also says "Allen's Put up for Prague Warner & Co.," apparently a quotation from a label. No label was present on the Fort Bowie specimen.

Shoe blacking under the trademark "Acme Blacking" was manufactured by Wolff and Randolph of Philadelphia. Three specimens of this product were recovered. George S. Wolff and Richard W. Randolph began manufacturing Pik-Ron brand blacking about 1880, according to Wilson and Wilson (1971: 132). Wolff is not listed in 1876 in *Gopsill's Philadelphia City Directory* but is listed in 1878 (Gopsill 1878: 1693) as one of the partners of Wolff and Randolph. The precise date of the introduction of Acme brand blacking remains undetermined.

Shoe polish was also present at Fort Bowie. One bottle reads 'Whittemore/Boston/U.S.A.' and has a reversed 'S' basemark. Tibbits (1964: 124) cites Whittemore as having produced shoe polish. *The Boston Directory* (Sampson, Davenport & Co. 1868: 956) lists Whittemore and Bean, 30 Pearl Street. In addition to machinery, inks, and varnishes, the listing advertises dressing and blacking. The designation "oval polish" for this shape of bottle is taken from a 1903 Illinois Glass Company catalog (Century House 1965: 23).

One snuff jar has been identified among the materials recovered at Fort Bowie. It is a mold-blown bottle similar to those illustrated in Munsey (1970: 79, lower right). The base is plain and does not have any of the dots that Ferraro and Ferraro (1964: 66) mention as representing the strength of the snuff in the bottle.

Hall and Ruckel were manufacturing chemists and jobbers in New York, according to Devner (1970: 12), who gives 1867 as the earliest date for which she was able to find a listing. One of their products was Van Buskirk's Fragrant Sozodont, a dentifrice represented at Fort Bowie by a ball neck panel bottle (Fig. 6 *f*). This product came in liquid form, according to the advertisement reproduced by Fike (1966: 14), which also gives 1848 as the date the firm was established. Another advertisement (Colcleaser 1967: 10) proclaims that "Beauty and Fragrance are communicated to the mouth by Sozodont," which renders the "Teeth pearly white, the Gums rosy, and the Breath sweet." Van Schaack, Stevenson and Reid (1874: 70) carried Van Buskirk's in their inventory at $6.25 per dozen bottles wholesale and gave the retail price as $.75 a bottle. The ingredients of this preparation were not determined.

TABLE 7

Glass Foodstuff Bottles

Contents	Manufacturer/Product	Shape	Volume (Ounces)	Finish	Color	Quantity
Condiment		Wide mouth round prescription	18	Bead	Light blue	1
Cranberry	Partial label: 'Refined cranberry'				Flint	1
Extract	Joseph Burnett & Co.	Panel, 2 sides	2	Patent/extract	Flint	2
Extract	E. R. Durkee	Panel, 4 sides	1½	Double bead	Light blue	1
Extract	E. R. Durkee Co.	Panel, 3 or 4 sides	2		Flint	1
Extract	Dr. Price's Delicious	Panel, 3 sides	2	Prescription	Flint	3
Extract	Dr. Price's Special	Panel, 3 sides	2	Patent/extract	Flint	8
Extract	Dr. Price's	Panel, 3 sides	2	Patent/extract	7 Flint; 1 SCA	8
Extract	Thurber	Panel, 3 sides	2	Patent/extract	Flint	2
Extract		Panel, 3 sides	2		Flint	3
Horseradish	H.J. Heinz Co.		4½	Patent/extract	Light green	2
Horseradish		Round horseradish	8	Bead	Light blue	1
Lime juice	L. Rose Co., Ltd.				Light green	2
Mustard	'—outar—'	French barrel mustard		Patent/extract	Flint; SCA	9
Olives			7		Light green	4
Olives		Oval olive bottle	8	Patent/extract	Medium green	1
Olive oil		Eclipse olive oil	16	Patent/extract	Light green	6
Peppersauce		Gothic peppersauce	6	Double bead	Light green	5
Peppersauce		Square ring peppersauce	4		Light blue	3
Pickles		American pickle	18	Bead	Light blue	3
Salad dressing					Flint	1
Spice	'—elli & Co.'	Octagonal spice			Medium green	5
Worcestershire sauce	Lea & Perrins	Club sauce	6	Club sauce	Light green	21
Unidentifiable	E. R. Durkee & Co.				Flint	1

The second dental cleanser identified was Riker's Fragrant American Dentifrice. This preparation, however, is not one of the many products mentioned by Devner (1968: 80-1) in conjunction with the Riker firm. A family business, the company dated from at least 1878 as manufacturing druggists (Devner 1970: 18).

The tooth powder bottle was identified as such on the basis of its basemark, '902.' The 1880 catalog of bottle manufacturer Whitall, Tatum and Company (Pyne Press 1971: 23), lists model number 902 as a 1½-oz. oblong tooth powder with a sprinkler top. Embossing was available with this model but none was present on the recovered specimen.

The remaining bottle in this section is a small flint-colored bottle with the basemark 'CUTEX/J-5.' The glass has a "satin" finish on its exterior and as a result is not entirely transparent. It was not determined whether the 'J-5' in the basemark was a product code. It is presumed that this bottle is a post-occupation deposit.

Foodstuffs

The bottles that contained food products (except for fruit jars) are summarized in Table 7. It is interesting to note that of the 93 bottles in this category, all but 10 contained seasonings and flavorings such as spices, peppersauce, and extracts.

The first bottle on the list was identified as a condiment bottle on the basis of its size, shape, and finish, although neither the specific product nor the manufacturer could be determined. The fragments of another carried a label that read, in part, 'Refined Cranberry,' but it was too incomplete for the manufacturer's name to be ascertained.

Four firms have been identified as having produced extracts used at Fort Bowie. By far the most common extracts were Dr. Price's. Nineteen specimens were recovered representing two of his lines or brands. Those more frequently recovered were Dr. Price's Special Flavoring Extracts, while the others were Dr. Price's Delicious Flavoring Extracts, of which three specimens were identified. It is not clear at this time whether the two brands denoted different levels of quality, or whether the disparity in the frequency of recovery between the two brands has a temporal significance. Although listings were found dating to 1870 in St. Louis city directories, detailing changes in the firm's ownership and title until it emerged in 1873 as Steele and Price (Gould 1870, 1871, 1873), no information concerning product dates was located. Joseph Burnett and Company of Boston, represented by two specimens, was producing vanilla extracts as early as 1845 (Devner 1964: 32). E. R. Durkee and Company, New York (Fig. 6 g), began in the spice and extract business some five years later (Jones 1963b: [34]). The fourth manufacturer of extracts is represented by two bottles with the embossing 'Thurber's Best Extracts/New York.' The firm of H. K. and F. B. Thurber and Company is discussed above under *Proprietary Medicines.*

Horseradish is represented by three bottles, two of them identical and originally containing the product of the H. J. Heinz Company, Pittsburgh. The basemark is 'H 47,' which may well have been a product code. Although much remained of the labels, only parts of the words 'Evaporated Horse Radish' could be distinguished (Fig. 6 h). The company name changed from F. and J. Heinz Company to H. J. Heinz Company, and then to H. J. Heinz and Company. Devner (1964: 17-8) dates the H. J. Heinz Company bottles between 1888 and 1905.

Lime juice produced by L. Rose and Company, Ltd., is represented by fragments of two bottles, easily identified by the distinctive molded floral pattern on the exterior (Blumenstein 1965: 31-2). Devner (1970: 35) lists W. A. Rose & Bro., New York 1899 and 1900, as producers of West Indian Lime Juice and Oil of Lime Syrup. As of 1978 L. Rose and Company still markets lime juice in an embossed bottle similar to the Fort Bowie specimens.

Of the nine examples of mustard bottles, only one had embossing, a fragment reading '– outar– .' It appears to be quite similar to the bottle illustrated in Blumenstein (1965: 137) that reads 'Moutarde Diaphane/Louit Freres & Co.'

The bottles that contained olives are essentially the same shape as the Gulden condiment bottle illustrated in Blumenstein (1965: 121-2). The specific identification was made by comparison with labeled specimens recovered during the Tucson Urban Renewal excavations conducted by the Arizona State Museum. The olive oil bottles were identifiable because of their distinctive shape (Fig. 2 aa) – the "eclipse olive oil" illustrated in Putnam (1965). This is a case in which the bottle shape was virtually identified with a particular commodity.

The same can be said for the peppersauce bottles, three types of which were recovered. Cathedral or gothic peppersauce bottles (Fig. 2 dd) are frequently illustrated in bottle books, and a square-ring or ribbed peppersauce (Fig. 2 ee) is pictured in Blumenstein (1965: 121).

As with olive oil and peppersauce bottles, shape was diagnostic in identifying pickle bottles at Fort Bowie. Three specimens of the style identified as American pickle (Putnam 1965) were recorded (Fig. 2 bb). It is quite probable that many more were represented in the multitude of fragments that were too small to be identified.

Salad dressing produced by a firm located in New York was identified from the remnants of a label on a fragmentary bottle. This bottle was round, constricted below the finish (which is missing), and originally no taller than 7 in.

Spices appear to have been the contents of the five medium green bottles that had beveled edges or corners and concave front and back panels (Fig. 2 cc). Ferraro and Ferraro (1964: 52) note that partial labels found on several such bottles indicated contents of allspice and nutmeg, while a specimen of this type recovered by the Tucson Urban Renewal Archaeological Project had a label reading 'Ground Pepper.' This bottle shape is commonly seen with 'H. W. Hunnewell and Company, Boston' embossed on it; however, none labeled in this manner were found at Fort Bowie. Two partial specimens with embossing were recovered; they held the product of an unidentified San Francisco firm, '–elli & Co.' Another of the five specimens has the numeral '4' as its basemark.

Worcestershire Sauce was obviously extremely popular, as the listing of 21 specimens in Table 7 indicates. All of those recovered have the 'J.D.S.' basemark and 'Lea & Perrins' embossed on the side. The basemark represents John Duncan and Sons, who were the brokers or agents for the firm of Lea and Perrins. The 'J.D.S.' basemark dates these bottles as post-1877, according to Ferraro and Ferraro (1964: 50). Prior to that time, they state, the basemark was 'ACB Co'; one bottle with this mark was actually found at the fort after the analysis of the artifact collection was completed. Mold numbers accompanying the 'J.D.S.' basemark are 1-5, 7, 8, 28, and 34. Stoppers from Lea and Perrins bottles are discussed below.

A flint-colored body fragment was recovered from a bottle that almost definitely contained some sort of foodstuff. It bore the embossed partial inscription 'ERD– & – .' This inscription is quite similar to that on a six-sided peppersauce bottle in *Chips from the Pontil* (Tibbits 1964: Plate 12), which also bears a patent date. *The Official Gazette of the United States Patent Office* for February 17, 1874, shows that design patent #7,181 was granted to Eugene R. Durkee, Brooklyn, for a term of 14 years for a bottle design (USPO 1874b: 176). Although the Fort Bowie specimen is not this type of bottle, its embossing and the patent information suggest that it originally contained a Durkee food product.

Fruit Jars

Although fruit or "Mason" jars are technically not considered bottles, they have been incorporated into this section because of their close functional similarity. The 13 jars and 13 lids recovered at Fort Bowie represent at least six different manufacturers; however, only four of them can be positively identified.

Three jars made by the Hero Glass Works, Philadelphia, have been identified. All of these are fragments, but they are definitely from different vessels. Two of the fragments are partial bases and can be identified as "The Crystal" type on the basis of embossed patent dates, November 26, 1867, and February 4, 1873. The third fragment, a piece from a jar body, has part of the November 26 date. Toulouse (1969b: 82-3) notes that this patent, design patent #2,849, covered the shape of all Hero jars. The patent dated in February was assigned to Salmon B. Rowley, the owner of Hero and the holder of the November 26 patent, and referred to the threads in the jar mold and the making of the lids. Their "Crystal" pattern jar is dated by Toulouse to about 1873-80.

One body fragment was found from a jar manufactured by the Pacific Glass Works, San Francisco. This dates around 1867, according to Toulouse (1969b: 231).

Another San Francisco firm, the San Francisco Glass Works, is represented by a number of objects at Fort Bowie. The remains of seven separate jars made by this firm around 1869-76 have been recovered. These jars are termed "Victory" because of the embossing of that word on the body. The word is surrounded by two patent dates – February 9, 1864, and June 22, 1867 – which refer to the glass lid and metal screw-band seal with which these jars were equipped.

Two other fruit jars were found, but neither of them bears any identifying marks. One, nearly complete but with its base missing, has a screw finish and is 7-5/8 in. high. The second jar is represented by a part of a threaded or screw-type finish (Fig. 3 *m*).

The 13 fruit jars are equaled in number by glass lids or seals – the precursors of the metal seals used in home canning today. One seal of the Consolidated Fruit Jar Company, New York, was found. The company's name and monogram appear on the upper or exterior surface of a milk glass lid. A capital 'P' is embossed in the center of the under side. The 'P' might stand for Payne and Company, mentioned by Toulouse (1969b: 60) in connection with the Consolidated monogram. This firm was part of the Consolidated Glass Company, New Brunswick, New Jersey. No other information was found.

One lid has embossed on it 'Patented/Dexter Approved/August 8, 1865.' This patent deals with a glass lid and metal screw band. The manufacturer may have been the Franklin Flint Glass Company, Philadelphia, which operated from 1861 until 1930 (Toulouse 1971: 91, 120).

Hero Glass Works, the jar manufacturer mentioned above, also produced five of the lids that were recovered. Two styles of lid are present. One bears nine patent dates in the center; these are identified by Toulouse (1969b: 125) as those of Hero patents. The other style bears some of the same patent dates, but only around the circumference of the lid; the center of this second pattern consists of raised dots and pyramids in a circle, surrounding an embossed circle with the letter 'A' in the center. The first of these patterns is dated about 1882-84 by Toulouse (1969b: 125).

One lid has three patent dates embossed around its circumference: January 5, 1875; June 5, 1877; April 25, 1882. All of these patents are associated with the Lightning fruit jar, according to Toulouse (1969b: 404-6). Three firms are listed by Toulouse as having produced Lightning fruit jars: Lyndeboro Glass Company, New Hampshire (1866-86); Hazel Glass Company, Wellsburg, West Virginia, and Washington, Pennsylvania (1886-1902); and Atlas Glass Company, Washington, Pennsylvania (1896-1901).

In addition to the lids for which a manufacturer has been identified, five flint glass lids were recovered that bore no embossing or marks indicative of any particular firm. Three of these lids are identical in size and shape, and one was found with a metal screw band still around it. Only one of the five has turned sun-colored amethyst.

Bottles of Undetermined Contents

The bottles for which no specific product or contents could be determined are summarized in Table 8. It is organized on the basis of bottle shape, using the terminology illustrated in Figure 2. Of the 62 bottles in this category, only four merit any specific mention. One is a 12-oz. Philadelphia oval with the following embossing: 'A. Hamburger & Sons/Peoples Store/Los Angeles.' The earliest reference to this firm was found in the Los Angeles City directory for 1888 (Curran 1888). The proprietors are listed as Asher, Soloman, David, and Moses Hamburger. The store is not listed in 1891, but in 1895, Maxwell (1895: 649) lists for the Peoples Store " . . . dry goods, shoes and boy's clothing, gents furnishing goods, drugs and general outfitters." While the bottle might have contained a medicinal product, there is no real evidence to support such an inference, and it has therefore been included in this category.

Two other bottles are sample vials (Fig. 2 *v*) with embossing. The 2-dram vial has 'W.H. Smith & Co.' on it, while the 2-oz. vial reads 'C.A. Murdock & Co./Kansas City.' Unfortunately, nothing was learned about either of these companies, so that no specific product can be attributed to them.

The last of these four bottles is unique among the Fort Bowie materials. It is a round medium green, bottom portion of a bottle. The diameter of the base is approximately 2 in., and it bears the scar of a 1-in.-diameter bare iron pontil. Portions of an illegible red label with black printing remain on the side. Still discernible is raised embossing that reads, '– ETCHU– /– ALTIMOR– .' Although the specimen probably originated in Baltimore, it is doubtful that the '– ETCHU– ' refers to ketchup, in view of the color and shape of the bottle. More likely, this is part of the name of the manufacturer of the contents.

GLASS STOPPERS

There are two basic types of glass stoppers represented among the 119 stoppers and fragments found at Fort Bowie. They are ground shaft and peg type stoppers. The former type has a shaft that is tapered and ground to fit exactly with the ground opening of the bottle. The peg stopper has a straight, unground shaft that was originally covered with a piece of cork tubing. There are 38 peg stoppers, 37 of which are identical. These are light green, 1¼ in. long, and ½ in. wide. The grasp has the name of the manufacturer of the bottle's contents embossed on its top: 'Lea & Perrins.' The only other peg type stopper is also light green and has the

TABLE 8

Glass Bottles of Undetermined Contents

Shape	Volume (Ounces)	Finish	Color	Basemark	Quantity
Baltimore oval	5	Prescription	Flint	1 with 'R.D. Co.'	2
Baltimore oval	16	Prescription	Flint		1
French square	1	Prescription	Flint	1 with 'C'	2
French square	1½	Prescription	Flint		1
French square	2		Light green		1
French square	2		SCA	Reversed '3'	1
French square	4	Prescription	Flint		1
French square			Light green		7
Indiana oval	2	Prescription	Flint		1
Octagonal			Flint		2
Oil sample vial	½ dram	Patent/extract	Flint		1
Oil sample vial	2 drams	Prescription	Light green		1
Oil sample vial	1	Prescription	Flint		1
Oil sample vial	1¼	Prescription	Flint		3
Oil sample vial	1½	Prescription	Flint		1
Oil sample vial	2	Patent/extract	Flint		1
Panel		Patent/extract	Flint		1
Panel	1½	Patent/extract	Flint	1 with 'B' or 'R'	2
Panel	2	Patent/extract	Light blue		2
Panel	2¼	Patent/extract	Light green		2
Panel			SCA		1
Philadelphia oval	2/3	Prescription	Flint		1
Philadelphia oval	1	Prescription	Flint	'M'	1
Philadelphia oval	1¼	Prescription	Flint	'M'	1
Philadelphia oval	2	1 Prescription	Flint		2
Philadelphia oval	2½	Prescription	Flint	'T'	1
Philadelphia oval	4	Prescription	Flint	1 with 'T,' 1 with 'H'	6
Philadelphia oval	4½	2 Prescription	Flint	2 with 'T,' 1 with 'H'	3
Philadelphia oval	6	Prescription	Flint		2
Philadelphia oval	6		SCA	⋀	1
Philadelphia oval	12	Prescription	Flint		1
Philadelphia oval			Flint	(mark: ENT 25 / 1825)	1
Philadelphia oval			SCA		1
Union oval	2½	Prescription	Flint		2
Union oval			Flint		3
Cylindrical			Medium green		1

same dimensions but is without embossing on the upper surface (Fig. 6 *i*). It does have embossing in the form of raised nodules around the outer edge or perimeter of its disc-shaped grasp. There is a depression 9/16 in. in diameter in the upper side of the grasp.

Stoppers with ground shafts are twice as numerous as peg type stoppers. The 80 whole and partial examples recovered are summarized in Table 9. The most important statistic in the table is probably the maximum shaft diameter. This measurement is generally the same as the opening or mouth of the bottle that held the stopper. There are 16 dif-

ferent styles represented. Ten of these have been given a name and a style number (Table 9) from the Whitall, Tatum catalog for 1880 (Pyne Press 1971: 6). Three of the designations, Carmine, Cologne, and Half Ball, are used by Freeman (1964: 302, 384). There are three ground shaft stoppers that do not appear to match any published description or illustration (Fig. 6 *j-l*). One of these (Fig. 6 *l*) is hollow, with cut or ground decoration on the top and around its circumference; the size and hollow construction clearly set it apart from all of the other stoppers. It is possible that this grasp belonged to a decanter rather than to a bottle.

TABLE 9

Glass Stoppers with Ground Shafts

Style	Style Number	Range of Lengths (Inches)	Maximum Shaft Diameters (Inches)	Color	Quantity
Ball	702	1½-2¼	½; ¾	Flint	5
Carmine		1¼-1¾	½	Flint	2
Chloral	719	1¼	1	Flint	2
Cologne		2½	½	Light blue	1
Flat head	703	1-2½	½; ¾; 1	Flint; SCA; light green	23
Half ball		1½	½; ¾	Flint	3
Lubin	705	1½-1¾	¼; ¾	Flint; light blue; SCA	5
Mushroom salt mouth	709	1¾	1	SCA	1
Mushroom tincture	701	1½-2	¾; 1	Flint; SCA	7
Oblong head	725	1½	¾; 1	Flint	2
Pear	717	2	½	Flint	1
Square head	704	1¼-2	½; ¾; 1	Flint; SCA; dark green	7
Teat carmine	713	1¾	¾	Flint	1
		2	½	Flint	1
Hexagonal		3¼	¾	Flint	1
Spherical			1½	Flint	1
Unidentified fragments			½	Flint; medium brown	2
Unidentified fragments		½-1½	¾	Flint; SCA; light blue; dark blue	10
Unidentified fragments		1	1	Flint; SCA; dark brown; light green	5
Unidentified fragment		¾	1¼	Light green	1

Source: Styles and style numbers from Pyne Press (1971: 6); Freeman (1964: 302, 384).

PRESSED AND CUT GLASS

"Pressed glass" and "press-mold glass" are essentially terms that denote a technique of manufacture. A molten blob or gather of glass is formed to shape in any one of various types of molds (Lorrain 1968). Frequently surface decoration is molded at this time. "Cut glass" is a term used to describe an item that has been decorated by cutting the surface after the piece has been formed either by pressing (as above) or perhaps by free-blowing.

Ninety-six fragments of pressed glass and one of cut glass have been identified. They have been divided into three classes, based on degree of identifiability. Seventy of the pieces are assigned to the first group, consisting of parts of identifiable items – goblet, mug, tumbler, and so on. The second group is composed of pieces of bases, feet, handles, or stems that cannot be assigned to a specific type of object. The remaining 16 pieces are essentially unidentifiable fragments.

In the first group, that of identifiable items, one section of what was probably a coaster was recovered. It is sun-colored amethyst (SCA), with an edge or rim that is 5/8 in. high and was probably 4¼ in. in diameter. The main decorative element is an arrangement of grapes and leaves. This piece represents the only coaster found.

Another unique item in the collection is the footed base to what may have been a creamer. A similar base is pictured in a United States Glass Company catalog for 1904 (Pyne Press 1972b: 155).

Parts of 10 stemmed pressed glass goblets have been identified. One nearly complete specimen (Fig. 7 a) is 5-3/4 in. high and 3¼ in. in maximum diameter. It is very similar, but not identical, to a style called "New York goblet" in a catalog of King, Son and Company, dated about 1870-75 (Pyne Press 1972b: 22). Elsewhere, a similar pattern is termed "New York Honeycomb" (McKearin and McKearin 1941: Plate 208). A portion of another goblet appears quite similar to the style termed "Mitchell D, No. 122" in the King, Son and Company catalog (Pyne Press 1972b: 23). Another goblet fragment resembles "No. 125 cocktails" in the same catalog (Pyne Press 1972b: 22). In addition to these three items, portions from the bowls of three goblets and the stems of four other goblets have been identified. The stems are all of a type with six sides or facets ending in a smooth round ball just above the base.

The single example of cut glass is a fragment from the bowl of a goblet. It is flint glass with a fern design cut into its exterior surface (Fig. 7 b).

Portions of one definite and one probable medicine glass have been identified. Both items have a base diameter of 1-7/8 in. and have thick, weighted bases. One of the specimens is graduated, with tablespoon and teaspoon marks etched into it (Fig. 7 c). It is similar to the glass illustrated in the 1880 catalog of Whitall, Tatum and Company (Pyne Press 1971: 64).

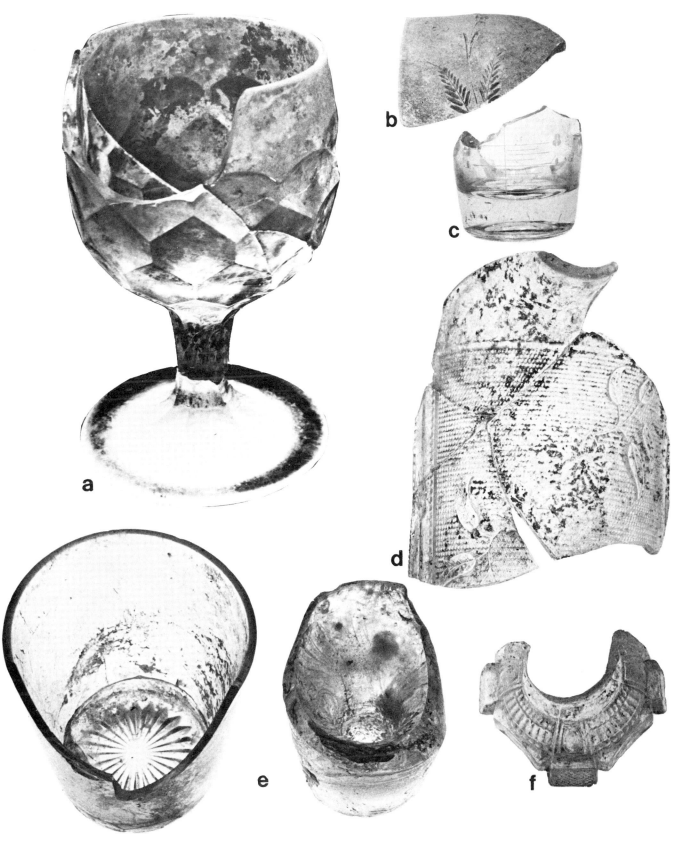

Fig. 7. Pressed Glass
a. Goblet   *c.* Medicine glass   Base diameter of *c:* 1-7/8 in.
b. Cut glass fragment   *d.* Pitcher fragment   *e.* Tumblers
    f. Footed base fragment

The remains of 11 mugs, probably beer mugs, have been recovered and identified. Some of these are round, while others have fluted or faceted sides. All have concave or indented bases, ranging in depth from 5/16 in. to 1¼ in. Those fragments that come from the section of the body beneath the handle invariably have a raised rib or reinforcing about 5/8 in. wide. This rib does not occur above the top of the handle.

One portion of a pressed glass pitcher was found. Most of the spout and a small segment of rim remain, and the raised floral decoration on the patterned background is clearly visible on the body (Fig. 7 *d*). This piece is 5¼ in. high and has a diameter of approximately 4½ in.

A piece survives from an octagonal holloware flint glass vessel that may have been a salt or pepper shaker. The base is 1¼ in. wide, and there is neither etching nor embossing on the parts of sides that remain. The fragment, which is 2-11/16 in. high, allows no estimate of the original height of the vessel.

One object collected appears to be a spout. It is flint glass, 3-3/16 in. long, and tapers from the base to an opening ¼ in. in diameter. This spout appears similar to those of whale oil lamp fillers shown in *American Glass* (McKearin and McKearin 1941: Plates 58A, 60).

Portions of 11 pieces of stemware have been recovered. Eight are bases and the others are stem fragments. One of the bases has a portion of a six-sided stem attached to it. Two others appear similar to the style called "Pearl" in *Pennsylvania Glassware 1870-1904* (Pyne Press 1972b: 23). The diameters of the bases range from 1¾ to 3-1/8 in. The three stem fragments are round and are otherwise undiagnostic.

Tumblers constitute the largest group of artifacts within the pressed glass category. The two major sizes are illustrated in Figure 7 *e*. Portions of nine plain round tumblers have been distinguished. Measurable base diameters range from 1-7/8 to 2½ in., while indentations in the bases are 3/8 to ½ in. deep. These glasses are all simply designated as "tumblers" in the King, Son and Company catalog (Pyne Press 1972b: 18-9); the smaller sizes probably served as whiskey or bar tumblers.

Pieces of three thin-walled round tumblers or glasses were found. The one nearly complete example is 3-5/8 in. high and has a diameter at its mouth of 2-5/16 in. The thickness of the wall at the rim is .38 in. The second item is a rim fragment 7/8 in. wide. It has an etched inscription below the rim that reads '- - ME GL- -.' The third piece is a rim fragment with the words 'FALKS MILWAUKEE' etched into it, obviously for advertising purposes. This brewery was not listed in an 1860 census, although by 1866 it was the fourth largest manufacturer of beer in Milwaukee – a ranking that remained constant through 1872, according to Milwaukee Chamber of Commerce statistics (Cochran 1948: 56). On February 15, 1893, Frank Falk became treasurer of the Pabst Brewing Company when that firm purchased the Falk operation (Cochran 1948).

Fluted tumblers are even more numerous than plain or round tumblers. Portions of five tumblers that cannot be identified as to specific style were present. Three of these have eight flutes each, one has six flutes, and the number of flutes on one cannot be determined. The rim diameter of two of these items was estimated as 4 to 4-5/8 in.

In addition, examples of three specific styles have been identified by comparison with the King, Son and Company catalog (Pyne Press 1972b: 18-9). Portions of two fluted tumblers are at least similar to a 1/2-pt. "Huber," another may have been a 1/3- or 1/2-pt. "Star" fluted tumbler, and a fourth looks like a 1/2-pt. "Kate," an unfluted design.

The five items tentatively classified as whiskey or bar tumblers include both fluted and unfluted styles. Two specimens appear to be similar to the style called "Gill Plain." One has a basal depression of approximately ½ in.

Fragments of four wine glasses were recovered. Three of the four appear to be either champagne or claret glasses of a style termed "Mitchell C" (Pyne Press 1972b: 23), which has a six-fluted stem and a body with straight sides tapering toward the bottom. The fourth piece is a fragment of a body with part of a round stem attached.

The second group of pressed glass artifacts consists of fragments of 12 objects, none of which can be identified as to use. One is a light SCA base, 3-3/16 in. in maximum width, retaining three of the four feet upon which it originally sat (Fig. 7 *f*). A round foot on a small segment of rayed flint glass was recovered from Building 35 (Fig. 8 *a*). The bottom of the foot is well scratched, indicating fairly heavy or long-term use of this object, which is presumed to have been holloware.

Portions of six pressed glass handles were recovered, but they cannot be assigned to any particular object. Five of these pieces are flint or SCA in color, while the sixth is a medium blue. One of the fragments is oval in cross-section, another has six sides or facets, and the remainder are round.

Two stems from unidentified holloware objects have been recovered. Both are flint glass, one 3¼ in. high and the other 4-3/8 in. high. The taller specimen has a maximum diameter of 2 in.; it has eight facets and is hollow. The shorter specimen is solid and has six facets.

There are also partial bodies from two unidentified holloware objects, both of flint glass. They could be from almost any kind of object – a bowl, a lamp font, or a vase, for instance.

Unidentifiable fragments of pressed glass, about which little or nothing could be learned, total 16 pieces. Three very small pieces of decorative flint glass with a rayed or starburst type of pattern were recovered. Two other flint glass fragments have rectilinear embossed decoration, one with squares and the other with truncated pyramids. Another piece exhibits a portion of an edge or rim and has raised nodules embossed on it. Two pieces of milk glass are very different in their decoration. One has a series of vertical, raised ribs beginning about 3/8 in. below a folded rim. The other is a holloware vessel, possibly a jar, showing a basket-weave pat-

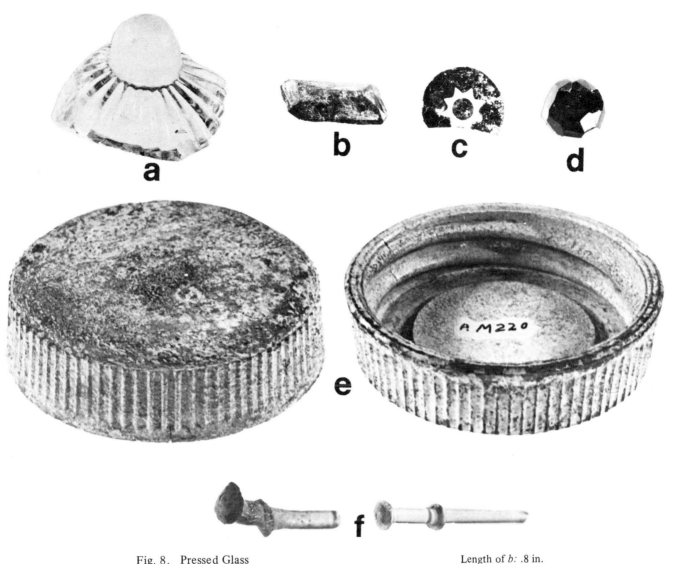

Fig. 8. Pressed Glass

Length of *b:* .8 in.

a. Footed base fragment	*c.* Button	*e.* Jar lid
b. Artificial amethyst	*d.* Button	*f.* Syringe plunger fragments

tern with a single weft, or horizontal element, woven over and under a pair of warps, or vertical elements. Another basket-weave pattern is found on two identical light green fragments, which may also have been part of a jar or bottle. This pattern has a single warp woven across bundles of three wefts.

Six pieces of glass are unidentified, but are clearly decorative in nature. Two rim fragments have a 2-in. colored band extending down from the rim. The coloring shades from a deep rose at the rim into a clear or flint color. These pieces belong either to the same object or to two objects from a set – possibly lampshades. Three other fragments, all possibly from the same object, show identical color patterns, each having a pink layer and a white layer; the white appears to be on the exterior surface, judging by the curvature of one of the pieces. The sixth fragment is a convoluted piece of rim with a white interior and a blue-green exterior.

MISCELLANEOUS GLASS

Artificial Gem

A piece of glass recovered from Building 8, room 2, was cut to imitate a large amethyst (Fig. 8 *b*) and originally was thought to be genuine. Analysis by a certified gemologist, using specific gravity as a test, revealed it to be only an excellent copy. This "stone" is rectangular, with hexagonal faceting and octahedral corner truncations. It measures .8 in. by .43 in. by .2 in.

Buttons

Most of the 70 glass buttons recovered at Fort Bowie are plain four-hole sew-through buttons of white milk glass. They range in size from 14 to 28 lignes (.35 in. to .657 in. in diameter), with the majority clustering at the smaller end of the scale (see p. 37 for definition of *ligne*).

Four buttons are plano-convex in cross-section and have a slight depression in the flat back side where a tab shank of some sort was apparently inserted. There are five decorated four-hole sew-through buttons, four monochrome blue and two monochrome black. Another button has two overglaze blue stripes on a white background.

Only two glass buttons are more elaborate in style. One has a white six-pointed star set into the navy blue body (Fig. 8 *c*); it measures 22 lignes and has a brass wire loop shank. The other, probably produced in a mold, is a black multifaceted sphere (Fig. 8 *d*); it measures 20 lignes and originally had a brass wire loop shank.

Beads

A total of 13 glass beads came from seven proveniences at the post. All beads recovered are either red, white, blue, or black monochrome. These beads are summarized in Table 10. The specific shape, color, and glass type designations utilized are those presented by Kidd and Kidd (1970). The only pertinent information not contained in Table 10 concerns one of the two faceted beads. The smaller one was probably produced in a mold, the most common method of producing faceted beads. The large blue bead, however, was apparently shaped by grinding. It has no visible mold seams, yet the edges of each facet are fairly sharp and well defined. Under a 10x hand lens, the surface of each facet displays a series of shallow parallel striations.

TABLE 10

Glass Beads

Type of Manu-facture	Shape	Color	Diameter (Inches)	Glass
Wire wound	Round	Light aqua blue	.375	Opaque
Tube	Circular (ring)	White	.203	Opaque
Tube	Circular (ring)	Light aqua blue	.215	Opaque
Tube	Circular (ring)	Light aqua blue	.229	Opaque
Tube	Circular (ring)	Light aqua blue	.244	Opaque
Tube	Circular (ring)	Light aqua blue	.236	Opaque
Tube	Circular (ring)	Light aqua blue	.278	Opaque
Tube	Circular (ring)	Apple green	.152	Opaque
Tube	Circular (ring)	Redwood	.122	Translucent
Tube	Circular (ring)	Light aqua blue	.095	Opaque
Tube	Circular (ring)	Aqua blue	.071	Opaque
Molded(?)	Round faceted	Black	.30	Opaque
Ground(?)	Round faceted	Bright blue	.65	Translucent

Source: Terminology from Kidd and Kidd 1970.

Insulators

The 12 incomplete glass insulators recovered at Fort Bowie belong to three types. Six are "Pony" insulators, or type CD 102, according to Milholland and Milholland (1971: 21). Three of the specimens have two patent dates molded

on them: January 25, 1870, and January 14, 1879. The 1870 patent is for a hand press for making insulators, invented by Homer Brooke (USPO 1872a: 40). The second date is design patent #10,981 for telegraph insulators, granted to James M. Brookfield (USPO 1879b: 33).

One threadless signal-type insulator fragment was recovered. This piece belongs to the Milhollands' type CD 138 (1971: 59) and bears no embossing.

"Single Petticoat Side Groove Style," type CD 126, is the Milhollands' terminology for the remaining five insulators found at the fort. Of the three manufactured by Brookfield, two bear the patent dates mentioned above, as well as an address: '45 Cliff St/N.Y.' This was the location of Brookfield Company from 1882 until 1890 (Milholland and Milholland 1971: 6). The third Brookfield insulator of this type apparently has the patent date of March 20, 1877, referring to design patent #9,858 for telegraph insulators by James M. Brookfield. This specimen also has 'W. Brookfield' embossed on it below the patent date.

Jar Lid

One jar lid (Fig. 8 *e*), which cannot be classified as a fruit jar lid, was recovered. It is light brown, has a diameter of 2-11/16 in. and is 11/16 in. high. Its edge is fluted and the interior is threaded.

Lamp Chimneys

Of the total of 48 flint glass lamp chimneys recovered, 28 have the shape or style of what is generally called a "student lamp" (Pyne Press 1972a: 121). This is the shape that the army adopted when it first introduced lamps as an item of issue in 1882 (Fig. 9; USWD 1881: facing p. 438). These lamps are discussed in greater detail in Chapter 3, *Metal*.

Two examples of the pearl top chimney (Pyne Press 1972a: 116-7) were recovered, as were 17 rim fragments of the scalloped top chimney and one base from an unidentifiable style of chimney.

Lamp Shades

The 11 fragments of glass lamp shades recovered almost certainly represent only six discrete specimens. Four fragments belong to a single shade made of bright yellow glass with a white slip or glaze. This shade is quite similar, if not identical, to that illustrated in a reprint of a Plume and Atwood catalog (Plume and Atwood 1965: 55). The same catalog shows a type of shade of which three white or milk glass fragments were recovered (Plume and Atwood 1965: 67). The remaining four fragments are of the same white glass and represent two shades of unidentified form.

Marbles

At least four, and probably all five, of the glass marbles recovered at Fort Bowie are handmade, rather than machine produced. Handmade glass marbles were commercially produced in Germany from 1846 to about 1920 and in the

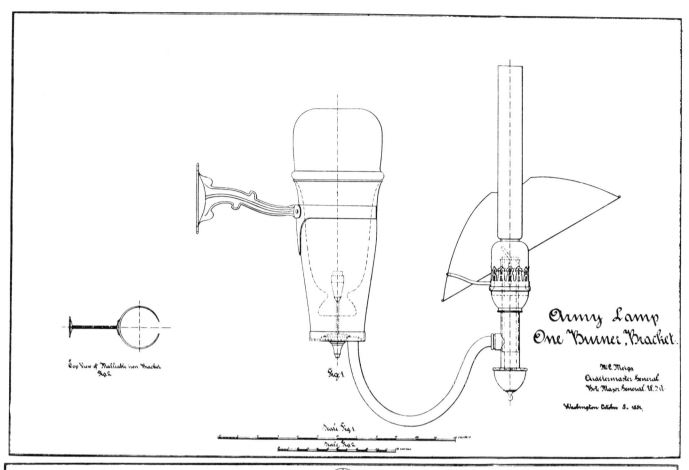

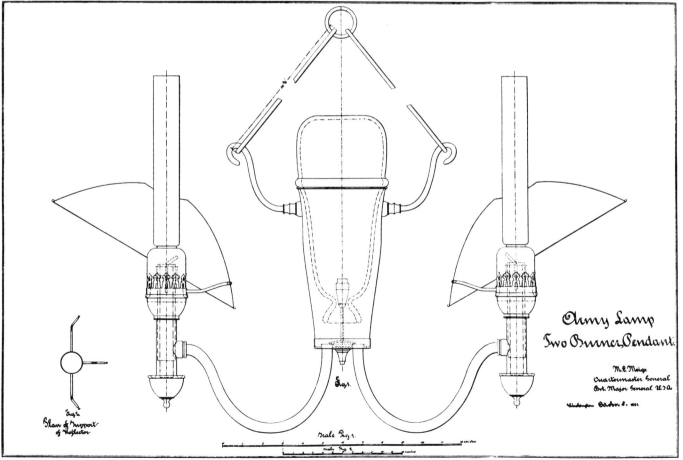

Fig. 9.   U.S. Army kerosene lamps (USWD 1881: facing p. 438).

United States by a firm in Iowa from 1880 to 1882 (Randall 1971: 104). A second American firm manufactured hand-made marbles, but not until 1897. The probability is fairly high, therefore, that the specimens are German imports.

The five marbles range in size from .58 to .73 in. and are of the style consisting of a spiral of colored ribbons contained within a clear glass. Three of the specimens have blue, white, and pink spirals, and one has a yellow and orange spiral. The fifth has a spiral composed of green, yellow, pink, blue, and white glass.

Medicine Droppers

Eleven fragments of flint glass medicine droppers have been identified. These have barrel diameters of 3/8 in., 7/16 in., and ½ in. Rubber bulbs or nipples were still attached to two specimens.

Mirror

One small mirror was recovered. It is round and has a diameter of 1-7/16 in., including its brass frame. Only remnants of the reflective backing, probably of tin amalgam or silver, remain.

Syringe Parts

Five fragments of flint glass syringe plungers are recognizable (Fig. 8 *f*). The longest piece measures 2-5/16 in., while the diameters of the shafts range from .15 to .20 in. Two of the five plungers have striations or corrugations at the end that was to be pressed, apparently to provide a non-slip surface.

Tubing and Rod

One piece of glass rod was recovered. It is 7/8 in. long and has a diameter of .205 in. It may be a fragment of a syringe plunger, but there is no way to verify this.

Twenty pieces of flint glass tubing were found. The inside diameters range from .10 to .27 in. and the outside diameters from .163 to .36 in. The smallest wall thickness is .02 in., while the largest is .054 in.

Window Glass

Fifty-five small pieces of window glass were collected. The largest piece recovered is 6¾ by 4¾ in. It would seem that the most relevant dimension for window glass is thickness. Table 11 clearly shows a clustering from .08 in. to .2 in. There is no ready explanation for the presence of the single specimen that is .31 in. thick.

TABLE 11

Window Glass

Thickness (Inches)	Number of Specimens
.050-.059	2
.060-.069	4
.070-.079	9
.080-.089	15
.090-.099	10
.100-.199	14
.31	1

3. METAL

Metal is by far the most abundant of all the materials recovered at Fort Bowie. Several thousand artifacts and fragments have been recorded and identified, and as might be expected, these include both military and civilian items. As is usually the case with excavated metal, the state of preservation ranges from very good to extremely poor. Many of the metal artifacts were cleaned, either fully or in part, when it was felt that the effort and expense would be repaid by more numerous or more complete identifications. In many cases the degree of deterioration effectively prevented any detailed study. Considerable effort has been made to search out manufacturers' names, locations, and histories. Where the condition of the artifacts allowed, fairly exhaustive research was conducted into their patent histories, utilizing the *Official Gazette of the United States Patent Office* and the *Annual Report of the Commissioner of Patents* for the years 1862 through 1899.

The metal has been divided into the following categories: Accoutrements, Apparel, Arms and Ammunition, Coinage, Communication, Hardware and Construction Materials, Household Items, Personal Items, Tools, Transportation, Miscellaneous and Unidentified Artifacts, and Scrap. As with the subdivisions created for glass artifacts, the intent has been to provide function-oriented classifications and to interpret the artifacts within the context of daily life at Fort Bowie.

The term "pattern," used in phrases such as "pattern 1851 belt plate" and "pattern 1872 dress helmet," appears frequently in this chapter (and in Chapter 5, *Leather*). This was standard Quartermaster terminology of the period, used to define the official configuration of Army issue items – shape, dimensions, materials, and so forth. The use of the term arose from the practice whereby an inventor or manufacturer presented a model or "pattern" of an item when seeking its adoption by an examining board of the relevant Army branch. An accepted model became, in turn, the "pattern" for the items that were to be manufactured to specification.

ACCOUTREMENTS

Accoutrements, while not actually parts of garments, were worn by soldiers and were thus as much a part of the uniform as shirts, trousers, or helmets. Items considered accoutrements include belt plates, bayonet scabbard parts, carbine slings, cartridge belts and boxes, haversack or canteen straps, saber belts and slings, and spurs. In all, 258 artifacts compose this subcategory.

Bayonet Scabbard

The only evidence of a bayonet in the materials collected is one bayonet scabbard tip (Fig. 10 *a*). The scabbard type to which this tip belonged was used from 1841 until superseded by an all-metal scabbard in 1874.

Belt Plates

Two pieces of the pattern 1851 belt plate were recovered. The one nearly complete specimen is lacking the applied silver wreath and has the number '569' stamped on the back in two places. Both specimens are the narrow tongue style, indicating production between 1851 and the early 1870s (Brinckerhoff 1972: 24). Seven examples of the plate loop part of the buckle were found. Five of these have stamped serial numbers: 31, 92, 353, 701, and 714. According to Brinckerhoff (1972: 23) "serial numbers between 1 and 999 are found stamped on the back of these buckles produced during the Civil War"; the number was recorded when the belt was issued to a soldier. It should be remembered that these plate loops could belong to the 1874 or 1884 cavalry saber belt, as well as to the 1851 belt plate.

Buckles

A buckle frequently found at military posts of this period is a brass wire buckle accommodating a strap ¾ in. wide. Thirty-six of these were recovered at Fort Bowie. Buckles of this type and size were used on at least three different pieces of military accoutrements and equipment. One buckle was used on each spur worn by mounted troops, one was used on each flap of the haversack, and six were used on the saddle bags used by the cavalry from 1879 until 1902. None of the specimens recovered at Fort Bowie retained any leather, so that it was impossible to assign them to the specific artifacts.

Bugles

Twenty brass parts from bugles were recovered, primarily from the trash dump, although pieces also were found in Buildings 18 and 39, the supposed stage station, and

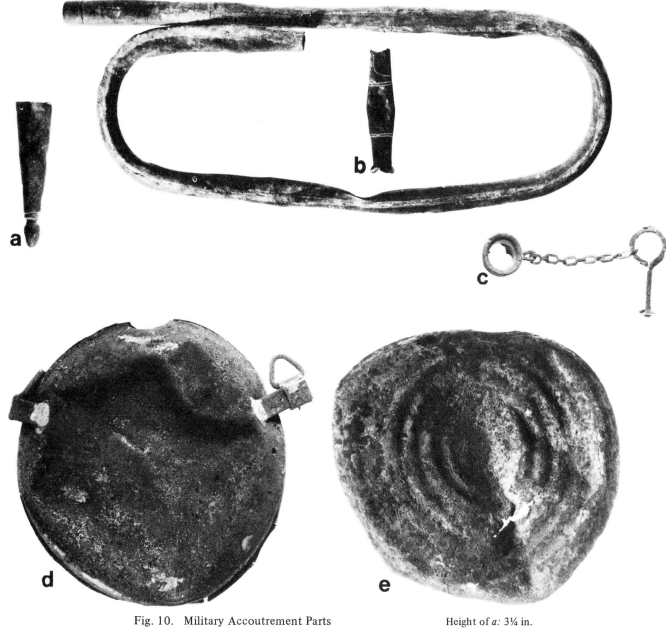

Fig. 10.   Military Accoutrement Parts
a.   Bayonet scabbard tip
b.   Bugle parts
c.   Canteen stopper pull, chain, and spout

Height of *a:* 3¼ in.
d.   Canteen pattern 1882
e.   Canteen pattern 1861

Reservoir A. Among the specimens recovered were a coil from a B-flat bugle and a complete mouthpiece (Fig. 10 *b*), as well as a tuning slide, a fingerpost, and a cut fragment of a second mouthpiece. One other item, recovered from Building 18, has been tentatively identified as a part of a valve from a musical instrument, perhaps a trumpet.

Buttons

Ten metal buttons recovered may have been used on military equipment. Seven are iron buttons with brass rivet "shanks"; they measure approximately .7 in. in diameter.

These specimens are virtually identical to buttons on a canvas blanket bag in the collection of the Arizona Historical Society, Tucson; this is apparently the pattern 1881 blanket bag described in the 1881 *Annual Report of the Secretary of War* (USWD 1882a: 285-6). Another button of the same design, but measuring .58 in. in diameter, was found. Two other buttons recovered, also .58 in. in diameter, are made of a nonferrous metal, perhaps a lead and zinc alloy. They are constructed of three pieces (front, back, and shank), and one button still holds a brass rivet in its shank. These buttons are essentially the same form as the iron buttons and may have been haversack or perhaps blanket bag buttons.

Canteens

A total of 95 items from or related to canteens were recovered, primarily from the trash dump. Two spouts were collected, one complete with a brass spout ring, brass chain, and iron stopper pull (Fig. 10 *c*). The spout ring was first adopted in 1874 (USWD 1875). Among 50 other specimens of spout rings, chains, and stopper pulls was one iron washer on a stopper pull, which had originally sat atop the cork stopper. In 1878, a new pattern of canteen was submitted for trial; it was adopted in 1881 and issued in 1882. This canteen differs from earlier patterns in that it has two rectangular tin strap loops, one on either side of the spout, to which an iron wire triangular loop is soldered (Fig. 10 *d*). Thirty-seven of these loops, which served as points to which the shoulder strap was hooked, were recovered. The shoulder strap was also modified in 1882, with an adjustable leather strap replacing the cloth strap. Three brass wire hooks, 1-7/8 in. long, are thought to be examples of the hook used for adjusting the length of the pattern 1882 shoulder strap.

Two canteens of the 1882 pattern were recovered, both lacking spouts. One half of the earlier corrugated or "bull's-eye" canteen was also found (Fig. 10 *c*). This canteen, adopted in 1861, is approximately 7½ in. in diameter. Although new specifications were adopted after the Civil War, it appears that the pattern 1861 canteens were modified and reutilized for many years. In the 1898 report on the operations of the Rock Island Arsenal, for example, it is stated that "until this year no canteens had been made at this arsenal, the supplies left over from the war of 1861-1865, when repaired and recovered being sufficient to meet the ordinary needs of the Army" (USWD 1899: 66).

Carbine Sling Parts

Metal remains from several carbine slings were recovered. Each sling originally had a buckle, a tip, a swivel, a D-ring with roller, and a snap-hook. Three examples of each of these pieces, except the snap-hook, were located. This pattern was in use for at least seven years before Fort Bowie was established in 1862. It was superseded in 1885 with the promulgation of *Ordnance Memoranda No. 29* (USWD 1891), which prescribed the use of a narrower sling.

Cartridge Belt Parts

Two parts from two different patterns of the Mills cartridge belt were recovered. The earliest of the two specimens is a pre-1885 cast plate loop (Fig. 11 *a*). Identification of the precise pattern is difficult, since the specimen is the same height (3-7/16 in.) as the 1880 or 1881 pattern but has the ridge indicative of the 1883 pattern (Brinckerhoff 1972: 28-31). The second item is also a plate loop. This piece is stamped rather than cast, is 3¼ in. high, and therefore is definitely the 1885 pattern.

Cartridge Box Parts

In addition to cartridge belt fragments, there are three items identifiable as parts from cartridge boxes. Using specimens in the collection of the Arizona Historical Society for comparative purposes, a portion of a brass hinge pin (Fig. 11 *b*) can be identified as belonging to the pattern 1874 McKeever cartridge box. The hinge pin has a diameter of .165 in., while the escutcheon (Fig. 11 *c*) is oval shaped and measures 1 by 13/16 in. A second escutcheon is circular and measures 7/8 in. in diameter. This item cannot be assigned to any single pattern of box, but could have been part of any one of several.

Haversack Parts

Another piece of equipment represented at Fort Bowie is the haversack. Ten haversack strap hooks and two D-rings have been recovered and are known to postdate 1884. In 1885, the War Department adopted a haversack with "2 double brass wire hooks ... with rollers in fold." The haversack and strap are illustrated in *Ordnance Memoranda No. 29*, Plate XIII, and the strap itself is detailed in Plate XV (USWD 1891)

Hooks

Three of the adjustment hooks recovered (Fig. 11 *d*) may have been part of haversack straps. They are made of 1/8-in. brass wire and are 2¼ in. wide at the point of fastening to the belt. Comparison with specimens at the Arizona Historical Society shows that this adjustment hook might have been used on the 1885 haversack strap, the 1872 canteen strap, or an 1874 saber belt. More specific identification is not possible. The same is, unfortunately, the case for two other adjustment hooks found (Fig. 11 *e*). These are made of sheet brass and are 2-7/16 in. long. Each specimen has two rivets with rather large heads, the largest of which is 3/8 in. in diameter. That these hooks belonged with a belt holding a fair amount of weight is an inference based on their size and the size of the rivets. Military specifications and collections examined for comparison have failed to yield a more positive identification.

Adjustment hooks are also among the 42 artifacts associated with various saber-related accoutrements. Comparison with known specimens made possible the identification of eight pre-1874 saber belt adjustment hooks (Fig. 11 *f*), as well as two hooks from the pattern 1874 belt (Fig. 11 *g*). The two patterns are easily distinguishable, since both shape and dimension changed in 1874 (U.S. War Department 1874b: 56). Saber belt shoulder straps in the collection of the Arizona Historical Society have adjustment hooks of two sizes, both of which were found at Fort Bowie. Two examples of the larger front hook have been identified, one of which still has a remnant of the leather strap (Fig. 11 *h*); it is made of sheet brass, is 2¾ in. long, and the strap is fastened to the hook with two rivets. The one smaller rear adjustment hook found is also of brass and has two rivets, and is 2 in. in length (Fig. 11 *i*).

Saber-Related Items

The evolution of saber attachment devices can be seen in the artifacts from Fort Bowie. Nine examples of the saber

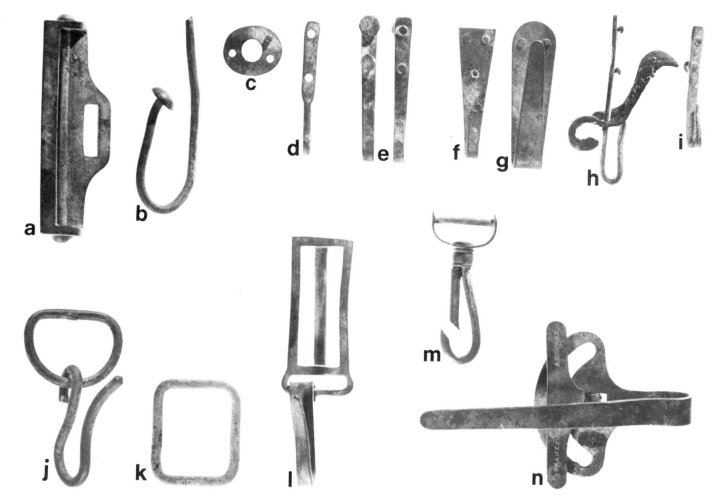

Fig. 11. Military Accoutrement Parts

Width of *k:* 1¼ in.

a. Cartridge belt buckle part	*f.* Pre-1874 saber belt adjustment hook
b. McKeever cartridge box hinge pin	*g.* Pattern 1874 saber belt adjustment hook
c. McKeever cartridge box escutcheon	*h.* Saber belt shoulder strap hook (front)
d. Haversack adjustment hook	*i.* Saber belt shoulder strap hook (rear)
e. Adjustment hooks	*j.* Saber belt hook and D-ring

k. Rectangular belt loop
l. Pattern 1874 saber belt slide
m. Pattern 1879 saber snap-hook
n. Stuart saber attachment device

hook and D-ring (Fig. 11 *j*) were recovered. These were used from at least 1841 through 1873, as were the two rectangular belt loops recovered (Fig. 11 *k*; also illustrated on a belt in Chappell 1972: 5). These items were replaced in 1874 by saber belt slides (Fig. 11 *l*). As an illustration in *Ordnance Memoranda No. 18* shows, each belt had one slide with a hook and one slide without a hook (USWD 1874a: Plate 5). Recovered at Fort Bowie were two examples of each, as well as a part of a third hook. In 1879 a brass saber snap-hook (Fig. 11 *m*) was introduced (USWD 1879: 42). As a Bannerman catalog (1936: 290) states, the "U.S. Arsenal made heavy gilt slinghooks, for snapping the sling straps in the scabbard rings." Although two hooks were used per saber, only one specimen was found. The mechanism was changed once again in 1885. In that year, the modified Stuart saber attachment (Fig. 11 *n*) was adopted, according to *Ordnance Memoranda No. 29* (USWD 1891: 15, Plate XV). This item, which had been patented in 1859 by James E. B. (Jeb) Stuart (Hutchins 1970: 15), was modified slightly and made part of the equipment. Four of these saber attachments were found. Two of them have a "cross-bar" bearing the inscription 'Frankford

Arsenal' (as seen in Fig. 11 *n*), while the other two lack this piece. The cross-bar is not illustrated in *Ordnance Memoranda No. 29* and may have been experimental.

Other saber-related artifacts include eight saber sling studs. Three of these are approximately 11/16 in. in diameter, while the remaining five are 5/8 in. It has been suggested that the larger specimens are of an earlier date, but no specific supporting documentary evidence has been found. *Ordnance Memoranda No. 13* (USWD 1872b: 15) and *No. 18* (USWD 1874b: Plate 5) indicate a sling width of 1 in., and *Ordnance Memoranda No. 29* (USWD 1891: Plate XV) indicates a sling width of ¾ in. as of 1885. While these specifications seem to suggest a change from the larger to the smaller sling stud in 1885, specimens in the Arizona Historical Society collection, which are believed to be well dated, are not consistent in the matter.

Spurs

The last military issue accoutrement that can be specifically identified is the spur. The remnants of five brass spurs, all without the iron rowel, were recovered. One specimen has the number '53' stamped on the inside surface. Attempts to pinpoint the precise date these spurs were introduced as an issue item have thus far been unsuccessful. The type recovered is illustrated in Plate IX of *Ordnance Memoranda No. 29* (USWD 1891). Also recovered was one non-issue iron spur.

Miscellaneous Accoutrements

Four additional artifacts believed to be military accoutrement parts were recovered, but they have defied specific identification. One is a wire hook identical in all respects to the haversack hook described above, except that the latter is 2 in. long, whereas this specimen is only 1½ in. long. This item is not unique, however, for identical hooks have been recovered at Fort Buchanan, Fort Crittenden, and Fort Lowell; these specimens are in the collection of the Arizona Historical Society. No mention of this item has yet been located in any documentary source. Two brass D-rings were recovered that do not match the dimensions for any other identified item. Finally, a brass wire rectangular loop with interior dimensions of 2-1/16 in. by 3/8 in. was recovered. The item to which this belongs has not yet been identified.

APPAREL

Buckles and Other Fastening Devices

Buckles for clothing were relatively common among the artifacts found at Fort Bowie. Sixty-two buckles were recovered (apart from those discussed above under *Accoutrements* and below under *Shoe Parts* and *Suspender Parts*). The 10 buckles not recognizable as military issue items accepted straps ranging from 5/8 in. to 1-3/8 in. in width. One is a flat oval shape and has a floral pattern on the brass body (Fig. 12 *a*).

Six of the buckles (Fig. 12 *b*) are of a type used on ladies' shoulder braces and hose supporters, as seen in the Sears, Roebuck catalog of 1897 (Israel 1968: 322-3).

Military trouser buckles are common and are easily recognized. The earliest reference found for this buckle is in the report of an 1875 Army board considering clothing and equipage, which recommended that a "strap and buckle on the back" be adopted as one of several modifications to issue trousers (USWD 1876: 205). Nine years later, the *Annual Report of the Secretary of War* (USWD 1885: Plate 1) has an illustration of what is termed a "Gilt Buckle," which is virtually identical to 52 examples found at Fort Bowie (Fig. 12 *c*). At least five different manufacturers produced these buckles, as evidenced by the initials on the buckle frames: 'C.J.'; 'H.B. & Co.'; 'H. B. & Co. 11^D'; 'J. R. M.'; 'MI & Co./PARIS'; and 'T. G. H.'

The initials 'T.G.H.' undoubtedly stand for Thomas G. Hood, Philadelphia. Under the name Hood and Company, this firm operated from 1850 through 1860 as importers and merchants of dry goods (McElroy 1850; Cohen 1860). From 1861 until at least 1888, Thomas G. Hood was one of the proprietors of Hood, Bonbright and Company. Either Hood,

Bonbright or, as is more likely, Horstmann Brothers and Company were the manufacturers of the 11 buckles with the initials 'H. B. & Co.' Horstmann Brothers and Company operated under that name in New York from 1859 to 1862 and in Philadelphia during the years 1859-1863 and 1867-1893 (Jacobsen 1972c. [1]).

One other artifact was recovered that must have been a fastening device for an article of apparel, probably a corset. This item (Fig. 12 *d*) consists of a spring steel band, ½ in. wide, to which two brass eyelets remain riveted. The initials 'W C C,' of an unidentified firm, are inscribed on both eyelets. The supposition that this piece was one part of a two-piece item was confirmed through discovery of the illustration for patent #191,467, which is entitled "Corset-Clasps" (USPO 1877a: 961). Virtually identical items, from the Tucson Urban Renewal Archaeological Project excavations, consist of two spring steel bands, 13 in. long, that fasten together by means of eyelets riveted to one piece and corresponding tabs riveted to the other.

Among the other fastening devices are seven safety pins. These range from 1-1/8 to 2¼ in. in length. Also recovered was one clasp, which is illustrated in the Marshall Field catalog (1892-3: 170); there it is listed as the Wizard Scarf Holder at $.50 per dozen pairs. The Fort Bowie specimen (Fig. 12 *e*) bears the same patent date: June 6, 1882. This patent, #259,002, was registered by Henry C. Frank, New York, and is titled "Clasp or Dress-Supporter" (USPO 1882b: 1722).

Buttons

The largest group of metal artifacts relating to apparel are the 362 metal buttons. Not surprisingly, 336 (or 93 percent) are from military clothing, while only 26 are from civilian apparel. The sizes of almost all military buttons were specified in official documents in fractions of an inch; however, there was considerable variation from these specifications, and therefore the measurements of the military buttons recovered are given in decimal fractions for greater accuracy. The civilian buttons are described in terms of lignes. A "ligne" (the French term), or "line," is the unit of measurement used in the button trade to describe buttons in terms of their diameter. There are 40 lignes to the inch, so that the ligne scale may be converted to inches by multiplying the number of lignes by .025.

Civilian Buttons

The 26 civilian buttons were recovered from seven buildings (8, 18, 26, 27, 28, 35, and 106) and the trash dump. The more ornate decorated buttons were equipped with metal loop shanks, while the plainer and undecorated specimens are of the sew-through type, having either two or four holes. The smallest button, measuring only 10 lignes, is clover-shaped and is made of brass; the back is filled with lead, which holds the shank in place. Two buttons decorated with embossed animals were found. One bears a snarling wolf's head (Fig. 12 *f*), while the other shows a squirrel sitting on a tree limb (Fig. 12 *g*). Both buttons measure ap-

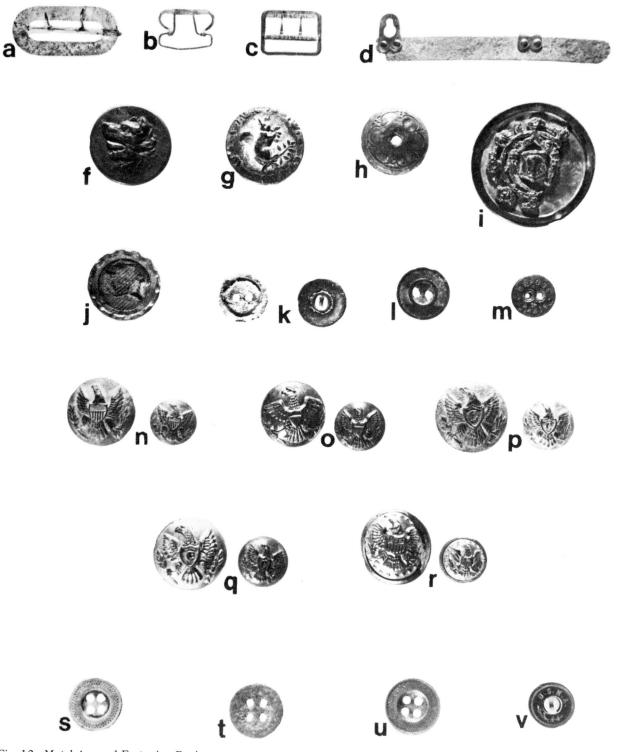

Fig. 12. Metal Apparel Fastening Devices

a. Oval buckle with floral decoration
b. Shoulder brace and hose supporter buckle
c. Military trouser buckle
d. Spring steel band with eyelets
e. Wizard scarf holder

Scale (a–e): Length of a, 1-3/8 in.

f. Button with wolf's head
g. Button with squirrel
h. Hemispherical button
i. Button with attached shield
j. Brass button with fabric center
k. Fabric-covered buttons
l. Two-hole sew-through metal button
m. Brass button reading 'DÉPOSÉ/PARIS'
n. General service buttons, early style

o. General service buttons, later style
p. Line eagle device buttons, early style
q. Line eagle device buttons, late style
r. Staff buttons
s. Suspender button
t. Suspender button
u. Overall, stable frock, and drawers button
v. U.S.M.A. button

Scale (f–v): Diameter of j, 15/16 in.

proximately 38 lignes. Another brass button, hemispherical in shape and measuring 34 lignes, has a floral and geometric pattern stamped into its surface (Fig. 12 *h*); although a hole is present in the center, the hollow underside is still partially filled with lead, indicating that a loop shank of some sort was employed. The largest button recovered at Fort Bowie measures 60 lignes; it has a shield and floral design, probably made of pewter or lead, attached to a brass backing (Fig. 12 *i*). One of the very few pieces of fabric recovered at the post is contained in a button consisting of a brass bezel and an iron backing (Fig. 12 *j*); a loop shank was probably used on this specimen, which measures 36 lignes. One part of a button produced by or for the Levi-Strauss Company, San Francisco, was recovered from the trash dump. This brass fragment, measuring 24 lignes, is the front portion of the same type of metal shank button that is riveted to the waist of Levi-Strauss blue jeans today. Patented rivets used by Levi-Strauss were also recovered and are discussed below.

The nonmilitary sew-through buttons range in size from 16 to 26 lignes. Several two-hole buttons were originally fabric-covered (Fig. 12 *k*), while others are all metal (Fig. 12 *l*). A two-hole button recovered from Building 26 bears the legend 'DÉPOSÉ/PARIS' (Fig. 12 *m*). The Levi-Strauss button mentioned above is the only nonmilitary metal button for which the manufacturer or dates of manufacture could be ascertained.

Three of the four collar buttons recovered are the two-piece separable type illustrated in an 1889 catalog (Busiest House in America 1889: 455). There are several styles of "Gents Collar Buttons, Rolled Plate, Separable," whose prices range from $1.50 to $6 per dozen.

Military Buttons

Considerably more can be said about the 336 military buttons recovered than could be said for the nonmilitary specimens. Military buttons identified include general service buttons; line eagle devices; staff buttons; helmet side buttons; fly, suspender, and overall buttons; and several miscellaneous items. The military buttons with backstamps, the dates for the firms that produced them, and the style and size of the buttons are presented in Table 12.

As a group, the 239 general service buttons were the most frequently recovered type. First authorized by General Order No. 1, Adjutant General's Office, on January 20, 1854 (Ludington 1889: 40), this button was issued to all enlisted men from 1855 until 1902 (Brinckerhoff 1972: 5). It is a three-piece button consisting of a loop shank, a backing or shank plate, and a convex front. The decoration consists of an eagle, invariably facing to the left, with a lined shield on its breast. This button occurs in two general sizes – a coat size and a smaller vest, cuff, or jacket size – and in two styles, the latter distinction having chronological significance. The smaller general service button was also used to attach the chin strap to the kepi or forage cap.

According to Brinckerhoff (1972: 5), the earlier style of general service button (Fig. 12 *n*), which was regulation issue until 1884, is characterized by a wide, recessed lined shield on the eagle's breast, and longer, narrower wings than occur after 1884. Using these criteria, 150 coat buttons and 41 cuff buttons have been identified as belonging to this period. Although specifications called for these items to be 7/8 and 1/2 in. respectively in outside diameter, these measurements were not, in fact, adhered to. Early-style coat buttons in the collection range from .76 to .84 in. in diameter and the cuff buttons vary from .56 to .63 in. The variation in size is undoubtedly due in part to the number of different contractors from whom these buttons were purchased.

The discrepancy between the dates of issue and the dates of manufacture for the 22 general service buttons with backstamps of 'SCOVILLS & CO.' requires a short comment. The firm of this name operated from 1840 to 1850 (Albert 1976: 464), but these buttons obviously cannot predate the regulations of January 20, 1854, that authorized them (Albert 1976: 40). This contradiction implies either that backplates manufactured prior to 1850 were used on later buttons or, more probably, that a backplate die dating prior to 1850 was used by the firm's successor, Scovill Manufacturing Company, to make buttons after 1854 or 1855. Emilio (1911: 47) suggests the latter practice in the case of another button with a backstamp of a company that had long been out of business when the button was produced.

The later style of general service button was apparently used from 1884 until 1902. On both the coat and cuff buttons the eagle has shorter, wider wings and a longer neck, and the raised shield on the eagle's chest is smaller (Fig. 12 *o*). It should be noted, however, that cuff buttons with the later raised shield occur with both wide and narrow eagle's wings. The specifications for the later coat buttons remained at 7/8 in., and the 25 specimens collected ranged from .80 to .83 in. The regulation size for the cuff buttons also remained constant, at ½ in., and the 23 recovered examples ranged from .61 to .63 in.

One artifact recovered from Building 18 consists of two cuff-size general service buttons attached to each other by the shanks, apparently to make a cufflink. One of the buttons is the early style, while the other has the raised shield of the post-1884 style.

That only 22 specimens of the button known as the line eagle device were recovered is not surprising in view of its restricted use. It was adopted as early as 1821 by the artillery and infantry for both officers and enlisted men, but was specified for use solely by officers in 1854, eight years prior to the founding of Fort Bowie (Brinckerhoff 1972: 3-4). The line eagle device coat and cuff buttons represent 8.5 percent of the total sample – a figure not very much out of line with the ratio of officers to enlisted men at the fort.

The line eagle device (Fig. 12 *p*) is not very different in appearance from the general service button. The major distinction between the two is the presence of a letter inside

TABLE 12

U.S. Military Buttons with Backstamps

Backstamp	Company Dates	General Service 1854-1884	General Service 1884-1902	Line Eagle 1851-1884	Line Eagle 1884-1902	Staff
HENRY V. ALLIEN & CO. N. Y.	} 1877–1948[b]	13 coat				
HENRY V. ALLIEN & CO •NY •			1 coat			
H. V. ALLIEИ & CO. И. Y. *			1 cuff			
D. EVANS & CO. * ATTLEBORO MASS *	{ 1847–1911+[c]				2 coat	
D. EVANS & CO. SUPERFINE	{ 1848–1945[b]			1 cuff		
EXTRA * QUALITY *				1 coat		2 cuff
EXTRA ★★★QUALITY ★★★		3 coat				
EXTRA·∴·QUALITY·∴·		2 coat				
⟩ FINE GOLD PLATE ⟨ ⤚				1 coat		
H. C. HARPER •PHILA. •			1 cuff			
THOS. G. HOOD •PHIL. •	ca. 1850–1860[g]		6 coat; 2 cuff			
HOOD BONBRIGHT &. CO. • PHILA. •	1861–1888+[g]		1 coat			
HORSTMANN BROS. & CO. •PHIL. •		13 coat				1 cuff
HORSTMANN BROS. & CO. •PHIL•					2 coat	
HORSTMANN BRO.S & CO ⊙ PHILᴬ ⊙		8 coat				
HORSTMANN BROS & CO. •PHILᴬ •		25 coat	10 coat			
HORSTMANN BROS & CO., PHILᴬ	} 1859–1863,	11 coat				
HORSTMANN BROS. & CO. •PHIᵀᴬ •	1867–1893[d]	1 coat				
HORSTMANN BROS. & CO. •PHIᴸ. •		8 coat				
HORSTMANN BROS & CO •PHI •		3 cuff	5 cuff			
HORSTMANN BROS. & CO. • PHIL. •			1 coat			
HORSTMANN BROS & Cᵒ • PHILᴬ •			10 cuff			
HORSTMANN PHILᴬ & NEW •YORK •				1 cuff		
HORSTMANN'S N. Y. & PHI.				1 cuff		
HORSTMANN & CO •NY & PHI •		1 cuff				
M. C. LILLEY & CO. COLUMBUS O.	1879-1927[e]				1 coat	

the shield on the eagle's chest, representing one of the various branches of the Army. The same change in shield style occurs with the line eagle device as with the general service button; it was presumably in 1884 that the shield became slightly smaller and was raised (Fig. 12 *q*). Of the line eagle device buttons found at Fort Bowie, all but two are for the cavalry, the infantry being represented by only one coat and one cuff button. Although the line eagle device buttons of the style found at Fort Bowie were first authorized in 1851 (General Order No. 31, Adjutant General's Office; Ludington 1889: 36, paragraphs 27, 31, 32, 33), the 20 cavalry buttons obviously can date no earlier than 1855, the year in which the cavalry was first organized as a branch of the U.S. military.

The 14 line eagle device coat buttons found range from .88 to .91 in. in diameter, against the 1851 specification sizes of 3/4 (.75) in. for enlisted men and 7/8 (.875) in. for offi-

cers. Three of the coat buttons have a stippled background in the shield, which Brinckerhoff (1972: 4) believes to be a fancy variation dating no earlier than the late 1880s. The one infantry coat-size specimen has the backstamp 'FINE GOLD PLATE' and therefore can be identified as an officer's button; the 1851 specifications cited above also prescribed for the first time gilt buttons for infantry officers and yellow metal for enlisted infantry soldiers.

The specification for the cuff-size line eagle device button remained at 1/2 in. until 1888, when it was increased to 9/16 (.565) in. (Ludington 1889: 61). The examples recovered have diameters larger than specification size: the cavalry specimens range from .60 to .63 in., while the single infantry specimen measures .575 in. The latter button has one of the 'SCOVILLS & CO.' backstamps that cannot be reliably dated, for the reason discussed above.

The five staff buttons recovered include two coat size

TABLE 12

(continued)

Backstamp	Company Dates	General Service 1854-1884	General Service 1884-1902	Line Eagle 1851-1884	Line Eagle 1884-1902	Staff
* PLATE & CO. * S.F. CAL.	ca. 1875–1886[h]			2 coat		
SCOVILLS & Cº· EXTRA	1840–1850[b]			1 cuff		
SCOVILLS & Cº • EXTRA •		7 cuff				
SCOVILLS & Cº • EXTRA •		15 cuff				
SCOVILL MFG Co • WATERBURY •		11 coat				
SCOVILL MFG Cº WATERBURY		1 coat				
SCOVILL MFG Cº •WATERBURY •		3 cuff				
SCOVILL MFG CO •WATERBURY •	1850–1960[b]	8 coat				
SCOVILL MFG CO. •WATERBURY. •			2 cuff			
SCOVILL MF'G Cº • WATERBURY •		1 cuff				
SCOVILL MF'G CO. ★ WATERBURY ★		11 coat				
SCOVILL MF'G CO. WATERBURY		1 coat		3 coat		
SHANNON MILLER & CRANE NEW – YORK						1 coat
SHANNON MILLER & CRANE ✳ NEW – YORK ✳	1868–1901[f]				1 coat	
S M &C NEW-YORK				1 cuff		
WALTON BROS ⊙ NEW YORK ⊙	1875–1880[f]	3 coat				
WATERBURY BUTTON CO •		1 cuff				
WATERBURY BUTTON CO. •		1 cuff	2 cuff	1 cuff	1 cuff	
WATERBURY BUTTON CO. *	1849– [b]			1 coat		
WATERBURY BUTTON CO. ★		2 coat		1 cuff		1 coat
WATERBURY BUTTON CO. ★ ★		8 coat				
WATERBURY MANUFACTURING CO ★	1837–1919+[i]		3 coat			
J. H. WILSON. ★PHILA ★	1873–1904[a]	11 coat				
Total		140 coat; 32 cuff	22 coat; 23 cuff	8 coat; 7 cuff	6 coat; 1 cuff	2 coat; 3 cuff

Sources: [a]Albert 1976: 456   [b]Albert 1976: 464   [c]Emilio 1911: 28   [d]Jacobsen 1972a   [e]Jacobsen 1973   [f]New York City Directories   [g]Philadelphia City Directories   [h]San Francisco City Directories   [i]Waterbury City Directories

and three cuff size (Fig. 12 *r*). These buttons were used by general officers and by staff officers of the Medical, Quartermaster, and Signal branches. They are distinguished by a high convex front, a circle of stars surrounding the eagle, and a number of stars in the upper portion of the shield. All the staff buttons found at Fort Bowie were used after 1872, for prior to that time the center shield contained only vertical lines (Brinckerhoff 1972: 6). The size specifications for staff buttons appear to be identical with those for the line eagle device. The three cuff size buttons, all measuring .59 in., are fairly close to the 1889 regulation of 9/16 (.565) in.

In 1885 the *Annual Report of the Secretary of War* (USWD 1885: 603) stated that "neat black japanned suspender and fly buttons, adding greatly to the appearance of the trousers, have been adopted and are now being purchased and used on these garments. Similar buttons of white metal will be used on the drawers, stable frocks, and overalls." The

regulations stated that the style was to be a four-hole metal-back button, the fly buttons to be 22 lignes and the suspender buttons to be 27 lignes (USWD 1885: 678). It is believed that all three of these types have been identified among the buttons from Fort Bowie. Thirty two-piece buttons measuring 27 lignes, some showing evidence of having been black-japanned, are believed to be suspender buttons. They occur in two styles, one with a band of cross-hatching on the front (Fig. 12 *s*) and the other plain (Fig. 12 *t*); several of the former style are made of brass, while all of the latter are of iron. Fourteen fly buttons measuring 22 lignes occur in the same two styles. Thirteen buttons believed to be the overall, stable frock, and drawer buttons mentioned in the report also were found. Measuring 27 lignes, they are one-piece white metal buttons with a band of cross-hatching (Fig. 12 *u*), making them very similar in appearance to the cross hatched style of suspender and fly buttons described above.

Three other brass buttons are described at this point because they are believed to be military buttons, although they cannot be conclusively identified (and have therefore been omitted from Table 12). Two identical specimens are similar to the plain style suspender buttons described above. These four-hole metal-back sew-throughs measure 27 lignes. On the front, the inscription 'J. Reed's Sons Phil' provides the name and location of the manufacturer. Jacob Reed's Sons, established in 1824, operated under this name as merchant tailors, clothiers, and manufacturers of military uniforms from 1879 until at least 1899 (Philadelphia City Directories). The third brass button is a two-piece sew-through believed to have been designed and produced originally for use at the United States Military Academy at West Point. This specimen measures 22 lignes and has the initials 'U.S.M.A.' on the front above a pair of crossed laurel(?) branches (Fig. 12 *v*). The backstamp reads 'DOHERTY'S PATENT,' a reference that could not be traced to a patent or manufacturer.

Finally, 10 buttons ranging from .58 to .70 in. in diameter are believed to have been military issue but could not be specifically identified.

Buttonhooks

Two apparel-related items recovered are iron buttonhooks. One is 4-7/8 in. long and the second is 3¼ in. long. The latter has the inscription 'WEINSTOCK LUBIN & Co.' Two references to this firm have been found. One is a listing in the New York City directory from 1890 to 1892, which states, "dry goods 56 Worth [St]" (Trow 1890, 1892). The second reference is from a perfume bottle listed by Fike (1965: 35); it bears the embossing 'Weinstock Lubin & Co. Sacramento.' No dates for the California location were obtained and it is not known whether the two operations functioned simultaneously or sequentially. The three years during which the company was listed in the New York City directory, therefore, cannot be specified as the sole period of manufacture and distribution of the buttonhook.

Clothing Rivets

Although most of the rivets are discussed below under *Miscellaneous Hardware,* five copper specimens recovered are definitely from articles of apparel. These rivets all have the inscription 'L.S. & Co S.F. PAT MAY 1873' around the head. The Levi-Strauss Company, San Francisco, was one of the assignees of patent #139,121, dated May 29, 1873. On that date Jacob W. Davis, Reno, Nevada, was granted a patent for a method of fastening pocket openings to prevent the pocket from tearing at the corners (USPO 1873: 569). Levi's have achieved such extraordinary popularity that it is worth quoting the claim of the original patent in full:

> As a new article of manufacture, a pair of pantaloons having the pocket openings secured at each edge by means of rivets, substantially in the manner described and shown, whereby the seams at the points named are prevented from ripping, as set forth.

Dress Stays

Three tips from dress stays were found. The stays were originally lined with rubber and covered with cloth (which came in eight colors), and they were sold in sets of nine, according to a 1902 catalog (Crown Publishers 1969: 947). One of the tips found at Fort Bowie is 5/16 in. wide, while the other two are ½ in. wide.

Epaulettes

A distinctive piece of apparel worn at Fort Bowie was the "shoulder scale." This brass ornament, which had the appearance of an epaulette without a fringe, was worn on each shoulder by enlisted men. It was first introduced in 1833 on the dress uniform of enlisted dragoons, and a new, lighter pattern was prescribed in 1854 for all enlisted men in the Army. After 1862 it generally was used only with the full dress uniform, but even then it was sometimes omitted. The "shoulder scale" was omitted entirely in the new patterns of uniform prescribed in 1872 and issued in 1873 (Brinckerhoff 1972: 31-4; Chappell 1972: 9). One complete specimen and 21 parts and fragments of the "shoulder scale" were found at Fort Bowie.

Garters and Armbands

Five parts of a coil spring garter or armband have been recovered. This type of garter consists of two parallel coil springs attached to clasps. Each of the two clasps found bears a February 15, 1876, patent date, which corresponds with patent #173,440 assigned to George S. Bishop, of Bridgeport, Connecticut, for coil spring garters. The essence of the patent describes an elastic garter with end clasps, either of which may be used as a hook or eye (USPO 1876b: 314). The Sears, Roebuck catalog for 1897 (Israel 1968: 335) pictures "Patent Duplex Ventilated Men's Arm Bands or Ladies Garters," at eight cents a pair, that appear identical to the Fort Bowie specimen. A similar item is listed in the 1892-3 Marshall Field and Company catalog (p. 401) as Armstrong's garters and armlets. A check reveals that patent #365,770 was issued to Frank Armstrong of Bridgeport, Connecticut, on July 5, 1887, for a garter whose description sounds identical (USPO 1888a: 3). There is probably some difference between the two in addition to the 11 years between patents, but it was not discernible from the written description.

Another item of apparel is represented by six parts of hose support apparatus. Three of these are of the spring clasp type, and the other three work in conjunction with a button, very much like the type illustrated in the 1902 Sears, Roebuck catalog (Crown Publishers 1969: 940).

Hat and Helmet Parts and Insignia

The 105 hat and helmet artifacts identified are all from military apparel. The pattern 1872 and the pattern 1881 dress helmets are both amply represented. One pattern 1872 insignia for mounted troops and the Signal Corps (Chappell 1966: 3) has been recovered. This specimen may have been

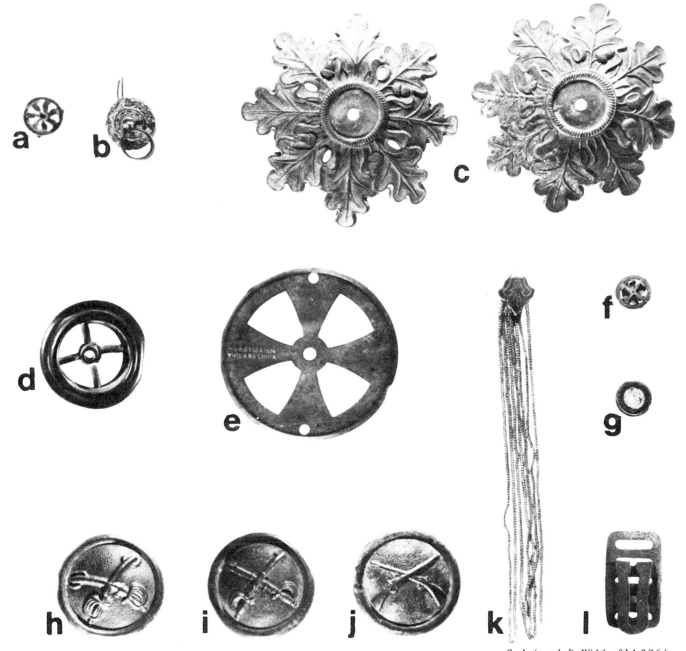

Fig. 13. Metal Apparel Artifacts
- a. Helmet ventilator
- b. Helmet scroll and ring
- c. Pattern 1881 helmet socket bases
- d. Helmet ventilator socket
- e. Helmet open disc or washer
- f. Fatigue hat revolving ventilator
- g. Campaign hat wire gauze ventilator
- h. 1877-81 cavalry helmet side button
- i. Pattern 1881 cavalry helmet side button
- j. Pattern 1881 infantry helmet side button
- k. Bracelet or watch fob part
- l. Military field shoe buckle

Scale (a–g, k–l): Width of l: 1-9/16 in.
Diameter of h–j: 1 in.

gilded, but it lacks perforations on the shield over the eagle's breast and is therefore probably from an enlisted man's helmet. Fourteen whole or partial plume sockets, socket base plates, and their fastening ornaments have been identified. These items, as well as the seven helmet plume pins, are described along with their specifications in the *Annual Report of the Secretary of War* (USWD 1877b: 263-7). These dimensions cannot be taken for granted, however, since specifications were not always complied with. The plume pins, for example, are 3/16 in. in diameter, whereas the official specification is 1/4 in. The specifications were particularly useful, however, in identifying four slightly concave brass

washers of 1-7/8 in. diameter; these are part of the plume socket attachment device for the pattern 1872 helmet. The ventilator pictured in Figure 13 a, of which two examples were recovered, is the type used on the pattern 1872 helmet and the pattern 1872 shako (or full dress cap). All specimens of the plume socket base plates that were found have oblong rather than round holes through the four points of the base.

Several recovered items were used on both the pattern 1872 and the pattern 1881 helmet – for instance, the scroll and ring (Fig. 13 b), of which three specimens were found. The one concave brass washer that is 1¼ in. in diameter could have been used on either pattern.

There are 37 pieces from the pattern 1881 helmet in the collection of materials from Fort Bowie. Examples of the three spikes, one infantry insignia, seven cavalry insignia, three sockets, and four bases recovered may be seen in Chappell (1966: 19, 22, 33, 38). The significance, if any, of the presence of four "acorn holes" in one base and their absence in three others (see Fig. 13 *c*) is unexplained at this time. A total of 18 fragments of helmet ventilator sockets (Fig. 13 *d*) were found, representing from 9 to 15 separate helmets. This ventilator was an integral part of the helmet, in contrast with the one removable open disc or washer (Fig. 13 *e*) that was made to be screwed inside the helmet on the plume pin to provide support. Both of these items are shown in plates in Appendix N of the 1884 *Annual Report of the Secretary of War* (USWD 1884a).

Other hat and cap items recovered include one infantry insignia of the 1875-95 pattern, and 10 cavalry insignia from the period 1876-96 (Brinckerhoff 1972: 13), worn on the fatigue hat. Also found were one brass eagle device of the type worn on one side of the 1855-72 full dress "Jeff Davis" hat, and one brass insignia used on either an 1872 dress shako or a pattern 1872 chapeau de bras of a general or staff officer (Brinckerhoff 1972: 17-8). The two brass numerals ('2' and '6') and two brass company letters ('B' and 'C'), all ½ in. high, were most likely worn on a forage cap in accordance with regulations adopted on February 24, 1885 (USWD 1885: 672). It is possible, however, that the numerals were worn on a coat during the period from 1877 (USWD 1877b: 266-7) to 1884 (Chappell 1972: 37-8).

Six helmet, hat, or cap chin strap parts were recovered. The four flat brass slides, with an inside dimension of 5/8 in., fitted on straps that could have come from the pre-Civil War dress cap, pattern 1858 forage cap, pattern 1872 enlisted man's shako, pattern 1872 enlisted or officer's helmet, pattern 1881 enlisted man's helmet, or pattern 1881 sun helmet. The two slides that accommodated ½-in. wide chin straps could have belonged to pattern 1872 infantry and dismounted officer's shakos, or enlisted men's forage caps worn from 1872 to 1895.

A "revolving ventilator in each side" (Fig. 13 *f*) was part of both the officer's and enlisted man's pattern 1876 fatigue hat (USWD 1876: 226). A later type was a wire gauze ventilator (Fig. 13 *g*), which first appeared on the pattern 1881 fur campaign hat (USWD 1884a: 673). A ventilator of this type has also been noted on an 1872 enlisted man's helmet in the collection of the Arizona Historical Society. Four of these gauze type ventilators and two of the revolving or "spinner" type were recovered.

A number of buttons used on helmets were recovered. Included in this category are seven stamped brass side buttons. The pattern 1872 and 1881 dress helmets each required two of these buttons. As Chappell (1966: 12-3) has noted, the *Annual Report of the Secretary of War* for 1877 gives an increase in dimension from 7/8 to 1 in. in diameter. The seven specimens recovered all meet the latter specification and therefore must be dated no earlier than 1877. Three buttons were used on cavalry dress helmets between 1877 and 1881, and three others were worn on pattern 1881 cavalry helmets. The three early specimens, measuring 1 in. in diameter, have a pair of short, curved, crossed sabers (Fig. 13 *h*); in contrast, the 1881 pattern buttons, according to Brinckerhoff (1972: 20), have crossed sabers that are straighter and longer (Fig. 13 *i*). The one remaining button is an infantry helmet side button (Fig. 13 *j*) displaying the crossed rifle branch insignia on a stippled background. This button was introduced with the infantry helmet in 1881 (USWD 1881: 304), and the recovered specimen has a sheet brass attachment loop, which, according to Chappell (1966: 35), replaced the early brass wire loop by 1885.

Jewelry

One of the few pieces of jewelry found is seen in Figure 13 *k*. This fragment consists of seven braided chains of silver-colored metal soldered to what is probably part of a clasp. This item may have been an inexpensive bracelet or, perhaps, a watch fob.

Shoe Parts

The bulk of the shoe material is discussed in Chapter 5, *Leather*. However, six metal shoe parts that were recovered retained no leather: one semicircular iron heel tap, which measures 2-1/16 in. by 1½ in.; one shoe eyelet, with an inside diameter of 1/8 in.; three shoe hooks; and one field shoe buckle. The latter (Fig. 13 *l*) is interesting if only for chronological reasons. It was adopted on April 24, 1884, along with a new style of field shoe (USWD 1884a: 682, Plate 34) that was "to be closed with an automatic buckle on the outside." This buckle apparently proved unsatisfactory in some way, for it was only in use for approximately one year (Sidney B. Brinckerhoff 1973: personal communication).

Suspender Parts

The military adopted suspenders as an issue item on September 4, 1883. Nineteen buckles were recovered that belong with the apparatus seen in full in Figure 14, a reproduction of the original War Department illustration (USWD 1884a: Plate 24). According to the report, "to supply a long-felt want, the Secretary of War approved the recommendation . . . that the enlisted men be supplied with suspenders at the rate of one pair per year" (USWD 1884a: 614).

In addition to the military issue suspenders, 20 metal parts have been identified as having come from non-issue or civilian suspenders. These parts, mostly buckles, accommodated suspenders ranging in width from 1 to 1-5/8 in. Two names, 'Russell' and 'Rockford,' were found on a few recovered pieces, but the companies remain unidentified. Three patent dates on other suspender parts – March 17, 1885, November 5, 1889, and May 19, 1891 – are all in the name of Charles R. Harris and refer to improvements on such parts as the frame, fixed tooth cross bar, and presser bar (USPO 1885c: 1043; 1890b: 890; 1891: 877). Animal figures appear on three of the buckles; one has an embossed spaniel, and two that form a pair are decorated with foxes.

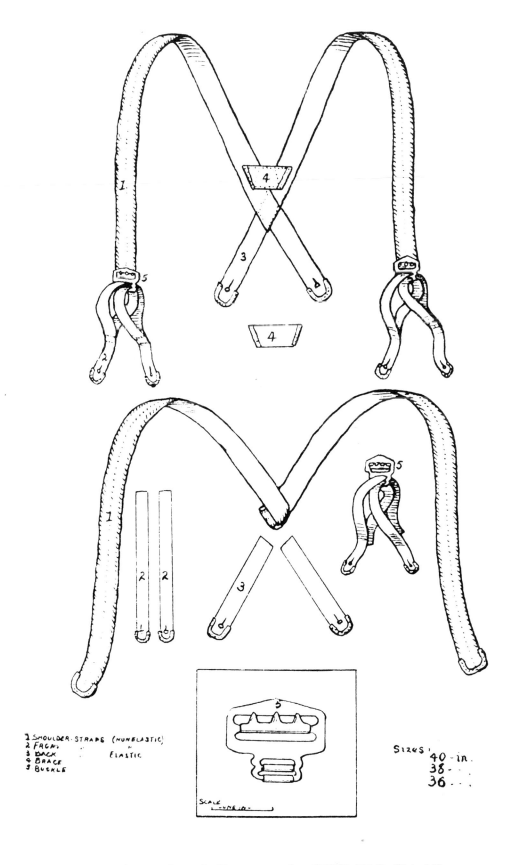

1 SHOULDER STRAPS (NONELASTIC)
2 FRONT   "
3 BACK   ELASTIC
4 BRACE
5 BUCKLE

SIZES:
40 in.
38 -
36 -

SCALE

Fig. 14. Drawings of military suspenders (USWD 1884b: Plate 24).

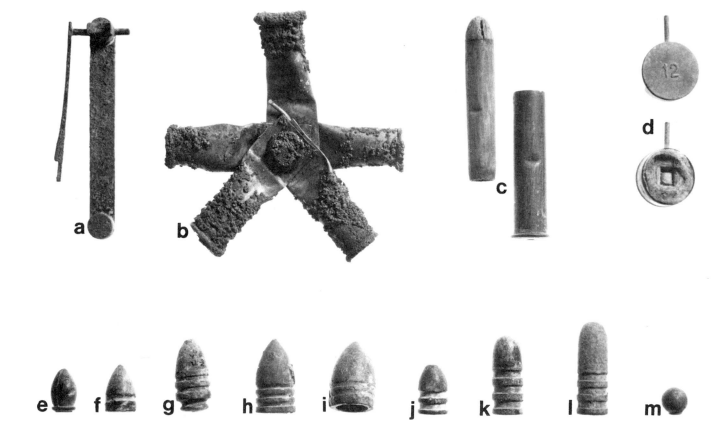

Fig. 15. Weapon Part, Cartridges, and Bullets

    a. Ramrod stop and band spring

    b. Benét primed cartridges riveted together

    c. "Dummy" .45-70 cartridge

    d. Pinfire shotgun shell

    e. .36-caliber combustible cartridge bullet

    f. .44-caliber conical bullet

    g. .52-caliber Sharps bullet

    h. .58-caliber Minié

    i. .69-caliber Minié

    j. .45-caliber revolver bullet

    k. .45-55 carbine bullet

    l. .45-70 rifle bullet

    m. .36-caliber ball round

Diameter of *h:* .57 in.

ARMS AND AMMUNITION

Arms

Only 15 weapons parts and pieces of cleaning equipment were found, in contrast to the great number of cartridges and other types of ammunition recovered.

One iron butt plate was recovered that measures 5 by 1¾ in. An iron rod with a brass head at one end probably belonged to a muzzle-loading shoulder weapon. The brass head has a diameter of approximately .38 in. It is believed that this item was part of a ramrod.

One nearly complete revolver was recovered. Although it cannot, because of its condition, be identified by exact caliber or manufacturer, it is either a .30- or .32-caliber, 5-shot, sheath trigger, metallic cartridge revolver. It appears to be very similar to an illustration of a .32-caliber White Star Revolver in *Firearms Identification* (Mathews 1962: 279). There were, however, literally hundreds of such "suicide specials" manufactured, so that precise identification is often difficult even for specimens in good condition.

Also recovered was a length of shotgun barrel, which was part of a 12-gauge, double-barrel weapon. Sections of both barrels remain; the longest remaining portion measures 22¾ in.

Six weapons parts are more specifically identifiable than those discussed above. One firing pin from the so-called trapdoor Springfield rifle, Model 1870, was found. From another Springfield, Model 1873, came a ramrod stop and band spring (Fig. 15 *a*). These parts were utilized on both the .45-70 rifle and the .45-70 carbine (McLean 1969: 26-8), and therefore the stop and spring may have belonged to either of these. The ramrod stop has an inscription reading, 'PAT AUG 16, 1870.' This date refers to patent #106,405, entitled "Ramrod Stop," filed by Samuel W. Porter, Springfield, Massachusetts (USPO 1872a: 657). The claim consists of a physical description of what is termed an improved ramrod-stop.

Other items for the Springfield .45-70 include a rear sight base from a Model 1873 or Model 1877 carbine. The government publication entitled *Description and Rules for the Management of the Springfield Rifle, Carbine, and Army Revolvers. Caliber 45* (USWD 1874a: 18) specifically details the differences between the rifle and carbine rear sight bases.

The former is graduated to 400 yards, while the latter goes to 500 yards. The Fort Bowie specimen has four elevation "steps" and is therefore clearly a carbine sight. (The rifle sight base, with three such "steps," is represented by an 1873 Springfield model in the collection of the Arizona Historical Society, Tucson.) Since the carbine sight that was recovered lacks the leaf, the part that is diagnostic for the model, determination of the particular model year is not possible.

The other rear sight recovered is a Model 1879 "Buckhorn." Given the condition of the artifact, this identification is as specific as possible, even with the detailed description of the four forms of the Model 1879 sight provided in Hicks's *Notes on United States Ordnance* (1940: 99-100).

One breech block and level action assembly from a Model 1865 Spencer carbine or rifle was recovered. It was possible to distinguish between the Model 1860 and the Model 1865, since the latter has a cut-out and a coil spring not present on the earlier model. Despite the extremely rusted condition of the artifact, an X-ray revealed the cylindrical hole that accepted the coil spring, clearly showing it to be the later model.

The barrel and part of the receiver of a Model 1906 slide action Winchester .22-caliber rifle were also found. This popular weapon, which came with a barrel 20 in. long, originally retailed for $9.50 (Madis 1971: 467). The recovered specimen was obviously deposited after the Army had ended its occupation of the fort.

Five accessories or appendages for weapon cleaning and repair were recovered. Four of these are parts of brass bore brushes, with diameters ranging from .29 to .43 in. One of these, the base to which the brush was attached, has a threaded shaft. The other parts have a threaded socket to receive the brush base, and each was originally attached to either a wooden rod or a leather thong. Both the rod and the thong type of bore brush were used for handguns of the period. The fifth accessory is an L-shaped double-bladed screwdriver, 3¼ in. long and made of iron. Edwards (1953: 285) illustrates a screwdriver that appears to be virtually identical to the Fort Bowie specimen; it belonged with a Colt New Model 1857 pistol. This tool was probably used with other weapons as well.

Ammunition

The 2,850 specimens of ammunition recovered at Fort Bowie include 1,965 cartridges, 129 shotgun shells, 59 bullets, three ball, three pieces of shot, and 691 primers.

Cartridges

A total of 1,978 metal cartridges was recovered at Fort Bowie. The 42 different rounds identified range in size from .22 through .56 caliber and display a variety of headstamps (Fig. 16). Several of the categories of cartridge recovered – for example, the .22-caliber – were deposited both during and after the occupation of the post.

.22-Caliber. Four types of .22-caliber cartridges were identifiable among the 59 specimens collected. The most frequent type identified was the .22-caliber Long or Long Rifle, of which 51 specimens were found. The .22 Long was developed as early as 1871 as a black powder revolver load, while the .22 Long Rifle was developed in 1887 by the J. Stevens Arms and Tool Company (Barnes 1965: 274); they utilized cases of identical dimensions. Eight different headstamps discernible (Fig. 16) include several that positively date to the fort's occupation, several that definitely postdate it, and two that are unidentified.

Four .22 Short cartridges are examples of the oldest commercially produced, self-contained metallic cartridge (Barnes 1965: 273). This round, which was developed by Daniel Wesson in 1857 for the Smith and Wesson (S&W) First Model revolver, is still extensively loaded and used today. One .22-caliber Winchester Rimfire (WRF), produced by Winchester, was recovered. This round was introduced in 1890 for Winchester's Model 1890 pump or slide action rifle, but has also been chambered in various Remington, Stevens, and Winchester rifles and several Colt revolvers. Three other .22 cartridges were collected – one fragmentary case and two .22-caliber shot rounds, a modern "snake-load."

.28-Caliber to .30-Caliber. One .28-caliber and four different .30-caliber rounds are among the cartridges that postdate the military occupation of Fort Bowie. These specimens, all introduced in 1895 or later, include one .280 Kynoch, two .30-06 Springfield, two .303 Savage, three .30 Luger, and three .30-30 Winchester cartridges (Fig. 16).

.32-Caliber. Seven cartridges representing five different .32-caliber loads were collected. The one .32 Long found is a rimfire cartridge introduced in 1861 for the S&W New Model No. 2 revolver. Colt's New Line revolvers were also chambered for this round (Barnes 1965: 277). The two .32 S&W rounds recovered (Fig. 16) could date as early as 1878. Originally designed for the S&W Model 1½ hinged frame, single-action revolver (Barnes 1965: 154), this round was later chambered in a large variety of handguns. Caliber .32 rifle loads identified include two .32 Winchester Centerfires (WCF), originally used in Winchester's Model 1873 repeating rifle, as well as in Winchester and Colt single shot rifles (Pacific Hardware and Steel 1902: 917). Also found was one .32 CLMR, "adapted to Colt's and Winchester Repeating Rifles" (Pacific Hardware and Steel 1902: 917). "CLMR" is the acronym of Colt's Lightning Magazine Rifle, a weapon first introduced in 1885 (Haven and Belden 1940: 180). The .32 CLMR cartridge, also known as the .32-20 Winchester, was introduced possibly as early as 1882 (Bearse 1966: 123). Another example of a cartridge postdating the fort is one .32 Remington, which was introduced in 1906 (Barnes 1965: 81).

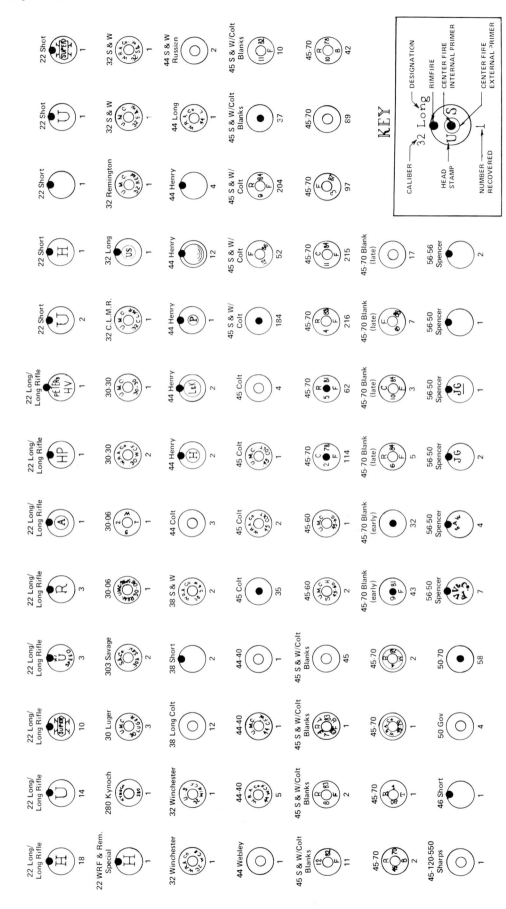

Fig. 16.   Cartridge types and headstamps recovered at Fort Bowie, arranged by caliber. Not to scale.

.38-Caliber. Twelve of the 19 .38-caliber cartridges collected are .38 Long Colts. Introduced in 1875 for Colt's New Line, this round was the official U.S. Army cartridge from 1892 until 1911 (Barnes 1965: 162). At least 9, if not all 12, of the cartridges recovered were blanks. Also recovered were two examples of the .38 Short, a rimfire cartridge dating to about 1866, when Remington's Model 1866 revolving rifle was available as a .38 rimfire (Barnes 1965: 278). This was a popular round — Barnes cites an 1876 catalog that lists this cartridge as being chambered in rifles of three separate manufacturers and in pistols produced by more than five different firms. Other .38-caliber cartridges recovered include three fragmentary rounds, possibly .38 Long Colts, and two .38 S&W cartridges (Fig. 16); the latter were introduced around 1877 by Smith and Wesson for their hinged frame revolvers.

.44-Caliber. The 36 .44-caliber cartridges are of seven identifiable types. The three .44 Colts could date as early as 1871, the year the round was introduced (White and Munhall 1967: 80-81); however, it is more likely that they date no earlier than 1873, since that is the year that the round became the official military revolver cartridge (Barnes 1965: 169). One of the earliest weapons chambered for this round was the metallic cartridge conversion model of the 1860 Colt percussion revolver. The .44 Colt was superseded in 1875 when the Army adopted the .45 Colt as the official load.

One fragment of an externally primed cartridge that lacks a headstamp may be a .44 Evans. There were two variants of this load, a long and a short. The former was introduced around 1875, while the latter was developed in 1877. The .44 Evans Short was available as late as the 1920s (Barnes 1965: 101).

The Henry was the .44-caliber cartridge most frequently recovered at Fort Bowie. A total of 21 of these rimfire rounds was recovered, but not all of them were fired in a Henry rifle. The Henry rifle has a distinctive firing pin, which leaves two marks on the head of the cartridge instead of the more usual single impression. In addition to the Henry rifle, the Ballard and the Wesson have been suggested as weapons that could have fired the round. The cartridge itself was manufactured from 1860-61 until 1934 (Barnes 1965: 280).

One example of a .44 long centerfire was recovered (Fig. 16). Introduced in 1875 or 1876, it was used in a number of single shot rifles. Two specimens were identified as .44 S&W Russian cartridges, which were used in Smith and Wesson's Model No. 3 single action revolver, manufactured from 1870 to 1875 (Logan 1959: 137). This model was followed in production by a commercial or civilian model in 1878 (Barnes 1965: 167). One other .44-caliber revolver round recovered is the .44 Webley. This round originated in 1868 and was used in at least one Harrington and Richardson revolver. The seven .44-40 (or .44 WFC) cartridges recovered were made for use in the Winchester Model 1873 rifle and the Colt single-action revolver. This was only the beginning, however; as Barnes states, "just about every American arms manufacturer has offered some weapon chambered for this round" (1965: 61). In addition to the above .44-caliber rounds, 13 fragments were recovered that may have been either .44- or .45-caliber cartridges.

.45-Caliber. By far the most commonly recovered cartridges at Fort Bowie were .45-caliber rounds. The 13 different types identified represent slightly more than 88 percent of all the metallic cartridges (excluding shotgun shells). As with much of the material from the fort, the .45-caliber rounds show the process of technological change; both internally primed cartridges and the newer externally primed cartridges are present.

Thirty-five specimens, all lacking headstamps, represent the early type .45 Colt round, which utilized the internal Benét primer introduced in 1873. It measures 1.26 in. in length. By December 1879, experimental solid-head reloadable cartridges were being manufactured at the Frankford Arsenal (Hackley, Woodin, and Scranton 1967: 10). Seven externally primed Colt revolver cartridges were recovered. Two bear the headstamp of the Winchester Repeating Arms Company (Fig. 16) and four lack a headstamp. One cartridge has the headstamp 'U.M.C./45 Colt' (Fig. 16), which identifies it as having been manufactured by the Union Metallic Cartridge Company prior to its merger with Remington in 1888.

The .45-caliber Smith and Wesson Schofield revolver was introduced in 1874. Like the Colt, it first used an internally primed round. The S&W cartridge was shorter than the Colt, measuring 1.1 in. Its production at the Frankford Arsenal began on August 20, 1874, and it bore no headstamp (Hackley, Woodin, and Scranton 1967: 19). One hundred eighty-four examples of this round were recovered. In 1882 an externally primed cartridge of the same length replaced the earlier model (Hackley, Woodin, and Scranton 1967: 205). This was the most common revolver round recovered. The 256 specimens are all headstamped and were manufactured from February 1883 through June 1887.

Although there is no record of blanks specifically manufactured for the Colt, 106 blanks for the S&W revolver were recovered. Prior to 1880, Benét internally primed blanks were manufactured at the Frankford Arsenal. By 1880 production was switched to externally primed rounds (Hackley, Woodin, and Scranton 1967: 14). Thirty-seven of the early type were recovered, none of which had headstamps. Of the 69 externally primed blanks, 45 bore no headstamp, indicating that they were manufactured as blanks (Hackley, Woodin, and Scranton 1967: 15). Those blanks that have headstamps were produced between November 1882 and August 1883 (Fig. 16).

In addition to the revolver cartridges discussed above, 10 fragments of .45-caliber, internally primed cartridges, all lacking headstamps, were recovered. More specific identification was not possible because of their incomplete state.

Three .45-60 rifle cartridges predating 1888 and bearing the headstamp of the Union Metallic Cartridge Company were recovered (Fig. 16). This round, introduced in 1880 (Barnes 1965: 110), was used in a variety of weapons, including those made by Colt, Kennedy, and Winchester.

In 1873 the Ordnance Department reduced the caliber of issue carbines and rifles from .50 to .45 caliber. The rounds for these weapons were internally primed .45-70 cartridges. The designation .45-70 is used here and in Figure 16 in a general sense, to include both rifle cartridges, which were .45-70 (.45 caliber and 70 grains of powder), and carbine cartridges, which were actually .45-55 (.45 caliber and 55 grains of powder). It is possible to distinguish between rifle and carbine loads for some, but not all, internally primed .45-70 cartridges, on the basis of headstamps.

Although production of .45-70 ammunition began in September 1873 at the Frankford Arsenal (Hammer 1970: 8), it was not until March 1877 that headstamping became standard practice (Hackley, Woodin, and Scranton 1967: 204). A total of 133 specimens of .45-70 internally primed cartridges lacking headstamps, and thus dating from the period September 1873 to March 1877, was recovered at Fort Bowie (these are not represented in Figure 16). Cartridges produced between March 1877 and April 1886 were headstamped with either 'R' (rifle) or 'C' (carbine), and with the month and year of manufacture (Fig. 16). The internally primed specimens recovered range in date from March 1877 through July 1882, including all the years but not every month. One hundred fourteen .45-70 carbine cartridges and 62 rifle cartridges were recovered, as were 15 specimens whose headstamps were indistinguishable. In all, 324 internally primed .45-70 cartridges were collected.

One interesting artifact recovered from Building 35, room 9, consists of five Benét internally primed .45-70 cartridges riveted together (Fig. 15 *b*). Only a small portion remains of a piece of copper wire that was also riveted to this object, which is covered with redeposited copper. The combination of the wire and the copper deposits suggests that this object may have served as a makeshift telegraph battery copper in place of the more common sheets of copper recovered at the post. (Telegraph battery parts recovered are described below under *Communication.*)

Externally primed .45-70 cartridges officially replaced the internally primed rounds in August 1882. The word "officially" should be emphasized, since 47 of the total 713 externally primed .45-70 rounds (excluding blanks) have headstamps dating their manufacture prior to August 1882 (Fig. 16); of the remainder, 137 either bear no headstamp or have an indistinguishable headstamp.

Two of 216 .45-70 rifle rounds produced at Frankford Arsenal were made prior to the official acceptance of the externally primed cartridge – one in January 1881 and the other in April 1882. Other headstamps on this type of round give a date of manufacture as late as February 1885. Headstamp dates on the 215 Arsenal-manufactured .45-70 carbine rounds range from August 1882 through April 1886 (Fig. 16).

In 1886 the government changed its headstamp, and the carbine and rifle designations on the cartridges were eliminated (Fig. 16). The 97 cartridges in this category were manufactured between July 1886 and September 1888.

One unique .45-70 cartridge, with a January 1887 headstamp, was recovered from wall debris of Building 6, one of the officers' quarters. This cartridge contained a dummy round carved from a piece of pine (Fig. 15 *c*). The dummy is 2-5/16 in. long and has a concave base so that it fits over the primer at the head of the cartridge.

Forty-eight of the .45-70 cartridges were produced by civilian manufacturers; all were externally primed. Of the 44 made by the Union Metallic Cartridge Company, 42 were produced in September and October 1878. One cartridge was manufactured by the Lowell Cartridge Company in April 1880, and one round produced by Winchester is undated. Two cartridges produced in April 1879 bear a headstamp 'R-79-W-4,' reading clockwise (Fig. 16); the manufacturer was not identified. It should be noted that all but three of these civilian-produced cartridges were definitely manufactured prior to the official date of transition to externally primed cartridges.

As with the other .45-70 cartridges, blank rounds were represented by earlier and later models at Fort Bowie. The early pattern is a Benét primed cartridge 1.6 in. long. Thirty-two of the total of 75 cartridges of this type bear no headstamp and therefore were either made prior to 1877, when headstamping began, or were originally produced as blanks. Hackley, Woodin, and Scranton (1967: 15) note that blanks made from fired cartridges or rejects normally had a headstamp, while those manufactured as blanks did not. This information seems to be incorrect for internally primed blanks, however, because some of these blanks were found with headstamps dating from July 1881 through October 1882 but lacking the carbine or rifle designation (Fig. 16); apparently, these specimens were originally manufactured as blanks.

Two characteristics distinguish the later .45-70 blank from the earlier one: it was externally primed and the case was 1.845 in. long. Fifteen of the total of 32 in this category fit the above description of remakes, since the headstamps bear the 'C' or 'R' model designation (Hackley, Woodin, and Scranton 1967: 15). The remaining 17 specimens of this later model have no headstamp and presumably were originally manufactured as blanks.

The last type of .45-caliber round to be discussed is the .45-120-550 Sharps. The one example of this centerfire cartridge, lacking a headstamp, has a case that is 3¼ in. long. According to Barnes (1965: 113), it was introduced in 1878-79 for the Sharps-Borchardt rifles, although other single-shot rifles were chambered for it.

.46-Caliber. The only .46-caliber round recovered was a .46 Short without a headstamp. This rimfire cartridge was designed for the Remington Army Single Action and other revolvers (Logan 1959: 69).

.50-Caliber. The cartridge that preceded the .45-70 in government issue was the .50-70. It was the official U.S. military rifle cartridge from 1866 to 1873, and was the first centerfire cartridge in general use by the military. Fifty-eight examples of the early internally primed Benét-type rounds, all lacking headstamps, were recovered. Also found were four externally primed .50-70 cartridges, which were called ".50-caliber Governments." These four rounds could have been chambered in a number of single-shot and repeating rifles as late as the early 1900s (Barnes 1965: 115).

.56-Caliber. The largest caliber rifle cartridges recovered at Fort Bowie were a number of .56-caliber Spencer rounds. Fifteen specimens of the .56-50 Spencer have been identified. This round was first used in the Model 1865 Spencer repeating carbine (an action from this weapon is described above, under *Arms*). The .56-50 was listed in a 1918-19 Remington catalog as being adapted to Spencer, Remington, UMC, Sharps, Peabody, and other rifles and carbines (Barnes 1965: 781). Headstamps on the 15 examples recovered include the marks of Fitch, Van Vetcher and Company, New York; Jacob Goldmark, New York; and Sage Ammunition Works, Middletown, Connecticut (Fig. 16).

Two examples of an earlier Spencer cartridge, the .56-56, were recovered. Patented in 1860 and manufactured in great quantity beginning in 1862, this round was loaded by manufacturers as late as 1920 (Barnes 1965: 281). Neither these cartridges nor another fragmentary .56-caliber Spencer round were headstamped.

In addition to the cartridges described above, fragments of six other cartridges were recovered, but they were too incomplete to allow determination of size or manufacturer.

Shotgun Shells

A total of 129 shotgun shells was recovered during the work at Fort Bowie. Shells were found in gauges 8, 10, 12, 16, and 20. Since a 20-gauge Springfield was the only shotgun issued by the army for other than prison and paymaster duties during the period of the fort's occupation (Hanson and Jackson 1965: 52), most of the recovered shells were apparently used in privately owned weapons. General Crook, for example, was said to travel with a rifle and a shotgun (Bourke 1891: 110).

8-Gauge. The largest shotgun shells recovered were three 8-gauge shells. These paper-cased rounds were manufactured by the Union Metallic Cartridge Company beginning in 1874 (Fellows 1969). In fact, all shotgun shells recovered were paper-cased, with the exception of the 20-gauge brass shells produced by the government.

10-Gauge. Twelve 10-gauge shells were recovered, and their headstamps show manufacture by two companies. Eight Winchester 'No. 10' shells were found. Four other shells, bearing three different headstamps, were produced by the Union Metallic Cartridge Company. The earliest, a U.M.C. 'No. 10,' could have been produced as early as 1874. The two 'Club' brand rounds were produced between 1888 and 1891 (Moos 1968: 40). The one 'New Club' brand shell found was produced no earlier than 1891, at which time it replaced the 'Club' brand.

12-Gauge. The 12-gauge shotgun was obviously the most popular size at Fort Bowie. In all, 102 12-gauge shells or fragments, representing the products of four different companies, were recovered.

Four brands appear among the 37 Union Metallic Cartridge Company shotshells recovered. The one 'U.M.C. Co./No. 12' was produced beginning in 1874 (Fellows 1969), while the 33 'No. 12/Club' shells were produced by U.M.C. beginning in 1891 to replace the 'Club' brand. The one 'No. 12/Nitro Club' recovered was a brand first produced in 1899 (Fellows 1969).

The dates of manufacture are not as well defined for the shotgun shells produced by the U.S. Cartridge Company. The company was founded in 1864, and ammunition was marketed under its name into the late 1920s (Vinson 1968: 92-3). Three 'Star,' three 'Climax,' and 14 'First' shells were found. These brands were noted in an 1891 U.S. Cartridge Company price list (Fellows 1969). The other 12-gauge shell made by this company has the headstamp 'U.S. Second/Quality.' The dates of its production were not ascertained.

The Winchester Repeating Arms Company produced 31 of the 12-gauge shotgun shells found at Fort Bowie. The three 'W.R.A. Co./Rival' shells could have been produced any time between the late 1870s and the early 1900s, while the one 'Winchester/Leader' was introduced in 1894 (Vinson 1968: 91). The dates for the 'Star,' 'Repeater,' and 'NuBlack' brand shells could not be pinpointed. Twenty-two 'Winchester/No. 12' and five 'S.Q.' (Second Quality) shells were also recovered.

Eight 12-gauge shotshells or fragments that were found could not be dated or identified by company. They are the brass bases of paper-cased Lefaucheux pinfire shells (Fig. 15 *d*) with an embossed '12' for a headstamp. Patented in France in 1835, the Lefaucheux pinfire cartridge was exported to the United States in limited numbers (Barnes 1965: 301). It was used only to a limited extent during the Civil War, and its appearance at an isolated western cavalry post is therefore something of a surprise.

16-Gauge. Only two 16-gauge shotgun shells were recovered. One shell is a 'Leader,' a brand introduced in 1894; the dates for the one 'Repeater' specimen are uncertain. Both brands were produced by Winchester.

20-Gauge. A Winchester 'No. 20 Repeater' paper-cased shotshell is one of only 10 20-gauge shells recovered. The remaining nine are brass-cased shells produced by the government's Frankford Arsenal. The five shells with discernible dates on the headstamp were manufactured between December 1882 and September 1884. These rounds were issued for use in the 1881 Springfield 20-gauge shotgun that the Army issued to western posts specifically for hunting (Hanson and Jackson 1965: 52). The Springfield 20-gauge was in general use by the Army until 1904. An interesting sidelight is that none of the first 250 Springfields were issued to cavalry regiments (Hanson and Jackson 1965: 52), and it was not until 375 more were manufactured in 1882 that they were available to mounted troops.

Bullets, Ball, and Buckshot

The 65 projectiles in this category include buckshot, bullets not attached to metallic cartridges, and combustible-cartridge bullets.

Bullets. The smallest combustible-cartridge bullet found is .36 caliber (Fig. 15 *e*). This single specimen, probably used in a percussion pistol, weighs 135 grains. The two .44-caliber conical revolver bullets recovered (Fig. 15 *f*) were probably used with a skin cartridge; they weigh approximately 207 grains each. Although it was not possible to determine the weapons for which most of the combustible-cartridge bullets were intended, two .52-caliber Sharps bullets (Fig. 15 *g*) were identified. The specimen illustrated weighs 453 grains. Originally called the 32-Bore Sharps Paper, this round was used in the Model 1859 Sharps B.L. (breech loading) percussion military rifles and carbines (Logan 1959: 14).

Six .58-caliber "Minié balls" were recovered. These were intended for use in the 1855 Springfield rifle-musket. Indeed, it was the development and introduction of the Minié ball, a decided improvement over the round ball used in smooth-bore firearms, that led to the production of the .58-caliber rifle-musket. Minié balls, which were conical in shape (Fig. 15 *h*), were used with paper cartridges. The recovered specimens weigh 35 to 39 grains less than the 500 grains that Logan (1959: 16) lists as the specified weight. The diameters range from .568 to .573 in. and are somewhat less than the diameter of the musket bore. This difference between the bore and bullet diameters facilitated loading, since the bores of blackpowder weapons were most often fouled, and it also allowed for the expansion of the hollow base of the Minié projectile.

One .69-caliber Minié bullet was recovered (Fig. 15 *i*). This projectile was not to be used in the .69-caliber musket, first adopted in 1795 (Hicks 1962: 126), but in the .69-caliber

rifled musket. Despite the general trend toward reduction in caliber of issue arms, the latter weapon was introduced around 1855, at approximately the same time as the .58-caliber rifle-musket, and its bore was rifled after manufacture specifically to exploit the advantages of the Minié ball. The .69-caliber rifled musket is known to have been carried as late as 1862 (Lewis 1956: 169).

The bullets from metallic cartridges recovered at Fort Bowie are not as varied as the combustible-cartridge bullets. All but one in this category are .45-caliber. The exception is a .38-caliber round-nosed bullet. It weighs 143 grains and has two grease grooves, but the weapon from which it was fired was not identified.

Eighteen .45-caliber revolver bullets were recovered, some of which had been fired. The bullet from this common round (Fig. 15 *j*) weighs 230 grains and is identical for both the Colt and the Smith and Wesson Schofield.

Twenty-eight bullets that were either used in or intended for use in government-issued .45-caliber rifles or carbines were recovered. Sixteen carbine bullets (Fig. 15 *k*) were readily distinguishable from 11 rifle bullets (Fig. 15 *l*), while one round was too fragmentary to be identified specifically. Distinguishing characteristics of the two rounds are: (1) weight – 405 grains for the carbine, 500 grains for the rifle; (2) length – 1-1/8 in. for the carbine, 1-5/16 in. for the rifle; and (3) base shape – the carbine bullet has a concavity nearly 3/16 in. in diameter, whereas the rifle bullet has a depression only 1/16 in. in diameter. This last distinction is quite useful in identifying deformed bullets.

Ball. Only three ball rounds from percussion pistols were recovered. One is rather small, apparently intended for a .28-caliber weapon. It weighs 31.2 grains, varies from .269 to .285 in. in diameter, and displays both sprue and mold marks. The sprue mark is also evident on the other two ball rounds. One, a .36-caliber ball (Fig. 15 *m*), weighs 83.7 grains and has a diameter of .382 in. The other is either .44- or .45-caliber, and weighs 137.7 grains.

Buckshot. The absence of mold and sprue marks as well as the presence of small surface facets makes it possible to distinguish three pieces of buckshot from the percussion ball rounds discussed above. Two of the three are No. 0 buck, while the remaining specimen is No. 000 buckshot.

Primers and Percussion Caps

Two types of percussion caps were recovered at Fort Bowie. One is called the musket or "top-hat" percussion cap (Fig. 17 *a*); 17 examples were recovered. The second type is called the ground edge percussion cap (Fig. 17 *b*); 12 of these were recovered. Although the caps came in several sizes, the nipples onto which they fit were interchangeable from weapon to weapon, so that a correlation from percussion cap to specific firearm is not possible.

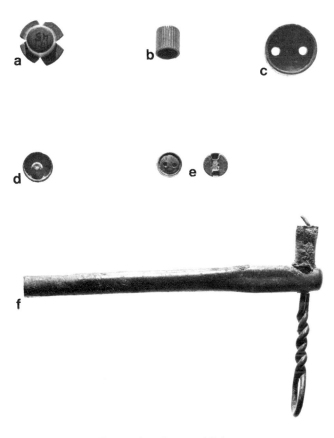

Fig. 17. Percussion Caps and Primers
    a. Musket or "top-hat" percussion cap
    b. Ground edge percussion cup
    c. Underside of Benét primer
    d. Expended Berdan primer
    e. Boxer primers
    f. Cannon friction primer
Length of *f:* 2-3/8 in.

The Benét-type primer was used by the military in their .50-70 and early .45-70 metallic cartridges. It was an internal primer, which could not be replaced for reloading purposes – a characteristic that led to its replacement by external, replaceable primers. The Benét cup primer (Fig. 17 *c*) is an integral part of a cartridge, and only one specimen was found not attached to a cartridge.

Expended primers from centerfire, externally primed metallic cartridges were a common artifact at Fort Bowie. Two basic types, totaling 625 specimens, were recovered. The Berdan primer (Fig. 17 *d*), of which six specimens were recovered, was a cup containing the fulminate mixture but no anvil; the anvil was an integral part of the primer pocket in the cartridge. The more recent type of external primer is the Boxer type, which is still in use. Many variations of this primer, which has an anvil as part of the primer itself, have been developed over the years. Two kinds of Boxer primers, mostly expended, were recovered (Fig. 17 *e*).

Probably the only artifactual evidence of weapons other than small arms at Fort Bowie is the 36 cannon friction primers recovered (Fig. 17 *f*). A lanyard was attached to the serrated wire, which was twisted and extended from the body of the primer, and the wire was pulled to detonate the powder sealed inside. In 1882 a new model of primer was introduced (USWD 1884b: 154). The changes consisted of having the primer "made from cartridge copper instead of brass, and in having the end stopped with a tinfoil cup instead of a wax plug." The specimens recovered at Fort Bowie appear to be of the latter type.

COINAGE

Coinage recovered at Fort Bowie can be divided into three subcategories: U.S. currency, foreign currency, and tokens. Because the 20 pieces of currency recovered are very common or are in poor condition, or both, none can be considered particularly valuable specimens.

U.S. Currency

Seven denominations are represented among the 18 coins of United States currency (Table 13). The dates indicate that all but the two quarter-dollars were minted within the period during which the fort was occupied.

Foreign Currency

Of the two foreign coins recovered, one is an 1882 Mexican 10-centavo piece. The mint mark shows it to have been produced at the Hermosillo mint, and it is 90 percent silver in content. The second foreign coin is more unusual. This badly worn silver coin is .84 in. in diameter and .03 in. thick. One side of the coin has the silhouette of a male bust facing to the right, and the legend around the rim, 'Carolus II− DEI GRATIA.' The date '1783,' directly below the bust, is almost illegible, and the reverse side has been worn smooth. A biconically drilled suspension hole apparently altered the original numeral 'III' to a 'II,' since the year 1783 falls within the reign of Charles III of Spain, 1759-1788.

Tokens

A total of nine tokens was recovered during the stabilization of Fort Bowie. One, reading 'Warren Bisbee Bus Line/Student Token,' obviously postdates the fort's occupation. The remaining eight, all of brass, are of three different types.

The first is a circular token, .88 in. in diameter (Fig. 18 *a*). One side reads 'POST TRADER FORT BOWIE A.T.' ('A.T.' stands for "Arizona Territory"), while the reverse side reads 'GOOD FOR ONE DRINK.' The date at which a trader was first established at Fort Bowie is uncertain. A map of the first fort shows a building labeled "Mr. Anderson

TABLE 13

United States Coins

Denomination	Date, Mint Mark, Type	Number
Silver dollar	1883-s	1
Half dollar	1871-s	1
	1875	1
Quarter-dollar	1861	2
Dime	1869-s	1
	1871	1
	1899-s	1
Half-dime	1868	1
Five-cent piece	Shield type without rays, probably 1869	1
	Shield type with rays, 1866	1
	Liberty head with 'CENTS,' 1883	2
One-cent piece, Indian head	1871	1
	1887	1
	1891	1
	(Illegible)	1
Unidentifiable (possibly one-cent Indian head)		1
Total		18

Fig. 18.   Tokens
    a. 'POST TRADER/FORT/BOWIE/A.T.'
    b. 'POST CANTEEN/FT. BOWIE A.T./ 5/¢'; overstamped
    c. Obverse: 'GOOD FOR ONE GAME/ TROOP 'G'/4TH U.S./CAVALRY'; Reverse: 'THE BRUNSWICK BALKE/ COLLENDER/COMPY./CHECK'; overstamped 'C'

Diameter of *a:* 7/8 in.

Trader" (Sheire 1968), and Murray (1951: 153) notes that a trader was located at the new post at least as early as 1869. The latest possible date for this drink token is 1890, the year the post trader's store was replaced by an official post canteen (Murray 1951: 292).

This same year, 1890, is the earliest that two recovered coins of military scrip could have come into use. On both specimens, one side is blank, while the other reads 'POST CANTEEN, FT. BOWIE A.T.' around the perimeter. One coin is a 10-cent piece and the other (Fig. 18 *b*) is a 5-cent piece. The post canteen functioned until the post was abandoned in 1894.

The five examples of the third type of token were all coined by one company, The Brunswick Balke Collender Company. These tokens are pool or billiard checks. On the obverse is the company name and a depiction of a pool table (Fig. 18 *c*). On the reverse (Fig. 18 *d*) is the legend 'Good for one Game' and a troop designation of a U.S. Cavalry unit. Two tokens bear the designation 'Troop 'C'/4th U.S./Cavalry,' and two read 'Troop 'G'/4th U.S./Cavalry'; on the fifth token the specific troop of the 4th Cavalry cannot be discerned. In addition to the minted embossing, there is a legend overstamped on four of the tokens. Two read 'G 9th I,' while two have a large 'C' on one side. In all, three Army units are

represented by these tokens, which may be dated through documentary sources giving the dates during which the units were stationed at Fort Bowie. Troop G, 4th Cavalry, was at the post between June 1884 and September 1888. Troop C, 4th Cavalry, arrived in May 1885 and stayed until June 1890. The overlapping periods may explain why tokens originally coined for Troop G were overstamped with the Troop C designation; they were probably used by Troop C after the departure of Troop G. Company G, 9th Infantry, arrived at the post in September and October 1887 and departed in June 1890. The two tokens with the 'G 9th I' overstamp were probably also modified after Troop G, 4th Cavalry, left the post in 1888.

COMMUNICATION

"Communication" is a term of broad application, but it is utilized here to refer essentially to written and electrical communication, the two forms for which metal artifacts have been identified in the Fort Bowie collection. Remains of the heliograph, which played such an important part in Miles's campaign in 1886, were not noted among the materials recovered.

The written word was an important part of life at Fort Bowie. Not only were letters written and received, but numerous Army reports had to be written in the Indian War

Fig. 19. 'CARTER'S INKS' patented pen rack, shown with a hard rubber penholder. Length of penholder: 6-15/16 in.

period, just as they are today. Representing these activities are 25 metal writing implements, parts, and accessories.

Six pen points made by two firms were recovered. Esterbrook's #048 Falcon, #305 Colorado No. 1, and #314 Relief, and Joseph Gillot's F Warranted 404 were identified. They are all listed in the 1892-93 Marshall Field catalog (pp. 160-1), selling for $.30 to $.57 per gross. Ten penholders for these points were also recovered (Fig. 19). One was manufactured by the Eagle Pencil Company, while six others were produced by the Eberhard Faber Pencil Company. The Faber penholders bear a patent date of March 27, 1877, which refers to design patent #9,870. This was granted to Phillip Schrag, New York, who assigned it to the Eberhard Faber Pencil Company, Port Richmond, New York, for the 14-year term of the patent (USPO 1877b: 504). The Faber firm was established in 1861 (G. Smith 1972: 142) and is still in operation as of the late 1970s. Two pencil ferrules were also found, but the manufacturers could not be identified.

In addition to pen and pencil parts, one complete pen rack and six fragments were identified. This item, illustrated as it was used (Fig. 19), is stamped with the legend 'CARTER'S PAT. JULY 21ST 68 INKS.' On that date, William E. Clarke of Attleborough, Massachusetts, was granted patent #80,140, which he assigned to Henry F. Marsh of Boston (USPO 1870: 258). Henry Marsh may have been employed by Carter's, which was established in 1858 and first advertised in the Boston City directory in 1869 (Nelson and Hurley 1967: 72). It is not known whether Carter's sold these racks or distributed them as a promotional device.

Two forms of electrical communication are known to have been used at Fort Bowie. A telephone line was constructed between the post and the town of Willcox in 1890 and was torn down just before the post was abandoned in 1894 (Murray 1951: 289). No artifact could be identified as related to this line. However, a number of artifacts were identified as part of the telegraph line that was operating at

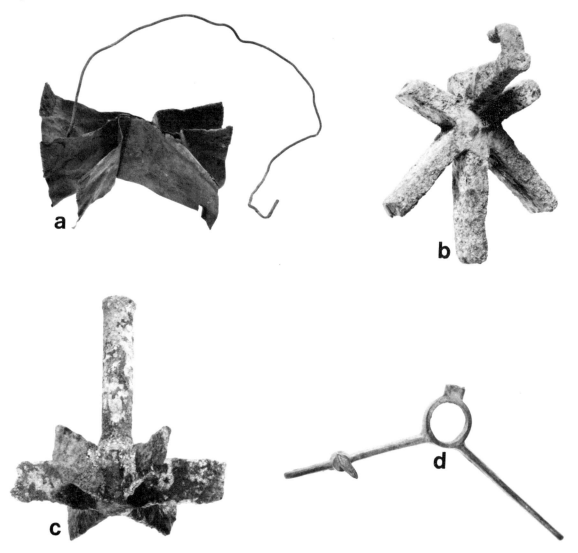

Fig. 20. Telegraph Battery Parts
    a. Copper sheets and wire riveted together
    b. Zinc "crow foot"
    c. "Six-toed" battery zinc
    d. Bracket for "six-toed" battery zinc
    Width of *d:* 6½ in.

the post by the spring of 1877 (Murray 1951: 177). The batteries consisted of a glass jar filled with acid in which two metal parts were immersed; the resulting chemical reaction produced an electrical current. One of the metal components was a series of copper sheets riveted together in the middle with a length of copper wire riveted to one of the sheets (Fig. 20 *a*). The other, called a crow foot battery zinc, was found in two different forms at Fort Bowie. One type (Fig. 20 *b*) was suspended from the side of the jar, its shape obviously giving rise to the term "crow foot." The complete apparatus is illustrated in the 1895 Montgomery Ward catalog (Dover 1969: 215). The second type (Fig. 20 *c*) has six "toes" radiating from the base of a post; it was suspended from a brass bracket (Fig. 20 *d*), which rested on the rim of the glass jar. These batteries were sold through the early part

of the 20th century, and two sizes were offered in the 1913 catalog of H. G. Lipscomb and Company (Lipscomb 1913: 409). In all, 34 whole and fragmentary telegraph battery parts were recovered.

Two other objects most likely associated with the telegraph are pieces of 10- and 11-gauge iron and steel wire, 11-12 in. long, apparently cut from the original line. Attached to both pieces are loops of wire, approximately 2¾ in. in diameter, which held the telegraph wire to a glass insulator.

HARDWARE AND CONSTRUCTION MATERIALS

This section is not concerned with all items that may be found in hardware catalogs of the Fort Bowie period, but rather with items of hardware that do not properly belong

TABLE 14

Nails

	Penny (d) Size															Fragments	Total
	2	3	4	5	6	7	8	9	10	12	16	20	30	40	60		
Hand wrought	1	2	2	5	1	1	6		1	2				2	1	35	59
Square cut common		5	23	9	29	30	12	5	22	7	25	8		4		141	320
Square cut finishing	1		1	2	2	2	1			2						3	14
Wire	1		1		2		3		1			1	1	4	3	1	18

in the more specific categories of metal such as transportation, tools, and household. In order to facilitate the locating of particular items, the hardware has been subdivided into four categories: Construction, Builder's (mainly window and door items), Plumbing, and Miscellaneous.

Construction Hardware

In addition to some of the more obvious pieces of construction hardware, such as nails, bolts, and screws, a number of other generalized construction items have been included in this section – for example, the majority of brackets, braces, and corner irons, which cannot be related specifically to items of furniture or to wagons.

Sixty whole and fragmentary braces or brackets were recovered from more than 17 separate proveniences at Fort Bowie. These are handmade, not manufactured items, which were undoubtedly used for a variety of functions. Of varying shapes, these iron braces range up to 27 in. in length and ½ in. in thickness. Nineteen have eyeholes at one or both ends, with diameters up to 1 in. Although a few of the holes are square, probably to accept a carriage type bolt, most holes are round and have been punched rather than drilled.

A corner iron is a type of small bracket with two arms, generally of equal length; the arms form a right angle, so that the holes in one arm are perpendicular to those in the other. The 15 specimens recovered, like the braces discussed above, came from a number of proveniences and were undoubtedly used for a variety of purposes. Although many of the pieces have countersunk holes, probably to accept flathead wood screws, this is not always the case. At least two corner irons have a bolt or large rivet still present in the hole, and one still has two brackets fastened to it.

One variant of the corner iron is called a flat corner plate; as its name implies, it differs from the corner iron in that the holes in the two arms are in the same plane. The one handmade specimen identified has arms of unequal length, a feature that sets it apart from the manufactured corner plates illustrated, for example, in the 1910 Sargent and Company catalog (p. 914).

Four hooks that were recovered have been categorized as gate hooks, since their length, ranging from 4½ to 7¾ in., exceeds that of the small hooks and eyes frequently used on doors. These hooks are all fashioned of iron wire or rod.

One interesting piece of construction hardware recovered was a drainspout or *canale* (Fig. 21 *a*). The purpose of the *canale* was to drain water from the flat roofs of adobe buildings, which were enclosed by the exterior walls. Although it was flattened when found, this light-gauge galvanized iron spout originally had a diameter of approximately 3 in. Even if the provenience of this artifact had not been recorded, it would have been safe to surmise that it came from the post trader's store, since photographs show that this was probably the only flat roofed building at the fort near the end of the occupation of the post (Sheire 1968).

Nails, which total 411 (excluding horseshoe nails), constitute the largest category of construction hardware at Fort Bowie. It is not surprising, therefore, that all three major types of nail technology – hand-wrought, machine-cut, and wire – are represented. Nelson (1968) notes that hand-wrought nails were used well into the 19th century and that wire nails were introduced in the 1850s. Table 14 summarizes the types and sizes of nails recovered from all areas of the fort.

Several varieties of spikes are represented among 76 recovered specimens, although many are too fragmentary or rusted to be identified by type or size. The most common type of spike identified was the square cut spike that is actually just a very large cut nail (Fig. 21 *b*). At least 40 of the total sample are square cut spikes; these range from 3 to 12¾ in. in length. A boat spike has a square shaft, a chisel-like point, and a head with five facets (Fig. 21 *c*). The eight boat spikes that were found range in length from 5½ to 6¾ in. Also recovered was a railroad spike 4¾ in. long (Fig. 21 *d*). The remaining spikes range in size from 4 to 13 in., but are too incomplete to permit more detailed identification.

Like other types of construction hardware, staples were found scattered throughout the post. The 29 staples recovered range in size from 1¾ to 5 in. in length, although 18 are 3 in. or less. Only a few of the staples were manufactured; most were handmade from round iron rod.

Bolts of many sizes were recovered from 23 different proveniences throughout the post, the largest quantity coming from the test trenches in the dump. Among the total of 139 bolts and bolt fragments are the following: 84 carriage bolts, 17 stove bolts, 15 machine bolts, 7 tire bolts, and 16 bolt shafts without heads. Despite their names, all these types

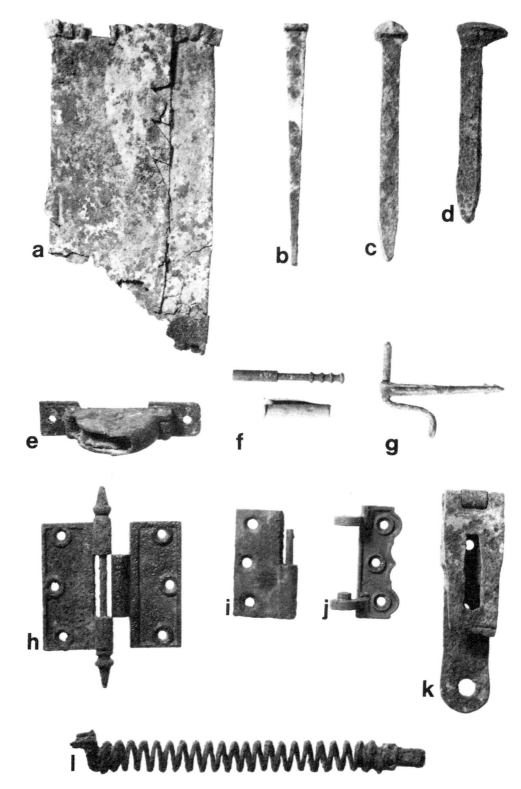

Fig. 21. Construction and Builder's Hardware   Length of *l:* 9¾ in.

a. Drainspout *(canale)*   g. Brace hook
b. Square cut spike   h. Loose pin butt hinge
c. Boat spike   i. Loose joint butt hinge
d. Railroad spike   j. One half of spring hinge
e. Window frame (sash) pulley   k. Hinge hasp
f. Window frame bolt   l. Door spring

of bolts were used on a variety of objects, and there is a wide range in size. Carriage bolts, for example, range from 1¾ to 13¼ in. in length, with the majority measuring less than 5 in. Of the 51 nuts used on these bolts, almost all (49) are square; only two hexagonal nuts were recovered. Considering the number of nuts and bolts recovered, it is somewhat surprising that only 53 washers were found. Almost all of these came from either the trash dumps, Building 18, or Building 39. The washers are in standard sizes from 1/8 to 15/16 in. inside diameter, the majority from 3/8 to 5/8 in. Only four washers are brass; the rest are iron.

In addition to nails, nuts, and bolts, 66 screws were recovered. They are all of one type – iron flathead wood screws. As with the bolts, the majority of the screws were recovered from the test trenches in the trash dump and from Building 18, the corral. Lengths range from 5/8 to 2-7/8 in., with shank diameters of 1/8 to 5/16 in.

Builder's Hardware

The term "builder's hardware" is used by the hardware trade to refer to a specific group of items that includes the various types of door and window hardware. The locks and hinges included in this section, for example, are exclusively those used on doors, and other types of these items are dealt with in other sections.

Window Hardware

Relatively little window hardware was recovered at Fort Bowie. One complete window frame (or sash) pulley (Fig. 21 *e*), as well as fragments of three others, came from the trash dump. This item, also called an axle pulley (Huntington Hopkins Company 1890: 488), was intended to be mortised into a window frame and served to carry the rope and the sash weight, which were ordinarily attached to the window sash to counterbalance its weight and thereby facilitate its opening and closing.

One device for holding a window open is called a window spring bolt. It consists of an iron bolt, 3-1/8 in. long, riding in a barrel (Fig. 21 *f*). The bolt extends horizontally through the side of the sash so that one end, in front of the glass, can be grasped; the other end fits into a hole or socket in the window frame. The exact type found at Fort Bowie is listed in the catalog of Huntington Hopkins Company (1890: 507) at $2.90 to $7 per gross, depending upon finish. The 1866 Sargent and Company catalog (p. 77) lists window spring bolts at $2.75 and $3.75 per gross.

Five examples of a brace hook used in conjunction with a hinge were found (Fig 21 *g*). Used for window blinds hung outside the casing, the hook was driven into the casing and provided a pivot point or a pintle for the blind. An illustration in the Huntington Hopkins Company catalog (1890: 642) shows a hook that is virtually identical to the Fort Bowie specimens. The listing cites Washburn's blind hinges at $.13 per set, which includes the hook and a hinge. A similar item listed in another catalog is called Orr's Brace Hook (Baker and Hamilton 1889: 523). On the same page this catalog also lists Washburn's blind fast. One badly rusted specimen closely resembles this item, which was intended to hold a blind either open or closed.

Door Hardware

The bulk of the builder's hardware consists of 129 items of door-related hardware. Six types of door hinges were found, including three kinds of butt hinges. Ten parts from loose-pin butt hinges were recovered from five separate buildings and the trash dump. This type of hinge (Fig. 21 *h*) has two pieces joined by a removable pin. The hinge pin in the illustration has what is termed an acorn tip; one pin with a round tip was also recovered. Ten examples of the second type of butt hinge, termed a loose joint hinge (Fig. 21 *i*), were recovered, mostly from the trash dump. This hinge has a metal rod or pin in one half that fits into a shaft on the other half. In contrast to the loose pin hinge, the pin in the loose joint hinge is not removable, nor does it extend above or below the hinge. The third type of butt hinge is called a fast joint butt hinge. Nine hinges of this type were recovered. This style is distinctive in that it uses no pin and cannot be disassembled. Five other fragments of butt hinges were recovered but were too incomplete to type. All the butt hinges are iron, the most common sizes (opened) being 2½ or 3 in. by 2½ or 3 in.

Two specimens of the same half of a patented spring hinge were recovered (Fig. 21 *j*). The legend on the back reads 'Pat. Aug. 8, 1882.' On that date, patent #262,400 was granted to William Gilfillan and assigned to Sargent and Company, New Haven, Connecticut (USPO 1883a: 464). A 1910 Sargent and Company catalog (p. 546) lists a 3-in. cast iron spring hinge, at $1.70 per dozen pairs, that appears to be identical with the specimens recovered. However, the catalog gives a patent date of February 6, 1883. While this 1883 patent (USPO 1883b: 517) makes no reference to the 1882 patented hinge, the assumption is that the 1883 patent is an improved version of the earlier model. It would appear, therefore, that the Fort Bowie specimens were manufactured sometime between August 1882 and February 1883.

Twelve incomplete specimens were recovered that could have been from either strap hinges or T-hinges. They came primarily from the dump. The largest recovered, which is almost complete, measures 10-5/8 in. in length.

Nine whole or fragmentary hinge hasps, a variation on the strap hinge, were recovered (Fig. 21 *k*). A hinge hasp was used with a padlock and locked a door from the outside in a much more substantial fashion than did the rim locks of the period. Many of the recovered specimens, including the one illustrated, were handmade. Most are 9 to 12 in. long, but one extraordinary specimen from the post trader's store is 3 ft. in length.

Also recovered were six fragments of hinges that are too incomplete for the specific type to be determined. Like all the hinges discussed thus far, these are of iron.

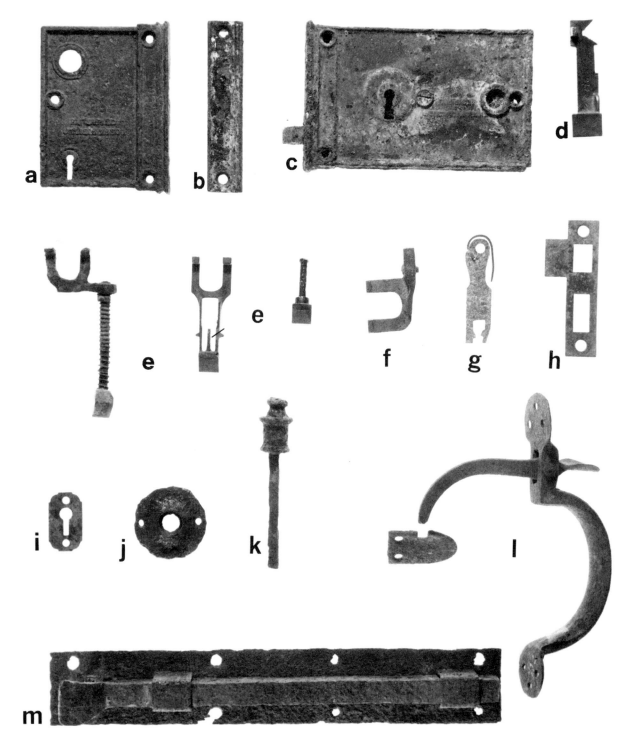

Fig. 22. Door Hardware

Length of *m:* 12 in.

a. Upright rim lock case
(P. and F. Corbin Company)
b. Rim lock striker
c. Horizontal rim lock
(Davenport, Mallory and Company)
d. Rim lock bolt
e. Mortise lock bolts
f. Mortise lock tailpiece

g. Mortise lock tumbler
h. Mortise lock striker
i. Keyhole escutcheon
(P. and F. Corbin Company)
j. Rosette
k. Doorknob shank and spindle
l. Thumb latch and catch
m. Square bolt

One iron or steel spring (Fig. 21 *l*) was originally part of a spring hinge that closed a door. It appears quite similar to, and may actually be, the Star pattern spring hinge illustrated in a Pacific Hardware and Steel Company catalog (1902: 518). The complete hinge was 11 in. long and sold for $1.50 per dozen.

A relatively large number of door locks and parts were recovered from the post. In all, 43 locks, parts, and keys could be identified as door hardware. The most common type of lock found is the rim lock. The upright rim lock (Fig. 22 *a*) was screwed onto the inside of the door, while the striker (Fig. 22 *b*) was attached to the door frame. The horizontal rim lock (Fig. 22 *c*) was merely a different style. The manufacturer of this item, 'D. M. & Co.,' has been tentatively identified as Davenport, Mallory and Company, a firm that was in operation in New Haven, Connecticut, about 1868 (Bishop 1967: 433). The total of 25 rim lock parts recovered includes cases, case covers, strikers, and internal parts. A typical rim lock bolt, made of brass, is shown in Figure 22 *d*; the numbers '0470' stamped on the shaft represent a model produced by the P. and F. Corbin Company, New Britain, Connecticut. Similarly, the case in Figure 22 *a* can be identified as a Corbin lock, since it has '0460' cast in raised numerals on the inside of the case. A Corbin catalog (1885: 519) lists model No. 0460 as a Reversible Lever Upright Rim Knob Lock. The exterior of the case bears a patent date of June 8, 1880, further confirming the identification, since the patent was assigned to P. and F. Corbin Company by William E. Sparks on that date (USPO 1880b: 1313-4).

Although rim locks were apparently the most common, mortise locks were also in use at the post. A mortise lock, the type that has come to be used almost universally today, is set (mortised) into the edge of a door. Among the 13 mortise lock parts recovered were three bolts (Fig. 22 *e*), a tailpiece (Fig. 22 *f*), a tumbler (Fig. 22 *g*), and a striker (Fig. 22 *h*), as well as fragments of two Corbin cases.

Of the five door keys found, at least two appear to belong to Corbin locks. They are of brass and are quite similar in design to keys illustrated in an 1885 Corbin catalog (p. 616). The remaining three keys are of iron.

Two keyhole escutcheons, which were attached to a door on the side opposite a rim lock, were also recovered. One is of brass (Fig. 22 *i*) and was manufactured by P. and F. Corbin (Corbin 1885: 570). The second, a type called a drop escutcheon, is a movable cover to protect the keyhole; it is similar to models pictured in the 1885 Corbin catalog.

Figure 22 *k* shows a doorknob spindle fitted into a metal shank, to which a ceramic doorknob was originally attached. The spindle, one of two recovered, was the most common size sold, ¼ in. square. The shank, which is of iron, is one of six recovered. Door rosettes or roses (Fig. 22 *j*) are essentially decorative items, used to cover the hole in the door through which the doorknob spindle passes. They were used on both sides of a door with a mortise lock, or

on the outside of a door with a rim lock. Three examples of such rosettes were found.

When a doorknob and lock were not used, a thumb-type latch was commonly employed. One complete latch and one catch (Fig. 22 *l*) were recovered from separate proveniences at the post. Also recovered were three handmade parts from thumb latches. Along with the thumb latch, a barrel, spring, or square bolt was frequently installed on the inside as a locking device. One complete square bolt (Fig. 22 *m*), one spring bolt, and part of a spring or square bolt were also recovered.

Plumbing Hardware

Plumbing was a late addition at Fort Bowie. Initially water was hauled from springs to the post in wagons. It was not until the fall of 1885 that water works were installed (Murray 1951: 170). Bids advertised in 1884 called for laying a total of 6800 feet of 1-in., 1¼-in., and 2-in. iron pipe. In 1889 the 2-in. pipe from the spring proved to be inadequate and was replaced by 4-in. pipe (Montgomery 1966).

Considering all the pipe that was laid and replaced, it was somewhat surprising that only 72 artifacts relating to plumbing were recovered. The majority, 32 pieces, are small lengths of various kinds of pipe. Diameters range from 3/8 to 5¼ in., but most of the pieces measure from ½ to 1½ in. The pipe recovered is obviously small scrap, for only five pieces are longer than 12 in. While iron pipe is the most common, four pieces of lead pipe were also recovered.

The 11 iron pipe fittings collected are standard couplings, plugs, caps, or elbows. The four brass fittings recovered include one coupling and three sink drains or flanges. The metal cores from three sink stoppers were found, as were two pipe hooks of iron.

One brass water faucet (Fig. 23 *a*), complete with a 2-in. diameter collar at the intake end, was recovered from the trash dump. The intake and outlet diameters are both ½ in. on this unlabeled faucet. The proper term for this item, according to a Pacific Hardware and Steel Company catalog (1902: 1131), is "lever handle bibb."

Two iron valve handles were recovered. Also recovered were a type of metal washer that was probably part of a steam valve handle and a brass object believed to be an interior moving part from a water valve.

A good deal of the above material was found in the trash dump, and most of the remainder came from buildings known to have been connected to the water line. The one anomaly is a 1¼-in. diameter iron coupling recovered from Building 109 at the old fort. There is no record of the old fort having been connected to the water line, even though it was used throughout the second fort's occupation as married soldiers' quarters. Therefore, the presence of the coupling in Building 109 is almost certainly not related to working plumbing at that location.

Fig. 23. Plumbing and Miscellaneous Hardware
  a. Lever handle bibb
  b. Possible sink drains
  c. Grommet
  d. Glue brush handle and jar cover
  e. Flanged lid or "tin can screw"
  f. Lid with stamped floral design
  g. Padlock shackle and locking bolt
       (Ames Sword Company)

Length of *l:* 3 in.
  h. Padlock drop escutcheon
  i. Padlock key
       (D. K. Miller Lock Company)
  j. Scandinavian type padlock key
  k. Tent pole ends
  l. Tent slips
  m. Bale tie

A large iron nut from Building 30 may have been a plumbing fitting. It is 1-3/16 in. high with an interior diameter of 2-7/16 in. A flange 1/16 in. wide projects into the interior diameter of this specimen, apparently to hold a pipe or fitting in place. Eight facets around the top of the exterior clearly indicate that the object was designed to be tightened with a wrench.

The precise use of 14 iron fittings recovered from the kitchen of the post trader's store (Building 31, room 8) is uncertain, but they are believed to be related to plumbing. These fittings (Fig. 23 *b*), which are possibly sink drains, have interior diameters ranging from 3/4 in. to 7/8 in. There is 3/4 in. of wood thread below the flange on the exterior surface, but no thread on the interior.

Miscellaneous Hardware

The 871 artifacts grouped in this section are truly a miscellany, since many of them are pieces from larger objects, or items to be affixed to or used in conjunction with other objects. Barrel parts and buckets, some electrical material, a few small pieces of machinery, padlocks and keys, and rivets are among the items included. All of the items described here are to be found in various hardware catalogs of the period; however, none properly fit into any of the more specific functional categories of metal, and some almost certainly were used for a variety of purposes.

Buckets

Buckets, of which 15 complete and fragmentary specimens were found, might have been used to carry water for cooking, drinking, or washing clothes or to water horses, among other things. One copper and two galvanized iron buckets were found. Of the 10 bucket or kettle ears recovered, some still had rivets attached for fastening the ears to metal buckets, while several appeared to have been used on wooden buckets. Two pieces of an iron band, found at the old fort, are thought to have been fastened to the rim of a wooden bucket; two iron D-rings rotate in brass hinges that were riveted to the band.

Barrel Hoops

Twenty fragments of barrel hoops were found, many still retaining one or more rivets. Widths of these bands range from ¾ to 1¾ in. on 12- to 19-gauge iron. The size of the barrels from which these pieces came could not be determined since most of the pieces were less than 12 in. long.

Chain

Essentially four types of chain are present among 41 lengths and individual links recovered (this figure does not include those pieces of chain that are parts of harness, which is discussed below under *Transportation*). Twenty-two pieces of long and short straight-link iron chain and iron twisted-link chain were found. Also recovered were three lengths of brass chain. Eleven iron end links and five chain repair links were found. Although much of the iron chain was doubtless used on wagons, less than a third of the chain was recovered from the corral. The iron chain was made from rod ranging from 3/16 to 7/16 in. in diameter and was sold not by length, but by the pound. The 1890 Huntington Hopkins Company catalog (p. 314) lists prices for short straight-link iron chain ranging from 8½ cents per pound for the heavier chain to 12 cents per pound for the lighter chain.

Grommets

Of the 70 specimens of two- and three-piece grommets found at Fort Bowie, only one is made of iron; the remainder are of brass (Fig. 23 *c*). Interior diameters range from .18 to .64 in. The most common sizes have interior diameters close to ½ in., and exterior diameters ranging from 1.1 to 1.25 in. These grommets were probably used on a variety of articles, including tents, tarpaulins, and wagon covers. Only one specimen still had some cloth clamped in the groove.

Handles

Sixty-five handles of various sizes and shapes, not attached to any object, were recovered. Seven identical specimens are sufficiently distinctive to be identified as the handles of brushes, probably from small jars or pots of glue. One of these (Fig. 23 *d*) is still in place in the center of the jar cap. The remaining specimens are all carrying rather than grasping handles. Most are not singular enough to be specifically identified, but many may have been attached to large tin cans. The vast majority are wire and are either rectangular, oval, or D-shaped. Three are cast iron movable, drop-type handles.

Lids and Covers

Like handles, metal lids and covers were common objects and were found scattered throughout the fort. The most prevalent type is listed under "Tinners' Trimmings and Supplies" in a catalog of Holbrook, Merrill and Stetson (1911: 94-5). These 22 specimens, called tin can screws, are threaded tin caps for cans and jars. Some are straight-sided, while many have a short beveled flange at the bottom edge (Fig. 23 *e*). Inside diameters range from 1 to 4 in., and most of the measurable specimens are 1¼ in. in diameter. One of the other 10 lids recovered is brass, and two are heavy cast iron. One unique lid, 3¼ in. in diameter, is covered with an intricate stamped floral and scroll design (Fig. 23 *f*). In the center is the legend 'E.A.P. Paris,' which may stand for Ed. Pinaud, a Parisian perfumer, but this could not be verified.

Rings and Loops

Another group of items whose specific use was unverifiable consists of 122 brass and iron rings and rectangular iron loops. While rings of two specific sizes have been placed with the harness trappings, those described here could not be positively identified as having come from harness or saddle goods, although the likelihood is high. Nine brass rings have interior diameters ranging from 7/16 to 7/8 in., while the 91 iron rings vary from ½ to 3½ in.; the most common diameters are 5/8 and 1¾ in. The iron rectangular loops, like the rings, are probably harness items. For example, the cavalry halter in *Ordnance Memoranda No. 29* (USWD 1891: 36, Plate VII) utilized two iron loops; their precise size is not specified, but they were sewn to leather straps 1¼ in. wide. Of the 22 rectangular loops recovered at Fort Bowie, the most common size is 1¼ by 1½ in.

Grease Cup

One complete grease or oil cup and a cap from a second were recovered. These small reservoirs, both of brass, were undoubtedly used on some type of machinery, as they are today, to lubricate gears, bearings, or bushings by dripping oil or grease onto the appropriate part.

Padlocks and Keys

Along with the hinge hasps described above, padlocks were used at Fort Bowie. Four padlocks and ten padlock parts were recovered. One of the padlocks was produced by the Yale and Towne Manufacturing Company, Stamford, Connecticut. Their catalog for 1884 (p. 224) identifies the lock found at the post as Model No. 813, "Spring Padlock, 3 brass tumblers, 54 changes, size 1 in., finished bronze, $12.00/dozen." This little lock is interesting in that it has four patent dates stamped on one side: February 1, 1876; July 10 and November 27, 1877; and September 24, 1878. All of these patents were granted to Warren H. Taylor of Stamford, Connecticut, the latest in conjunction with Henry R. Towne, and all were assigned to the Yale Lock Manufacturing Company (USPO 1876b: 220; 1878a: 63, 64, 931; 1879a: 450). It is interesting to note that only two of these patents refer to padlocks, while the other two are for drawer or cabinet locks.

Part of a padlock produced by 'W. W. & Co.' was recovered. These initials probably refer to William Willcox and Company of Middletown, Connecticut, which was granted a padlock patent on January 27, 1874 (USPO 1874b: 112). Two brass padlock shackles collected were stamped with the name of Romer and Company, of Newark, New Jersey. Little more is known of these two companies.

One shackle and two locking bolts were recovered from a padlock manufactured by the Ames Sword Company, Chickopee, Massachusetts (Fig. 23 *g*). This firm dates from at least 1834, when the Ames Manufacturing Company was organized (Gardner 1963: 6). The various Ames companies are generally thought of as manufacturers of firearms and edged weapons, and Ames is still in operation as of the late 1970s. The brass shackle bears the Ames name and also a patent date of September 18, 1882. The company must have secured rights to that patent subsequent to that date, since padlock patent #264,445 granted to Charles C. Dickerman, Boston, does not mention the Ames firm (USPO 1883a: 952-3). The illustration accompanying the patent gives the term for the locking bolt seen in position below the shackle in Figure 23 *g*.

One other padlock part is a brass drop escutcheon (Fig. 23 *h*). Although this specimen has 'U.S.' clearly stamped on the front, it appears to be virtually identical with a commercially sold escutcheon illustrated in Blumenstein (1968: 101-2) on tumbler padlocks 306 and 314. In any case, padlocks were issued by the military, as an 1876 War Department report indicates: "A new standard padlock has been adopted during the year ... for the cavalry service the 'Goodenough' (both iron and steel), the 'Burden' and the 'Schoenberger' were the most suitable" (USWD 1876: 236).

In addition to the locks, 12 keys were recovered. Two identical padlock keys (Fig. 23 *i*) were made by the D. K. Miller Lock Company, Philadelphia. This firm was established in 1871, incorporated in 1904, and merged with Yale and Towne in 1925 (Porter 1925: 1633). This shape of key was used on Miller's Champion 6-Lever padlocks numbers 1, 7, and 10 (Pacific Hardware and Steel 1902: 481). Another key is known to have been manufactured by Yale and Towne; it is illustrated in their catalog (1884: 236) as "No. 77 ... for all padlocks of 1½ and 1¾ in. size." The blanks sold for $1.25 per dozen. One other key (Fig. 23 *j*) is noted in a Sargent and Company catalog (1910: 1049) as a key for a Scandinavian type padlock. This iron key is 2-13/16 in. long.

Rivets

Rivets were a common item at Fort Bowie; 285 copper rivets and burrs and six iron rivets were recovered. The iron rivets range from 2¼ to 4¼ in. in length. Many of the copper rivets and burrs found were undoubtedly related to harness equipment, since 56 percent of those recovered came from the harness room at the corral. However, rivets were also used on such articles as clothing and tents, and they are included here with the iron rivets, which are not ordinarily used on harness.

Tent Parts

Murray (1951: 169-70) notes that housing was often insufficient at Fort Bowie and that "between 1880 and 1886 it often became necessary to erect tents on the parade ground." Thirty-seven artifacts in the collection reflect such tenting activity. The 12 iron tent pins recovered range from 9¼ to 17 in. in length. Although an Army board on equipment and uniforms noted that "experience on the frontier and in the winter season has fully established the advantages of iron tent pins" and recommended that they be manufactured and issued (USWD 1879: 19), most, if not all, of the tent pins found appear to be handmade. Also recovered were four metal tent pole ends (Fig. 23 *k*) of the type illustrated in an annual report of the Secretary of War (USWD 1884b: Plate 75). The same report (pp. 644-5) mentions metal tent slips purchased from Isaac Townsend of Philadelphia. Twenty-one of these tent slips were recovered (Fig. 23 *l*); they bear a November 30, 1880, patent date, which refers to patent #234,896, granted to Henry B. Townsend and assigned to Isaac Townsend, Philadelphia (USPO 1881: 1239). The slips were used to provide tension on the ropes that ran from the tent to a tent pin. Although three sizes are noted in Plate 38 of the 1884 report, only size Number 1, which is 3 in. long, was found.

Wire

Recovered from the trash dump and 15 separate buildings at the fort were 134 pieces of iron, steel, brass, and copper wire. Only three pieces of barbed wire, all the same type, were found. They appear to be Burnell's Four-post barbed wire, a successful double-strand variety patented by Arthur S. Burnell of Marshalltown, Iowa, on June 19, 1877 (McCallum and McCallum 1965: 251). Other single- and double-strand iron or steel wire, ranging from 1 to 18 gauge in size, consists mostly of scraps less than 12 in. long and constitutes 66 percent of the wire collected. The 32 pieces of copper or brass wire found range in size from 8 to 23 gauge. Like the iron wire specimens, these are obviously scraps — only four pieces are longer than 9½ in. Ten iron or steel bale ties, all but one found in the trash dump, are the type commonly seen on baled hay; the combination of a loop and twisting on 13- to 15-gauge wire (Fig. 23 *m*) makes these items fairly distinctive. A fragment of one brass wire screw hook was made from wire .132 in. in diameter.

Miscellaneous

A small alligator clip, 1¼ in. long and made of steel, was found. This is the type of clip generally used to make temporary electrical connections. Although it bears a February 11, 1879, patent date, this item was not found in the patent records.

Other pieces of miscellaneous hardware recovered include three heavy-duty wing nuts for 3/8-in. bolt or threaded rod, and two parts of clamps for wire rope or cable. The manufacturers cannot be identified, since there are no markings.

Two small pieces of hardware recovered are parts from small wooden boxes, perhaps jewelry boxes. One is a small brass plate, ½ by 15/16 in., that has an incised scroll design on its upper surface and a small hook on the underside. The other piece is a small decorative hinge only 1¼ in. long and ½ in. wide.

One small brass T-shaped device was listed in a Marshall Field catalog (1892-3: 175) under "McGills Patent Fasteners" and was described as "for fastening and binding of all descriptions, sampling all kinds of drygoods, etc." While bearing no patent date, the specimen is virtually identical to the item described in the catalog. Clips of this type are still used to fasten papers together.

Three small iron coil springs were recovered, two of them from the first fort. None could be linked with any specific use or piece of hardware.

Several parts of metal vessels, trays, or bowls were recovered. They all are too fragmentary or crushed to be identifiable, but one of the two copper objects may have been an oval bowl approximately 22 by 11 by 4 in. Two other fragments are tin or galvanized iron.

HOUSEHOLD ITEMS

The title of this category is intended to be understood in its broadest sense. While some families did live at Fort Bowie during its occupation, most of its inhabitants — enlisted men, officers, and civilians alike — were single men who lived in barracks. Kitchens were most often not part of the living quarters, but were located in separate buildings behind the barracks. The term "household" is used here to refer to metal kitchen and table wares, interior furnishings, and tin cans and parts of containers, most of which undoubtedly held food. Many of the 734 artifacts were recovered not from kitchens and living quarters, but from various parts of the trash dumps.

Kitchen and Table Wares

In all, 143 items of kitchen and table ware were identified, including such things as pots and pans, cutlery and flatware, coffee mill parts, salt shaker tops, and locking cocks from kegs. While much, if not most, of this material was probably purchased and distributed by the Army Quartermaster, it is noteworthy that very few items can be definitely identified as having been Army issue.

Exceptions to this general rule are nine pieces of Army-issue flatware. Two forks, two knives, and three spoons, as well as two fork or knife handles, all appear to be identical with those described and illustrated in a set of 1885 regulations (USWD 1891). Both the spoons and the forks (Fig. 24 *a*) are 7½ in. long; the spoons are made of tinned iron, while the forks and knives are made of steel and have a depressed central area.

The remaining 46 pieces of flatware and cutlery were not issue items. Iron and steel are the most common materials, but a number of silver or silver-plated spoons and forks were recovered. The non-silver ware includes five spoons, only one of which is complete. It is a teaspoon 5½ in. long, with a "tipped" handle, a common pattern. Of 11 knives or knife fragments found, only one had an all-metal handle; of the remaining 10, only three had remnants of the bone or wood handles that had been riveted in place. One of these (Fig. 24 *b*) is a wood-handled butcher knife with 5½ in. of its blade remaining. Two other fragments are also portions of butcher knives. At least five of the seven non-plated forks recovered had attached handles. One small brass four-tined fork (Fig. 24 *c*) had originally been hafted, but nothing remains of the handle. Two iron forks still had portions of their bone handles intact; one of these (Fig. 24 *d*) is a small carving fork with a crudely executed geometric design carved in the handle. Of eight additional iron or steel handle fragments, only one is noteworthy. This item, possibly a knife, has a depressed area like that on the fork pictured in Figure 24 *a*, and the initials 'L.F. & C.' are embossed in the hollow. It is possible that this knife was produced by Landers, Frary and Clark of New Britain, Connecticut, a firm incorporated in May 1853 (Moodys 1920: 254).

At least four manufacturers are represented among the 15 pieces of silver or silver-plated ware recovered. One fork or spoon handle bore the name 'Wm. Rogers & Son AA.' This firm was organized in 1865 by William Hazen Rogers and

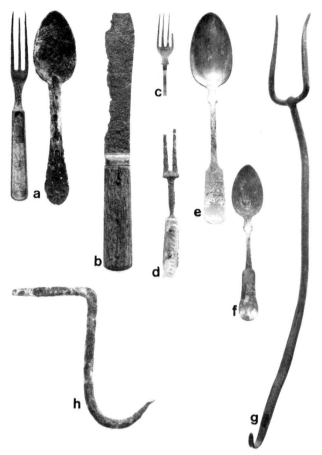

Fig. 24. Kitchen and Table Utensils
    a. Military issue fork and spoon
    b. Butcher knife
    c. Brass four-tined fork
    d. Carving fork
    e. Silver tablespoon (Brown and Brothers)
    f. Monogrammed silver teaspoon (J. B. LeBeau)
    g. Flesh fork
    h. Meat hook

Length of *a:* 7½ in.

his son, William Rogers, Jr. It was one of the companies that combined in 1898 to form the International Silver Company (Rainwater 1966: 152). A tablespoon with the common tipped pattern on the handle (Fig. 24 *e*) was produced by Brown and Brothers, of Waterbury, Connecticut. The hallmark on the back of the handle was patented on September 21, 1875, for use on brass, German silver, and silver-plated goods (Rainwater 1966: 24). Brown and Brothers was out of business by 1904. A monogrammed silver teaspoon (Fig. 24 *f*) bears the hallmark 'J.B. LeBeau/St. Louis, Missouri' on the back of the handle shaft, but no information concerning this firm could be located. No manufacturer could be identified for an 8-in. fork with the hallmark 'CP' or for a 6-in. plated teaspoon with 'R&B White Metal' on the handle shaft. It is possible that the latter was a product of Rogers and Brothers, but this is not certain (Rainwater 1966: 145). The firm of Rogers and Hamilton, of Waterbury, Connecticut, was incorporated on February 14, 1886. The secretary

and partner, William H. Rogers, a Hartford cigar dealer, was obviously included in order to capitalize on the similarity of his name to the famous Rogers Brothers (Rainwater 1966: 148). All 10 pieces of Rogers and Hamilton plated ware – seven forks and three fork or spoon handle fragments – were recovered from three rooms at the post trader's store. They are all the very plain, unadorned Windsor pattern, judging by illustrations in a Pacific Hardware and Steel Company catalog (1902: 860-1).

One iron fork, 17 in. long (Fig. 24 *g*), is called a flesh fork and was apparently used primarily by cooks to handle large cuts of meat. Wrought iron flesh forks like the one found at Fort Bowie, but 18 in. in length, were sold for $2.25 per dozen by one dealer in 1911 (Holbrook, Merrill and Stetson 1911: 15). One meat hook was recovered (Fig. 24 *h*). It measures 5½ in. from the base of the hook to the top of the shaft, and was designed to be driven into a wooden wall or post to hold large cuts of meat. This particular specimen, however, was recovered from Building 18, room 4 – a harness room at the corral – and therefore was more likely used to hold harness or tack.

Cast iron cooking vessels were commonly used at Fort Bowie. All but five of 46 fragments recovered came from the trash dump. While most are too fragmentary for the type of vessel to be identified, four pieces are from dutch ovens, eight from frying pans, and two probably from a kettle. Many of the pieces appear to be parts of fairly sizable vessels. One frying pan, for example, was approximately 11 in. in diameter. Another fragment, possibly the bottom of a skillet, was nearly 12¼ in. in diameter.

One other piece of cast iron cooking ware recovered is the top half of a waffle iron. It is 8 in. in diameter, and the cooking surface is divided into quadrants. This design (Fig. 25 *a*) is referred to as the "American Pattern" in several catalogs of the period.

Several blue enamel tinware objects were found. One is an oval pan or bowl 12 by 8 by 2 in. Another is probably the body or cup from a water dipper; a blue enamel dipper handle was found nearby in the dump, as were two other iron or tin dipper handles. A piece of tinware with four concentric rows of holes, each approximately 3/32 in. in diameter, is probably a small part of a colander or strainer. One other tinware object recovered is a grocer's scoop, 8 in. long and with a wire reinforced rim. Only a ring of solder remains where a tubular tin handle had been fastened. Also found was a wire handle from a skillet or griddle.

Six handles from the Army issue mess kit, or "meat can," were recovered, one from one of the officers' quarters, and two from Building 20, a kitchen behind one of the cavalry barracks. One complete but badly rusted handle (Fig. 26 *b*) is 10 in. long, including the hinge. Near the end opposite the hinge, the letters 'U.S.' are still faintly visible. These handles are described in *Ordnance Memoranda No. 19* (USWD 1874b: 56-7) as follows: "To the deeper dish or plate is attached a light iron handle, which folds over and holds the

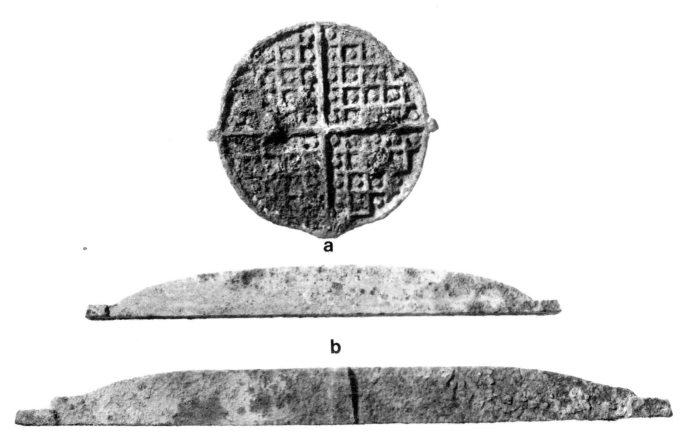

Fig. 25. Waffle Iron and Oven Grate Bars Diameter of *a:* 8 in.
a. "American Pattern" waffle iron half *b.* Two sizes of oven grate bars

two [halves] together." No examples of either the deep or shallow half of the kit were found at Fort Bowie.

Five pieces from coffee or spice mills were recovered, including one handle and three grinding wheels. Both the upright box type (Fig. 26 *c*) and the wall type are represented. The fifth piece is a small brass tag (Fig. 26 *d*) with two small blobs of solder on the back. The tag reads 'Charles Parker's/Best/Quality/Meriden, Conn.' Although the name of Parker is most frequently associated with quality shotguns, the various Parker companies in Meriden actually manufactured a much wider range of products over the years. Established in 1832 as a manufacturer of coffee mills, the firm expanded to include other types of hardware 10 years later, and continued to produce coffee and spice mills for a long time. A 1910 catalog of Biddle Hardware Company, Philadelphia (Lantz 1970: 91), shows a wall-type Parker spice mill with a tag similar to the Fort Bowie specimen fastened to the case.

A part of an ice cream freezer was identified by the name and date embossed on it (Fig. 26 *e*). Patent #67,133 was granted on July 23, 1867, to Charles W. Packer, Philadelphia, for his ice cream freezer (USPO 1868: 1012). The gist of the patent was that the paddles and the can revolved in opposite directions. A part of a strap or T-hinge that was

recovered appears to have been fashioned into an ice chipper. One end of this piece has been modified to produce a row of seven teeth (Fig. 26 *f*) and has a good deal of similarity to an ice chipper illustrated in a Pacific Hardware and Steel Company catalog (1902: 688). Use of the ice cream freezer, if not the chipper, may postdate August 1887, when an ice machine was installed at the post (Murray 1951: 283).

Several items for use at the table were recovered from the trash dump. These include three salt shaker tops (Fig. 26 *g*), ranging from 1 in. to 1¼ in. in diameter. One is iron or steel and two are of an unidentified white metal. Also found was a pair of sugar tongs (Fig. 26 *h*) only 3½ in. long; they may have originally been gilded. The significance of the name 'Allegretti,' which is stamped on both handles, could not be ascertained; it probably identifies either the manufacturer or the pattern or style.

Of the seven artifacts used in dispensing liquids from kegs, several are not strictly household items but were utilized in other settings such as the post trader's store. One brass lock cock and its key (Fig. 26 *i*) were recovered from the billiard room at the trader's store (Building 35, room 7). It was made by the Haydenville Manufacturing Company, Haydenville, Massachusetts, according to the legend stamped on the cock. This particular cock was made to be threaded

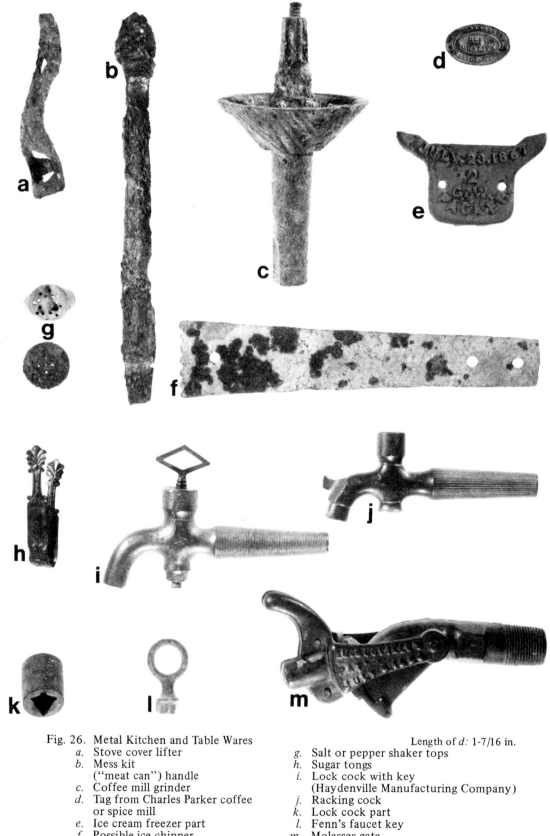

Fig. 26. Metal Kitchen and Table Wares   Length of *d:* 1-7/16 in.

a. Stove cover lifter
b. Mess kit
      ("meat can") handle
c. Coffee mill grinder
d. Tag from Charles Parker coffee
      or spice mill
e. Ice cream freezer part
f. Possible ice chipper

g. Salt or pepper shaker tops
h. Sugar tongs
i. Lock cock with key
      (Haydenville Manufacturing Company)
j. Racking cock
k. Lock cock part
l. Fenn's faucet key
m. Molasses gate

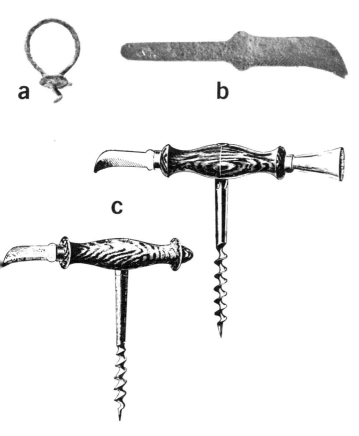

Fig. 27. Corkscrews   Length of *b:* 3-1/16 in.
   a. Wire cork ring
   b. Knife from corkscrew
   c. Illustration from catalog showing hafting of *b*
      (Huntington Hopkins Company 1890: 261)

into the keg. A different type of cock (Fig. 26 *j*), found in the same room, was made to be driven in. A similar item, called a brass racking cock, is illustrated in a Hibbard, Spencer, Bartlett and Company catalog (1891: 757) and sold for $12 per dozen. A part of one other lock cock (Fig. 26 *k;* Blumenstein 1968: 88), found in the trash dump, was made to accept a key with an unusual shape. Like the other two cocks, it is made of brass. Two keys (Fig. 26 *l*), made of some type of nonferrous metal, were to be used with Fenn's Keyed Faucet (Blumenstein 1968: 89); however, the faucet itself was not recovered. One of these keys was found in the sales room at the trader's store (Building 35, room 2). One "Perfection" molasses gate (Fig. 26 *m*) was found on the surface. Made of brass, with a bore diameter of ¾ in., it was designed to be screwed into a keg or barrel. This gate bears the inventor's name and the patent date; Elijah U. Scoville of Manlius, New York, was granted patent #301,759 on July 8, 1884 (USPO 1885a: 168). The Pacific Hardware and Steel Company (1902: 692) sold this size "Perfection" molasses gate for $12 per dozen.

Portions of seven corkscrews were recovered at Fort Bowie. Three of these are called wire cork rings (Fig. 27 *a*). They are illustrated in catalogs of Whitall, Tatum and Com-

pany (Pyne Press 1971: 69), a bottle manufacturer, and of the Sanford Ink Company (Cummings 1971). One unusual corkscrew part (Fig. 27 *b*) is actually a small knife used for cutting the wire that held the cork in place. It was hafted in the rosewood handle of two models of corkscrews sold by Huntington Hopkins Company (1890: 261). The illustration from the catalog is reproduced as Figure 27 *c*.

Furnishings

As in the case of the metal kitchen and table wares, the majority of the 203 whole and fragmentary metal furnishing items recovered at Fort Bowie are of civilian manufacture and sale.

Since the fragmentary nature of the 60 stove parts prevents discriminating between large cooking stoves and the smaller heating stoves used by the military during this period, they are all grouped together here. Four round stove covers or lids ranging in diameter from 7-3/8 to 10 in. were recovered, as were four stove or range doors. One of these doors, measuring 9 in. wide by 9½ in. high, was the only stove part identifiable as to manufacturer. An oval plaque bolted to the front reads, 'Holbrook Merrill/&/Stetson/COR. Market/&/Beale St/San Francisco Cal.' This stove was produced no earlier than 1881, for in that year the company moved to its location at 225-229 Market and 1-17 Beale, according to *Langley's San Francisco City Directory* (1880: 449; 1881: 475). One other door has a large 'B' embossed on the front but could not be attributed to a particular firm. Other recognizable parts recovered are legs, grates, a short center section from a stovetop, made to support a 10-7/8-in. cover, and a long center top section, 5 by 16 in., that served to support the short center sections.

Sixteen whole and fragmentary grate bars were recovered. It was on these bars that the fuel was stacked. Two grate sizes, 17¾ and 24¾ in. long, were found (Fig. 25 *b*), but neither can be definitely linked to the two cooking ranges described and illustrated in an 1882 Army publication (USWD 1882b: 94-6, Plates *R, S*). Replacement grate bars sold in lengths of 12 to 25 in., at 18 cents per pound, in 1911 (Holbrook, Merrill and Stetson 1911: 263). Also recovered was one stove pipe elbow with a diameter of 7 in.

Four fragments of cast iron recovered from Buildings 26 and 28 and from the surface appear to be pieces of grate of some sort. They are probably from a heater or stove, although the rectilinear pattern that they display is not illustrated in the trade catalogs examined. Two stove cover lifters were also recovered. One of these (Fig. 26 *a*), of the type illustrated in the Britton, Holbrook and Company catalog (1871: 229), originally had a wooden handle. The other is a fragment of an all-metal lifter.

Four casters and four metal wheels from casters were recovered, mostly from the trash dump. The wheels range from 1 to 4¾ in. in diameter. One of the casters has a small porcelain wheel, while the others are all metal. One other re-

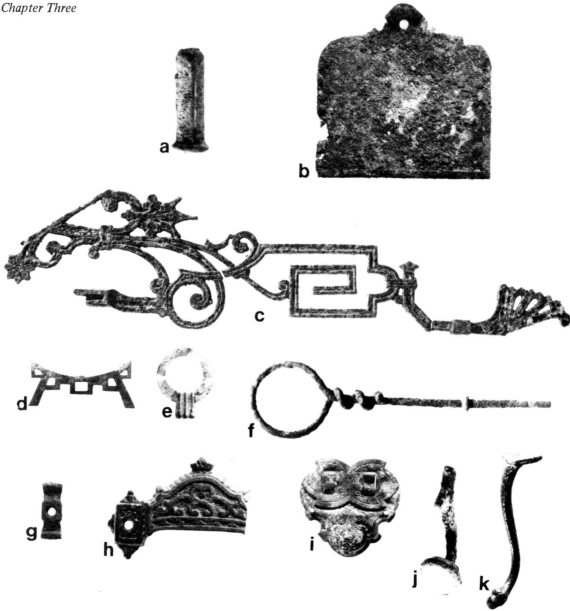

Fig. 28. Household Furnishings
a. Caster socket
b. Card receiver from military bed
c. Bracket
d. Alarm clock part (see Fig. 29)
e. Curtain retainer loop
f. Fire lighter handle (?)

Scale (*a–b, d–k*): Length of *f:* 6¼ in.
Length of *c:* 20¼ in.
g. Door button
h. Drawer pull (Parker and Whipple Company)
i. Furniture drop handle backing plate
j. Patented coat and hat hook fragment
    (Sargent and Company)
k. Acorn tip coat hook

lated item recovered is half of a divided caster socket (Fig. 28 *a*). The metal shaft of a caster was inserted into the socket, which allowed the caster to swivel. An 1866 catalog (Sargent and Company 1866: 97-8) noted that such divided sockets were commonly used for bed casters.

One artifact known to be part of a bed is an item of military issue called a card receiver (Fig. 28 *b*). It is illustrated in an annual report of the Secretary of War (USWD 1884b: plate 39). The device was fastened at the foot of the Coyle Army bunk and served to hold a piece of paper or card giving the name of the bed's occupant. According to an 1876

publication, "the Coyle Army iron gas-pipe bunk [was] favorably reported on and admitted to competition in future contracts" (USWD 1876: 129). This design replaced the iron bunk of the Composite Iron Company, New York (USWD 1876: 225), which apparently was the iron frame bunk first installed in the company quarters at the fort around 1874 (Murray 1951: 160). The only other artifact identified as part of a bed is an iron ornamental bedpost cap, clearly from a civilian rather than a military bed.

Five pieces representing two identical brackets were recovered from the post trader's store. These ornamental cast iron brackets (Fig. 28 *c*) served to hold a flower pot or perhaps a lamp. Although the recovered portions are 20¼ in. long, the complete brackets were even longer. Eight other cast iron fragments of what were most likely shelf brackets were recovered from the trash dump. A series of connected arcs fills the area between the two perpendicular arms of the bracket.

Of the 11 parts of clocks found at the fort, only two were recovered from buildings. The parts, which are all from small table-size clocks, include dial faces, gears, a mainspring, a frame and works, and a brass bell from an alarm clock. The most distinctive piece identified is the support for an alarm clock (Fig. 28 *d*). The complete clock (Fig. 29) is shown in an 1896 Marshall Field catalog (Schroeder 1970: 35), where

NUTMEG LEVER—ALARM. Nickel Plated.
(Seth Thomas.)
Dial, 3 inches.
One-Day Time, Alarm..............................$2 00

Fig. 29.   Seth Thomas alarm clock,
from 1896 Marshall Field catalog
(Schroeder 1970: 35).

it is identified as the "Nutmeg Lever" alarm clock produced by the Seth Thomas Clock Company. The October 24, 1876, patent date visible on the clock face in the illustration refers to patent #183,725, which concerned clock cases; it was granted to Seth E. Thomas, who assigned it to the Seth Thomas Clock Company, New York (USPO 1877a: 697). This firm dates to 1808, when Seth Thomas purchased an existing shop in Thomaston, Connecticut, from an Eli Terry (Lathrop 1909: 31). The only other clock company that could be identified from the Fort Bowie artifacts was the Ansonia Clock Company, which was formed in 1878 to take over the production of clocks from the Ansonia Brass and

Copper Company (Lathrop 1909: 86). This firm made one of the four winding keys recovered, all of which may have been used on a large variety of clocks.

Only four artifacts, all from the trash dump, could be identified as relating to the use of curtains or drapes. One drapery hook and one curtain retainer loop (Fig. 28 *e*) were found, the latter similar to an illustration in the 1897 Sears, Roebuck catalog (Israel 1968: 298). It is brass, with an embossed floral design on one side, and has a 1¼-in. outside diameter. The other two items are identical and have the legend 'Judd's Pat./Feb. 4th 1873' stamped on them. The patent records for that date note patent #135,561, for a cord tightener for curtain fixtures, granted to Hubert L. Judd of Brooklyn (USPO 1873: 140).

Open fireplaces were used at Fort Bowie, at least through the mid-1870s, but they were eventually replaced by stoves as the chief source of indoor heating (Murray 1951: 160). Two handmade pokers and a pair of tongs were found, as was the end of a brass handle, most likely from a fireplace tool. The tongs are 20 in. long, while one of the pokers, recovered from the cavalry barracks, is 3 ft. 4½ in. long. One other item (Fig. 28 *f*) may be the handle from a fire lighter. The Waverly Heating Supply Company catalog (1932: 119) illustrates an implement for lighting fires with a handle and shaft very similar to the artifact recovered at Fort Bowie.

Five of 12 pieces of furniture hardware were recovered from buildings at the post. A small door button (Fig. 28 *g*) was frequently used on cabinet doors. One iron drawer knob and a drawer pull (Fig. 28 *h*) were also found. The latter was patented on February 28, 1871, by Pietro Cinguini and assigned to Parker and Wipple Company (USPO 1872b: 146). This company was in existence at least through 1876; Romaine (1960: 173) lists a catalog with that date presenting "door knobs, locks and builders hardware of all sorts." One handle and a backing plate from a furniture drop handle (Fig. 28 *i*) were recovered, as were three small fast-pin bolt hinges. Door lock parts that were found include an iron cabinet or chest lock strike, the brass backing plate from a wardrobe lock, and two brass interior parts from a cabinet or chest lock.

Portions of seven coat or hat hooks and two ceiling hooks, generally used to suspend lamps, were collected. The cast iron ceiling hooks, 2½ in. long, were listed in a Rice and Miller Company catalog (1919: 88) at $2.40 per half-gross box. One fragment of a coat and hat hook (Fig. 28 *j*) has a porcelain knob at the end. This item was listed in an 1866 Sargent and Company catalog (p. 63) as an "Oak Leaf and Stem Pattern Patent Coat and Hat Hook." The August 1860 and April 1, 1862, patents listed in the catalog were not located. The other type of coat hook recovered was cast iron with the so-called acorn tip (Fig. 28 *k*).

By far the largest group of metal furnishings was the 74 parts of lamps and lighting devices recovered. The earliest method of lighting is represented by five pieces of three separate brass candlesticks. Two are the same type (Fig. 30 *a*), with a base 5½ in. in diameter and a height of 4½ in.

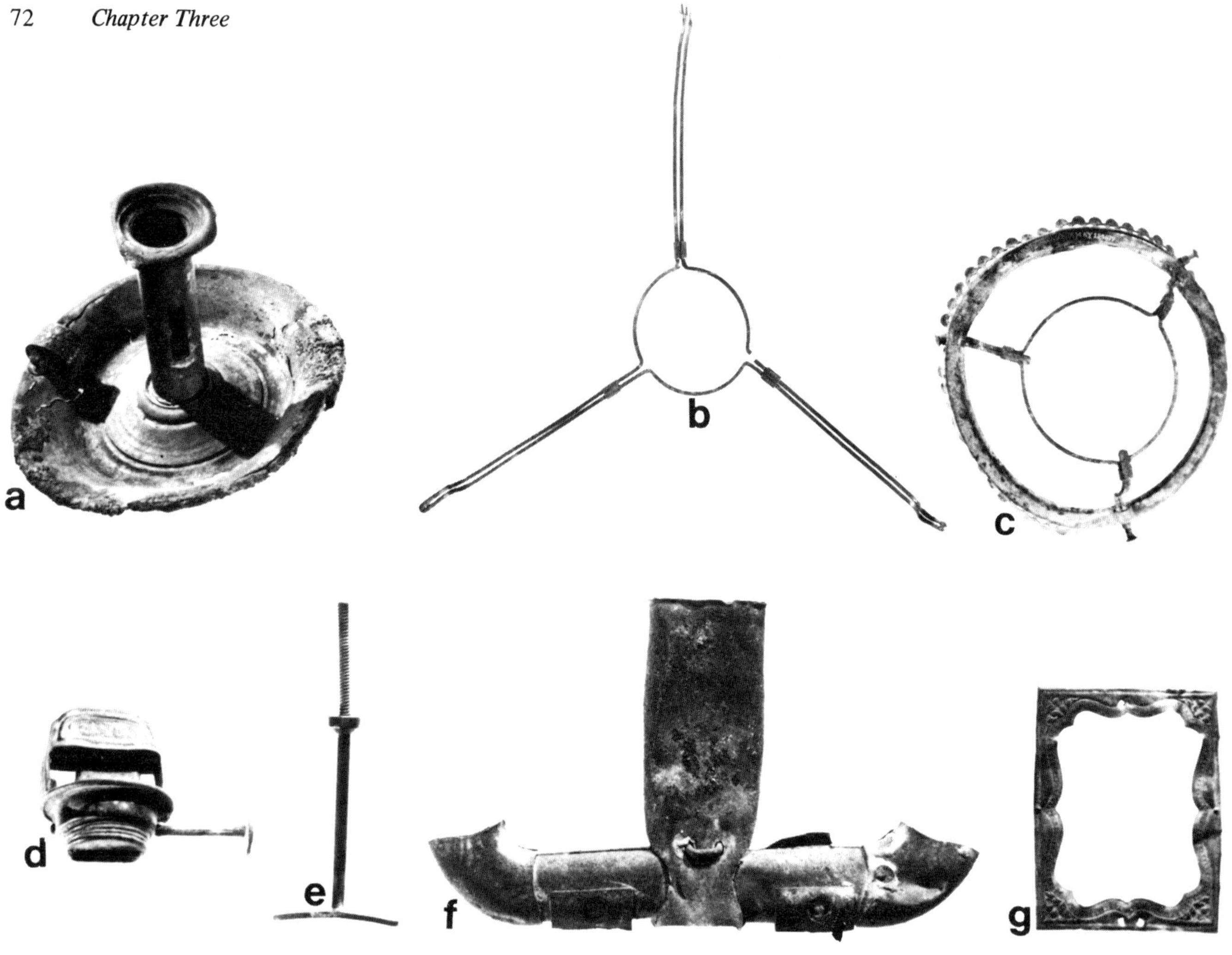

Fig. 30. Metal Lighting Devices and Tintype Frame
    a. Brass candlestick (height: 4-3/8 in.; diameter: 5-1/2 in.)
    b. Lampshade holder (diameter of central portion: 2-1/4 in.) (Plume and Atwood)
    c. Lamp globe ring (diameter: 5-3/8 in.) (Plume and Atwood)
    d. Lamp ratchet burner (height: 1-9/16 in.)
    e. Lamp valve part (height: 3-3/16 in.)
    f. Railroad lantern part (height: 3-1/4 in.; length: 5-13/16 in.)
    g. Tintype frame (height: 2-1/2 in.)

This type of candlestick had a "hog scraper" candle stub ejector, with a spring and tab, but these parts were no longer present.

It is not clear precisely when lamps replaced candlesticks at Fort Bowie, but the change was surely made by 1885. In 1880 it was the suggestion of the Quartermaster General that his department should furnish lamps and kerosene oil (USWD 1880: 501-2). The following year, a board that had convened to consider the lighting of barracks issued its report (USWD 1881: 225), recommending the selection of one of three models of lamps tested. They suggested that two styles of one model manufactured by the Manhattan Brass Company of New York City be selected – a two-light pendant or hanging lamp and a one-light bracket lamp. Perhaps the fact that the model selected, at $4.40 apiece, was the cheapest of those tested had something to do with the

decision. Twenty-seven parts and pieces of these Army issue lamps were recovered at Fort Bowie. These parts include a reflector, burners, chimney holders, font holders, a font holder bottom (from the two-burner pendant lamp), and one iron bracket from the one-burner bracket lamp. The original Quartermaster diagrams of these lamps are reproduced in Figure 9, in Chapter 2.

Patent dates on two different parts aided identification of the Army issue lamps. Fragments of the brass font holder bear the legend 'Pat. Mar. 5.72/Reissued Nov. 28.81.' Both patents were granted to William Brown of Newbury, Massachusetts, who in turn assigned the reissue to the Manhattan Brass Company. Two complete chimney holders and one fragment have the name 'Manhattan Brass Co.' stamped on them, in addition to three patent dates. The patents of May 23, 1876, and December 25, 1877, were both granted to Joseph Funck of Tompkinsville, New York, the first for burners for lighthouse lamps and the second for lamps (USPO 1876b: 994; 1878a: 1104). The last date, May 20, 1879, refers to patent #215,506 granted to Henry L. Coe, Clifton, New Jersey, for his student lamp; it was assigned to the Manhattan Brass Company (USPO 1879b: 796).

The lamp business was obviously competitive – 42 other lamp parts show no less than seven different patents. Several items were produced by the Plume and Atwood Manufacturing Company of Waterbury, Connecticut. These include shade holders (Fig. 30 *b*), patented on June 1, 1870, and a globe ring (Fig. 30 *c*), patented on July 29, 1873, and again on May 15, 1877. The 1873 date refers to two patents, #141,251 and #141,252, granted to Lewis J. Atwood and assigned to Plume and Atwood (USPO 1874b: 113). The 1877 patent refers to design patent #9,971 for shade rings, also granted to Lewis J. Atwood and assigned to Plume and Atwood (USPO 1877b: 833). According to Lathrop (1909: 67), the firm of Holmes, Booth and Atwood, which was organized in 1869, became Plume and Atwood in 1871 by court order, but Lathrop does not state the reason for this legal action.

One hinged burner bears a patent date of August 10, 1875, which refers to patent #166,670, granted to S. R. Wilmot for lamp burners (USPO 1876a: 272). This patent was assigned to the Bridgeport Brass Company, which appears to be represented by the legend 'Lincoln/Bridgeport' on the ratchet handle knob of this burner. However, the burner also bears a patent reissue date of December 7, 1880, which refers to reissue patent #9,498, granted to Hiram J. White of Boston, and assigned to Holmes, Booth and Haydens of Waterbury, Connecticut (USPO 1881: 1338). This company name does not correlate with that of the earlier patent assignee, and no information was found to clarify the relationship of Holmes, Booth and Haydens to the earlier Waterbury firm of Holmes, Booth and Atwood, mentioned above in connection with other patents for lamp parts.

The earliest patent date found on the Fort Bowie material – March 1, 1864 – appears on a ratchet burner (Fig. 30 *d*) along with a brand or company name, 'Convex.' This patent was granted to E. Hobbis and Alexander McNair, both of New Jersey (USPO 1865: 316). It was not assigned to a company, and the manufacturer of this item remains unknown.

Three objects were identifiable as lamp valves only through the May 16, 1882, patent date that appears on one of them (Fig. 30 *e*). Patent #257,965 was granted on that date to Montgomery C. Meigs of Washington, D.C., for a "constant-level lamp" (USPO 1882b: 1477). The patent claim mentions ". . . an elastic material, capable without injury, of being pushed through a narrow neck. . . ." The "elastic material" may have been cork, as a piece of cork was still present on one of the three specimens. It is interesting to note that the drawings for the Army issue kerosene lamp, dated October 1881, bear the name of M. C. Meigs,

Quartermaster General, Brevet Major General, U.S.A.

Two other pieces represent another kind of lighting device. One piece was part of a "railroad" lantern, while the second (Fig. 30 *f*), is a portion of the frame from a tubular lantern. These lanterns were common types in the late 19th century, and the manufacturer could not be ascertained for either piece.

Many of the parts of lighting devices were recovered from the trash dump. The notable exceptions were the Army issue lamp fragments. Roughly two-thirds of them came from the bar room at the post trader's store or canteen (Building 35, room 10).

Finally, four small brass frames and plates believed to be furnishings of some type were recovered. At least two seem to be frames for photographs of the period – tintypes, ambrotypes, or daguerreotypes. One of these (Fig. 30 *g*) measures 2 in. by 2¼ in. and has 'Emerson's Patent Applied –' and 'Providence R.I. No. 42' embossed in very small letters near the edge. This manufacturer could not be traced.

Containers, Covers, and Parts

Of the 388 artifacts in this category, only 14 (3.6 percent) are known to have been used for substances other than food or drink – for instance, ink, mucilage, and boot blacking. While not all of the remaining 96.4 percent were definitely food or drink containers, the indications are that the large majority of them were.

One hundred two artifacts are parts of bottle or jar closures. Ten metal foil bottle covers, of a type still being used on champagne bottles (Fig. 31 *a*), were recovered. They represent at least six different firms: Crosse and Blackwell, London, producers of jams and jellies; L. Rose and Company, London, distributors of lemon and lime juice; Tennent's Pale Ale, Well Park Brewery; Mallinckrodt Chemical Works, St. Louis; Charles Heidsieck, Rheims, France, a vintner; and one other, unidentifiable firm. The Mallinckrodt cover dates no earlier than 1883, the year the company name was changed from G. Mallinckrodt and Company (Gould 1883).

A variety of metal caps for bottles were recovered. Four patented mucilage bottle caps (Fig. 31 *b*) were the invention of Thomas N. Hickcox, Brooklyn, New York. The patent dates of October 2, 1866 (patent #58,417), and April 20, 1868 (#89,222), appear on these caps and make specific identification possible. Both patents concern caps and handles for mucilage bottles.

Another 81 caps were designed to cover and protect the corks that stoppered bottles. Those most commonly found are a flat type that was used on the top of beer bottles to prevent the wire from cutting through the cork. They are 13/16 in. in diameter and have a circle of bumps or nodules around the perimeter to keep the wire from slipping (Fig. 31 *c*). Thirteen of these also have the letter 'S' in the center (Fig. 31 *d*), possibly signifying the Joseph Schlitz Brewery. Another type used on beer bottles has a raised perimeter and a hole in the center (Fig. 31 *e*). Two caps from Ross's Bel-

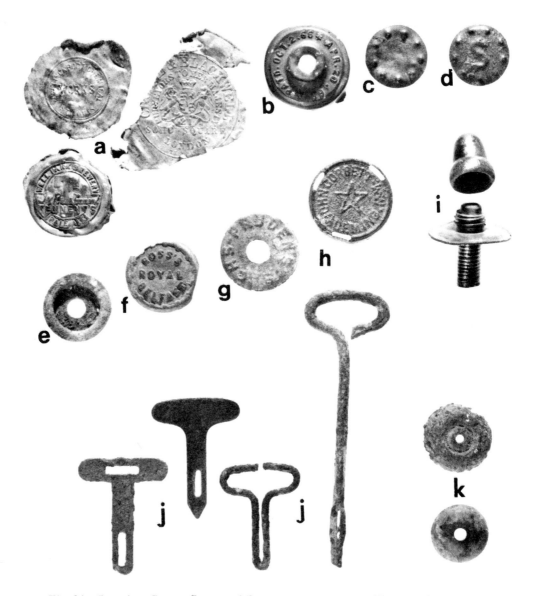

Fig. 31. Container Covers, Parts, and Openers   Diameter of *c:* 13/16 in.
    a. Foil bottle covers   *g.* Sachs-Prudens cork disc
    b. Mucilage bottle cap   *h.* Bernardin patent bottle cap part
    c. Tin cap   *i.* "Acorn" sprinkler
    d. Tin cap   *j.* Strip-type can openers
    e. Tin cap   *k.* Tin can "handle ears"
    f. Ross's Royal Belfast cork disc

fast mineral water were found (Fig. 27 *f*). Other embossed caps include five with a central hole and the legend 'Sachs-Prudens' (Fig. 31 *g*), and one large cap, 1-13/16 in. in diameter, with the legend 'Universal Re-form Goldpaonium/Ges. Gesch: Deutche Manufactur.' It is not known what products these two legends refer to.

Three metal caps bearing the name 'John Corbett, Deming, N.M.' were recovered. In 1881 John Corbett moved to Deming from Socorro, New Mexico, and opened a bottling firm as he had in Socorro. Corbett joined the Bank of Deming when it was organized in 1892, although it is not

clear whether he was still in the bottling business (Deming Headlight 1918). Labels on several Corbett bottles collected at the fort indicate that the contents were soft drinks. The caps that were found (Fig. 31 *h*) date no earlier than 1885, however, since they are examples of a closure patented by Alfred L. Bernardin, of Evansville, Illinois. The three caps recovered at Fort Bowie are clearly identical to the illustration that accompanies patent #314,358, granted to Bernardin on March 12, 1885 (USPO 1885c: 1135-6). Bernardin also held patents on tin beer-bottle caps similar to those discussed above (Lief n.d.: 15).

Six sprinkler or powder tubes were recovered. These items are actually two-piece tops (Fig. 31 *i*) from bottles that contained either liquid or powder. The specimen illustrated is called an acorn top and was used on bottles for several products such as tooth powder, according to a Whitall, Tatum catalog (Pyne Press 1971: 63).

One other metal jar closure found at the fort is a screwband, or screw-cap, with a cut-out center; it was used on a Mason or fruit jar of the continuous screw-threaded top seal variety (Toulouse 1969b: 432-3). It has a diameter of 2-3/8 in. and is apparently made of some form of nonferrous metal, probably a zinc alloy, for it is completely free of rust.

Four strip-type openers and four sardine can style openers (Fig. 31 *j*), types frequently used today on a variety of canned meats, were recovered, as were three of the discarded strips. In the late 19th century, lard cans, among others, generally had wire handles that were attached to the can by "handle ears." Four of these ears, two iron and two brass (Fig. 31 *k*), were found in the trash dump.

A total of 253 tin cans, lids, and parts was recovered; only 81 cans and lids are complete or nearly complete. Forty-nine percent of the total sample are round cans, fragments, or lids, and 16.2 percent are rectangular cans, fragments, and the like. The 20 caps from hole-in-top cans, 7.9 percent of the sample, range in diameter from 1-3/16 to 1-15/16 in. Three tops from oval cans measure 2½ by 1½ by ½ in. Nine assorted can spouts range in diameter from 3/8 to 1-15/16 in. and are made of tin, iron, lead, and zinc. Slightly more than 22 percent of the cans are body fragments from which the original shape of the can could not be determined.

Although crushing and deterioration of the specimens made measurements difficult and imprecise, some observations can be made. The round cans range in diameter from 1-5/8 to 7-1/4 in. and in height from 1 to 6-3/4 in. Round lids range up to 9-1/4 in. in diameter. Estimated content ranges from as little as 2 or 3 fluid ounces to approximately 100 fluid ounces. However, the contents of cans in the 19th century were most frequently measured in pounds, and this, of course, cannot be estimated from the empty cans, since the original weight was a function not only of volume but also of the density of the contents. Rectangular cans range from 3/4 by 1-1/16 in. up to 5 by 5 in., and heights vary from 1 to 9-1/2 in. Of the cans with an identifiable method of construction, 78 percent have soldered seams and 22 percent have crimped seams.

Twenty-six cans or lids have printed or stamped information concerning contents, manufacturer, or patents. The majority are food or food related. Six cans, representing three brands of baking powder, were recovered. Four of these contained Golden Gate Baking Powder, the most expensive of the various brands produced by J. A. Folger and Company (Newhall n.d.: 34). The firm first used the name J. A. Folger and Company in 1865 (Newhall n.d.: 31). Two cans contained Royal Baking Powder. A lid from another can, 2 in. in diameter, reads 'Baking Powder/¼ lb/Full Weight.' One

fragmentary imported can originally contained prunes. The stamping on the top of this can reads, 'BAYLE & FILS FRERES/PRUNES D'ENTE/BORDEAUX.' Also found was a tin disc, 1-5/16 in. in diameter, with the stamping 'Gail Borden Eagle Brand Condensed Milk.'

One can labeled 'Pure Refined Family Lard' was produced by N. K. Fairbank and Company, Omaha. At Fort Berthold II, G. Smith (1972: 144) recovered several Fairbank lard pails with labels showing locations in Chicago, New York, and St. Louis, as well as Omaha. Nine 'Topocan Brand' cans all have three patent dates on the top: June 25, 1878; March 27, 1888; and April 10, 1889. The earliest date refers to patent #205,309, granted to G. W. Simpson of Somerville, Massachusetts, for butter cans (USPO 1878b: 1150). On March 27, 1888, another patent for butter cans, #380,211, was granted to John E. Levasseur of Monticello, Iowa, and assigned to Greenlief W. Simpson of Somerville, Massachusetts (USPO 1888b: 1375). The April 10, 1889, patent was not located, but another butter can patent granted to John E. Levasseur and assigned to Greenlief W. Simpson was recorded on May 7, 1889 (USPO 1890a: 801). The one complete 'Topocan Brand' can is a round container 6¼ in. in diameter and 3½ in. high, with soldered seams.

Two lids from non-food products were recovered. One, 3 in. in diameter, has a badly corroded picture of a mansion in its center and the words 'Universal Blac-' above it. This can most likely held either boot and shoe blacking or stove blacking. The legible print on the other lid reads, 'Putz Pomade/Chemische Fabrik/Herr Ahn & Adolf /Lubszynski/ Berlin So.' The legend on a can of German putz pomade illustrated in a Marshall Field catalog (1892-3: 256) indicates that this product is a metal cleaner.

The information on the five remaining cans was too fragmentary to enable either product or manufacturer to be identified. Two unusual brass cans have a spiral twist seam on a body measuring 1-7/8 in. in diameter and 5¾ in. high. Stamping on the cans reads, 'Hotchkiss Patent Paris.' One rectangular can, 3 by 2 by 3-7/8 in., has 'LM & L/Chicago' stamped on the top. A lid 4 in. in diameter has only part of its printed message remaining: '-ONCO THESFRA-.' The remaining lid, made of tin with a rotating copper center, has a September 1, 1868, patent date stamped on it, but the patent could not be located.

Eighteen pieces recovered represent parts of at least eight brass opium containers. All but one of these pieces were collected outside the south wall of Building 35, room 3, which was functioning as the officers' club room in 1889 (Montgomery 1966). The parts recovered are lids that are 2-5/8 in. long, 1-11/16 in. wide, and 9/16 in. high. Two types of markings are present on these lids. The first is a series of three Chinese characters (Fig. 32 *a*) that has been stamped into all eight specimens. The significance of the translation, "source (or origin) of the musk deer," is not understood. The other type of marking consists of paper duty stamps, portions of which are present on five of the eight lid tops

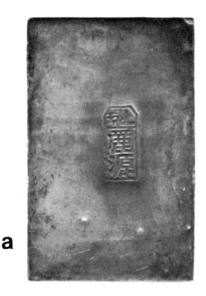

a

b

Fig. 32. Opium Tin Lids
a. Lid showing Chinese character
b. Lids with U.S. Treasury duty stamps

Length of *a:* 2-5/8 in.

recovered. The design, with two sailing ships depicted in black, together with the inscription 'Duty Paid' (Fig. 32 *b*), dates these stamps as having been used between 1890 and 1907 on imported smoking opium (Alfano 1974: 180).

It is interesting to note that the Chinese characters on the containers clearly indicate the ultimate origin of the contents, despite the fact that by 1880 an immigration treaty between the United States and China prohibited each country from importing opium into the other's ports (A. Taylor 1969: 16). These containers, then, presumably originated in China, were exported to Japan or some other country, and from there were imported into the United States. Smoking opium ceased to be legally imported into the United States after April 1, 1909 (Alfano 1974: 185).

PERSONAL ITEMS

Since sampling was not uniform or systematic during the stabilization at Fort Bowie, it is difficult to gauge how representative the 84 artifacts identified as personal items may be. Fairly small in quantity but wide in variety, this category includes such personal possessions as musical instruments, pocket knives and pocket watches, smoking paraphernalia, children's toys, and items for personal hygiene.

In the latter category are two fragmentary and one complete enema or douche tubes. All three are made of an unidentified nonferrous, lead-like metal and are essentially identical in form to two composition rubber enema tubes also recovered. The one complete metal specimen is 4½ in. long and has five holes in the rounded distal end. The proximal end has an inside diameter of ¼ in. and is threaded to allow for attachment to a flexible tube that ran to a reservoir bag.

Two key tags and one patented key ring were collected. One key tag is a manufactured brass disc with the numeral '1' embossed on one side. It was sold by Huntington Hopkins Company (1890: 865) at $1.50 per hundred. The other tag had been handmade from copper sheet, 1/32 in. thick, in a sunburst design (Fig. 33 *a*). Several edges indicate that it was cut rather than sawed from a larger piece. The numeral '33' is stamped on one side, while a '3' is stamped on the other side. The key ring (Fig. 33 *b*) is 1-5/8 in. long and made of nickeled brass. In one catalog it was called the "Puzzle, Nickel plated" key ring and sold for $1.75 per dozen (Hibbard, Spencer, Bartlett 1891: 554). A patent date of November 11, 1879, appears on one side. On that date George W. Jopson of Meriden, Connecticut, was granted patent #221,571 for a key ring that was an improvement of an earlier patented model (USPO 1880a: 812).

Ten parts from non-issue musical instruments were recovered. One is the badly rusted iron frame of a jew's harp (Fig. 33 *c*). A jew's harp of the same size, 2¼ in. wide, with a tinned iron frame and brass-tipped tangs, was sold by Marshall Field (1892-3: 235) at $1.20 per dozen. Eight reed plates and one exterior cover from harmonicas were recovered. The reed plates are from harmonicas with 10 to 20 reeds each and range from 3½ to 5½ in. in length. The brass cover (Fig. 33 *d*), which has the name 'Richter' stamped on the outside surface, is the only piece for which the manufacturer could be determined. Neither location nor dates were ascertained for this firm, although the 1892-3 Marshall Field catalog (p. 212) lists several models of Richter harmonicas.

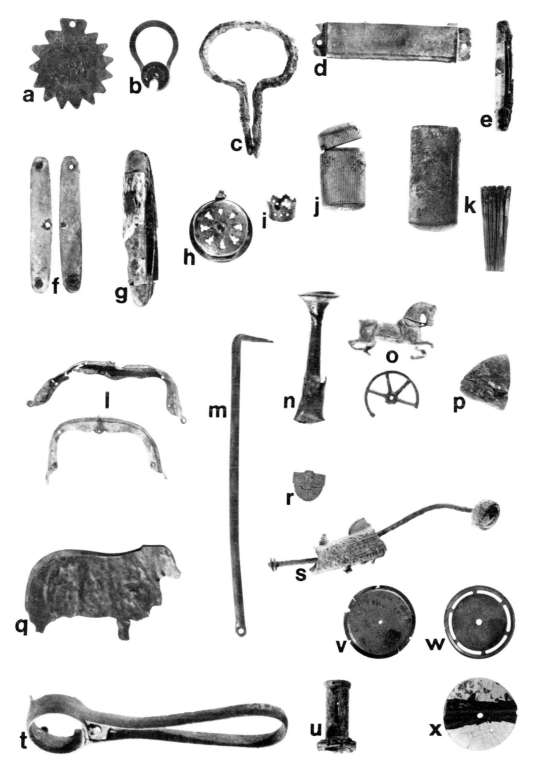

Fig. 33. Personal Items

- *a.* Key tag
- *b.* Key ring
- *c.* Jew's harp frame
- *d.* Harmonica part
- *e.* Penknife
- *f.* Silver penknife handles
- *g.* Knife with stag handles
- *h.* Pipe bowl cover
- *i.* Pipe stem ferrule
- *j.* Match safe
- *k.* Match safe ('Compliments/of/Pabst/ Brewing Co./') and wood matches
- *l.* Coin purse frames

Height of *b:* 1-5/8 in.

- *m.* Purse frame
- *n.* Toy bugle mouthpiece
- *o.* Lead horse and iron wheel
- *p.* Brass frog's head
- *q.* Tin sheep
- *r.* Belt and shirt front
- *s.* Train or rifle part
- *t.* Shoe dauber frame
- *u.* Umbrella part
- *v.* Pocket watch part
  (New England Watch Company)
- *w.* Pocket watch part
- *x.* Watchface

Seventeen recovered parts from pen and pocket knives display a variety of style and quality. The smallest knife, 2-1/8 in. long, is a two-bladed penknife with mother-of-pearl on the handle (Fig. 33 *e*). This curved style is termed a "Congress Pen" (Ferguson 1972). The two handles from another penknife are labeled 'Hallmark Sterling' and are adorned with a scroll design (Fig. 33 *f*). Other handles in the collection are made of bone, composition rubber, and stag. The specimen with the stag handle (Fig. 33 *g*) is called an easy opener (Ferguson 1972) because of the elliptical depressions in the bolster linings, which make it easier to grasp the blades when opening the knife. All of the knives found apparently had either two or three blades, but many examples are too fragmentary for this to be determined with certainty. The largest pocket knife, for example, is 4¼ in. long but consists only of a bolster lining and one German silver bolster.

Two broken pieces from straight razors were recovered. They are in a poor state of preservation and essentially consist of the tang, a brass rivet, and part of the blade. The more complete of the two has a blade ¾ in. wide.

One half of a small pair of scissors was recovered from the old fort. It is 6 in. long overall and has an oval handle and a 2-in. cutting edge on the blade. In style it most closely resembles sewing scissors illustrated in various catalogs of the period – for instance, that of Pacific Hardware and Steel Company (1902: 823).

The eight pieces of metal smoking paraphernalia include six pipe parts and parts from two match safes. Four brass pipe bowl covers recovered range from a very plain hinged specimen, 1-1/16 in. in diameter, to an ornate cover and bezel (Fig. 33 *h*) with incised floral decoration and perforations in the cover. Another cover and bezel, 1½ in. in diameter, were both ornamented with a geometric design of perforations. The same technique was used to embellish two very similar pipe stem ferrules (Fig. 33 *i*); the bottom edges are scalloped and two rows of holes ring the circumference.

One of two match safes found (Fig. 33 *j*) is brass and measures 1-7/8 by 1 by 3/8 in. It has a spring-action button opener, and a longitudinal ribbed pattern covers the exterior surface. It is interesting to note that when found in the trash dump, this match safe contained not matches, but six pen points. The second match safe is larger, measuring 2-3/8 by 1-3/16 by 9/16 in. (Fig. 33 *k*). This nickel-plated brass safe also had a hinged top and a spring-action button opener, both of which have deteriorated into fragments. There is a ribbed or corrugated section on the bottom that served as a striking surface. A bundle of 24 wooden matches was found inside this safe. One side has the inscription 'Compliments/of/Pabst/Brewing Co./Milwaukee Wis./U.S.A,' while the other side has a 'B' superimposed on a hops leaf within a circle and the words 'Trade Mark' below the circle. The 'B' is undoubtedly a symbol of the Phillip Best Brewing Company, which became the Pabst Brewing Company in March 1889. The firm began advertising and distributing promotional materials shortly thereafter, and the style of logotype appearing on

this item was used between 1890 and 1905 (Grace Ellis, Pabst Brewing Company, 1971: personal communication to John B. Clonts).

Eight brass frames from several sizes of cloth or leather purses were recovered. Two frames from a small coin purse (Fig. 33 *l*) were recovered from the trash dump. Figure 33 *m* shows one of three identical frame parts believed to be from a woman's purse or pocketbook; they measure 7 in. in length. The remaining three pieces are too fragmentary to permit identification as to size or style.

Among eight metal toy parts is a mouthpiece from a toy bugle or trumpet (Fig. 33 *n*). Unlike a full-size mouthpiece, it was fashioned of soldered tin rather than turned brass and was not removable from the body of the instrument. The toy had been bent back and forth until it broke just forward of the mouthpiece. Other toy parts found include two lead horses and a spoked iron wheel 1-5/16 in. in diameter (Fig. 33 *o*). Doll carts with wheels of this general type were not uncommon in the late 19th century (White 1966: 176-7). The horses are 2 in. long and 1-9/16 in. high; each has a hole 1/8 in. in diameter through the neck, undoubtedly for attachment to a hitch. The bodies are painted red and the saddle blankets are blue. A set of reins is depicted although a saddle is not.

Two other animal toys are a hollow brass frog's head (Fig. 33 *p*) and a tin sheep (Fig. 33 *q*), the latter consisting of two halves soldered together at the mouth. One fragment recovered is a flat cast replica of a belt and a shirt front (Fig. 33 *r*). Measuring only ¾ by ¾ in., it still bears remnants of gilding on both front and back. The remaining toy (Fig. 33 *s*) seems to be part of a train or perhaps of a rifle. The cast white metal body is covered with a floral decoration and has a panel on each side containing illegible writing.

One other item, probably a toy, is made of a disc of nonferrous metal, 3¾ in. in diameter, which appears to have been cut from a jar lid. On one side of this disc the words 'PRIV DEPUTY U S MARSHALL' have been incised or scratched. Since this specimen was recovered from Building 26, listed as the guardhouse on an 1889 map of the fort, it is tempting to speculate that it was made as a joke either by a guard or by one of the prisoners.

The iron frame from one Royal brand shoe dauber (Fig. 33 *t*) was recovered from the yard of the commanding officer's quarters (Building 25). The pointed tang on the head is a mudscraper. This particular item was located in the catalogs of Marshall Field (1892-3: 292), Huntington Hopkins (1890: 303), and Hibbard, Spencer, Bartlett (1891: 804), who sold it for $1.50, $3.00, and $4.00 per dozen, respectively.

Two identical parts were from umbrellas or parasols (Fig. 33 *u*). This piece, made of tin and black japanned, was the one to which the ribs were attached; it slid up the handle and locked into place to hold the umbrella open.

At least four domestic firms and one foreign firm are represented among 20 parts of pocket watches. The import, a case back 1-13/16 in. in diameter, reads in part, 'Bethoud

Adams & Cie/Paris/4 Holes Jewelled.' It is one of six watch parts recovered from the post trader's store. One other case from the same location had the trademarks 'Obelisk' and 'Silverex' on an interior surface. These marks were used by Byron L. Strasburger and Company, New York (Jeweler's Circular Publishing Company 1915: 169). The firm was listed in the New York City directory from 1887 through 1892 (Trow 1887-1892). The word 'Swiss' below the trademarks probably indicates that a Swiss movement was installed in this case.

Another case, bearing the brand name 'Monitor,' was recovered with two of its internal parts from the same provenience. It is quite likely a product of the Illinois Watch Case Company of Elgin, Illinois (Jeweler's Circular 1915: 182), since one of the movement parts found inside this case bears the name of the Elgin National Watch Company, a firm also located in Elgin, Illinois. The Illinois Watch Case Company was incorporated on November 13, 1888 (Porter 1931: 3171), and the Elgin National Watch Company was incorporated on August 27, 1864 (Moodys 1920: 553).

A fifth firm, the New England Watch Company of Waterbury, Connecticut, was identified on the basis of its logotype, which appears on an internal part (Fig. 33 *v*) (Jeweler's Circular 1915: 164). Below the logo of two interlocking 'W's and a 'C' is a model designation, 'Series C.' Two other parts (Fig. 33 *w, x*) bear no trademarks or manufacturer's name. One of these is a watchface that still has a substantial amount of "porcelainized" surface (Fig. 33 *x*); it also has a small hole and a slight depression, 9/16 in. in diameter, showing the position of the small off-center second hand, a common feature in pocket watches. At least three of the watches found at Fort Bowie had this type of second hand.

TOOLS

Although a wide variety is present among the 118 tools and tool fragments recovered at Fort Bowie, nothing in the collection is out of the ordinary or unexpected. Forty-four percent of the specimens are woodworking tools; the balance includes metalworking and blacksmith tools, mechanical tools such as pliers and wrenches, implements for working the soil, and several miscellaneous tools and unidentifiable fragments.

Of the fifty-two woodworking tools found, over half came from various parts of the trash dump. Five axes and five hatchets represent at least five different patterns. All 10 specimens have burred or peened heads, resulting from heavy pounding or hammering. The hatchets include one shingling hatchet, three small eared hatchets, and one fragment of unidentifiable type. The eared hatchets (Fig. 34 *a*) are of the type that was issued by the Army (USWD 1884b: Plate 47); however, they are so rusted that the 'U.S.' that was stamped on the side near the head of issue hatchets is not discernible. Illustrations in Blumenstein (1968: 73) show that three of the five axes are the Ohio pattern (Fig. 34 *b*), one is a Yankee pattern, and one is called the Georgia Long Bit pattern (Fig.

34 *c*). The latter two patterns have ears, while the Ohio pattern does not.

One splitting wedge, probably used to split firewood, was found near the fireplace in Building 106 of the old fort. It is 6½ in. long and weighs nearly 6 lbs. Wedges were sold by weight; the Huntington Hopkins Company (1890: 13) offered similar cast steel Eureka Falling wedges, in a range from 5 to 12 lbs., at \$.25 per lb.

Two parts of a wood brace were found, quite possibly from the same tool. One is part of the chuck (Fig. 34 *d*), while the other is part of a sweep reinforcement strap (Wildung 1957: 40). The reinforcement strap is brass, as is the chuck, and has 'R 22' stamped on the inner side.

Six bits for a hand brace were also found. One is a "L'hommedieu" pattern twist drill bit, ½ in. in diameter (Fig. 34 *e*). The remaining segment, which is 3-5/8 in. long, is the working end of the bit, the upper portion having broken off. One nearly complete spoon bit (Fig. 34 *f*) is 5/16 in. in diameter and 6½ in. long. One snail pattern countersink bit (Fig. 34 *g*) was recovered from Building 30, which is listed on an 1889 map of the fort as the laundresses' quarters. The bit is 4¾ in. long and is capable of providing a countersink 9/16 in. in maximum diameter. Also recovered were two gimlet bits, both 4½ in. long and lacking tips, and a screwdriver bit 3-11/16 in. long (Fig. 34 *h*).

Twelve pieces of boxwood rule frames were recovered, two with small pieces of wood still attached. A boxwood rule, the equivalent of the modern carpenter's scale, was a folding ruler with a metal frame. The frame pieces recovered (Fig. 34 *i*) are of brass. A part of another carpenter's measuring device is the brass facing plate from a try square (Fig. 34 *j*). A small portion of the iron blade, which was fixed at a 90-degree angle to the handle and facing plate, remains wedged in the slot at one end of the plate. The facing plate measures 4½ by 1/8 in.

One fragment of a C-clamp was recovered. It is similar in style to a carriage maker's clamp in an 1890 hardware catalog of the Huntington Hopkins Company (p. 109). It was not possible to determine the original size of the clamp.

A badly rusted claw hammer was recovered. The claw is sharply curved, in contrast to the nearly flat claw on some models, but more specific identification of the model or style is not possible. Three metal wedges that held the wooden handle firmly in place are still lodged in the burnt portion of the handle remaining in the hammer head. A nail claw is an implement used to get nails from the keg in which they are shipped and stored. The example recovered (Fig. 34 *k*), of handwrought iron, is 9-3/8 in. long. Both these tools were found in the dining room of the post trader's store or canteen (Building 35, room 9).

Two parts of planes were collected. One is the badly rusted, but almost complete, body of what was probably a block plane (Fig. 34 *l*). It is 7 in. long and has a 1-5/8-in. aperture for the blade or plane iron. The other part, a double plane iron (Fig. 34 *m*), is 2 in. wide and is therefore too large to belong to the body recovered.

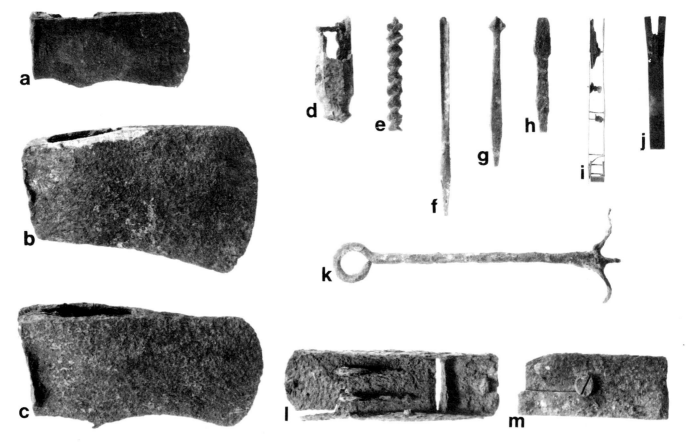

Fig. 34. Woodworking Tools
  a. Eared hatchet
  b. Ohio pattern axe
  c. Georgia Long Bit pattern axe
  d. Wood brace chuck
  e. Twist drill bit
  f. Spoon bit
  g. Countersink bit

Height of *f:* 4¾ in.
  h. Screwdriver bit
  i. Boxwood rule frame
  j. Try square facing plate
  k. Nail claw
  l. Plane
  m. Double plane iron

The five pieces of saw blades recovered represent several types of saws. A nose from a crosscut saw has five teeth to the inch. Another portion of a saw blade (Fig. 35 *a*), with eight points to the inch, shows four arcs where pieces were cut out of the blade; presumably the saw broke and was then cut up to make something else. Two tips from compass saw blades were recovered (Fig. 35 *b*), in addition to a fragment of a rectangular saw blade, 1 in. wide and with 12 points to the inch, indicating that it might have been used on metal or, perhaps, bone. Butcher's saws in several catalogs had blades of this shape and came in ¾- and 1- in. widths. Five saw screws (Fig. 35 *c*), which attach the wooden handle to the blade, were recovered; the head diameters range from 9/16 to 1 in. The two screws illustrated were the product of Henry Disston and Sons, Philadelphia, a firm incorporated in December 1886 (Moodys 1920: 491) and still in operation in the mid-1970s.

Four wood chisels and one draw knife were the other woodworking tools identified. Three of the chisels, measuring ½, 9/16, and ¾ in. in width, were manufactured socket firmer type tools. The fourth was apparently fashioned from a file and is 11 in. long and 1-1/16 in. wide. The draw knife (Fig. 35 *d*) is a broken fragment, 5½ in. long, with a blade slightly more than 1-1/8 in. wide. The numeral '12' is stamped on one side of the remaining portion of the handle and may indicate the original length of the tool. Judging by the severe peening on the back of the blade, this knife was frequently misused as a splitting tool.

Splitting or cutting tools are also represented among the metalworking implements found at the fort. Eight cold chisels were recovered, ranging from small fragments to complete tools 18 in. long. Most appear to have been improvised from pieces of bar stock, as was one example, 18 in. long, which was made of a piece of stock 11/16 in. square. Three, however, were probably manufactured chisels made from octagon-shaped rod 3/4 and 7/8 in. in diameter.

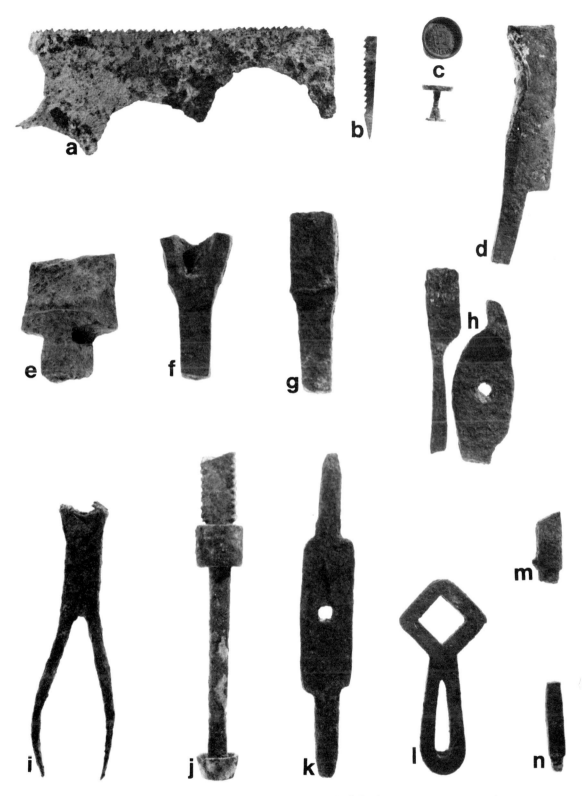

Fig. 35. Woodworking, Metalworking, and Mechanical Tools   Height of *n:* 2-1/8 in.

a.	Saw blade fragment	*h.*	Blacksmith's tong parts
b.	Compass saw blade	*i.*	End cutting nippers
c.	Saw screws (Henry Disston and Sons)	*j.*	Adjustable wrench
d.	Draw knife fragment	*k.*	Tap wrench handle
e.	Blacksmith's hardy	*l.*	Wrench
f.	Round stock cutter	*m.*	Soldering iron tip
g.	Creaser	*n.*	Unidentified tool

At least five tools are blacksmith's or farrier's metal-working tools. One hardy (Fig. 35 *e*) and one round stock or rod cutter (Fig. 35 *f*), were recovered. A tool that appears to be a creaser (Fig. 35 *g*) was found in Building 10, one of the cavalry barracks. Both the rod cutter and two ends of blacksmith's tongs (Fig. 35 *h*) were found at the corral, Building 18. A fragment of what may have been another creaser was also found at the corral. These tools were identified from descriptions and illustrations in *Blacksmiths' and Farriers' Tools at Shelburne Museum* (H. Smith 1966).

Another item, recovered from the trash dump, is part of the handle and blade of what is believed to be a farrier's knife. The fragment is only 3 in. long, but its curvature and a ridge just below the handle are characteristic of farrier's knives illustrated in a Huntington Hopkins Company catalog (1890: 135).

The 15 files and rasps found were probably used primarily by blacksmiths and farriers at the post. Included are four small triangular files, 5 to 6½ in. long, which were commonly used to sharpen saws; two fragments of half-round files; five whole and fragmentary mill files; a tang from a flat file; and three rasps. The rasps, which have the rough rasp cut on one surface and a finer double-cut file surface on the opposite side, could have been used on wood or on horses' hooves. One rasp was recovered from the harness room at the corral (Building 18, room 4).

One apparently handmade tool recovered from Building 18 is similar to the buffer, or clinch cutter, that is described and illustrated by H. Smith (1966: 169); it served to straighten and cut clinched nails. Another tool discussed by Smith (1966: 236) is a wagon tire and axle upsetter. This large device was used, in part, in applying an iron or steel tire to a wooden wheel. A large handle, 21½ in. long, recovered from Building 10, appears to be a part of this type of implement. The head of this piece has both the grooves and the shaft for pivoting that are characteristic of a tire upsetter.

Among eight tools of a generally mechanical nature are parts of two pliers. One is a handle, broken just above the joint, while the other is half of a pair of 6-in. flat-nosed pliers. One badly rusted tool is a remnant of a pair of end cutting nippers, 6½ in. long (Fig. 35 *i*). Like several of the woodworking tools, it was recovered from the dining room at the post trader's store (Building 35, room 9). A broken portion of an adjustable wrench (Fig. 35 *j*) appears quite similar to an illustration of a Taft Pattern screw wrench produced by L. and A. G. Coes, Worcester, Massachusetts (Blumenstein 1968: 49). This firm, established in 1839 and in existence at least as late as 1891 (Drew, Allis and Company 1891: 112), operated under various other names, including Aura G. Coes and Company, Lorins Coes and Company, and Coes Wrench Company. Two other handles of steel and wood are believed to be parts of a different style of adjustable wrench.

An item recovered from the blacksmith's shop at the corral (Building 18, room 1) is believed to be a handmade tap wrench handle (Fig. 35 *k*). The tool is 7-5/8 in. long and

the rectangular hole in the middle measures ¼ by 5/16 in.

Another wrench (Fig. 35 *l*) is 4-5/8 in. long and has an aperture 13/16 in. square. This cast iron tool is similar to an illustration of a "malleable iron wrench for steam and gas cocks" (Fairbanks Company 1906: 135) and to an illustration of a valve handle in a Pacific Hardware and Steel catalog (1902: 1116).

Sixteen tools for working the soil were recovered, the majority from the trash dump. The only complete tool is one of two picks that were found. It is a 4-lb. drifting pick measuring 15 in. in length. At least six of nine rakes recovered had 14 to 16 tines or teeth. Both straight and curved-tooth rakes are represented, as are straight and bow-braced shanks. Portions of the three shovels found include two blades and a D-handle. While one blade is too fragmentary for its original shape to be determined, the other is a square or straight-blade shovel measuring 9½ in. square. Two trowels with welded shanks were recovered from the trash dump. Judging from the remaining portions of the blades, they were probably pointing trowels – that is, trowels with flat triangular blades.

The remaining tools and fragments include a surveyor's pin, 15½ in. long; two punches (one a modern nail set made by Millers Falls Company); the tip from a soldering iron (Fig. 35 *m*); a cast T-handle, possibly from a gimlet; and several badly deteriorated parts of chisels or files. One enigmatic object (Fig. 35 *n*) measures 2-1/8 by 3/8 by 5/16 in. and has what appear to be file teeth on one side. A groove on the opposite side, however, seems to eliminate the possibility that this is part of a square file.

TRANSPORTATION

Metal artifacts relating to transportation at Fort Bowie include 56 wagon parts and 508 pieces of horse and mule trappings. The latter category encompasses handmade items as well as both military issue and civilian specimens.

Horse and Mule Trappings

The 153 horseshoes and 84 muleshoes collected account for 46.7 percent of the horse and mule trappings that were identified. They were found in 16 distinct proveniences as well as in the four test trenches in the trash dump. Only 40 shoes (16.9 percent) came from the corral and its work rooms, while 128 shoes (54 percent) were recovered from the trash dump. Other proveniences include seven buildings and the surface of the new fort, and the surface and five buildings of the old fort.

On the basis of shape, 112 (73.2 percent) of the 153 horseshoes recovered could be identified as coming either from a front hoof or from a hind hoof. As Berge notes in a paper on the horseshoes from Camp Grant, Arizona (1966: 17), front shoes are nearly circular at the toe and quarters, and wider at the heels, while hind shoes are more pointed at the toe and quarters and usually narrower at the heels.

Using these criteria, 57 front and 55 hind horseshoes were distinguished. The remaining shoes were too fragmentary to permit identification. Hayes (1960: 448) also states that "since the outside wing or web of a hind shoe is always longer than the inside web, it is easy to distinguish between left and right rear shoes." Following this rule, it was established that the hind shoes include 30 from the right hoof, 22 from the left, and three indeterminate.

Only six horseshoes recovered were designed for corrective purposes. One bar shoe (Fig. 36 *a*) was found. As Clonts notes in his preliminary report on Fort Bowie (1971: 90), this type of shoe "can be used to give pressure to the frog and help a bruised or tender foot; enable the horse to do more than just walk; or, primarily, prevent further sand splitting of the hoof by strengthening the web." The other corrective shoes have a toe clip (Fig. 36 *b*), a device frequently used to prevent split or cracked hooves when an animal has a condition known as "clicking" (also called "forging" or "overreaching"). This is a product of a type of faulty gait in which the toe of the hind foot strikes the heel of the front foot. This very small sample of corrective devices, only 2.5 percent of all the horse- and muleshoes, indicates a generally healthy condition of the animals used by the Army. The same conclusion was reached by Berge (1966: 50), who found only two corrective shoes in a sample of 56 horse- and muleshoes from Camp Grant.

Probably the most unusual shoe recovered at Fort Bowie is a manufactured three-piece shoe (Fig. 36 *c*), two parts of which were recovered from separate rooms at the corral. This shoe was designed to be adjusted to the foot by moving the branches forward or backward in relation to the toe piece. The shoe required 13 nails rather than the normal eight. The only shoe that had been fastened with less than eight nails was a very small front shoe, probably for a colt; it used six nails.

Muleshoes, even when fragmentary, are easily differentiated from horseshoes; they are much narrower in relation to their length and have a distinctive flair at the end of each branch (Fig. 36 *d, g*). It is impossible, however, to distinguish the foot to which a muleshoe has been fitted. Among the 84 muleshoes recovered, the only corrective devices noted are three shoes with toe clips.

One muleshoe (Fig. 36 *e*) is unique in that it has apparently been fashioned into a large staple. This shoe shows very little wear, especially on the toe calk, although the nails present make it clear that it had been fitted on an animal. An interesting analog is a horseshoe recovered at Camp Grant, which has a similar staple-like shape (Berge 1966: Fig. 40).

Present in almost identical frequency on both horseshoes and muleshoes are calks – pieces of metal that project from the underside of a shoe and serve to improve traction. Forty-one of the horseshoes (26.8 percent) and 22 of the muleshoes (26.2 percent) have calks. Most horseshoes have forged toe and branch calks (Fig. 36 *f*), while the muleshoes have toe and heel calks (Fig. 36 *g*). On the muleshoes, the toe calk is a piece of metal that has been added on, while

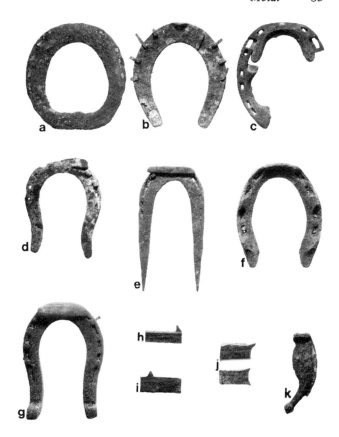

Fig. 36. Horse, Mule, and Ox Shoes
  a. Bar horseshoe
  b. Horseshoe with toe clip
  c. Three-piece horseshoe
  d. Muleshoe
  e. Re-utilized muleshoe
  f. Horseshoe with toe and branch calks
  g. Muleshoe with toe and heel calks
  h. Blunt pattern toe calk
  i. Sharp pattern toe calk
  j. Dubbing-off fragments
  k. Oxshoe

Height of *k:* 4½ in.

the heel calks have been made by bending over the ends of each branch. The longest muleshoe heel calk recorded is 1 in. long. Four toe calks that had never been welded to a horseshoe were also recovered. Three of these (Fig. 36 *h*) have a rectangular cross section and resemble the "blunt pattern" toe calks in a Lipscomb and Company catalog (1913: 412); the fourth (Fig. 36 *i*) has a triangular body in cross section and is similar to the "sharp pattern" in the same catalog. Lipscomb sold five sizes of toe calks in 25-lb. boxes.

Other related artifacts recovered include seven horseshoe nail fragments and 26 fragments resulting from dubbing off horseshoes (Fig. 36 *j*). Dubbing or dubbing off is the process of cutting off the ends of the branches of a horse- or muleshoe so that the shoe does not extend beyond the rear of the hoof. These pieces are usually ½ in. thick and are ¾ to 1-7/8 in. long. They are recognizable partly by their dimensions, but also because one end is relatively vertical

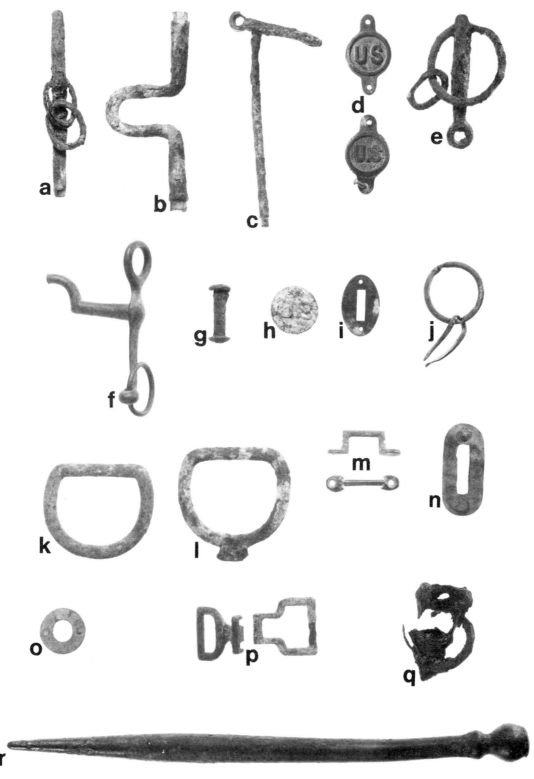

Fig. 37. Horse Trappings

Diameter of *o*: 1¼ in.

a. Bridoon bit
b. Mouthpiece from pattern 1861 curb bit
c. Lower crossbar and side branch from pattern 1861 curb bit
d. Shoemaker bit ornaments
e. Snaffle bit
f. Iron civilian bit
g. Halter strap bolt
h. Bridle blind insignia
i. McClellan saddle guard plate
j. McClellan saddle skirt ring and staple
k. McClellan saddle girth D-ring
l. McClellan saddle girth D-ring
m. Foot staples
n. Foot staple escutcheon
o. Saddle bag stud escutcheon
p. Side-line hook and hasp
q. Swivel from Lyons patent picket pin
r. Pattern 1861 picket pin

while the other is at an angle, the result of having been cut with a blacksmith's hardy or a cold chisel.

One oxshoe (Fig. 36 *k*) was recovered from Building 18, room 5. This piece is actually only half of the shoe, since the cloven hoof of an ox requires two separate halves. This shoe is 4½ in. long, has a forged heel calk, and was held on with four nails. It is the only artifact that indicates the presence of oxen at Fort Bowie.

Fragments from horsebits include both civilian and military issue specimens. Three side fragments from a bridoon bit of the Civil War period (Fig. 37 *a*) were recovered from Building 18, room 2. Also termed a snaffle or watering bit (L. Taylor 1966: 200), it was apparently used until 1885. The side pieces measure 5 by 3/8 by 3/16 in., while the oval chain links are 1½ in. long. Other parts from issue bits recovered include two mouthpieces (Fig. 37 *b*) from the Model 1861 No. 1 curb bit. The 2¼-in. port present on both these mouthpieces is quite large and is diagnostic of this model (USWD 1861: 155-6). This bit was discontinued in 1872 because it was "unnecessarily severe and injurious to the horses" (USWD 1872b: 11). One other fragment from a Model 1861 bit is a lower crossbar with a portion of a side branch (Fig. 37 *c*). Like the mouthpieces, the crossbar is for a bit that measured 4¾ in. between branches.

Two ornaments from the Model 1885 Shoemaker pattern curb bit were recovered (Fig. 37 *d*). The specifications required that each bit have "2 ornaments of cast brass . . . the letters U.S. raised thereon, riveted to the branches over ends of mouth piece" (USWD 1891: 10). The two ornaments recovered at Fort Bowie are slightly different from each other and are presumably the products of different contractors. There are slight dimensional differences between the two, and one specimen has a square period following the 'U' while the other does not.

Portions of two snaffle or watering bits were recovered that fit neither the 1861 nor the 1885 specification for Army issue watering bits. Both are of the pattern used by the military, with two mouthpieces linked in the center and with rings at the outer ends (Fig. 37 *e*). Although possibly civilian bits, these may have been issue bits purchased from a contractor who did not comply precisely with the Ordnance Office specifications.

Parts of two definitely non-issue bits were also recovered. One is a badly rusted side plate or branch. The other is an iron bit that has broken in half (Fig. 37 *f*); the side plate is 4¼ in. long and is riveted to a mouthpiece with a 1-in. port.

Three halter throat strap bolts (Fig. 37 *g*), of the type mentioned in *Ordnance Memorandum No. 29* (USWD 1891: 11), were recovered from the surface and the dump. The description details the throat strap as "embracing in its fold . . . a bolt which holds the ring of the halter swivel." This is not a true bolt, to be used with a nut, but a rod, 1½ in. long and ¼ to 5/16 in. in diameter, with a rounded head at either end. One bolt that was found together with a throat strap and an iron end ring is illustrated among the leather artifacts in Chapter 5 (Fig. 64 *d*).

One insignia from a bridle blind for a harness horse or mule was found (Fig. 37 *h*). It is brass, with 'U.S.' in raised block letters, and has a lead-filled back. This insignia, measuring 1-5/16 in. in diameter, is mentioned and illustrated in *U.S. Army Wagon Harness (Horse and Mule)* (USWD 1877a: 20, Plates 3, 8), but no dimensions are given. Conclusive identification was made by comparing this specimen to one still on a bridle blind in the collection of the Arizona Historical Society, Tucson.

A total of 55 metal artifacts from various models of the McClellan saddle was recovered. The most frequently found items were brass guard plate ovals (Fig. 37 *i*). These ovals, which were in use by 1874 (USWD 1874b: 49), served to protect the mortises in the saddle's pommel and cantle through which the four coat straps were passed. Seven of these guard plates were used on each saddle (USWD 1891: 8). Of the 25 guard plates recovered, 24 were found exactly where one would expect, in the harness room at the corral (Building 18, room 4). The same provenience yielded four of the five brass staples, 1¾ in. long, used to attach skirt rings to the saddle (Fig. 37 *j*). Also found were four of these brass rings, which have a 1¼-in. inside diameter.

The evolution of girth strap attachment devices can be seen in the artifacts collected at Fort Bowie. Three iron D-rings found (Fig. 37 *k*) are of the style first used in 1857. They measure 3 in. wide by 2¾ in. high. These rings were superseded about 1862-63 (James S. Hutchins 1978: personal communication to Jay Van Orden) by a D-ring with a separator tab (Fig. 37 *l*), of which one specimen was found. The girth and saddle devices were changed again in 1885, when the D-ring gave way to a simple circular iron ring 2¼ in. in diameter; four rings of this type were recovered. Also recovered were two iron rings, 4 in. in diameter, that were a part of the cincha (USWD 1891: 8, Plate VIII).

The remaining identifiable saddle trimmings are 11 brass foot staples (Fig. 37 *m*). *Ordnance Memoranda No. 18* (USWD 1874b: 49) indicates that foot staples were used on the McClellan saddle by 1874, but the most specific reference to them occurs in 1885. *Ordnance Memoranda No. 29* (USWD 1891: 8) specified that four foot staples, interior dimensions 1/4 by 13/16 in., were to be screwed to the saddle for use with the coat straps, and that two staples, interior dimensions 7/16 by 3/4 in., were used for fastening the saddlebags to the side bars. Ten of the smaller staples and one of the large staples were recovered, seven coming from various rooms at the corral.

The only portion of a stirrup identified is a piece that had been cut from the top of a brass Dragoon stirrup. It was used with the Grimsley saddle, which was regulation issue from 1841 until 1858, when it was officially replaced by the McClellan. It was used to some extent during the Civil War, however (Olsen 1955: 2). This fragment was found in a building in the old fort.

Ten metal artifacts from the 1879 and 1885 saddlebags were recovered from the trash dumps. Nine foot staple escutcheons (Fig. 37 *n*) were found. These were riveted, one

Fig. 38.　Rebuilt Comly side-line (used as a hobble).

on each side, to the seat of the saddlebag and protected it from tearing at the point where the foot staples passed through. One saddlebag stud escutcheon found (Fig. 37 *o*) has an outside diameter of 1¼ in. and an inside diameter of ½ in. It was riveted to the saddlebag seat at the point where it fit over the stud on the saddle. All 10 objects are brass.

Two types of devices for hobbling horses, hobbles and side-lines, were manufactured and issued according to the conditions of service or the preference of troop commanders (USWD 1891: 12). A hobble, properly speaking, links either both front legs or both hind legs of the animal, whereas a side-line links the front to the hind leg on one side. Remains of both types were recovered at the fort. The Butler and Varney "hobble" (actually a side-line) is represented by four hooks and two hasps (Fig. 37 *p*). These were used in lieu of buckles as fasteners on the leglets. The other type, the Comly side-line, is represented by one complete, but rebuilt, specimen (Fig. 38). The chain, swivel, D-rings, and iron buckles are all present, but two major modifications have been made. The leglets on this artifact are not the two-piece leather items that were specified (USWD 1891: Plate IX). The specifications state that side-lines were to be made in three sizes, varying according to the length of chain – 18 in., 24 in., and 30 in. Neither the length of the chain (6 in.) nor the size of the links (2½ by 1 in.) meets the specifications, which call for link chain measuring 3/4 by 3/8 in. The Fort Bowie specimen was obviously used as a hobble rather than as a side-line, and presumably was modified to meet someone's special personal preference, or had broken and was repaired with material at hand.

Four parts of picket pins were found. One, which came from the surface of the parade ground, is a Model 1861 Army issue pin (Fig. 37 *r*), lacking the figure-8 shaped lariat ring that went around the neck. The pin is 12 in. in length. Stamped 2½ in. below the neck and parallel to the long axis is the legend 'O.B. NORTH & Co.,' the name of a firm located in New Haven, Connecticut. Approximately 180 degrees around the pin the letters 'U.S.' are also stamped. One other part of an issue picket pin is the badly rusted swivel and ring (Fig. 37 *q*) from a Lyons patent picket pin. This model was adopted in 1885 (USWD 1891: 12), replacing the previously used Model 1861. The Lyons picket pin was originally patented by Wil-

liam Lyon on April 4, 1871, and was called a "swivel-pin for tethering animals" (USPO 1872b: 232). A complete 16-in.-long shaft from a picket pin not of Army regulation pattern was recovered. The shaft, which is 5/8 in. in diameter, bulges slightly around a ring hole located 1¾ in. below the head. A portion of another shaft recovered is 7½ in. long.

Of the 17 complete and partial curry combs recovered, 13 came from the trash dump. One complete curry comb (Fig. 39 *a*), measuring 4-7/8 by 3-7/8 in., has eight bars or rows of teeth. The protrusions from the sides of the body are called knockers, while the end of the handle is cut to serve as a hoof hook. This comb has 'U.S.' stamped on the handle. Two handles recovered have movable hoof hooks attached. One, with a 2½-in.-long hook that pivots off-center on the handle, is quite similar to the curry comb illustrated in *U.S. Army Wagon Harness (Horse and Mule)* (USWD 1877a: Plate 6). The other (Fig. 39 *b*) has a 3½-in.-long hook on a short recurved handle. The one curry comb identifiable by manufacturer (Fig. 39 *c*) is one of two combs that originally had wooden handles. It is illustrated and described in a catalog of Huntington Hopkins Company (1890: 300) as No. 234, Closed Back, Extra Heavy, made by Fitch, and selling at $3.75 per dozen. The body of this comb measures 4-9/16 by 4-1/8 in. Both the handle and the knockers are riveted on the body. The manufacturer, W. and E. T. Fitch Company of New Haven, Connecticut, was organized in 1848, according to its 1873 catalog (Diana McCain, Connecticut Historical Society, 1978: personal communication to Jay Van Orden). An earlier catalog (Hotchkiss and Sons 1861: 8) lists a very similar comb, No. 76, which has 'US' stamped on the cast steel back, one letter on either side of the riveted handle.

One interesting therapeutic item for horses was recovered from Building 30, listed as the laundresses' quarters on the 1889 map of the fort (Sheire 1968). It is a zinc and iron neck pad (Fig. 39 *d*) similar to one illustrated in a Lipscomb and Company catalog (1913: 519), but its 4¾-in. length is shorter than the 6, 6½, and 7 in. sizes listed. The description of another model of neck pad on the same catalog page explains the use of this item:

The most effective remedy for a sore on top of the horse's neck. The padded plate rests on the neck, surrounding the sore, while the elevated bar holds the

Fig. 39. Curry Combs, Harness Buckles, and Harness Hooks
Height of *d:* 4¾ in.

a. Military issue curry comb
b. Curry comb handle
c. Curry comb (W. and E. T. Fitch Company)
d. Neck pad
e. Cinch buckle

f. Bar buckle
g. Roller buckle
h. D-buckle
i. Harness buckle
j. Hame hooks

collar clear of the afflicted parts. It is kept in place by means of straps and buckles which attaches [*sic*] securely to the collar.

Ninety-six brass and iron buckles, probably used in some fashion on horse and mule harness or trappings, were recovered. Most of them fall into four categories based on shape and form. (Note that the ¾-in. brass wire buckles that were used on saddlebags and on spur and haversack flap straps are discussed above under *Accoutrements*.)

Only one circular buckle (Fig. 39 *e*) was found. It is a non-issue iron cinch buckle, 3 in. in diameter. Twenty-eight iron and 17 brass bar buckles (Fig. 39 *f*) were found, many in the trash dump. One is oval shaped and the rest are rectangular. The brass buckles were found in widths of 5/8, 3/4, and 7/8 in., and the iron buckles in widths from 9/16 to 1-3/8 in,

Fig. 40.   Harness T-bars and Hooks
a.   T-bars and chains
b.   Lash rope hook
c.   Harness snap hook
Length of *c:* 3¼ in.

The 31 roller buckles recovered (Fig. 39 *g*) are made of iron. Invariably greater in width than in length, these buckles are also generally rectangular, although four have curved, or "bow," sides. They range from 1 to 2 in. in width and from 3/4 to 1-1/8 in. in length.

D-buckles are so named because of the shape of the frame (Fig. 39 *h*). Of the 13 found, only four are made of brass. Six of these buckles are greater in length, three are greater in width, and four are equal in length and width. They range from 5/8 to 2 in. in length and from ¾ to 1½ in. in width.

In addition to five fragments of indeterminate shape and size, one unusual iron buckle (Fig. 39 *i*) is also believed to be from harness gear. This buckle is 1¾ in. long and was intended for a strap 5/8 in. wide. It is not clear whether one side of the strap passed under or was attached to the raised bar at the back of the buckle.

Two small rosettes, or standard spots, were recovered, one 5/8 in. and the other 9/16 in. in diameter. These harness ornaments were attached to the leather with the small tangs that project from them. A harness and saddlery catalog of the period (W. Davis and Sons n.d.: 196) lists rosettes of nickel and brass, ranging in diameter from ¼ to 1 in.

A total of 24 snaps, hooks, and chains has been identified as harness gear associated with the use of wagons. Two iron or steel hooks with staples (Fig. 39 *j*), recovered from the dump, are quite similar to hame hooks illustrated in 1877 as part of Army issue horse and mule harness (USWD 1877a: Plate 2). The specimens recovered at Fort Bowie are 3¼ and 4¼ in. long, but cannot be identified conclusively as Army issue since the specifications omit dimensions.

Six harness T-bars, three with lengths of chain still attached, were recovered from the corral and the dump. The T-bars are of various designs (Fig. 40 *a*), and several are obviously handmade. T-bars of this general configuration – that is, without a hook at one end – are shown as part of both horse and mule wagon harness in *U.S. Army Wagon Harness (Horse and Mule)* (USWD 1877a), specifically on neck chains, breast chains, and jockey sticks. Trace chains and bearing chains are invariably illustrated with the style of T-bar that has a hook.

Seven harness chain hooks were recovered, all but three of which were broken. These hand-forged, badly rusted iron hooks range in length from 2¼ to 7 in. At least one shows heavy wear on the concave, or inside, surface at the point where the hook doubles back on itself.

Two identical brass hooks (Fig. 40 *b*), recovered from the trash dump, are believed to have been used with either harness or pack saddles. Four brass rivets apparently attached a wide leather strap to this hook, which is 3¾ in. long and 1 in. thick at its maximum. Since the inside of the hook loop shows no wear, use with a rope rather than a chain is inferred. A crudely drawn illustration of the lash rope to be used with Moore's Pack Saddle shows a hook at one end that appears to be fairly similar to the Fort Bowie specimens (USWD 1882b: Plate 7 following page 81); however, neither the dimensions nor the type of metal is specified.

The remaining seven items are fragments of harness snap hooks (Fig. 40 *c*). The loop eyes, through which the leather strap passed or was attached, range from 1 to 1¼ in. in width. A catalog of the Huntington Hopkins Company (1890: 310) lists the size and type of snap hook illustrated in Figure 40 *c* (with a 1¼-in. loop) as selling for $15 per gross, packed ¼ gross per box.

Wagon Parts

The 56 parts that have been identified probably do not include all of the wagon parts recovered at Fort Bowie. Many braces, brackets, and pieces of bar and rod stock were undoubtedly parts for wagons, but are now either too fragmentary or not sufficiently distinctive in form to be identifiable. Not one of the identified parts bears a manufacturer's name or a patent date.

Nine complete wagon tongue caps, ranging in length from 16 to 24½ in., were recovered from Building 18. Eight have either oval or circular end loops, and one of the latter has a chain link connected to it (Fig. 41 *a*). These caps have holes for three bolts. The ninth tongue cap is different in several ways. It has a fancy end loop and two side loops welded in place (Fig. 41 *b*), and it has holes for four bolts, three of which are square to provide for the square shank portion on carriage bolts. The holes in the nine caps are for bolts 5/16 to 7/16 in. in diameter.

A hooked shaft, also recovered from Building 18, is believed to be either a wagon tongue part or a hook for pul-

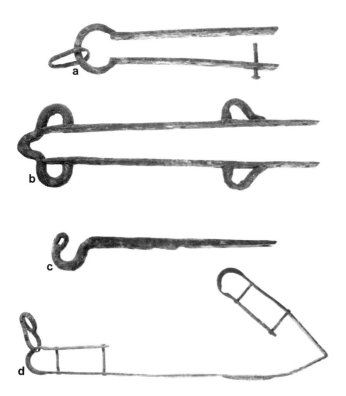

Fig. 41. Wagon Tongue Caps and Singletree Brace
a. Tongue cap with chain loop
b. Tongue cap
c. Hooked shaft
d. Singletree brace

Length of *c:* 21 in.

ling a trailer (Fig. 41 *c*). It is 21 in. long by 1-1/8 in. wide, and the rectangular shaft has three ½-in. holes for bolts. Also present is a rectangular hole, ½ by ¼ in., through the tip of the hook, which may have been used with some sort of catch or safety device to prevent a tongue cap loop or chain from coming out of the hook.

Six artifacts are recognizable as parts of singletrees or doubletrees, used to connect harness to the wagon tongue. One is a complete singletree strap or brace, 36 in. long, with a badly worn chain hook still in place (Fig. 41 *d*). This strap was used on a singletree that was 2 in. thick. The remains of five clips were found, three with rings. Judging by their size, only one (Fig. 42 *a*) was from a doubletree; it measures 4-3/8 by 3-3/16 in. and fits around a shaft 1¾ in. thick. The other clips are smaller (Fig. 42 *b*) and were probably single-tree parts.

Another piece of coupling and pulling gear is part of a wagon wiffletree coupling (Fig. 42 *c*). It is 4½ in. long, and the central portion has an outer diameter of 1¾ in. The pivot hole in the center is 11/16 in. in diameter, and the four screw holes are 3/16 in. in diameter. A similar coupling is illustrated in a Sears, Roebuck catalog (1905: 35).

Two rounded wagon axle clips and one smaller rectangular clip were found. The small clip (Fig. 42 *d*) is 1-3/8

in. wide and has threaded studs 5/16 in. in diameter. The size and shape indicate use on a buggy rather than on a wagon. The rounded clips (Fig. 42 *e*) are 1¾ and 2¼ in. wide inside, with threaded studs ½ in. in diameter. These clips all served to fasten the axle to the frame and were used with clip ties, or clip yokes (Fig. 42 *f*). The three clip ties recovered are too large to fit the axle clips found. The distances between the 5/8-in. holes range from 2-3/4 in. to 3-5/16 in., and the ties themselves are 4¾ in. long by 1½ in. wide. The spacing is wider than that on the clip yokes shown in the 1897 Sears, Roebuck catalog (Israel 1968: 61).

One of the pieces recovered is believed to be an axle fragment. This fragment of a rounded steel shaft is 1-5/8 in. in diameter, with a 5/8-in. hole located 1 in. from the end, which is not threaded. The hole apparently weakened the shaft, for there is a break on either side of it.

Two complete wheel hub bands were recovered, both made of stock ¼ in. thick. One is 1-3/8 in. wide and has a 4-5/8-in. inside diameter. The other, recovered from Building 18, room 4, has a 7-3/8-in. interior diameter and is 1¾ in. wide. One broken locking hub washer (Fig. 42 *g*) was recovered from the trash dump. It has a 3-7/8-in. outside diameter and was used on an axle with a 2-in. diameter. After the washer was placed on the axle, a pin or Woodruff key was inserted through an aperture in the side of the washer rim and into a hole in the axle. The washer was then rotated approximately 90 degrees so that the pin was covered by the solid area of the washer rim and was thus "locked" in place.

Two wagon wheel boxes of quite different types were recovered. One fragmentary steel box (Fig. 42 *h*) has an inside diameter tapering from 3 in. to 2-5/8 in. Three ribs originally projected from the exterior and prevented the box from slipping inside the hub. One complete skein box recovered (Fig. 42 *i*) is 5¾ in. long. It must be from a small vehicle, since the inside diameter of the small end measures only 11/16 in.

Four wagon wheel felloe plates (Fig. 42 *j*) were recovered from Buildings 18 and 39. Their widths are 1½ in. (two specimens), 1-5/8 in., and 1-7/8 in., all on the large end of the range of felloe plate sizes. Lipscomb and Company (1913: 428), for example, listed six sizes from ¾ to 1½ in. in width. The felloe plates held the wooden felloe sections together, with bolts running from the plates through the felloes and the iron or steel tires. Only three fragments of tires could be identified in the collection. These are short sections, ranging from 6-1/8 to 8-3/8 in. in length and from 1/8 to 3/8 in. in thickness. The widths are 2 in. (two specimens) and 1-7/8 in., common tire sizes for the period.

Seven braces used on wagons were recovered. These include five wagon box straps (Fig. 43 *a*), ranging from small fragments to complete pieces, one 17 in. long. The threaded end bolts are 3/8 in. in diameter. A piece believed to be a wagon rub plate (Fig. 43 *b*) was recovered from a building in the old fort. Rub plates were bolted to the sides of the box or frame of a wagon to prevent wear on the wood when

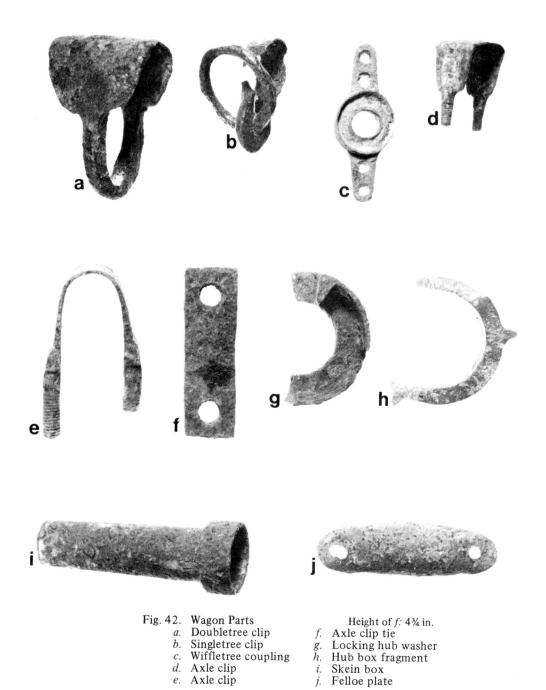

Fig. 42. Wagon Parts

    a. Doubletree clip
    b. Singletree clip
    c. Wiffletree coupling
    d. Axle clip
    e. Axle clip

Height of *f:* 4¾ in.
    f. Axle clip tie
    g. Locking hub washer
    h. Hub box fragment
    i. Skein box
    j. Felloe plate

the wheels were turned sharply and came into contact with the body or frame. One edge of this piece shows the type of wear that would have occurred.

One complete step, more likely from a buggy than from a wagon, was recovered from Building 39. This cast one-piece step (Fig. 43 *c*) has a ribbed platform, 3 by 3¼ in., and a sturdy bracket with two 3/8-in. holes for bolting it to the vehicle. Similar steps are illustrated in a catalog of the Barlow Hardware Company (1907: 240-1).

Four elliptical seat springs, both complete and frag-

mentary, and one heavier spring leaf were recovered. The one nearly complete seat spring (Fig. 43 *d*) is 26 in. long and 1½ in. wide. Other fragments range from 1¼ to 1½ in. wide. These dimensions are consistent with those of seat springs listed by Pacific Hardware and Steel (1902: 358), in lengths of 24, 26, and 28 in., and widths of 1¼ and 1½ in. The remaining spring leaf (Fig. 43 *e*) was probably from the suspension system of a buggy. Although it is 2 in. wide, its short 15-in. length indicates a relatively light vehicle. Also recovered was one wagon seat spring hook (Fig. 43 *f*). This speci-

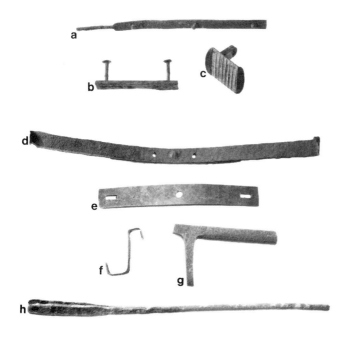

Fig. 43. Wagon Parts
   a. Box strap
   b. Rub plate (?)
   c. Buggy step
   d. Seat spring
   e. Elliptical spring
   f. Seat spring hook
   g. Brake traverse bar (?)
   h. Brake rod
   i. Brake shoe holder
   j. Brake bar hanger hook
   k. Trip-latch part

Length of *d:* 26 in.

Fig. 44. Wagon trip-latch (wagon on display
in Tombstone, Arizona).

men, which is slightly larger than the one listed in the 1897 Sears, Roebuck catalog (Israel 1968: 62), is 4 in. long and has 1¼ and 1¾ in. hooks.

Four wagon brake parts were found. One of these (Fig. 43 *g*), which came from the blacksmith's shop at the corral, appears to be a portion of a brake traverse bar, a rod that ran underneath the bed of a wagon to connect the right and left rear brakes. Also found were one section of a brake rod (Fig. 43 *h*), a brake shoe holder (Fig. 43 *i*), and a hook believed to be a brake bar hanger hook (Fig. 43 *j*).

One other artifact recovered from the corral may be part of a latch or chain closure device used on wagons (Fig. 43 *k*). This handmade item, 3¼ in. long, is very similar in size and shape to one part of a three-piece closure observed on the chain tailgate of a wagon on display in Tombstone, Arizona (Fig. 44). It is also similar to a part of a trip-latch used with a rough lock, which was a piece of chain that forced a pair of wagon wheels to drag, thereby reducing momentum

on downgrades (Eggenhoffer 1961: 43). The piece recovered at Fort Bowie is that part holding the device closed, in much the same way that a wire loop holds the lever bar closed on many modern western barbed-wire fence gates.

MISCELLANEOUS AND UNIDENTIFIED ARTIFACTS

Included in this section are 116 items that have been identified but do not fit any of the previous functional categories, and 277 items that could not be identified as related to any specific object.

A balance wheel from some sort of machine (Fig. 45 *a*) was recovered from the surface of the fort. This wheel, which still retains some of its black japanned finish, seems fairly heavy for its size. It is 7-3/8 in. in diameter, has a 7/16-in. straight shaft bore, and weighs approximately 6½ pounds. It is possible that this balance wheel, which was used with a V-shaped pulley belt, was part of a heavy-duty sewing machine, but it is not identical to any specimens located in trade catalogs of the period.

Four iron bands, virtually identical in form (Fig. 45 *b*), were recovered from the trash dump. They are made of iron strips, 3/8 and ½ in. wide, twisted together to form rings with inside diameters ranging from 1¾ to 3 in. Perhaps serving a somewhat similar function were three hinged iron clamps (Fig. 45 *c*). One of these was found at the commanding officer's house, while the other two came from the trash dump. Inside diameters range from 2 to 3½ in. and lengths from 4½ to 6 in.

A fragment of a partially hollow iron cone was recovered from the trash dump. The remaining portion is 7¼ in. long and has a cylindrical hole ¾ in. in diameter extending 1¾ in. into the cone. A small fragment of an iron nail is present slightly below the broken upper edge. It is believed that this object was fixed at the base of a wooden pole, perhaps a guidon, so that it could be driven easily into the ground.

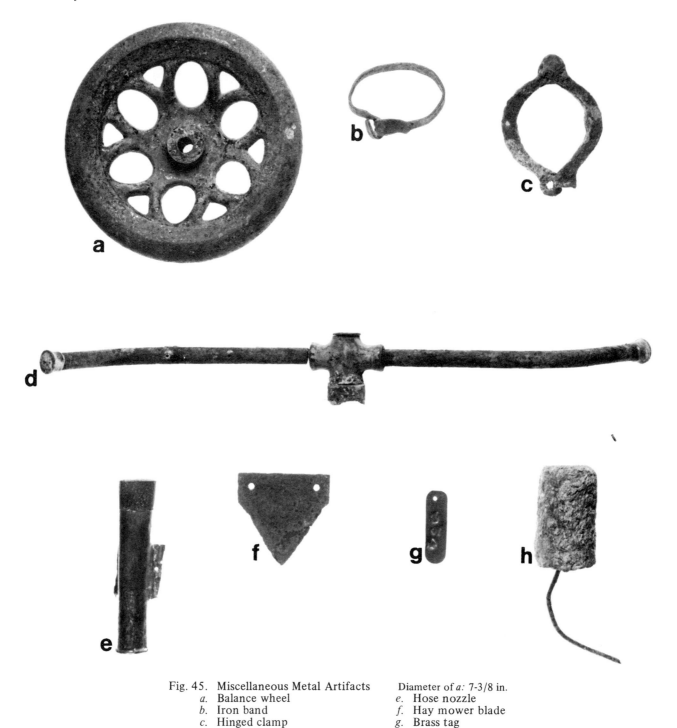

Fig. 45. Miscellaneous Metal Artifacts   Diameter of *a:* 7-3/8 in.
    a. Balance wheel   *e.* Hose nozzle
    b. Iron band   *f.* Hay mower blade
    c. Hinged clamp   *g.* Brass tag
    d. Lawn sprinkler   *h.* Lead weight

Thirty-five hooks of various sizes and shapes, and 15 metal eyes, were recovered from numerous buildings in both the old and new forts and the trash dump. One hook is made of sheet brass, one is of wire, and the balance are of forged and cast iron. The hooks range in size from ¾ in. to as much as 4¼ in. in length, but they are either too fragmentary or too generalized in form to allow any specific identification. The eyes, 14 iron and one brass, are mostly handmade and broken and are also unidentifiable as to specific use.

Thirteen brass bezels and rims and 27 brass and iron ferrules were recovered. Even those that are complete show no traits or characteristics that make specific identifications possible. Several of the bezels are threaded. One brass ferrule is stamped with the legend, 'Isaac H. Smith's Sons/New York, N.Y./Pat June 6, 1876.' Isaac H. Smith is listed in the New York City directory, variously as dealing in liquors, wines, and molasses. However, the only possibly applicable patent granted on June 6, 1876, is a whiskey trademark for the words

"Empire State," granted to Bryce and Smith, New York (USPO 1876b: 1068). The connection between this trademark patent, if indeed it is the correct patent, and the brass ferrule recovered is uncertain. One possible explanation is that the ferrule is part of a corkscrew that was used to promote the firm's product. It is also entirely possible that the patent date was improperly used and has no relationship to the object in question.

One fragment of a flat brass gear was recovered. It originally had a 4-in. diameter and bore ten square teeth to the inch. It is not known what sort of mechanism this piece belonged to, but the obvious possibility is a large clock.

Two pieces of an almost complete lawn sprinkler (Fig. 45 d) were recovered from the subsistence store house, Building 14. The central fixture, which swivels, and the tips screwed into the curved iron arms are brass. The entire implement was painted green. There are holes in the brass tip and on the inner curve of each iron arm, and the pressure of water coming through the arms caused the sprinkler to rotate. The bottom of the center piece is threaded, probably for attachment to a hose. The distance from tip to tip is 18½ in. Another object, thought to be a homemade garden hose nozzle (Fig. 45 e), was recovered from Building 19, an infantry barracks. It is 5-7/16 in. long and 1 in. in diameter. A tip, drilled or punched with six irregularly spaced holes, is soldered in place. A bracket of some sort was also soldered to the shaft of the nozzle, but has broken off. The open end is not threaded, but is reinforced on the outside by a 7/8-in. band soldered in place.

Five hay mower blades (Fig. 45 f) were recovered from Buildings 10 and 39. These triangular blades, each 3 in. wide, are of the type commonly found on a horse-drawn mower (Cayuga Chief Manufacturing Co. 1869: 15). Since hay was purchased by the government on contract, it is not clear why these replacement blade sections were at the fort.

One brass tag (Fig. 45 g), thought to be a packing tag, was recovered from the dump. It measures 2-5/16 by 11/16 in. The number '54' is stamped below a five-letter logotype, which consists of a 'B' inside a diamond surrounded by the letters 'NTWC.' What this designation symbolizes is not known.

Two of three fragments from a tobacco plug cutter were recovered from the trash dump. They appear to be similar, if not identical, to the Champion Knife Improved produced by the Enterprise Manufacturing Company of Philadelphia (Pacific Hardware and Steel 1902: 683). One of the fragments reads '– MAX TOBACCO,' and another fragment, a handle, exhibits the embossed legend 'LORILLARD'S – IN TAG TOBACCO.' One of the brands of Lorillard plug tobacco during the 1870s was Climax, and a price list for the same firm, dating around 1880, mentions Tin Tag Plug (Hermann 1960: 193). Lorillard apparently had plug cutters produced displaying their name and brands, either for sale or for free distribution as advertising.

A lead weight suspended on a 4½-in. length of iron wire was found (Fig. 45 h). The body of the object is 3 in. long

and weighs 1.9 pounds. Its specific use was not discovered.

Three late 20th century objects recovered from the surface include a shoe horn, a small louvered grate 4¼ in. square, and a key ring with a leather strap intended to be hung from a belt.

The 277 objects that are too incomplete to be identified account for less than 4 percent of all metal recovered. Since very little would be gained by detailing the vast majority of these items, only a few of the more complete and unusual pieces will be described.

A cast iron brace of some sort (Fig. 46 a) was recovered from Building 39. It has two hollow arms, with inside diameters of 1-3/8 in., which apparently served as collars to hold wood or metal shafts that were either screwed or bolted in place by means of holes in each arm. The rounded end, 3-1/8 in. in diameter, has a center hole, 1 in. in diameter, that is surrounded by a slight depression. A depression 1 in. wide and a projection ¾ in. long at the round end seem to have served as a stop. Little could be inferred about this object, except that it either rotated or was attached to something that rotated around it.

A brass cylinder resembling a lens hood from a large format camera (Fig. 46 b) was recovered from the surface of the new fort. It consists of three pieces of brass that are soldered together, and all of this was probably soldered to yet another piece at the smaller end. The diameters are 2-3/8 in. at the small end and 3¼ in. at the large end, and the length is 2¼ in.

Three broken sections of hexagonal brass rod (Fig. 46 c) were recovered from two rooms of Building 8, a cavalry barracks. The two short sections are 2¾ in. long and the third piece is 5¼ in. long. All are 5/32 in. in diameter and have a fish-scale design on their surface. Two of the pieces apparently fit together around the stud-like projection on the end of the third piece; the opposite end of this piece also appears to have had a stud, now broken off. A small pin has broken off in a hole at the point where the long piece is bent.

An unbroken artifact recovered from Building 18, room 5, is illustrated in Figure 46 d. Made of nickeled brass, this object is a rectangular bar 2-1/8 by 7/16 by 7/16 in., with a machined rectangular slot measuring 1-3/8 by 1/4 in. A thumb screw projects through one end into the slot, while a knurled round nut sits on a stud at the same end. The nut apparently held something in place between it and the rectangular body of the object. It seems likely that this object is a clamp from some piece of equipment akin to a surveyor's instrument or tripod, but this could not be verified. It was determined, however, that this object is not a heliograph part.

An iron barrel or pipe recovered from Building 30, the laundresses' quarters, has the general shape of a gun barrel (Fig. 46 e). There are no remaining markings on the object, however, nor is there any indication of rifling. The length of the object is 12¾ in., the outside diameter is approximately 7/8 in., and the thickness of the barrel wall is roughly 1/8 in. The impression of a weapon barrel is created by the pres-

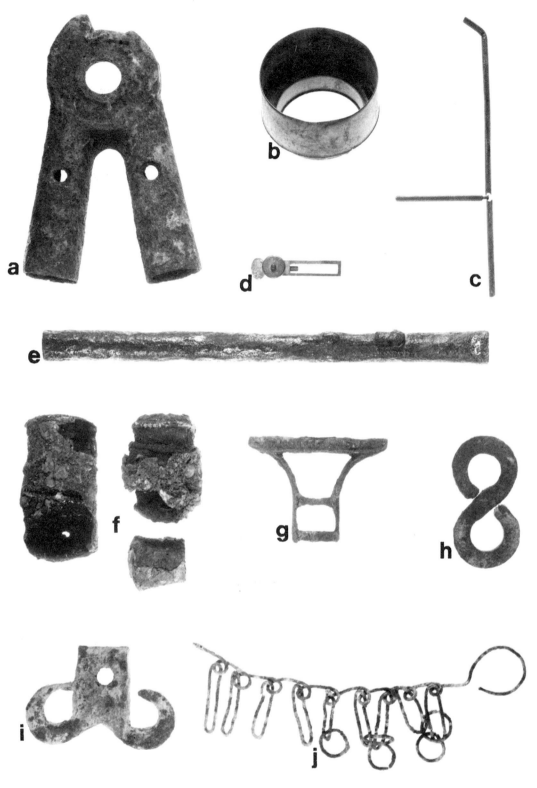

Fig. 46. Unidentified Metal Artifacts   Length of *e:* 12¾ in.
    a. Iron brace   *f.* Hollow iron objects
    b. Brass cylinder   *g.* Cast iron frame
    c. Brass hexagonal rods   *h.* Object in figure-eight shape
    d. Clamp   *i.* Iron object
    e. Iron pipe or barrel   *j.* Wire object

ence of what looks like the base of a rear sight mounted 2¼ in. from one end. This piece, also of iron or steel, is 3-5/16 in. long and was apparently fastened along the base and at one end. The other end of this "base" looks like a barbed, round-tipped hook, which may have interacted with another part.

Fourteen partial and fragmentary objects (Fig. 46 *f*) recovered from Building 33, the new hospital, are virtually identical. They consist of a series of three or four hollow iron or tin parts that are graduated in size and are nested, one partially inside another. Each piece is shaped somewhat like a rubber cane or crutch tip. The open ends of a smaller pair of the objects are inserted into each other, and this pair is enclosed by another pair fitted together in the same way. One seemingly complete outer shell is 4¼ in. long and has a diameter of 2-3/8 in. near the ends. It is not clear whether these objects are containers of some sort or, as is more likely, parts of some larger object.

A cast iron frame (Fig. 46 *g*) that was recovered may have been part of a tool or an implement. It is 3 in. long, 1-3/8 in. wide at its smaller end, and 4 in. wide at its larger end. Prongs at the narrow end may have held a handle, and a groove is present on the under side of the wide end. A series of raised block letters and possibly numbers on the upper side of the wide end may represent a patent date, but they are too oxidized to be legible.

An unbroken iron or steel object in a figure-eight shape (Fig. 46 *h*) was recovered from the corral. Handmade of a piece of metal varying from 1/8 to 3/16 in. in thickness, it is 3-13/16 in. long overall and has two loops, each with a 7/8-in. inside diameter. The object shows wear at one spot on the inner surface of each loop; this is just visible in the illustration at the points where the straight central portion begins curving around to form the loops. It is difficult to visualize how the object remained sufficiently stationary for wear to develop in those two areas.

It is unclear whether another unidentified object, recovered from the dump, is complete (Fig. 46 *i*). This item is 4-5/16 in. wide at its maximum, and has two loops with interior diameters of 7/8 in. The hole in the central portion is 7/16 in. in diameter. The center piece has been cut with a chisel or a hardy ½ in. above the hole, but it is not known whether this cut was made in order to form the object or to remove it as waste. This item might have been the ornamental end of a large strap hinge or a dual loop from which something was suspended.

An object most likely used to suspend a series of items was recovered from Building 8, room 2, a cavalry barracks. It consists of a piece of wire bent into a series of nine loops,

each holding a rectangular loop 2 in. in length (Fig. 46 *j*). Circular iron rings 7/8 in. in diameter are still attached to five of the rectangular loops. The object is 10 in. long and has two loops of unequal size at the ends. It is not known what specific function this handmade item might have served.

SCRAP

The balance of the metal material collected consists of 582 pieces of iron, brass, tin, and lead scrap. Thirty-five percent of the 142 pieces of rectangular bar stock collected was recovered from Building 18, the corral. Eighty of the pieces, ranging in thickness from 1/16 to 15/16 in., are less than 10 in. in length and have from one to nine holes. Only 9 percent of the bar stock is more than ½ in. thick.

The round or rod stock recovered tends to be slightly longer than the bar stock. Nineteen percent of the 106 pieces recovered are at least 12 in. in length. Diameters of the rod stock range from ½ to 1½ in., with 51 percent being ½ in. or less. Only three pieces are threaded, and 27 have varying degrees of taper at one end. Also recovered were four pieces of oval stock and seven pieces of half-round iron stock; all but one of these came from the trash dump or the corral.

Of the 101 pieces of iron and brass stripping recovered, half came from the trash dump. Most of the pieces have nail holes and are short fragments of reinforcing from wooden packing cases and crates. Few pieces are more than 8 in. long. Six of the 18 brass strips represent the narrowest stripping recovered, 3/8 in. in width. The rest of the material ranges in width from ½ to 1 in., the most common sizes being ½, ¾, and 1 in.

Ninety-seven pieces of metal sheeting were recovered, two thirds of them from Building 18 and the trash dump. These are irregularly shaped pieces of a nonferrous sheet metal, apparently some alloy of lead and zinc, which was probably used as roofing material. All of the sheeting is approximately .035 in. thick, and no piece is larger than 16½ by 9¾ in.

Twenty-nine pieces of melted lead refuse, weighing a total of 43.14 oz., were recovered, mostly from the trash dump. Twenty-four pieces of lead foil, weighing a total of 24.62 oz., were also collected from the trash dump. Among the remaining scrap are five small cut pieces of copper, 33 of brass, 18 of iron, and six of tin. Nine pieces of copper, brass, and iron tubing were found, as was one unusual piece of oval pipe. The latter is a segment 4½ in. long, 1 in. wide, and 7/8 in. high. It was made by joining two 3/16-in.-thick elliptical pieces of iron at their edges, thus creating an oval cross section. The use or function of this pipe is unclear.

4. CERAMICS

As with the glass and especially the metal recovered at Fort Bowie, the ceramics represent a wide range of activities carried on at the post. A total of 1,147 whole and fragmentary specimens of non-Indian ceramics was collected, the greatest number pertaining to the preparation, serving, and consumption of food. Other functions or activities represented are storage, personal sanitation, smoking, recreation, mining and assaying, and construction. Also recovered were ceramic parts and pieces of furniture or interior furnishings and a number of ceramic buttons. A small amount of Indian pottery, both historic and prehistoric, was collected.

Whenever possible, the specific purpose or function of artifacts has been used to organize the material within each of the broad categories mentioned above. In the section dealing with food preparation and table wares, for example, several kinds of bowls are discussed. The particular type and style of earthenware or porcelain is described in conjunction with the description of each bowl form identified. It is felt that this format will facilitate artifact identification for the non-specialist without hampering the professional archaeologist.

Three basic types of ware or ceramic body are present among the materials collected at Fort Bowie: earthenware, stoneware, and porcelain. White earthenware is defined by Ramsay (1939: 6) as having an opaque white or cream colored body, a granular fracture, and the tendency to absorb some moisture. Earthenware is not generally fired to the point where vitrification occurs, although some variants, such as "Ironstone" and "Stone China," approach that state. Other variations of white earthenware represented in the collection include granite, white granite, and semi-porcelain. Other types of earthenware represented are yelloware, cremeware, and redware.

The distinction made in this report between blue tinted and white tinted earthenware glazes is one that was made by manufacturers during the second half of the 19th century. Collard (1967: 130) indicates that the blue-grey tinted stone china and ironstone of Josiah Spode and Charles James Mason was originally intended as an imitation of Chinese porcelain, while the white tinted earthenware produced by British potters after 1850 was made to compete with the whiter French porcelain that had come into vogue. Another reference to the color distinction occurs in Jewitt's *Ceramic Art of Great Britain* (1970). Writing in 1883, he noted that

William Taylor, of Hanley, Staffordshire, produced "white graniteware for the United States and Canadian markets of both qualities – the bluish tinted for the provinces, and the pure white for the city trade" (Jewitt 1970: 504).

Stoneware, the second basic ceramic type, is a "hard, high-fired ceramic that, during the process of manufacture, has attained some degree of vitrification rendering it generally impermeable to liquids" (Miller and Stone 1970: 68).

The third basic type of ware is porcelain, which has been defined as a highly fired, fully vitrified, and more or less translucent ceramic (Miller and Stone 1970: 81). In the examination of specimens to determine the type of ware, it must be remembered that translucency is a characteristic that is highly variable.

KITCHEN AND TABLE WARES

The largest category of ceramics, accounting for nearly 54 percent of the material collected, consists of items used in the preparation of food, such as mixing bowls, as well as the more common items that were used in the serving or consumption of food. Some of the finer or more esthetic pieces may also have served secondarily for decoration or display.

Like the term "household," the terms "tableware" and "kitchenware" should be considered here in a broad sense. At least three types of kitchens and dining facilities existed at Fort Bowie. There were the mess halls, which prepared and served food in quantity for the enlisted men when in garrison; there were the kitchens in the individual quarters of the commanding and married officers; and there was at least one kitchen, the one at the post trader's store, that served as a restaurant for travelers and, possibly, as a bachelor officers' mess.

Bakers

A baker is a piece of holloware, generally oval shaped, used both for baking and for serving. This type of vessel, also called an oval vegetable dish, was sold in sizes ranging in length from 5¼ to 11½ in. (Hillcrest Shop n.d.). The fragments of bakers recovered at Fort Bowie were too incomplete to yield dimensions; like many of the ceramics recovered during the stabilization efforts, eight of the nine pieces of bakers were broken remains collected from the trash dump.

Both earthenware and porcelain are represented among the nine fragments of bakers. Four sherds are undecorated white earthenware. The other five baker fragments are of white porcelain and are minimally translucent. They are probably all of American manufacture. Only one bears evidence of a hallmark; this is a portion of the impressed mark of the Trenton China Company, Trenton, New Jersey (Fig. 47 *a*), a firm in existence from 1859 to 1891 (Barber n.d.: 68).

Bowls

A total of 95 recovered sherds are definitely known to have been parts of bowls. Slightly less than 79 percent of the bowl sherds were collected from various parts of the trash dump at the fort. On the basis of form and decoration, 95 percent of the sherds are classifiable into six bowl types.

Fourteen pieces of footed oyster bowls, made of either porcelain or earthenware, were recovered. A footed oyster bowl is a relatively small round bowl, with a diameter greater than its height (Fig. 48 *a*). One manufacturer, East Liverpool Pottery Company, sold footed oyster bowls in three sizes: 1 pt., 1½ pt., and 2 pt. (Hillcrest Shop n.d.). The partial bowl illustrated is 3 in. high and 5-5/16 in. in diameter, and has an estimated capacity of 1 pt. This specimen is the only footed oyster bowl recovered that is made of white earthenware with a blue tint glaze. It bears a printed black or dark navy blue hallmark of Charles Meakin (Fig. 47 *b*). This mark refers to the Burslem, Staffordshire, pottery manufacturers that operated from about 1876 to 1889 (Godden 1971: 77). Aside from being datable to a 13-year span, the mark is interesting in that it contains the word "England," a criterion commonly, but mistakenly, used to date ceramics as post-1890. As Liesenbein (1973: 6-8) has noted, there are at least 32 firms known to have used the designation "England" prior to the United States Tariff Act of 1890, which required that articles of foreign manufacture be labeled to indicate their country of origin. Some hallmarks that incorporate "England" definitely date to the 1870s (Liesenbein 1973: 1), as could the specimen described above. Ten fragments of footed oyster bowls were made of undecorated white earthenware with a white tint glaze. Six of these bear the complete or partial underglaze printed black hallmark, 'J & E Mayer Warrented/Stone China' (Fig. 47 *c*). This was a mark of the Mayer Pottery Company, Ltd., Beaver Falls, Pennsylvania, a firm that was in operation from 1881 through at least 1904. This particular hallmark dates between 1881 and 1891 (Barber n.d.: 33).

The remaining footed oyster bowl fragments are all white undecorated porcelain of American manufacture. Two have the underglaze printed brown hallmark 'KT&K/China' (Fig. 47 *d*), attributed to the Knowles, Taylor and Knowles Company, East Liverpool, Ohio. This firm was in operation from 1870 until at least 1921 (Barber n.d.: 108-9; Stout 1923: 64, 75), but more specific dates could not be ascertained for this hallmark. One fragment represents slightly less than half a bowl that apparently had a diameter of 6-1/8 in. A bowl of this shape and size would have a capacity of approximately 1½ pt.

Mixing bowls constitute the second category or type of bowl found at Fort Bowie. The 24 pieces recovered, all from the trash dump, apparently represent no more than three separate specimens, all of yellowware. Yellowware is, generally speaking, a kind of earthenware that was produced in the United States from the 1830s through at least the 1930s (Ramsay 1939: 23, 148, 151-2) and in Great Britain from about 1840 until apparently as late as 1900 (Collard 1967: 141-3). It has a creme or buff paste and is finished with a clear lead or alkaline glaze that intensifies the surface color, which may vary from pale buff to deep yellow. Examples of both domestic and imported yellowware were found. One domestic specimen is a mixing bowl, approximately 10½ in. in diameter at the rim, with a hand-applied underglaze decoration consisting of 11 blue and white concentric rings (Fig. 48 *b*). Another had a 1-7/8 in. wide white band encircling the body, which was bordered both top and bottom by an underglaze brown ring. A specimen that was apparently of British manufacture (Fig. 48 *c*) has a green underglaze mocha decoration 1¼ in. wide, bordered by brown rings on a yellow background. Mocha is a style of decoration that has "a typical tree-like effect produced by the chemical reaction of an acid colourant on an alkaline slip"; mocha-decorated items were produced from as early as 1799 to at least as late as the mid-1960s, and virtually all were manufactured in Great Britain (Godden 1963: 142-4).

Because of their distinctive nature, the 11 sherds of Oriental porcelain bowls are considered a separate category. These sherds represent eight different bowls, at least four being the relatively small footed bowls frequently referred to as rice bowls. Three have handpainted green, brown, or white underglaze enamel floral decoration, with a celadon type overglaze; they could have been manufactured in either 19th or 20th century China or Japan. A fragment of a fourth rice bowl is undecorated, except for a partial hallmark on its base and a greenish celadon type glaze; according to Quellmalz (1972), this type of bowl was produced in China during the 19th century. Little can be said about three other body sherds except that they were from small bowls of Chinese manufacture.

The four remaining Chinese porcelain bowl sherds are from a single large footed bowl (Fig. 48 *d*). Ornate handpainted overglaze enamel and gilt decorations cover both the interior and exterior. Birds, flowers, a waterfall, and human figures are depicted in red, yellow, blue, green, and black enamel. This bowl is Chinese "Mandarin ware," introduced as early as 1817 (Mudge 1962: 143).

The fourth category of bowl recovered is a shape called a St. Dennis (or St. Denis) bowl. As with the footed oyster bowl, catalogs of the late 19th century indicate that they were generally made in three sizes – 1, 1½, and 2 pt. – but

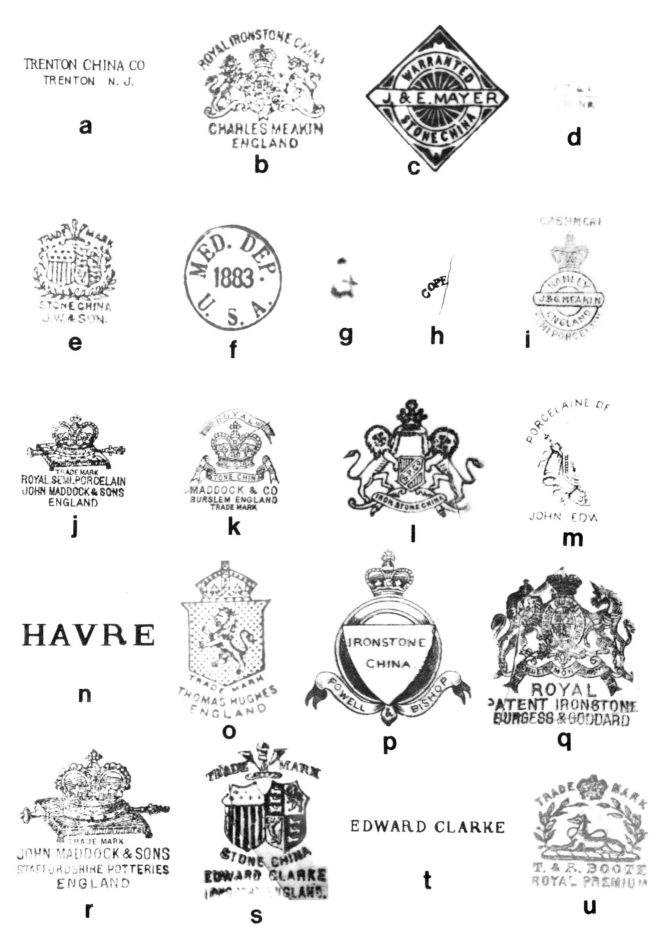

Fig. 47 . Ceramic Hallmarks

without a distinct foot at the base. The sides of a St. Dennis bowl are nearly vertical, flaring only slightly from the base to the rim. Of 20 pieces of St. Dennis bowls, 18 are white earthenware with a blue tint glaze; the remaining two fragments have a glaze of indeterminate color. The one restorable specimen recovered (Fig. 48 *e*) is 3¾ in. high, with a rim diameter of 5-3/16 in., and is the only decorated St. Dennis bowl in the collection. The decoration consists of a molded pattern of corn tassels and cobs extending as much as 2 in. below the rim.

Only one hallmark was found among the fragments of St. Dennis bowls. It is a printed underglaze mark in black, consisting of a pair of crests partially surrounded by a wreath and the words 'Trade Mark/Stone China/J.W. & Son' (Fig. 47 *e*). The manufacturer to whom this mark belonged was not identified, although comparison of the style and content of the hallmark indicates either American or British origin.

Twelve sherds from the trash dump represent three to five identical paneled bowls that are commonly called "fluted nappies" (Butler Brothers 1915). Made of white earthenware with a white tint glaze, they measure 3-11/16 in. high and have a rim diameter of approximately 7 in. The decoration consists of 14 molded panels covering the lower two-thirds of the exterior surface of the bowl. There is no evidence of a hallmark on any of these specimens.

Nine sherds of white porcelain compose a sixth category of bowl. Although the fragments are too small for definite identification, they appear to be from bowls similar in size to the paneled bowl described above. In addition to being porcelain of American manufacture, these bowls are distinct from the others in being military issue items. One base with a molded ring at its bottom (Fig. 48 *f*) and one rim sherd (Fig. 48 *g*) bear the initials of the United States Quartermaster's Department in a blue underglaze print. While no manufacturer's hallmark is present on these items, they were

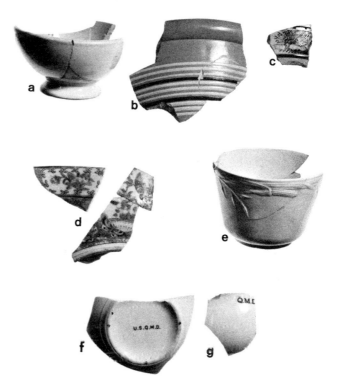

Fig. 48.   Ceramic Bowls
  a. Footed oyster bowl
        (Charles Meakin)
  b. Yelloware mixing bowl
  c. Mocha decoration on
        yelloware mixing bowl
  d. Chinese porcelain bowl
  e. St. Dennis bowl
  f-g. Military issue bowls

  Height of *a:* 3 in.

◄ Fig. 47.   Ceramic Hallmarks
  a. Trenton China Co. (drawing of impressed mark)
  b. Charles Meakin
  c. J. & E. Mayer
  d. Knowles, Taylor, and Knowles
  e. J. W. & Son
  f. U.S.A. Medical Department
  g. Untranslatable Chinese character
  h. W. T. Copeland & Sons (drawing of impressed mark)
  i. J. & G. Meakin
  j. John Maddock & Sons
  k. Maddock & Co.
  l. Steubenville Pottery Co.
  m. John Edwards
  n. John Edwards (drawing of impressed mark)
  o. Thomas Hughes
  p. Powell & Bishop
  q. Burgess & Goddard
  r. John Maddock & Sons
  s. Edward Clarke
  t. Edward Clarke (drawing of impressed mark)
  u. T. & R. Boote

  Hallmarks are actual size except *g,* which is 2x.

almost certainly produced by the Greenwood Pottery Company, Trenton, New Jersey. The initials 'U.S.Q.M.D.' on the illustrated base are virtually identical to those on Greenwood Pottery items in the Tucson Urban Renewal collection, Arizona State Museum; moreover, the same pattern of the 'Q.M.D.' on the bowl rim sherd appears on a saucer (Fig. 53 *f*) that also bears the impressed mark of the Greenwood Pottery Company (Fig. 52 *e*). This company was in operation from 1868 until at least 1893, and Barber dates the first use of its impressed mark to 1886 (Barber n.d.; 46-7, 68; 1893: 226-7). However, objects marked with the initials of the Quartermaster's Department apparently date no earlier than 1889, the year in which the Quartermaster's Department was "charged with the duty of issuing articles of tableware and kitchen utensils" (USWD 1889: 647). Other firms known to have produced ceramics marked with the initials of the Quartermaster's Department are John Moses & Sons Company (Barber n.d.: 51) and the Trenton China Company (Brose 1967: 54-5), both of Trenton, New Jersey.

The remaining five bowl sherds, all white earthenware, are too small to be identified as to size or shape. Only one fragment of a rim is of interest. It is decorated with the hand-applied overglaze polychrome insignia of I Troop of the 4th

Fig. 49.   Ceramic Cups
                                                                    Diameter of *a:* 3½ in.
    a. Military issue unhandled St. Dennis cup   *d.* Chinese green porcelain cup
    b. Military issue handled St. Dennis cup   *e.* Japanese saki (?) cup
       (Greenwood Pottery Company)   *f.* Rim sherd with luster resist decoration
    c. Ovide cup with blue transfer print   *g.* Creme-colored ware rim sherd

Cavalry. The crossed sabers have yellow blades with blue hilt and handles. Both the numeral '4' above the intersection of the sabers and the letter 'I' below are outlined in blue, as the sabers are in grey. This sherd must have been deposited at the trash dump at the post no earlier than July 1886 and probably no later than September 1887, the period during which I Troop, 4th Cavalry, was stationed at Fort Bowie (Murray 1951: 185, 279).

Cups

    Essentially three types of cups are discernible among the 57 fragments and 8 whole or restorable specimens recovered at the fort. Identifiable are St. Dennis shaped cups, with and without handles, ovide shaped cups, and oriental tea or saki cups. The majority of the material, however, must be described on the basis of the type of ware and decoration alone, for the fragments are too small to permit size and shape identification.

    One whole unhandled St. Dennis coffee cup and parts of three others were recovered (Fig. 49 *a*). They are made of white earthenware with a white tint glaze and have a capacity of 9 oz. A black underglaze printed hallmark on their base identifies them as military issue items used by the Medical Department, U.S. Army (Fig. 47 *f*). Also within this

1-in. circular hallmark is the apparent date of manufacture, 1883. The one complete cup (Fig. 49 *a*) and another restorable specimen were recovered from a privy next to Building 33; two other base sherds were found in the trash dump.

    Other St. Dennis cups include five white porcelain cups, also of military issue. Two specimens have the same blue underglaze basemark, the 'U.S.Q.M.D.' of the Quartermaster's Department (Fig. 49 *b*), that occurs on two white porcelain bowls; for the reasons discussed above, they are attributed to the Greenwood Pottery Company, Trenton, New Jersey. These two cups have the same molded ring around their base, as do the two 'U.S.Q.M.D.' bowls. One other cup fragment is also attributed to the Greenwood Pottery Company on the basis of a partially visible 'Q.M.D.' on the exterior surface just below the rim; a bowl with this same mark has been described above. Five additional fragments of white earthenware cups were also recovered, one with a handle fragment present. Neither size nor manufacturer was ascertained for these specimens.

    Two identical ovide shaped cups (Fig. 49 *c*) were recovered from Building 6, one of the officers' quarters. "Ovide" is a 19th-century term used to denote a cup shape with the mouth wider than the base and with a characteristically curved profile from rim to base (Butler Brothers 1915). They are white earthenware with white tint glaze and are decorated with a blue bird and foliage transfer print. The decoration covers the entire exterior and extends approximately 1¼ in. below the rim on the interior surface. Although no hallmarks are present, these cups can be dated to around 1880-1890, on the basis of the style of decoration. Saucers with the identical decoration are described below.

At least 12 of the 15 porcelain cup fragments of probable continental European origin are from ovide shaped cups. These sherds, all from the trash dump, represent at least five, but no more than seven, separate specimens. Two bases and one handle fragment are undecorated white porcelain, while a second handle has a molded decoration in addition to hand-applied gilt. The remaining three cups have overglaze hand-applied decoration. Two have polychrome and gilt floral designs; traces of a red overglaze are all that remains of decoration on the third. Little can be said about the date and place of manufacture of these pieces. This type of ware was produced in France beginning in the 1850s (Collard 1967: 189-90), and central European porcelains of this type began to appear in Canada, for example, in the 1870s (Collard 1967: 193).

A third distinct class of cup is represented by three oriental porcelain specimens. The first, a cup with a greenish exterior resulting from a celadon type glaze (Fig. 49 *d*), was recovered from Building 35, room 3, the officers' club room at the post trader's (Montgomery 1966). This type of cup is probably of 19th-century Chinese manufacture (Quellmalz 1972) and is most likely from a set that included the green porcelain bowl fragment previously described. A blue hand-written Chinese character on the base (Fig. 47 *g*) is essentially untranslatable. As written, the mark is closest to *ri* or *jih,* meaning "the sun" or "a day," but because the central element of the character is off-center, this interpretation is not certain. The second oriental porcelain cup (Fig. 49 *e*) is probably of 19th-century Japanese manufacture and is possibly a saki cup. It is 2¼ in. tall and is decorated with a hand-painted underglaze blue floral design; it has no hallmark. A third specimen is a fragment of a cup that is also Japanese in origin. It is decorated with a bird and floral design in brown and green hand-painted overglaze.

Several types of ware are present among the cup fragments of indeterminate size and shape. Both decorated and undecorated white earthenware were recovered. Three designs of underglaze blue transfer print are present on white tint earthenware. One cup fragment with blue tint glaze and brown transfer print decoration was recovered from Building 30; a fragment of a saucer with the same design was also found there. Items of this type were produced from the 1870s through the 1890s. One rim sherd of white earthenware with white tint glaze is decorated with a copper-colored overglaze luster band below the rim on both the interior and exterior surfaces (Fig. 49 *f*). The luster decoration is an iridescence or metallic sheen produced by applying a metallic film to the ceramic body. The copper color could have been obtained by utilizing either a gold or copper oxide (Bedford 1965: 8). Recovered from Building 101 in the old fort, this sherd was most likely produced in the 1880s or 1890s. All known manufacturers of this type of ware were British; they included A. J. Wilkinson, Taylor and Company, Mellor, and Meakin.

Seven sherds representing four cups made of creme-colored ware or cremeware, a variety of earthenware, were found. Creme-colored ware is a ceramic body that is similar to yelloware but has a slightly finer texture and a lighter tint (Ketchum 1971: 120). Five sherds are decorated with a blue underglaze floral print, one incorporating a band of geometric design at the rim and a 1-in. band of decoration extending down from the rim on the cup's interior surface (Fig. 49 *g*). Another small rim sherd has a green underglaze print decoration. According to Little (1969: 17), green was the first color to be used for underglaze printing, a process developed in the 1820s. The remaining fragment, the base of a cup with a grey underglaze floral decoration, was recovered from Building 5. With it was a saucer fragment exhibiting identical decoration. The saucer has a partial impressed mark (Fig. 47 *h*) that is probably the hallmark of W. T. Copeland & Sons, Ltd.; this Staffordshire pottery firm used an impressed mark from 1850 into the 20th century (Godden 1964: 171).

Dishes

"Dish" is a term applied to several types of objects, including flatware and holloware. One form of dish recovered was a serving platter, which is an oval-shaped piece of flatware, similar to a plate, but distinguished from the latter by its flat, footless bottom (Fig. 50 *a*). Fourteen undecorated white earthenware sherds, 11 with white tint glaze, representing 8 serving platters, were recovered from the trash dump.

Parts of two rectangular footed serving dishes were also recovered from the dump. Five sherds of a creme-colored ware dish are decorated with a brown underglaze print touched up by hand in underglaze red, yellow, blue, and green, and with an overglaze gilt band at the rim (Fig. 50 *b*). Eight sherds of another dish have an underglaze black floral print, common from the 1870s through the 1890s.

A third footed dish, recovered from Building 6, is 5½ in. in calculated diameter and has a slightly scalloped edge. The rim is 1 in. wide and is decorated with a blue-grey underglaze floral print (Fig. 50 *c*). It is probably either a fruit or ice cream dish. A complete hallmark on the base (Fig. 47 *i*) identifies the manufacturer as J & G Meakin of Hanley, England. This specimen is of a type known as semi-porcelain, which is a synonym of white granite, one of the many forms of white earthenware (Jewitt 1970: 478). Over the hallmark appears the word 'Cashmer' or 'Cashmere,' undoubtedly the name of the particular pattern, probably dating to about 1890. The firm of J & G Meakin was organized in 1851 and existed at least through 1971.

Finally, covered vegetable dishes are represented by 21 sherds from three different specimens. One is of creme-colored ware and is decorated with a blue underglaze floral

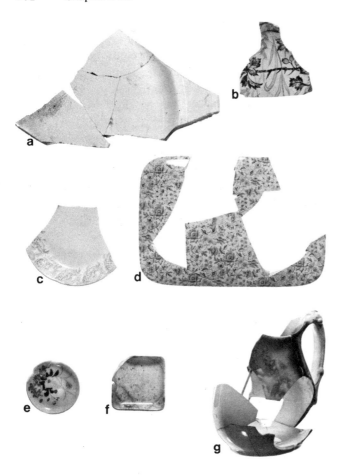

Fig. 50. Ceramic Dishes, Individual Butters, and Pitcher
  a. Earthenware platter fragment
  b. Rectangular footed dish fragment
  c. Fruit or ice cream dish (J. & G. Meakin)
  d. Vegetable dish cover
  e. Individual butter
  f. Individual butter (John Maddock and Sons)
  g. Pitcher (Maddock and Company)

Diameter of *e:* 2-11/16 in.

print (Fig. 50 *d*); parts of the dish body and handles, along with the cover, were found in the trash dump. A second cover, also recovered from the dump, is white earthenware with a white tint glaze, decorated with a grey underglaze floral print. Three remaining sherds, also of white earthenware with a white tint glaze, are from a rectangular cover. It is decorated with an overglaze brown print that has been touched up by hand with yellow and green, and with an overglaze gilt band around the edge. Molding is also part of the decoration, although the specimen is too incomplete to determine its nature. Judging from the style of decoration, this piece was probably manufactured in the 1880s or 1890s.

Individual Butters

Seven pieces representing six separate individual butters were recovered (Fig. 50 *e-f*). One is a rim sherd of white earthenware with the same underglaze blue floral print as the covered vegetable dish described above (Fig. 50 *d*); this butter was apparently 3 in. in diameter and 3/8 in. high. Another rim sherd of white earthenware with white tint glaze is decorated with three green overglaze bands below the rim on the interior surface. Two other fragments from the same item are decorated with an underglaze black print augmented by hand-applied green overglaze. This circular individual butter was approximately 3-5/16 in. in diameter and ¼ in. high. The design, though very incomplete, appears to be an oriental scene motif and indicates British production during the 1870s and 1880s. These four sherds were recovered from the dump.

The one porcelain individual butter (Fig. 50 *e*) is of 19th-century oriental manufacture. It has a green celadon type glaze as a background for the hand-painted underglaze and overglaze floral decoration in red, green, white, black, and gilt. There is also an overglaze gilt band around the rim of this piece, which is 2-11/16 in. in diameter and 9/16 in. high.

The remaining two pieces are parts of two identical rectangular individual butters recovered from Building 35, room 10. They are undecorated white earthenware, the one nearly complete specimen (Fig. 50 *f*) measuring 2-11/16 by 2¾ by 9/16 in. A complete hallmark on the base of this piece (Fig. 47 *j*) identifies the ware as Royal Semi-Porcelain, produced by John Maddock and Sons, England. Although this firm dates from about 1855 to at least 1971 (Godden 1971: 75), the presence of 'England' in the hallmark dates the piece no earlier than about 1880 (Liesenbein 1973: 7).

Ladle

The only ceramic ladle identified is represented by two sherds from the bowl and the handle. It is of white earthenware with a white tint glaze, with decoration consisting of an overglaze grey band around the rim. The bowl of this ladle was approximately 3 in. in diameter and 7/8 in. deep. A section of a round handle extends up from the side.

Mugs

The six sherds in this category represent three or four individual items. Since these specimens are far from complete, their identification as mugs is a matter of probability rather than of certainty. All were recovered from the trash dump. Two sherds, a handle and part of a body, are of white earthenware with a white tint glaze. A section of rim is at the level of the top of the handle, a typical conformation in mugs. Decoration consists solely of a molded thumb rest on the top of the handle.

The same shape is evident on a porcelain handle fragment of probable American origin. Another sherd of the same material is a base fragment with a foot and the remnant of a handle; it was on the basis of the latter portions that this sherd was identified as part of a mug, with a 3¾ in. diameter. The same types of foot and handle fragments were the basis for identifying two other sherds as probable mug fragments. The material is porcelain, most likely of continental European manufacture, and is decorated with molding and overglaze hand-painted enamel and gilt. A base fragment 3-5/16 in. in diameter has a foot and molded band that bulges slightly outward from the vertical side at the base; like the handle shape described above, this foot shape is typical of mugs.

Pitcher

Only one pitcher, reconstructed from nine sherds recovered from the trash dump, can definitely be identified (Fig. 50 *g*). It is made of white earthenware with a white tint glaze. It is approximately 6 in. high and has an oval base measuring 3 by 3½ in. Decoration is limited to the molding on the handle. The hallmark on the base of this pitcher (Fig. 47 *k*) is an underglaze blue-grey printed mark of Maddock and Company; although there is no date, the presence of 'England' in the mark suggests production no earlier than the 1870s (Liesenbein 1973: 1).

The distinction between a pitcher and a ewer, which is part of a toilet set, is based on the wideness or constriction of the throat. Many small sherds that might be fragments of either pitchers or ewers, therefore, cannot be specifically identified.

Plates

One hundred fifty-one plates and plate fragments were recovered, including nine whole and restorable specimens. Seventy-three of the specimens were recovered from the trash dump, most of the remainder coming from specific buildings at both the old and new forts. Except for 16 sherds of porcelain, all the plate fragments are of either white or creme-colored earthenware.

Of the 74 pieces of undecorated white earthenware, 26 are of the white tint variety, with measurable diameters ranging from 7-15/16 to 10-1/2 in. Two of these pieces are restorable specimens and bear hallmarks. One is an 8-1/8 in. diameter plate with a blue printed hallmark of the Steubenville Pottery Company, Steubenville, Ohio (Fig. 47 *l*). This mark was used on white granite ware produced by the firm, which was founded in November 1879 (Barber n.d.: 129-30). Actual production began in 1881 and ceased when the firm closed in 1921 (Stout 1923: 82). The second restorable white tinted specimen has both a grey printed and an impressed hallmark. The printed mark (Fig. 47 *m*) identifies the piece as a product of John Edwards, a firm located in Fenton, Staffordshire, England, and in operation from 1847 until 1900 (Godden 1971: 67). The ware, according to this mark, is "porcelain de terre," a type that the manufacturer distinguished from ironstone-china and white granite in an 1885 advertisement (Godden 1971: 107). An impressed hallmark, 'Havre' (Fig. 47 *n*), also appears on this plate, but its significance is not understood.

Of the 31 specimens of undecorated white earthenware with a blue tint glaze that were identified as plates, seven bear complete or partial hallmarks of six different firms. These items range in diameter from 8-7/8 to 10½ in. One

complete plate, 9-7/8 in. in diameter, bears the printed black hallmark of Thomas Hughes (Fig. 47 *o*). This English firm, located at Burslem and Longport, Staffordshire, produced "Granite" and "Ironstone China" from about 1860 to 1894 (Godden 1971: 73). It is not known when the company first used "England" in its marks.

A second complete plate with blue tint glaze was recovered from the privy next to Building 33. This specimen is 8-7/8 in. in diameter and has the black printed hallmark of Powell and Bishop (Fig. 47 *p*). Located at Hanley, Staffordshire, this firm was in business only from about 1876 to 1878 (Godden 1971: 83). A third firm, Burgess and Goddard, is represented by a blue-grey printed hallmark (Fig. 47 *q*) on a base sherd from a plate of indeterminate size and on a restorable plate 8-7/8 in. in diameter. An impressed 'U,' 3/16 in. high, is present to the right of the printed hallmark on the restorable plate, which was reconstructed from sherds collected at the trash dump. Two sherds with Burgess and Goddard printed hallmarks were also recovered at a ranch near Patagonia, Arizona, by Fontana and Greenleaf (1962: 95), who give the location of the firm as Longton, Staffordshire, England. Two other base sherds bear very incomplete black printed hallmarks. One is most likely that of J and G Meakin of Hanley, Staffordshire, a firm founded about 1851 and still in existence in 1971 (Godden 1971: 77). The earliest known use of "England" in this firm's hallmarks was about 1890 (Liesenbein 1973: 7). The other partial hallmark, also a printed black underglaze mark, most likely represents E and C Challinor of Fenton, Staffordshire, which was in existence from about 1862 to 1891 (Godden 1971: 61).

The final hallmarked specimen with blue tint glaze is a nearly complete plate, 10 in. in diameter, manufactured by Edward Clarke of Longport, England. It has a blue printed underglaze hallmark (Fig. 47 *s*) and an impressed mark (Fig. 47 *t*). This item apparently was produced around 1878-80 (Godden 1964: 147). The letters in the impressed mark appear to have a blue color, but this is attributed to the thickness of the blue tint glaze that has flowed into it.

Seventeen pieces of undecorated white earthenware plates with glaze tint of indeterminate color were recovered from the trash dump. The measurable specimens range in diameter from 9 to 10½ in. The first of two hallmarked specimens, a restorable plate 9½ in. in diameter, bears a dark blue printed mark of John Maddock and Sons (Fig. 47 *r*). As previously mentioned, this firm was founded about 1855 (Godden 1971: 75), and first used "England" in its marks about 1880 (Liesenbein 1973: 7). The second hallmarked specimen bears a printed black mark of T and R Boote (Fig. 47 *u*), a firm that has been in existence in Burslem since about 1842 (Godden 1971: 58; Godden 1968: 44). Also present on this 9-in.-diameter plate is a portion of an illegible impressed hallmark. The plate, according to the printed hallmark, is made of "Royal Premium" earthenware.

All of the plates discussed above are essentially flat dinner plates. Only one sherd from a soup plate has been

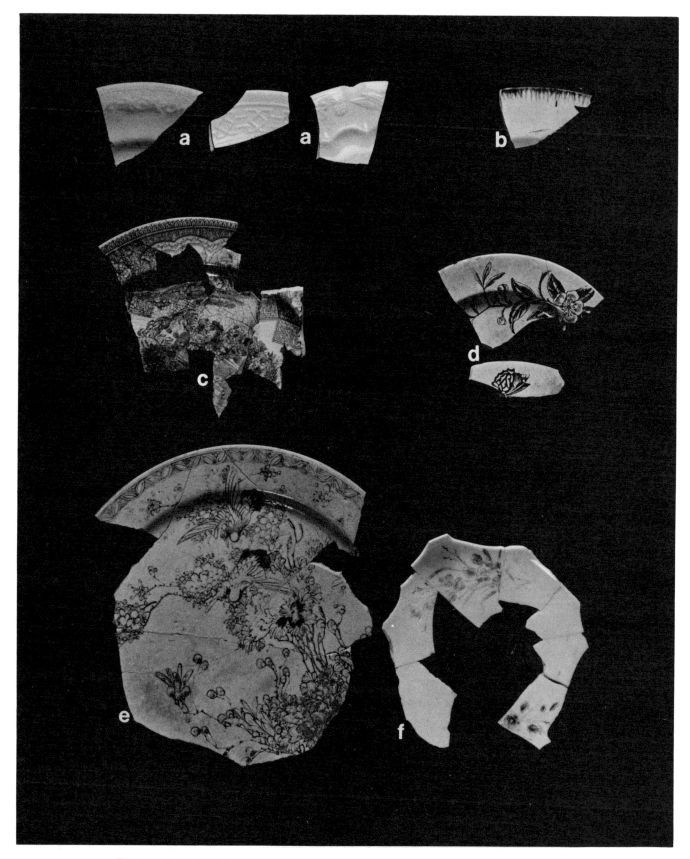

Fig. 51. Ceramic Plates
     a. Rim sherds with molded decoration
     b. Rim sherd of shell edge ware
     c. Blue transfer print on white
        earthenware

Width of *b:* 2-5/8 in.
     d. Butterfly and floral decoration on
        creme-colored ware
     e. Creme-colored ware plate
     f. Porcelain plate

identified in the collection. This specimen, from the corral at Building 35, is made of white earthenware with a white tint glaze and is decorated with a scalloped rim. It had a rim diameter of approximately 10 in., and a maximum depth of 1¾ in.

Thirty-two other decorated white earthenware sherds were recovered. Four have molded decoration below the rim (Fig. 51 *a*): one exhibits an indistinct design of interlocking curvilinear scrolls, another has a rectilinear design below the rim, and the remaining two have a molded floral decoration between the rim and the scalloped inner border.

White earthenware plates with molded and painted decoration are represented by 21 sherds, all of shell edge ware (Fig. 51 *b*), recovered from three separate proveniences at the fort. Measurable rim sherds indicate a diameter of 9½ in. The decoration includes a hand-applied blue underglaze enamel over the molded design around the edge. England is the only country known to have produced this style of decoration, which originally appeared on pearlware around 1779 and continued "well through the second quarter of the 19th century" (Noël Hume 1969: 393-4).

The balance of the decorated white earthenware plates are either printed or painted. Fifteen fragments, 11 of which compose one partial plate (Fig. 51 *c*), have a blue transfer printed design that includes geometric, floral, and scenic elements. A partial hallmark (Fig. 52 *a*) on the latter specimen, in the same blue underglaze as the decoration, is not sufficiently complete to identify the manufacturer; part of a word, believed to be 'Damascus,' is thought to be the name of the pattern.

Eighteen pieces of creme-colored earthenware recovered from the trash dump represent plates with four distinct designs. Five sherds are parts of one or more plates of the same design seen in Figure 51 *c*. Four other pieces are probably parts of one plate with a 7¾ in. rim diameter; the decoration is a floral and butterfly print in brown underglaze (Fig. 51 *d*). A restorable plate consisting of six fragments (Fig. 51 *e*) has a rim diameter of 10½ in. The finish is a clear liquid glaze, while decoration is a floral and bird design in polychrome hand-painted overglaze enamel and gilt. The enamel in some areas is exceedingly thick, measuring as much as .016 in. The same is the case for the remaining three sherds, probably all from one plate. This item, which originally had an 8½-in. diameter, is decorated with a floral design in polychrome hand-painted enamel overglaze, applied over a clear liquid glaze finish. Both of these last two specimens could have been produced in the United States beginning in the 1850s (Ramsay 1939: 152), or in England as early as the late 18th century (Collard 1967: 104-5); the style, however, indicates middle to late 19th-century manufacture.

The remaining 16 plate fragments are porcelain. Two fragments of a plate that was 8½ in. in diameter have a possible fugitive overglaze decoration. Another porcelain item is a restorable table plate with a coupe shape – that is, with an upcurved rather than flat rim (Butler Brothers 1915).

This plate is approximately 7½ in. in diameter and has hand-painted floral overglaze decoration in gilt and polychrome (Fig. 51 *f*). Both of these specimens are thought to be of continental European origin.

Seven other sherds are white American porcelain plate fragments. At least five, and probably all seven, were items of military issue from the Quartermaster's Department. A severely burnt plate recovered from Building 35, room 10, has a portion of a 'U.S.Q.M.D.' hallmark on the bottom that is very similar to one identified by Brose (1967: 54-5) as the product of the Trenton China Company; this specimen has a 9¾-in. rim diameter. Three rim sherds have the blue 'Q.M.D.' marking attributed to the Greenwood Pottery Company (cf. Figs. 48 *g*, 53 *f*). As noted above (see *Bowls*), while the impressed mark found on other Greenwood Pottery Company 'Q.M.D.' specimens was first used in 1886, according to Barber (n.d.: 68), it is believed that 1889 is the earliest year any tableware would have been marked with the abbreviation of the Quartermaster's Department.

Saucers

Of the 58 fragments of saucers recovered and identified, 19 are undecorated white earthenware. Two nearly complete specimens and four fragments are undecorated white earthenware with a white tint glaze. The two whole saucers are identical pieces and have the black hallmark of the U.S. Army Medical Department (Fig. 47 *f*); this is the same mark present on the base of white earthenware St. Dennis cups recovered from the same place, the privy of Building 33, the new hospital. Two other hallmarked fragments were recovered, both from the privy of Building 6. One bears a small portion of an impressed mark of the Mercer Pottery Company, Trenton, New Jersey (Fig. 52 *b*). Although the mark reads 'Mercer China,' the type of ware is actually a white granite produced by this company between 1868 and 1879 (Barber n.d.: 57). The other hallmark, also fragmentary, is a blue printed mark believed to belong to Henry Burgess. This pottery firm, located at Burslem, Staffordshire, England, was in existence from 1804 to 1892 (Godden 1964: 116).

Among the 10 pieces of undecorated white earthenware with blue tint glaze is one nearly complete 6-in. saucer. A printed black underglaze hallmark on its base identifies this piece as the product of Wedgwood and Company (Fig. 52 *c*). This firm, which has operated since about 1860 in Tunstall, Staffordshire, is not to be confused with the famous firm of Josiah Wedgwood, Etruria, Staffordshire (Godden 1971: 97-8). Other sherds with blue tint glaze include three specimens with parts of the black printed hallmark of E and C Challinor of Fenton, Staffordshire, a company in operation from about 1862 to 1891 (Godden 1971: 61). One of the pieces may have been produced during the last year of the firm's existence, since it appears to have included the word 'England,' an addition to Challinor's hallmark believed to date no earlier than 1891 (Liesenhein 1973:10).

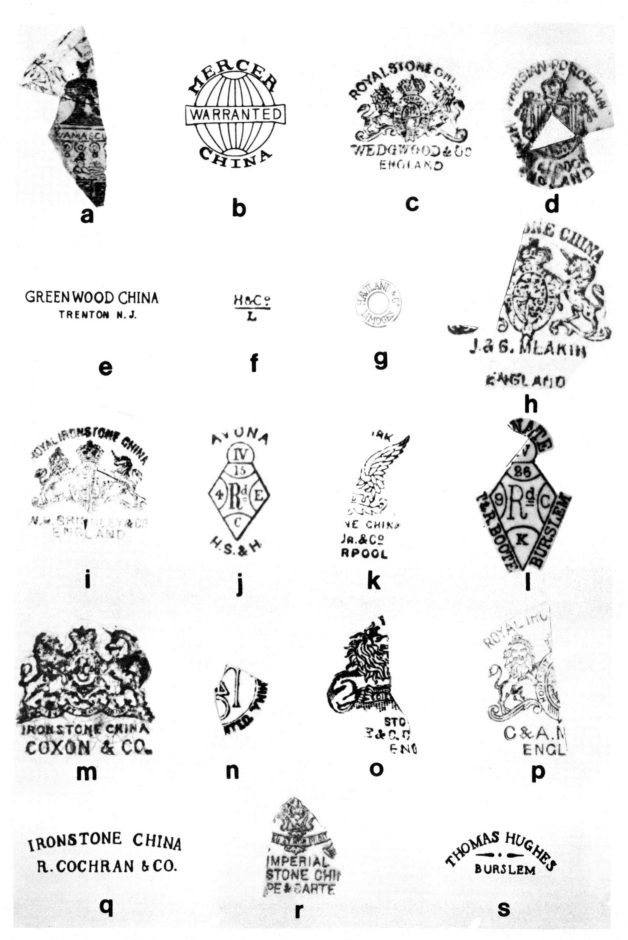

Fig. 52. Ceramic Hallmarks

Hallmarks are present on two of three pieces of undecorated white earthenware with glaze tint of indeterminate color. One is a nearly complete brown underglaze printed mark of Henry Alcock and Company (Fig. 52 *d*) on a nearly complete 6-in. diameter saucer. While the company was in operation from around 1861 to 1910 at Cobridge, Staffordshire, England, the presence of 'England' in this mark implies a date of manufacture no earlier than 1891 (Godden 1964: 26-7). The term "Parisian Porcelain," according to Jewitt, writing in 1883 (1970: 478), was simply another name for white granite. Also recovered was a saucer fragment with a partial Alfred Meakin hallmark. This printed black mark probably includes the ware name 'Ironstone China' and the word 'England.' The company was founded about 1875 in Tunstall (Godden 1971: 76), and the probable presence of 'England' in the mark indicates manufacture around 1891.

Seven different designs are present among 20 saucer fragments made of decorated white earthenware with white tint glaze. At least two saucers are represented by five sherds with the identical blue transfer print present on the ovide cup in Figure 49 *c*. These saucers were 5-5/16 in. in diameter and have no hallmark. Two other sherds with a blue underglaze transfer print design are probably from the same set as the "Damascus" pattern described above under *Plates*. Three fragments of at least two saucers with yet another blue floral transfer print (Fig. 53 *a*) were recovered from the trash dump and from Building 43. A partial printed blue hallmark on one of the sherds may be a portion of one of the hallmarks used by the American Crockery Company, Trenton, New Jersey. A mark reading 'American China/A.C. Co.' is illustrated in Barber (n.d.: 60), who states that it was printed in black about 1890 on white granite ware. The company was in operation by 1876 and continued at least through 1890. One sherd has a brown transfer print in a floral and geometric pattern (Fig. 53 *b*); it is from a saucer that was 5-13/16 in.

in diameter and that was probably produced during the 1880s or 1890s in Great Britain or the United States.

Four decorated fragments, probably from two 6-in. saucers, are made of white granite. They are decorated with an underglaze orange or peach colored band and four black overglaze bands (Fig. 53 *c*). Part of the impressed hallmark of the Mercer Pottery Company, Trenton, New Jersey (Fig. 52 *b*), places the date of manufacture of these pieces between 1868 and 1879 (Barber n.d.: 57).

Four sherds from two white earthenware saucers were decorated by a technique known as "sponge root," which consisted of stamping onto an unglazed piece generally bright-colored designs cut out of the roots of sponges. Another method of creating informal patterns was to dab the piece with a sponge impregnated with paint (Collard 1967: 144-5). These techniques were used from the 1850s into the early 20th century in the United States, England, France, Holland, Belgium, and Germany (Robacker 1971: 245-8). One rim sherd recovered from Building 106 at the old fort has sponge-root applied red decoration in conjunction with hand-painted green and black; it is from a 6-in. saucer of blue tint glaze white earthenware (Fig. 53 *d*). Three sherds, probably from one 6-in. saucer, have the same combination of sponge-root and hand-painted decoration. As on the preceding piece, the heads of the flowers are sponge-root applied, in this case in red and blue (Fig. 53 *e*), while the leaves and stem are hand-painted in green and black. A red band runs around the circumference of the saucer just below the rim.

The remaining 11 sherds of decorated white earthenware have a blue tint glaze. Nine sherds are from one or more saucers 6 to 6½ in. in diameter, recovered from Building 6. Decoration is a simple scalloped or undulating pattern. Another sherd, recovered from Building 30, has an underglaze brown print identical with that on a cup fragment found in the same building. The style of decoration is common to the period from the 1870s to 1890s. The final sherd, recovered from Building 106, is part of a saucer that was approximately 6 in. in diameter; it bears a sponge-root applied decoration.

Only two creme-colored ware saucer fragments have been identified among the materials recovered at Fort Bowie. One is from a saucer 4-7/8 in. in diameter, decorated with a grey underglaze floral print. A portion of an impressed hallmark is probably that of W. T. Copeland & Sons of Stoke, Staffordshire, England. Copeland used an impressed mark on earthenware from about 1850 into the 20th century (Godden 1964: 171). The second specimen is part of a saucer that was 5¾ in. in diameter. It has a green underglaze transfer printed decoration of oak leaves and acorns.

Only six fragments of porcelain saucers were recovered. One, recovered from Building 35, room 8, is an incomplete specimen 6-3/8 in. in diameter, with the initials of the Quartermaster's Department in blue underglaze ¼-in. letters below the rim (Fig. 53 *f*). A portion of an impressed hallmark on the base (Fig. 52 *e*) identifies the Greenwood Pottery Company of Trenton, New Jersey. Although this firm was in op-

◄Fig. 52. Ceramic Hallmarks
   a. Damascus (?) pattern of unidentified company
   b. Mercer China (drawing of impressed mark)
   c. Wedgewood & Co.
   d. Henry Alcock & Co.
   e. Greenwood China Co.
   f. Haviland & Co.
   g. Haviland & Co.
   h. J. & G. Meakin
   i. W. H. Grindley & Co.
   j. Unidentified British registration mark
   k. Unidentified
   l. T. & R. Boote
   m. Coxon & Co.
   n. Glasgow Pottery
   o. E & C. Challinor
   p. C & A. Meakin
   q. R. Cochran & Co. (drawing of impressed mark)
   r. Hope & Carter
   s. Thomas Hughes
Hallmarks actual size

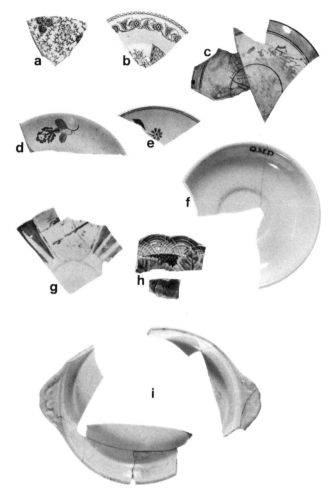

Fig. 53. Ceramic Saucers and Miscellaneous Fragments
- *a.* Blue transfer print rim sherd
- *b.* Brown transfer print rim sherd
- *c.* Saucer with overglaze and underglaze decoration (Mercer Pottery Company)
- *d.* Rim sherd with sponge root applied decoration
- *e.* Rim sherd with sponge root applied decoration
- *f.* Military issue saucer (Greenwood Pottery Company)
- *g.* Porcelain saucer with overglaze decoration
- *h.* Majolica flatware fragments
- *i.* Holloware fragments

Diameter of *f:* 6-3/8 in.

eration as early as 1868 (Barber n.d.: 467), documentation cited above (see *Bowls*) indicates that this specimen was manufactured no earlier than 1889. One other fragment of a white porcelain saucer is also attributed to the Greenwood Pottery Company. It has a partial 'Q' followed by the letters 'M.D.' printed in blue underglaze on its base.

Another porcelain sherd, found in the trash dump, is believed to be of continental European origin. It is a fragment of a saucer that originally had a rim diameter of approximately 5½ in. It has a scalloped rim and remnants of a fugitive overglaze floral print decoration. Also recovered from the trash dump was a porcelain sherd that is definitely French in origin. Two complete printed hallmarks on the underside of this piece identify it as the product of Haviland and Company,

Limoges. One of the marks (Fig. 52 *f*), printed in green, was the subject of trademark patent #10,525, granted on August 21, 1883 (USPO 1884: 708). It was granted to Haviland and Company, New York, for use on porcelain, earthenware, and glassware. Three other trademark patents granted to the firm on the same day include one (#10,527) for "the words Haviland & Co., Limoges," which constitute the second hallmark (Fig. 52 *g*) on this specimen. While the former, linear hallmark is printed in green underglaze, the latter, circular mark is printed in gold overglaze. The patents cited certainly do not preclude the possibility that this item was produced prior to 1883, especially since Haviland and Company dates to the 1840s (Collard 1967: 192). Although only a small part of the original decoration remains on this specimen, it was clearly an underglaze monochrome floral print touched up by hand with overglaze rose, grey, green, and yellow.

One last noteworthy porcelain saucer is thought to be continental European in origin because of its slightly dark body tint. It has a scalloped rim and both molded and painted decoration (Fig. 53 *g*), the latter a floral and geometric design executed in overglaze red, blue, grey, and gilt.

Sugar Box

One partial base recovered from the trash dump is believed to be from a sugar box. Made of white earthenware with blue tint glaze, this base measures 2-5/8 by 3-3/8 in. Although essentially rectangular, this is actually an eight-sided object, as the corners have been truncated. Period trade catalogs show that this octagonal shape is characteristic of a sugar box. A printed black hallmark on the base (Fig. 52 *h*) reads in part, 'J. & G. Meakin/England.' The earliest known use of "England" by Meakin is about 1890, although the company dates to about 1851 (Godden 1964: 427).

Unidentifiable Fragments

The total of 237 fragments constituting this category are summarized in Table 15. As the table indicates, it has been possible to identify a major portion (76 percent) of the material at a generic level of function, based on form – that is, flatware versus holloware. Included here are many sherds whose functional identification could not be restricted to less than two or three possibilities because of their incomplete condition – some rim sherds, for example, might have belonged to a dish, a plate, or a saucer. Although these miscellaneous fragments are all presented here under "Kitchen and Table Wares," it is recognized that a few pieces may be parts of toilet sets, a category of ceramics discussed below. Several handles, for example, may have belonged to ewers or to pitchers or jugs. These items, however, are few.

The descriptions given in this section are limited mainly to those pieces with hallmarks and those displaying a decoration of a type or style not described so far in this chapter.

A partial black printed hallmark of W. H. Grindley and Company of Tunstall, England, is present on a flatware base sherd (Fig. 52 *i*). This firm had its beginning about 1880 (Godden 1964: 294). Another flatware sherd has a portion

TABLE 15

Unidentifiable Ceramic Kitchen and Table Ware Fragments

Type of Ware	Flatware Decorated	Flatware Undecorated	Holloware Decorated	Holloware Undecorated	Indeterminate Decorated	Indeterminate Undecorated
White earthenware, white tint glaze	23	2	17	28	3	12
White earthenware, blue tint glaze			39			14
White earthenware, indeterminate tint glaze			1	14		5
Creme-colored ware	2		7		6	
Rockingham ware			3			
Majolica	2		1		3	
American porcelain				4		
Continental European porcelain	8	1	3		3	
Oriental porcelain	1		5		1	
Porcelain, unknown origin	2	1	3	7	5	4
Probable porcelain			3	4		
Total	38	4	82	57	21	35

of the 'S.P. Co.' printed hallmark of the Steubenville Pottery Company (Fig. 47 *l*), which is discussed above (see *Plates*).

A British design registration mark (Fig. 52 *j*) in red underglaze is present on the base of one other sherd; the design was registered with the British patent office on January 15, 1881 (Godden 1964: 526-7). This fragment is from a flatware object of creme-colored ware. The word 'Avona' on the sherd refers to the name of the pattern, but the manufacturer, 'H.S. & H.,' could not be identified.

Two flatware fragments of Anglo-American majolica (Fig. 53 *h*) were recovered from Buildings 105 and 107 at the old fort. These sherds are decorated in green and brown underglaze in conjunction with molding. Majolica of this type was produced in England beginning about 1850 (Collard 1967: 152) and in the United States as early as 1853 (Ramsay 1939: 109), with production apparently continuing in both countries until approximately 1900 (Godden 1966: xxv-xxvi; Hughes n.d.: 200-201).

A number of hallmarks are present on fragments of unidentified holloware objects. Part of an unidentified black printed mark (Fig. 52 *k*) appears on what may be a footed oval vegetable dish; the manufacturer was most likely a company located in East Liverpool, Ohio, but this has not yet been verified. A fragmentary black printed mark is probably that of C. Challinor and Company of Staffordshire, England; it closely resembles mark #834 in Godden (1964: 137), the only Challinor mark to include the word 'England,' which Godden dates between 1892 and 1896. A British registry mark of T and R Boote, Burslem, is printed in black (Fig. 52 *l*) on a piece manufactured after November 26, 1870, the date this mark was registered. On the base of a pitcher, jug, or ewer is the complete brown printed hallmark of Coxon and Company of Trenton, New Jersey (Fig. 52 *m*), a firm

that produced white granite ware between 1863 and about 1884 (Barber n.d.: 56). Four other pieces of white earthenware with blue tint glaze have fragments of the previously discussed hallmarks of J. W. & Son (Fig. 47 *e*), Charles Meakin (Fig. 47 *b*), J & G Meakin (Fig. 52 *h*), and Henry Alcock (Fig. 52 *d*); the latter mark is on the oval base of what was probably a pitcher or a ewer.

Among porcelain holloware fragments, two sherds have printed 'U.S.Q.M.D.' marks, and one of these also has a portion of the impressed mark of the Greenwood Pottery Company (see Fig. 52 *e*). Several fragments of a holloware object, probably porcelain, were recovered from the trash dump. It is a white circular vessel 6-3/16 in. in diameter with 1-3/16 in. high sides (Fig. 53 *i*). The two handles are decorated with molding. On the underside of one of the handles the word 'BAYEUX' is printed in a blue-green underglaze; it is not clear whether this is the name of the maker or of the pattern.

Among the 56 fragments of indeterminate form are sherds bearing 9 hallmarks that have not been discussed thus far. Three of these appear on sherds of undecorated white earthenware with white tint glaze. One is part of a black printed mark of the Glasgow Pottery, Trenton, New Jersey (Fig. 52 *n*); Barber (n.d.: 50) states that this mark was in use in 1884. The company was founded in 1863 and by 1904 was operating under the name John Moses & Sons Co. On a sherd of the same ware is an incomplete black printed hallmark of Thomas Furnival and Sons, Cobridge, England. The diagnostic feature of this fragment is the crest and the word 'MARK,' which is located below the royal arms. This crest was registered by the firm in 1878 (Godden 1964: 263-4). The third hallmark, also printed in black, is believed to be that of the Willets Manufacturing Company, Trenton, New Jersey. This partial mark matches one illustrated in Barber (n.d.: 45) for this company, which originated in 1879 and was still in operation in 1904, when Barber's book was originally published.

Three hallmarks that have not been described thus far appear on fragments of undecorated white earthenware with blue tinted glaze. One is a part of a printed black mark of E and C Challinor of Fenton, Staffordshire, England (Fig. 52 *o*). This firm operated from about 1862 until 1891 (Godden 1971: 61) and was the predecessor of C. Challinor, also of Fenton. Another printed mark is apparently that of C and A Meakin, England (Fig. 52 *p*). This fragment of the mark is identical to one on a specimen recovered by the Tucson Urban Renewal Archaeological Project and in the collection of the Arizona State Museum, Tucson. It is not clear how C and A Meakin fits into the chronology of the succession of Meakin potteries in Staffordshire, which date from around 1851 and were still operating in the mid-1970s. One clue is the presence of 'England' in the mark, since 1889 is the earliest known use of the word in a Meakin hallmark (Liesenbein 1973: 7). A portion of an impressed mark on one other sherd (Fig. 52 *q*) is that of R. Cochran and Company, which operated in Glasgow, Scotland, from about 1846 until 1918 (Godden 1964: 157).

Three additional fragmentary hallmarks of English firms appear on white earthenware sherds, the tint color of which is indeterminate. One is that of Hope and Carter (Fig. 52 *r*), a Burslem pottery firm in operation from 1862 until 1880 (Godden 1964: 334). Another very incomplete black printed hallmark is believed to be that of George Jones of Stoke-on-Trent, a firm founded about 1864 and in operation until 1957 (Godden 1964: 359). The last hallmark is an impressed mark of Thomas Hughes, Burslem (Fig. 52 *s*), which was used from around 1860 until 1894; the company produced "Granite" and "Ironstone China" primarily for the North American market (Godden 1971: 73).

BOTTLES, JARS, AND CROCKS

Several types of ceramic vessels and containers were recovered during the stabilization of Fort Bowie. The bottles, jars, and crocks that have been identified were used for packaging both food and non-food items. Ale, ink, and tooth powder, for example, were packaged by their manufacturers in ceramic containers for distribution to wholesale and retail outlets. The bottles and jars employed were almost surely designed with the thought of shipment to both domestic and export markets, and a great many were undoubtedly reutilized as storage containers.

Foodstuffs and Beverages

Parts of several fragmentary and restorable covered stoneware preserve jars, with an Albany slip on the interior and a salt glazed exterior, were collected (Fig. 54). Preserve jars of this form date no earlier than 1850 (Webster 1971; Ketchum 1970) and were apparently made as late as 1915

Fig. 54. Covered preserve jar.   *Height: 14-3/8 in.*

(Blair 1965: 51). These specimens are 14-3/8 in. high and 10 in. in diameter at the base. An impressed '3' on the body just below the neck denotes a 3-gallon capacity. One specimen has a small portion of what is probably a manufacturer's or wholesaler's overglaze printed mark. The only legible remnant of this mark locates the firm in New York.

Eight stoneware covers (Fig. 55 *a*) were probably used with preserve jars. Six have a salt glaze, one an Albany glaze, and one a colorless alkaline glaze. The diameters of these covers range from 4-7/8 to 6-3/16 in. The smallest specimen has an impressed '1½' on its upper surface, probably indicating that it fitted a 1½-gallon jar. The one complete cover, measuring 5¾ in. in diameter, fits the partially reconstructed 3-gallon jars in the collection. It should also be noted that covers of this general type were used on items other than preserve jars – for example, covered pitchers, herb pots, bean pots, spice jars, stew pots, and sugar bowls (Watkins 1950; Webster 1971); however, some of these items undoubtedly used smaller covers than the recovered specimens. Four sherds recovered, probably from the same object, are too incomplete to identify as to specific form, but are likely the remains of a preserve jar or a churn. The illustrations in Greer (1971: Figs. 7, 11, 16) show that it can be quite difficult to distinguish between a preserve jar and a churn on the basis

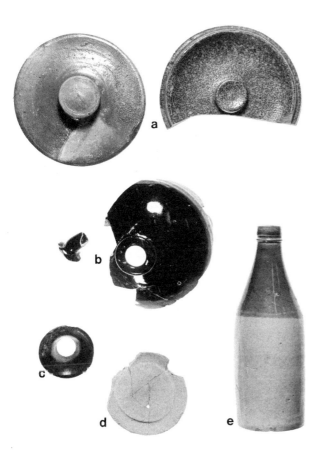

Fig. 55. **Food Storage Containers**
  a. Stoneware preserve jar covers
  b. Soy sauce jug
  c. "Tiger Whiskey" jug spout
  d. Bean pot cover
  e. Bristol glaze stoneware bottle

Diameter of *d:* 3-9/16 in.

the Fort Bowie specimen is part of the phrase 'Grand Medal of Merit Vienna 1873,' which is present on the jar illustrated in Blumenstein.

Twenty-six fragments of Chinese jugs were recovered from several proveniences, including the trash dump, the surface of the first fort, and Building 35, with the latter structure accounting for 17 sherds. Six sherds recovered from Building 35, room 7 (Fig. 55 *b*), are parts of a vessel identified by Munsey (1970: 138) as a Chinese soy sauce jug. A second style of spout recovered (Fig. 55 *c*) was part of a jug that contained a product labeled *ng ky pay* (or *ng ka pi*) and known as "Tiger Whiskey." A third type of Chinese vessel, which Munsey identifies as a bean pot, is represented by ten small sherds from Building 35, room 7. Three unglazed concave discs (Fig. 55 *d*) are thought to have been covers for the bean pots; two of these are 2-7/8 in. in diameter, while the third measures 3½ in.

One fragmentary stoneware bottle finish is probably part of a mineral water bottle. This fragment has a salt glaze over a brown slip and has a series of molded rings below the top. This type of bottle is reported to have been manufactured in Germany and Holland from the 1870s into the 20th century (Seger 1902: 809-17; Munsey 1970: 135). It is also possible that the bottle contained wine or spirits (Ferraro and Ferraro 1964: 39; Munsey 1970: 135, 139).

Another ceramic vessel known to have held a beverage is a complete stoneware bottle recovered from a privy west of Building 35 (Fig. 55 *e*). This bottle, which holds approximately 1 pint, is finished with an uncolored Bristol glaze on the interior and lower exterior and with a brown Bristol glaze on the top of the exterior. Although it almost certainly is British in origin, there is some question about the contents of this type of bottle. Switzer (1974: 9-14) advances an argument for ale as the contents of the specimens found in the steamboat *Bertrand,* while Munsey (1970: 135) identifies this type of bottle as having held beer.

Household and Personal Products

As many as 90 percent of the 61 pieces in this category are whole and fragmentary stoneware ink bottles. Seventeen fragments, from at least 11 separate bottles, held a product of the Sanford Manufacturing Company, Chicago. These bottles are of reddish-brown paste, with a brown slip and a salt glaze. One of the bottles had a capacity of ½ pint and at least seven others held 1 pint. These bottles most likely contained ink, although an 1882 advertising leaflet for Sanford shows that mucilage was also distributed in this type of bottle. The Sanford Manufacturing Company, organized in Worcester, Massachusetts, was moved to Chicago in 1866. The firm remained in Chicago, at various locations, until 1947, when it moved to Bellwood, Illinois (Cummings 1971: 7-8). Those bottles containing Sanford products can be identified by the complete and fragmentary impressed marks (Fig. 56 *a*) on the side of the bottle just above the base.

of an incomplete rim form. The exterior of these four sherds is olive green with an uncolored alkaline glaze, while the interior is finished with a brown colored alkaline glaze. One other sherd was probably a storage jar of some sort. It is of redware, a form of earthenware manufactured in the United States from about 1800 to 1900 (Ramsay 1939: 128). Both the interior and exterior of this vessel are covered with a greenish-brown liquid glaze.

Four earthenware sherds recovered from trash deposits are believed to be fragments of marmalade jars. While only one is decorated and definitely identified, all display essentially identical rim forms. The one decorated fragment is a sherd of white earthenware with a white tint glaze and retains a portion of underglaze black printing that reads, '–RIT VIEN– / –ER & Son's.' This legend appears to be identical to that on an illustrated marmalade jar that contained Dundee Marmalade, the product of James Keiller and Son, London (Blumenstein 1965: 137-8), a firm established in 1797 (Davis 1967: Plate 20). The first part of the inscription on

a # SANFORD MFG CO CHICAGO

b # CARTER'S INKS

c

J. BOURNE & SON,
PATENTEES,
DENBY POTTERIES,
NEAR DERBY.

d
VITREOUS STONE BOTTLES
J BOURNE & SON
PATENTEES

DENBY POTTERY
NEAR DERBY

P. & J. ARNOLD
LONDON

e
VITREOUS STONE BOTTLES
J. BOURNE & SON,

PATENTEES,
DENBY POTTERY,
NEAR DERBY.

P. & J. ARNOLD,
LONDON.

f
ENCRE JAPONAISE
N. ANTOINE & FILS

g
MAW
1

h

PRICE
P
BRISTOL

i

GROSVENOR
26
GLASGOW

Fig. 56. Drawings of Impressed Marks from Bottles and Jars *Marks actual size*

 a. Sanford Manufacturing Co.   *f.* N. Antoine & Fils
 b. Carter Ink Co.   *g.* MAW & Co.
 c. J. Bourne & Son   *h.* J. & C. Price and Brothers
 d. J. Bourne & Son/P. & J. Arnold *i.* Grosvenor/Glasgow
 e. J. Bourne & Son/P. & J. Arnold

A second American ink manufacturer represented in the collection is the Carter Ink Company. The firm was established in 1858 in Boston and by 1869 also had plants in New York and Chicago. The firm's official title was Carter, Dinsmore and Company from 1872 until 1901 (Nelson and Hurley 1967: 72), although 'Carter's Inks' is the legend impressed on stoneware bottles containing its products (Fig. 56 *b*). Of the four fragmentary Carter's bottles recovered, one had a 7- or 8-oz. capacity, while the others held 14 to 16 oz. All were of grey paste with white slip and uncolored Bristol glaze, and they most likely had cone tops (Blair 1965: 53). One interesting aspect of the Carter's bottles is the fact that at least two, and probably all four, were manufactured by the English firm of Joseph Bourne and Son. This firm, located near Denby, England, dates to about 1850 and is still in operation as of 1976. The impressed mark of J. Bourne and Son is present on the side of the two specimens, approximately 1 in. above the base (Fig. 56 *c*).

Impressed marks of J. Bourne and Son are also present on many of the 30 fragments and on one complete bottle (Fig. 57 *b*) that held the ink of P & J Arnold, a London firm founded in 1862 (Devner 1964: 45). These bottles are stoneware with a salt glaze over a slip that covers only the exterior surface. Three sizes of bottles have been identified among the pieces found at the fort: ½ pint, 1 pint, and approximately 21 oz. Although the lettering is identical on all three, the impressed mark is slightly different on the ½-pint size; it is enclosed by an impressed line that is part of the mark (Fig. 56 *d*). The mark on the two larger sizes of bottles, in addition to being larger, is not enclosed (Fig. 56 *e*).

The fourth ink manufacturer is represented by one nearly complete 1-quart bottle (Fig. 57 *a*) and by two fragments of a second bottle, probably with a capacity of 1 pint. These bottles are of grey paste and are covered with a brown liquid glaze on both the interior and exterior surfaces. An impressed mark of N. Antoine & Fils (Fig. 56 *f*) is present on both bottles. This French company was located in Paris, according to a paper label on a bottle illustrated by Nelson and Hurley (1967: 1).

Three recovered fragments of white earthenware with white tint glaze represent portions of two lids from jars that contained dental products. One sherd, believed to be from a jar of tooth powder, is decorated with an underglaze black print. Neither the specific product nor the firm was ascertained. The other two sherds are part of a lid from a jar of toothpaste (Fig. 57 *c*) produced by John Gosnell and Company, London. The lid is decorated with an underglaze green, yellow, and black print and with an overglaze gilt band. The complete legend on the lid, illustrated by A. Davis (1967: Plate 17), reads: 'CHERRY TOOTH PASTE/PATRONIZED BY THE QUEEN/FOR BEAUTIFYING AND PRESERVING THE TEETH & GUMS/PREPARED BY JOHN GOSNELL & C⁰ L^TD LONDON.' In the center is a portrait of the young Victoria, between the words 'EXTRA/MOIST.' According to Davis, this pot was introduced about 1853 and was produced in small quantities until 1940. Gosnell pots were manufactured by F. and R. Pratt and Company of Fenton, Staffordshire (Davis 1967: 39-40). This firm originated around 1780 and functioned under the above name from 1840 into the 20th century (Godden 1966: 265-6).

Three sherds from an incomplete tobacco jar are white earthenware with a blue tint glaze. Decorated with an underglaze brown print and molding (Fig. 57 *d*), this jar held Vanity Fair smoking tobacco produced by William S. Kimball and Company, Rochester, New York. Listings in various Rochester City directories supplied by the Rochester Historical Society (Mary Shannon 1974: personal communication) reveal that from 1868 until 1873 William S. Kimball was listed merely as a tobacconist. William S. Kimball and Company, manufacturer, was listed from 1873 to 1889. After that time, William S. Kimball was listed as a branch of the American Tobacco Company. Vanity Fair tobacco was listed from 1876 until 1893, first as a tobacco and later as cigarettes. The words "Vanity Fair" were, in fact, patented by Kimball as a trademark for smoking tobacco on August 22, 1876 (USPO 1877a: 293). As an interesting sidelight on this product, the author of a book of reminiscences mentions that in 1881 he purchased a pound tin of Vanity Fair tobacco and cigarette papers at Norton and Stewart's store in Willcox, Arizona Territory (Mazzanovich 1931: 197).

Vessels of Undetermined Contents

A total of 56 whole and fragmentary bottles, jars, or jugs were recovered for which specific contents could not be determined. Some were obviously storage vessels. The most frequently encountered forms were earthenware lidded cylindrical jars (Fig. 57 *e-g*). Of the 27 specimens recovered, 15 represent jars and 12 represent lids. Seven jar and lid sets can be fitted together, and two of these were found with the lids actually in place. Jars with the following capacities were found: 1 oz. (Fig. 57 *e*); 4½ oz.; 11½ oz. (Fig. 57 *f*); 18 oz.; and 21½ oz. (Fig. 57 *g*). The 1-oz. jar is the only specimen of this type with a hallmark. It is the impressed mark of MAW & Co. of Breseley, Shropshire, and Worcester, England (Fig. 56 *g*). The '1' below the company's name undoubtedly indicates the vessel's capacity. It is noteworthy that the seven complete jar and lid sets of this type were recovered from the privy of Building 33, the new hospital; from this it might be inferred that these jars held a medicinal substance or hospital supplies of some sort.

Five fragments of Bristol glazed bottles or jars were recovered, two of which bear impressed marks. One mark is that of J and C Price and Brothers, Bristol, England (Fig. 56 *h*), according to Jewitt (1970: 232-3). This pottery firm was established around 1735-40 and was still in operation in 1883. This piece cannot, however, predate 1842, when Bristol glaze was introduced at this pottery, according to Jewitt (1970: 232-3). The second impressed mark is that of F. Grosvenor, Glasgow, Scotland (Fig. 56 *i*). This firm was founded about 1869, and the absence of "& Son" most likely

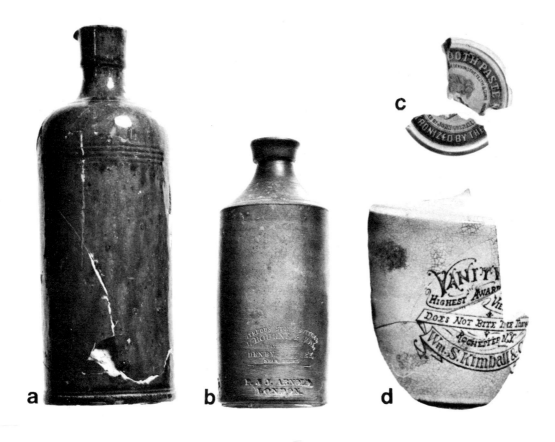
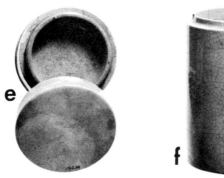

Fig. 57. Ceramic Storage Containers
a. N. Antoine & Fils ink bottle
b. P. & J. Arnold ink bottle
c. John Gosnell & Sons toothpaste jar lid
d. Wm. S. Kimball tobacco jar
e. Earthenware jar (1-oz. capacity)
f. Earthenware jar (11½-oz. capacity)
g. Earthenware jar (21½-oz. capacity)

Diameter of *b:* 3 in.

dates the specimen as having been produced prior to 1899 (Godden 1964: 295; Jewitt 1970: 621). Both of these hallmarked objects may have been ale bottles, since stoneware ale bottles with a 'Price/Bristol' impressed hallmark were recovered from the steamboat *Bertrand* (Switzer 1974: 12), and a 'Grosvenor/Glasgow' stoneware ale bottle was found at Fort Union, New Mexico (R. Wilson, In press).

Of the remaining 24 fragments, only five can be identified. These are stoneware sherds, with either uncolored or brown Bristol glazes; they probably were parts of jugs but are too incomplete to yield definite size or shape data.

STOPPERS

Two complete earthenware bottle or jug stoppers and the fragment of a third were recovered. The two complete examples, which are identical, measure 1½ in. in length and have a diameter of 7/8 in. at one end, tapering to 9/16 in. at the other.

TOILET SETS AND TOILETS

The material discussed in this section includes portions of two toilets and 42 fragments from several components of toilet sets. A toilet set in the late 19th century was a combination of several or all of the following pieces: ewer (a pitcher characterized by a narrow neck), basin, chamber pot (open or covered), combinet (a lidded vessel with a wire handle), jarette, brush vase, slop jar, pail, soap dish with drainer, and soap slab. Around 1894 a price list for the East Liverpool Pottery offered, in addition to individual pieces, sets consisting of 6, 10, and 12 pieces, with each cover counting as one piece (Hillcrest Shop n.d.).

Thirteen earthenware fragments, recovered primarily from the trash dump, represent six separate basins. Four are undecorated white earthenware, while a fifth is creme-colored ware decorated with an underglaze green floral printed design. The sixth basin had a 16-in. rim diameter and is decorated with an ornate oriental motif in underglaze black print, touched up by hand in both underglaze and overglaze (Fig. 58 *a*). Colors used include maroon, orange, pink, yellow, blue, and aquamarine. The technique and style of the decoration seem to indicate manufacture in England around 1870-1890.

Four fragments of a white earthenware chamber pot with a blue tint glaze were recovered from the dump. This vessel had a rim diameter of approximately 9 in. and probably was not covered. A printed black hallmark on the base identifies this piece as Royal Ironstone China, the product of W. H. Grindley and Company. This firm was formed about 1880 in Tunstall, England, and is still operating in the 1970s (Godden 1971: 70).

Three other fragments recovered from the trash dump are probably portions of chamberpots or combinets. Two of these are white earthenware with white tint glaze and have

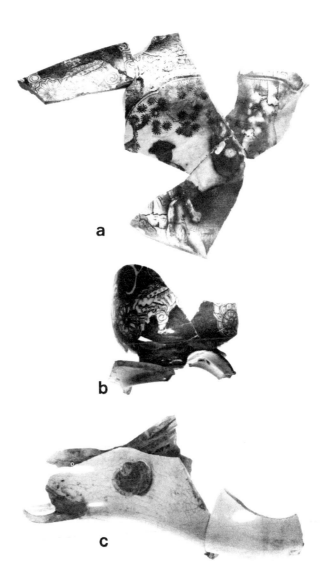

Fig. 58. Ceramic Toiletry Artifacts
    a. Basin
    b. Soapdish
    c. Male urinal
    Length of *c:* 7½ in.

overglaze decoration with hand-painted polychrome enamel and gilt.

Only three fragments of what was probably a ewer were identified. These sherds are white earthenware with white tint glaze and are decorated with an underglaze floral and geometric print in red. Although it is too incomplete for positive identification, this object was probably produced between 1870 and the 1890s, judging by the style of decoration.

Ten fragments from three earthenware objects are believed to be portions of soap dishes. Seven fragments are from a white earthenware object decorated with the same oriental motif that is present on the basin discussed above. This incomplete piece (Fig. 58 *b*) consists of a holloware body with three legs attached to a flat base, thought to have had a diameter of 6 in. The bottom of the holloware portion is perforated with a series of round drain holes. Such holes are also present on one of two other sherds believed to be fragments of a two-piece soap dish; the second sherd is a rim sherd from a vessel with an estimated 5½ in. diameter; it is decorated with a blue floral and geometric underglaze print. The floral aspect of the printed design probably dates the manufacture of this item to around 1880-1890.

Portions of the rim and body of a creme-colored ware vessel, also thought to have been part of a toilet set, were recovered from the trash dump. The flared rim had a diameter of approximately 5 in. and is decorated with an overglaze gilt band. Both the interior and the exterior of this vessel are finished with an uncolored liquid glaze.

One white earthenware object, not ordinarily part of a toilet set, is a fragmentary male urinal. Although far from complete, the unusual shape of this specimen (Fig. 58 *c*) leaves little doubt that it is identical in form to the urinal illustrated in a price list of the East Liverpool Pottery Company (Hillcrest Shop n.d.). The flat bottom, tubular spout, and position of the handle are diagnostic of this piece of toilet ware, which sold at wholesale for $4.50 per dozen.

One fairly complete white earthenware toilet (Fig. 59) and a fragment from another were recovered at Fort Bowie. The small fragment was found in the commanding officer's quarters and the specimen in the illustration was reconstructed from sherds found in Building 5, room 2 – one of the officers' quarters. These items were probably installed in 1889, when a sewage system was constructed at the fort (Sheire 1968: 83). This system serviced the hospital, officers' quarters, and the buildings on the eastern side of the parade ground, including the commanding officer's home. The remaining portion of the more complete specimen measures 17¾ in. long by 14-7/8 in. wide and 13 in. high, but an unknown amount of the base is missing. Three fittings at the back of the toilet provided intake for water that flushed the toilet both from holes in the rim and also from an outlet directly into the bowl. Water and effluvia were discharged at the front of the bowl and then down through the base. Sewage from this toilet and other sources was fed into a 4-in. ceramic feeder pipe, which was connected to a cast iron 6-in. main. This main ran approximately 1,000 ft. from a point opposite the south end of Building 8 to a cesspool (Montgomery 1966).

FURNISHINGS

Twenty-seven whole and fragmentary objects have been classified as ceramic furnishings. Three pieces recovered from Building 35, room 3, are part of an oriental porcelain candlestick (Fig. 60 *a*). The base was basically triangular in outline,

Fig. 59. Earthenware toilet   *Height: 13 in.*
(rear view, showing intake fittings).

with the hypotenuse a convex curve; the finger grip is located at the apex of the two straight sides, which were 3¾ in. long. Two concentric triangular foot rings are present on the bottom. Decoration is both molded and painted, the latter in a floral and geometric design utilizing red, yellow, green, and pink enamel, and gilt. This candlestick is probably Japanese in origin, most likely post-1854.

One fragment of molded Rockingham earthenware from Building 26 is believed to be part of a spittoon. Although incomplete, it shows a similarity to items illustrated in *Bennington Pottery and Porcelain* (Barret 1958: 128-9).

Six white porcelain drawer pulls were recovered, two from Building 35, room 10, one from Building 27, and three from the trash dump. These drawer pulls or knobs (Fig. 60 *b*) are round and range from 1 to 1½ in. in diameter. The metal shaft for attaching the pull to a drawer was held in place in the knob with lead.

One porcelain caster wheel was recovered from Building 106 at the old fort. It is 1½ in. in diameter by ½ in. thick and has a 3/16-in. hole for an axle. The type of furniture on which this wheel was used cannot be determined.

Fourteen earthenware doorknobs were recovered at Fort Bowie. Two came from Building 35, one from Building 19, and the remainder from the trash dump. Five of the 14 have a brown marble-like glaze referred to as a "mineral finish" (Fig. 60 *c*). Diameters range from 2 to 2-1/8 in. The nine white "porcelain finish" specimens are slightly larger, ranging from 2-3/16 to 2-3/8 in. in diameter. Five doorknobs retained all or part of the iron spindle (Fig. 60 *d*), and one of these still held its ½-in. square shaft.

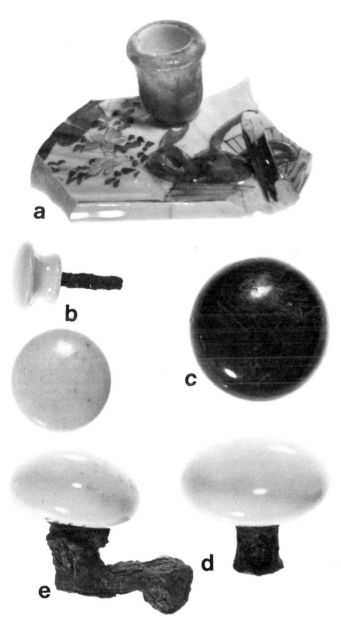

Fig. 60. Ceramic Furnishings
   a. Candlestick
   b. Drawer pulls
   c. "Mineral finish" door knob
   d. "Porcelain finish" door knob
   e. Crank handle

Diameter of *c:* 2-1/8 in.

One white "porcelain finish" knob, 2 in. in diameter, remains attached to an offset iron shaft (Fig. 60 *e*). Hardware catalogs of the period call this style of knob and handle a "crank handle."

The last piece of furnishing is an incomplete white earthenware tile. It has a white tint glaze on all original outer surfaces and is undecorated. It is ½ in. thick and measured at least 4½ by 3¾ in. This item was recovered from the trash dump.

BRICK

The one common fired brick that was recovered measures 8-5/8 by 4-3/16 by 2-3/8 in. A panel 7-3/8 by 1-9/16 in., impressed into the brick, bears the legend 'Evens & Howard/ St. Louis' in barely legible letters 9/16 in. tall. A similar but not identical brick was recovered at Fort Stevenson, North Dakota (G. Smith 1960: Plate 52 *k*). There is some confusion about the history of Evens and Howard in the sources. G. Smith (1960: 215) states that the firm of Evens and Howard was established in 1857 by R. J. Howard and John C. Evens, who had purchased a plant in operation at St. Louis since 1832. The earliest listing for Evens and Howard in the St. Louis city directory is an 1865 listing of the Evens and Howard Fire Brick Company (Lenore Harrington 1974: personal communication). An 1877 newspaper article discusses the Cheltenham Fire-Clay works "where all the celebrated Evens & Howard brands are made." The article goes on to say that the factory was started in 1865 and in 1877 consisted of three works at "Howard Station, Missouri Pacific R. R., four miles from the city"; the superintendent was Mr. F. T Howard, and, according to the 1877 St. Louis city directory, R. J. Howard, E. N. Leeds, and L. J. Howard were proprietors and John C. Evens was clerk (Missouri Historical Society 1960). In later years Evens and Howard manufactured primarily sewer pipe, and they remained in business until at least 1952 (G. Smith 1960: 215).

SMOKING PIPES

The 160 artifacts in this category include 129 pieces of white clay pipe bowls and stems, 29 pieces of red clay bowls and stems, one fragment from a Chinese redware opium pipe bowl, and one ceramic cigar holder. In the descriptions below, the pipes are oriented with stem toward the smoker.

The white clay pipes are all of the type with a nondetachable stem. It should be noted that white clay pipes were made of ball-clay, not the commonly mentioned kaolin (Walker 1974: 161). The most frequently identified manufacturer of pipes at Fort Bowie was the McDougall Company of Glasgow, Scotland. This firm was in existence from either 1810 or 1846 until 1967 (Humphrey 1969: 17-8). Three white clay bowls and 28 pieces of stems produced by McDougall were identified. One incomplete pipe, apparently identical to a specimen recovered at Old Sacramento (Humphrey 1969: 18), has an impressed 'TD' on the side of the bowl facing the smoker, and two dates on the left side of the spur (a projection at the base of the bowl). On the stem, either the numeral '1' or the letter 'I' appears halfway between the bowl and the impressed name 'McDougall,' which is enclosed by a frame in relief. The other two McDougall bowls also bear the 'TD' on the side facing the smoker; one of these has the Roman numeral 'II' between the bowl and the frame on the stem, and the other lacks frames around the 'McDougall' on the left side and 'Glasgow' on the right side of the stem but has a '1' or 'I' midway between the firm's name and the bowl. A number of other variations are to be seen on the McDougall stem pieces: the words 'McDougall' and 'Glasgow' are both enclosed within an embossed, ornamental frame; the letters 'H,' 'E,' 'V,' a reversed 'N,' the numeral '5,' and three embossed dots appear variously within and outside the loops preceding and following 'McDougall' and 'Glasgow.'

The second most frequently encountered manufacturer of white clay pipes was W. White of Glasgow, Scotland. Eight fragments of stems produced by this firm were found. The designation '78' precedes 'W. White' on the left side of five stems. One other stem fragment believed to be a W. White product has the number '79' in the same size and style as the '78.' One fragment of a bowl has a raised '2' on both sides of the spur; a similar feature is found on W. White bowls described by Sackett (1934: 74).

Five pieces of stems manufactured by Peter Dorni were recovered. Dorni was apparently a pipemaker in northern France around 1850, but no well-established dates for the company were found.

Two white bowls whose manufacturers were not identified are worthy of mention. One is a type described by Humphrey (1969: 25-6) as a 13-star patriotic pipe. It has the letters 'TD' surrounded by 13 stars on the bowl facing the smoker, as well as a row of stars around the bowl rim. A row of what appear to be embossed flowers is present on both sides of the mold seam on the side away from the smoker. The other bowl is a fragment with a portion of an embossed fouled anchor design similar to that on a specimen described by R. Wilson (1971: Fig. 33 *K*).

Red clay pipes are represented at Fort Bowie by 11 whole and fragmentary bowls and 18 stem fragments. There are no identification marks of any sort on the stems. Four of the bowls are complete unglazed examples of the "elbow" style, which has a detachable stem (Fig. 61 *a*). One of these has been crudely incised by hand with an 'XX' over 'D.S.' on the side of the bowl away from the smoker, presumably to identify the owner. One fragmentary unglazed elbow pipe, which had a detachable stem, bears the impressed inscription 'BONNAUD/MARSEILLE' on the left side of the stem socket. Above the 'BONNAUD' the number '296' is present in relief, presumably indicating the model number. No company history was located for this French firm.

The only two glazed pipes collected are of red clay and are the type with an elbow and a detachable stem. Although differing in size, both are decorated with a series of raised dots, or nodules, that cover the bowl (Fig. 61 *b*). The brown liquid glaze covers only the exterior surface of both items. No manufacturer's name or model number is present on either specimen.

In addition to two bowl fragments of unknown style, one complete bowl of red clay was recovered. Lacking decoration or distinguishing marks, this bowl is from one of the two red clay pipes recovered with non-detachable stems. The other example, also lacking any manufacturer's identifica-

Fig. 61. Ceramic Pipes and Cigar Holder
    a. Plain "elbow" pipe
    b. Glazed "elbow" pipe
    c. "Elbow" pipe with steamship decoration
    d. Cigar holder

Length of *d:* 1-5/8 in.

tion, is decorated on both sides of the bowl with an embossed representation of a steamship (Fig. 61 *c*). An interesting feature is that on the left side of the bowl, smoke emerging from the smokestack is blowing in the opposite direction from the flags flying at both bow and stern of the ship; this discrepancy does not occur on the opposite side.

One small sherd recovered from the surface of the first fort is a fragment of a red clay Chinese opium pipe bowl. Comparison with specimens collected by the Tucson Urban Renewal Archaeological Project has shown this fragment to be from an octagonal bowl having a diameter at its base of 2-5/16 in. The presence of this artifact is not surprising, considering the presence of lids from Chinese opium tins (see Chapter 3: *Containers, Covers, and Parts*).

One nearly complete ceramic body from a cigar holder was recovered from one of the officers' quarters. The tubular body (Fig. 61 *d*) is 1-5/8 in. long with an opening at the distal end 9/16 in. in diameter. The proximal end is threaded and contains a threaded wooden shaft, which served to connect the holder to a stem or mouthpiece.

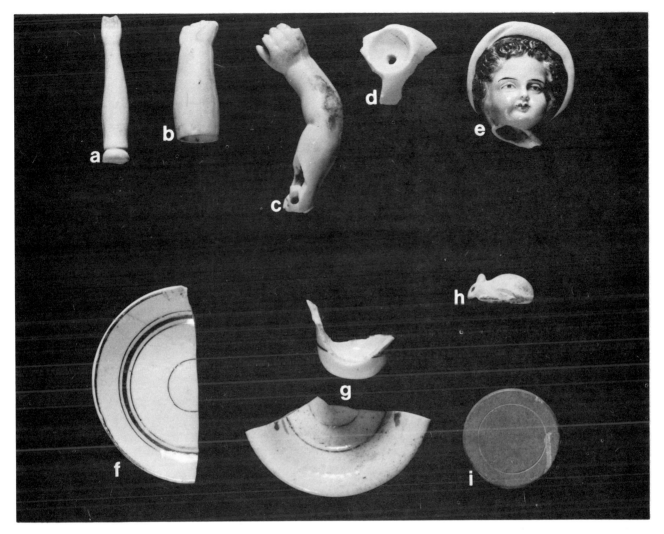

Fig. 62. Ceramic Toys and Gaming Piece   Length of *a:* 2 in.

a. Molded doll arm	*f.* Toy saucer
b. Hollow doll arm	*g.* Toy cup and saucer
c. Articulating doll arm	*h.* Mouse
d. Doll body part	*i.* Poker chip
e. Doll or figurine head	

TOYS AND GAMES

Three of eight ceramic doll parts recovered were found in the trash dump, while the others came from Buildings 27, 30, 35, and 106 at the old fort, and from the privy of Building 6. Five of these artifacts are arms from dolls. Two are solid molded arms made of porcelain, one with a clear glaze and the other bisque (unglazed) (Hillier 1968: 143). One of these is a nearly complete specimen, 2 in. long (Fig. 62 *a*), with a groove just below the proximal end for attaching the arm to a cloth or kid body; the material was stretched over the arm and threads were wound around the arm, pressing the material into the groove and thereby holding the parts together (White 1966: 28).

At least one specimen and possibly a second compose another category of doll arm. An incomplete white bisque arm, which is missing the fingers (Fig. 62 *b*), has a hollow interior and no apparent means for attachment to the doll; this arm was probably part of a doll made of kid, in which case it would have been glued to the kid that covered the upper part of the forearm. The second hollow arm is missing its proximal end, so that the means of attachment cannot be determined.

A fifth arm is the only example of an articulating doll limb recovered (Fig. 62 *c*). It is bisque and has been painted a pale pink. Measuring 2-11/16 in. long and 9/16 in. in diameter, this specimen is almost intact, missing only part of the top and the tips of several fingers. The hole at the shoulder end indicates that this arm was attached to a shoulder socket by a string, a wire, or perhaps some type of elastic material.

Three pink bisque fragments from doll torsos were recovered. One is probably a shoulder fragment, as it contains a hole 1/8 in. in diameter for attaching an arm. Another piece (Fig. 62 *d*) has a circular depression with a hole at the bottom; the concavity, which is either a neck or shoulder socket, is 5/8 in. in diameter at the rim, while the hole is approximately 3/32 in. in diameter.

A hollow porcelain head from either a doll or a figurine (Fig. 62 *e*) was recovered from the privy of Building 33. This molded head has painted pink skin; brown hair, eyebrows, and eyes; and red lips and nostrils. The hat is unpainted. This head measures 1-5/8 in. high, 1 in. wide, and 1-1/8 in. from front to back.

Six pieces of toy dishes were recovered, all but one from the trash dump. The exception, found in the privy of Building 6, is a porcelain saucer fragment 2¾ in. in diameter (Fig. 62 *f*). Decoration consists of four overglaze gilt bands and one overglaze grey enamel band. A saucer fragment and a portion of a cup (Fig. 62 *g*), apparently a set, have identical decoration. The saucer, with a diameter of 2¾ in., has a gilt band around the cup depression and an overglaze grey band, in addition to an overglaze blue and green floral design. The side of the saucer is painted pink from the grey band to the rim. A row of molded small bumps or nodules is present approximately 5/16 in. below the rim. The incomplete cup also displays the grey, pink, green, and blue painted decoration, in addition to a series of molded nodules running parallel to the cup rim.

Two other cup fragments recovered are undecorated white porcelain. The remaining piece of a toy dish, also porcelain, is possibly a fragment of a teapot; the exterior is decorated with a floral design in overglaze red, green, and brown enamel.

One small molded, unglazed porcelain mouse figurine (Fig. 62 *h*) was either a toy or a piece of furnishing bric-a-brac. It is 15/16 in. long and 3/8 in. high.

Four and possibly five of the eight marbles recovered at Fort Bowie appear to be ceramic. Two that were recovered from rooms 2 and 9 of Building 34 are made of clay and are approximately ¾ in. in diameter; one is white, the other pink or faded red. Two other marbles are quite hard, approximately 7 on Mohs' scale, but show neither temper nor structure diagnostic of any lithic material; they are presumably some sort of ceramic. The larger of the two, 1 in. in diameter, is white, while the other, 5/8 in. in diameter, is light tan. The clay marbles probably date no earlier than 1884 if they were made in the United States, since that is the first year in which clay marbles are believed to have been commercially produced (Randall 1971: 103).

Fourteen whole and fragmentary poker chips were recovered from Buildings 8, 10, 18, 26, and 35 and from the trash dump. Diameters vary from 1¼ to 1½ in., and thickness ranges from .11 to .13 in. All but two have a crack running around the entire edge; this is a seam, which apparently

resulted from joining two halves together in manufacture. The chips display a variety of colors, including white, red, maroon, blue, yellow, and brown. While most are unmarked, one complete chip and fragments of two others have an incised circular groove on both sides, 3/16 in. in from the edge (Fig. 62 *i*).

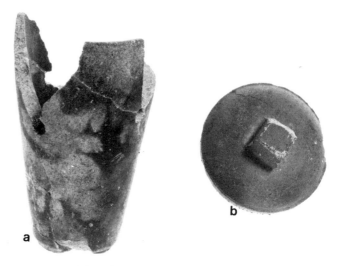

Fig. 63. Assay Crucible and Lid
   a. Assay crucible
   b. Crucible lid

Diameter of *b:* 3¼ in.

ASSAY ARTIFACTS

Some mining activity is known to have occurred quite near Fort Bowie. In the late 1860s a number of prospectors worked the Apache Pass area, but these relatively minor operations apparently ceased by May 1871 (Murray 1951: 149). A structure called Anderson's Steam Quartz Mill appears on one early map of the fort and its immediate vicinity (Montgomery 1966) and was apparently associated with the mining activity.

Only five ceramic artifacts relating to assaying were recovered from Fort Bowie. One partially intact assay crucible (Fig. 63 *a*) and three additional crucible bases were recovered from the cavalry barracks, the laundresses' quarters, and the post trader's store. The crucible illustrated is 5½ in. high with a 2-in. base diameter. A ½-in. hole has been drilled through the base and four 5/16-in. holes have been drilled through the sides approximately 2½ in. down from the rim. These holes give the distinct impression that the crucible, which was found in one of the cavalry barracks, had ceased to function in the assaying process and was serving as a hanging planter. Recovered from the post trader's store was one assay crucible lid with a diameter of 3¼ in. (Fig. 63 *b*). It is the correct size for the assay crucibles recovered.

A circular object with a concave top appears to be of porcelain. Glazed on its side and upper surface, it measures

1¼ in. in diameter and ¼ in. high. Although not as tall, it is of the same general shape as the bone cupel described in Chapter 6. The glazing suggests that this object was probably used for testing ore or mineral samples with acid.

HISTORIC AND PREHISTORIC INDIAN POTTERY

A small amount of Indian pottery was recovered in the course of work at Fort Bowie. A total of 61 sherds of historic Papago pottery was recovered not only from the trash dump, but also from the post trader's store (Building 35) and from Building 45, identified by Morris (1967) as the stage station. The presence of this material comes as no surprise, since the Papago are known to have produced pottery, especially ollas, for sale to Anglos for more than 70 years. Numerous photographs depict Papago women selling ollas in Tucson prior to the turn of the century (Fontana, Robinson, and others 1962: 25). Some Papago were also observed camping outside of Mexican towns and producing pottery for sale (Underhill 1939: 105).

A small amount of prehistoric Indian pottery was also collected both on and near Fort Bowie during the stabilization of the fort. Some of this material probably comes from several sites that are reported to be close to the post (Don Morris 1974: personal communication). Other material may have been collected and brought back by the soldiers, or brought in by historic Indians. Types present among the sample of 83 sherds are St. Johns Polychrome, unidentified White Mountain redwares, Mogollon corrugated wares, Playas Red Incised, and several types of unidentified smudged and unsmudged plainwares. This very small sample, which was not systematically collected, is mentioned primarily to point out the presence of prehistoric remains in the area.

5. LEATHER

Leather artifacts constituted only about 1½ percent of the total collected during the stabilization of Fort Bowie. Sixty-eight percent of the 253 pieces were recovered from 11 separate buildings, with the remaining 32 percent coming from the trash dump and general surface of the fort. Buildings 18 and 35 are the proveniences from which leather was most frequently recovered, the former accounting for 25 percent of the total sample and the latter for 21 percent. The types of leather artifacts recovered are fairly limited: parts and fragments of shoes and boots represent 57 percent of the total, pieces of harness and straps 11 percent, leather accoutrements 2 percent, miscellaneous items 2 percent, and scrap 28 percent.

ACCOUTREMENTS

Two pieces recovered from Building 18, room 2, fit together (Fig. 64 *a*). They appear to be part of the strap by which the Model 1885 carbine boot was suspended from the McClellan saddle. *Ordnance Memoranda No. 29* (USWD 1891: 9, Plate VIII) gives the specifications for this strap as 17 in. long by 7/8 in. wide. Although the Fort Bowie specimen is only 3/4 to 13/16 in. in width, the shape and placement of the two original holes is believed to be diagnostic. The difference in width is attributed to drying and shrinkage of the artifact.

Two parts of a leather strap, thought to be a saber belt shoulder strap, were recovered from Building 10, one of the cavalry barracks. These specimens are strap ends doubled back around a brass hook, which was riveted to the strap (Fig. 64 *b*). The specimen with the complete hook tapers to a width of ¾ in., while the other is 7/8 in. wide. Comparison with complete specimens in the collection of the Arizona Historical Society, Tucson, strongly indicates that these two pieces are the ends of the saber belt shoulder strap that was issued as early as 1841 and was listed in the 1861 Ordnance Manual. This strap was superseded in 1872 by the saber sling prescribed by *Ordnance Memoranda No. 13* (USWD 1872b: 15).

A third type of leather artifact is a cap visor (Fig. 64 *c*). This item measures 4¾ in. in maximum length by 1¼ in. in maximum width and is approximately 1/8 in. thick. Judging from the shape and thickness of specimens at the Arizona Historical Society, it is thought that this visor is probably from a post-1872 pattern kepi, or forage cap, although other possibilities are the 1859-1872 kepi and the pattern 1872 dress shako.

FOOTGEAR

One hundred forty-five fragments of footgear were recovered from seven buildings, the trash dump, and the surface of the new fort. This material has been categorized into three major groups on the basis of the method of construction: sewn, nailed, and screwed. There are, of course, differences within each category that will be described in the appropriate section below. Although several specimens of women's and children's shoes are present, the majority of the collection consists of examples of men's boots and shoes, many undoubtedly of military issue.

Military footgear was a source of innumerable problems and complaints, mostly pertaining to durability and fit. Rickey (1963: 123-4) notes that many cavalrymen resorted to wearing Indian moccasins instead of regular shoes. Other men purchased civilian shoes with their own money because the issue items were so unsatisfactory. When inspecting Fort Lowell, Arizona, for example, Major J. C. Breckinridge "found men of the Twelfth Infantry wearing citizen's shoes, and was told that they were better, cheaper and more comfortable except for marching than the government shoes" (USWD 1883: 489). The use of civilian or non-issue shoes is important from an analytical point of view, since it virtually precludes positive identification of any of the archaeologically recovered specimens as items of military issue. Furthermore, the dates assigned to recovered specimens for any particular method of construction on the basis of army regulations must not be considered as absolute dates, but as approximations.

Complicating the chronology further are the shortages and irregularities that occurred in the supply of footgear. Until the military prison at Fort Leavenworth assumed sole responsibility for the manufacture of footgear in 1877 (USWD 1883: 490), boots and shoes were purchased primarily from civilian contractors. In October 1875, the Quartermaster General ran short of shoes of the type specified by prevailing regulations and authorized the purchase of 10,000 pairs on the open market, with the method of attachment of the soles to the uppers intentionally left unspecified (Brinckerhoff 1976: 11).

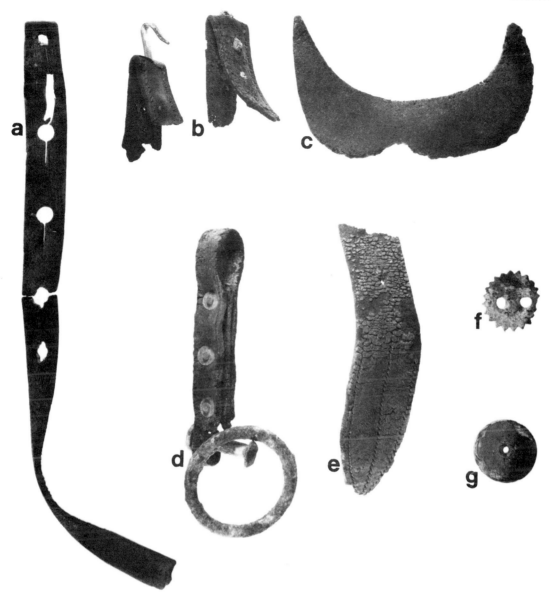

Fig. 64. Leather Artifacts Diameter of *g:* 1¼ in.
    a. Carbine boot strap   *e.* Strap end
    b. Saber belt shoulder strap ends *f.* Button
    c. Cap visor   *g.* Washer
    d. Halter throat strap

Until 1872 the Army was supplied with hand-sewn boots and shoes. As early as 1862, however, the need for a change was seen. The Quartermaster General, M. C. Meigs, wrote in a letter that he had seen a shoe ". . . in which the threads of the sewed shoe, or the wooden pegs of the pegged shoe, are replaced by brass wire screwed throughout its length," and he authorized the purchase of some examples for trial (USWD 1862). This description undoubtedly refers to an 1862 patent granted to Eugene Lemercier for a machine for attaching shoe or boot soles to uppers.

The use of screws in footgear is a somewhat complicated matter. The technique apparently began in France in the early 1860s. On December 16, 1862, Eugene Lemercier of Paris, France, as administrator of the estate of Louis Soles Sellier, was granted U. S. patent #37,201 (USPO 1864: 706-7). The patented machine, which served as a prototype for later developments, not only cut threads into a continuous strand of wire, but also screwed it into the shoe and cut the screw off after it was inserted the proper distance. Other devices for using screws to construct shoes were also developed. In 1881, *Knight's American Mechanical Dictionary* (Knight 1881: 1649-50) described Sargent's Pegging Machine, which took a continuous strand of screw-threaded wire and cut it into lengths that were fed into position through a tube and then "driven home by a plunger." The same source (Knight 1881: 1647-8) also describes how a continuous strand of screw-threaded wire was made by twisting wire that was not round, but diamond-shaped in cross-section. Sargent's machine and the technique of twisting wire to create threads are mentioned to point out that the shoe industry of the period employed more than one method to produce similar results. The possibility exists that government shoes, many of which were purchased from civilian contractors, were constructed by methods other than Lemercier's, which was apparently employed at the shoe shop of the Federal Prison at Fort Leavenworth. Boots were purchased for trial at least as early as 1864 (USWD 1871: 164), and in 1872 the Quartermaster General made brass-screwed boots and shoes standard issue for the Army (USWD 1872a: 179).

Twenty-three specimens of brass-screwed footgear were collected at Fort Bowie, primarily from the trash dump. Figure 65 *a* shows one of these fragments, with two rows of screws holding fragments of the insole to the outer sole. At least one specimen is definitely not an item of military issue; this is a fragment of a child's shoe, 6¾ in. long (Fig. 65 *b*). The sole was originally fastened with brass screws spaced at intervals of 3/8 in. A half-sole was later attached with serrated brass nails. Also present is an iron stiffener, or shank, situated between the insole and the outer sole in the instep.

With one possible exception, the rest of the brass-screwed specimens are men's boots or shoes. The incomplete nature of the uppers makes it impossible to distinguish boots from shoes; like almost all Army footgear of the period, these specimens all have square toes. The most complete example recovered (Fig. 65 *c*) is 9¾ in. long and 3½ in. wide across the ball of the foot. As is the case with all shoes from Fort Bowie, the heel is fastened with iron nails, and the brass screws that fastened the sole to the upper extend around the entire side. The spacing between screws on the men's footwear ranges from 3/16 to 5/16 in.

The original sole of one specimen recovered from the trash dump was fastened with brass screws; however, a half-sole studded with seven rows of iron hob-nails has been applied. While this boot may have been an item produced to an individual's requirements, the possibility exists that it is government issue. In reference to problems with footgear in "the stony and rocky country of Arizona . . . instructions [were] given to have the soles of the boots issued in those regions studded with broad-headed nails" (USWD 1871: 164). It is not clear how long this practice was continued.

Examination of the 23 specimens of brass-screwed shoes and boots revealed that three kinds of screws were used. The variation is not surprising in light of the fact that military shoes were purchased from a variety of civilian contractors, in addition to being manufactured at the prison at

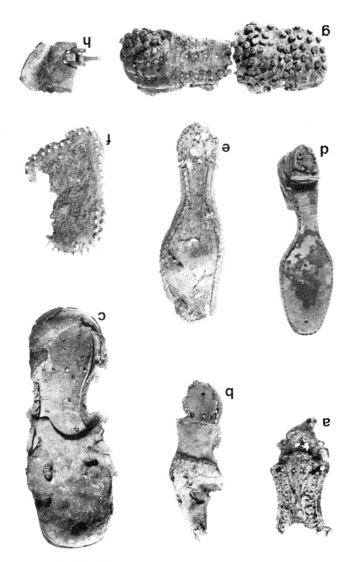

Fig. 65. Shoes
    a. Sole with brass screws
    b. Child's shoe
    c. Brass screwed boot or shoe
    d. Woman's shoe
    e. Insole with Goodyear welt (underside)
    f. Nailed half-sole
    g. Hob-nail boot sole (heel at right)
    h. Fragment with buckle part

Length of *c:* 9¾ in.

Fort Leavenworth, Kansas. As noted above, the spacing between screws varies from 3/16 to 5/16 in.; this range exceeds the specifications for boots adopted in May 1876, which required "five spaces to every two (2) inches" (USWD 1877b: 268). Allowing for the diameter of the screws, this specification works out to approximately 3/8-in. spacing. The most frequently encountered screw is approximately 7/16 in. long and .10 in. in diameter, with a thread that is almost rectangular in cross-section (Fig. 66 *a*). The screws in one specimen are slightly different, measuring approximately ½ in. in adopted (USWD 1884b 612-3). Thirty-five specimens with soles originally machine-stitched to uppers and insoles were recovered. All of these specimens had the heel nailed to the sole, and several display remains of half-soles that had been nailed into place.

The 35 sewn specimens were collected from Buildings 6, 18, 26, and 35, as well as from the surface of the new fort and the trash dump. Apparently all machine-stitched, rather than hand-stitched, they represent two types of manufacture. The majority were produced with a McKay-type sewing machine, a device patented by Gordon McKay in 1862 (Anderson 1968: 59), which eliminated the need for wooden pegs and hand stitching. The entire edge of the shoe was sewn, leaving a characteristic row of stitching on the foot side of the insole. Among the 33 pieces of McKay-sewn shoes are one man's hob-nailed boot sole and the insole and heel from a woman's shoe. The latter (Fig. 65 *d*) is 7¾ in. long, 2¼ in. wide across the ball of the foot, and 1-7/8 in. wide across the instep. It is sewn with five stitches to the inch. McKay-stitched examples in the collection generally exhibit from four to eight stitches to the inch; only one insole examined is more finely sewn, with 16 stitches to the inch. A single row of stitching occurs on all but one of the McKay-sewn specimens. The exception is an insole from a woman's shoe that has two parallel rows of stitching, seven stitches to the inch.

The second general type of sewn shoe has what is known as the Goodyear Welt construction, which was introduced in 1875 (Anderson 1968: 61). A welt was sewn to the upper and to the sole simultaneously, in a one-step rather than a two-step operation. The process utilized a rib on the underside of the insole, eliminating the uncomfortable row of stitching on the foot side of the insole left by the McKay system. One example of Goodyear Welt construction is a shoe insole, 9 in. long, recovered from the dump. The shoe had been half-soled with both brass and iron nails. The underside of this shoe insole is illustrated in Figure 65 *e*.

One of the most unusual artifacts recovered during the stabilization of Fort Bowie was a man's right shoe manufactured with Goodyear Welt construction (Fig. 67). This shoe measures 10 in. in length, 3 in. across the ball of the foot, and 2-1/8 in. in width at the instep. The unique aspect of this shoe is that it is the only known extant example of footwear constructed with a patented thread known as "metalin." Patent #342,679 granted to Edward L. Brown of Rockland, Massachusetts, on May 25, 1886, describes "an improved sewing-thread, composed of shoe maker's wax, a wire or wires, and one or more strands of flax or a vegetable or animal material" (USPO 1886: 972). The wire provided the core for the thread, thereby greatly increasing its strength and durability. Figure 67 also shows a photographic enlargement of the thread. The core, believed to be either brass or copper wire, is surrounded by a flax or vegetable thread. There are seven stitches per inch. The trademark patent for the word "metalin" stated that the term had been in use since February

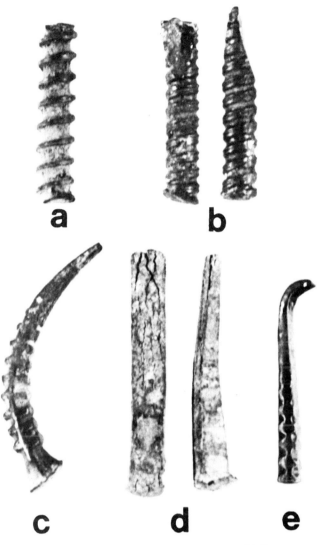

Fig. 66. Boot and Shoe Screws and Nails
   a. Brass screw
   b. Brass screws
   c. Brass nail
   d. Lead/zinc nails
   e. Brass "clinching screws"

Length of *e:* ½ in.

length and .09 in. in diameter, but having a distinctly rectangular cross-section to the thread. The unique aspect of these screws is the presence of a shallow groove in the outer edge of the thread (Fig. 66 *b*). Another variant is an iron screw 3/8 in. long and .10 in. in diameter, which was used on what may have been a woman's shoe, recovered from Building 35. Unfortunately, the screws of the latter type are so deteriorated that the details of shape are obscured.

Complaints about the government issue brass-screwed shoes and boots, appearing in literature as early as 1879, continued until the specifications for issue footgear were changed in 1884. At that time boots and shoes with sewn soles were

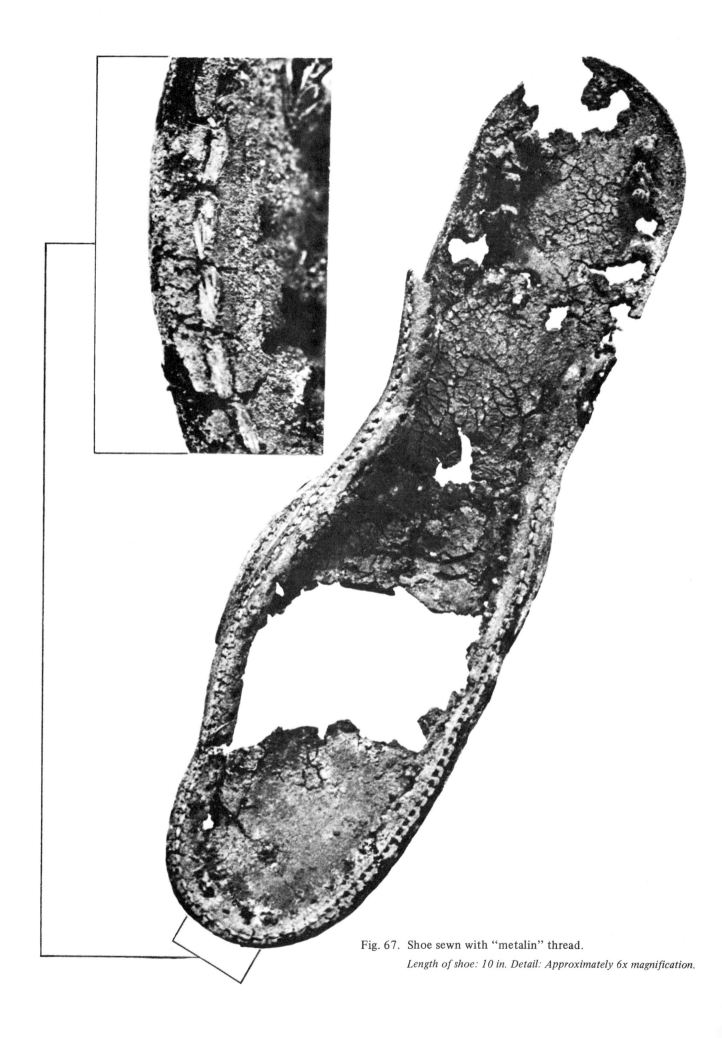

Fig. 67. Shoe sewn with "metalin" thread.

Length of shoe: 10 in. Detail: Approximately 6x magnification.

1, 1886 (USPO 1887: 458). In 1887, in the *Report of the Secretary of War* (USWD 1887: 512-3), the Quartermaster General noted that "soles of the boots and shoes now made at the prison [at Fort Leavenworth, Kansas] are sewed upon the machine by means of thread known to the trade as metalin." It is therefore believed that the Fort Bowie specimen was most likely not of civilian manufacture, but an article of military issue produced at Leavenworth no earlier than 1887. It is not known how long metalin thread was used, either by the military or by civilian shoe manufacturers.

Twenty-seven specimens of nailed boots and shoes were recovered from the trash dump and from Buildings 18, 26, 35, and 44. This total includes only five shoes originally constructed with nails, the balance being fragments of half-soles and other repairs that utilized nails. The nails used to attach the original soles to the uppers are all of brass; they measure ½ to ¾ in. in length and have small, slightly serrated heads (Fig. 66 *c*). Brass nails of this type, as well as iron nails, were used to attach half-soles to shoes. One half-sole recovered from the trash dump (Fig. 65 *f*) utilized wedge-shaped nails or pegs that are rectangular in cross-section and are believed to be made of an alloy of zinc and lead (Fig. 66 *d*).

Generally, the nailed fragments are too incomplete for identification of the type of shoe or boot. One exception is the sole and heel of a man's hob-nail boot, whose sole had been attached to the upper with brass nails (Fig. 65 *g*). The hob-nails used are iron, approximately 9/16 in. long, with heads 3/16 in. in diameter, placed randomly on both the heel and the toe end of the sole. Only the instep of this specimen lacks hob-nails.

The Army never adopted specifications for using nails to attach soles to the uppers of boots and shoes, with one exception. In 1876 the specifications for boots were modified to allow the use of the "Estabrook and Wise patent clinching screw, which is driven into the leather with a hammer, and not screwed in" (USWD 1877b: 268). Although the Estabrook and Wise patent was not found, a patent entitled "Screw Peg for Boots and Shoes" was granted to J. M. Estabrook of Milford, Massachusetts, on December 29, 1868 (USPO 1870: 731); the illustration (USPO 1869b: 1596) shows a headless "screw," which is actually a serrated nail. One specimen recovered at Fort Bowie has a series of wedge-shaped, headless, serrated brass nails that appear to be virtually identical to this patent illustration. They are ½ in. long with a chisel- or wedge-shaped end, as in the published description and illustration, and have a series of ridges below the top to create a serration (Fig. 66 *e*). Although the specimens recovered at the fort cannot be definitely identified, it is certainly plausible to suggest that they are examples of the Estabrook and Wise "patent clinching screw."

The remaining shoe material consists of 27 leather heel and heel-lift fragments, 10 pieces from uppers, and 23 scraps. Of this material, only one item is noteworthy. A scrap from a shoe upper recovered from the surface of the new fort bears an iron clasp or buckle (Fig. 65 *h*), which is 1-7/8 in. long in the open position and is attached to the leather by two

clips on the back of the buckle. This buckle, which is almost identical to those used on modern rubber galoshes or snow-shoes, may be the "automatic buckle" mentioned in the 1884 specifications for Army leather field shoes (USWD 1884b: 682, Plate 34). The drawing accompanying the specifications illustrates a buckle with a definite resemblance to the artifact recovered at Fort Bowie, although a documented specimen for comparative purposes was not located. The 1884 field shoe was produced for only one year. It was replaced in 1885 by a "campaign" shoe utilizing laces instead of the metal buckle (USWD 1885: 604, Plate 13).

HARNESS

Not a great deal can be said about the 28 pieces of harness leather recovered. All but two pieces are fragments of straps ranging from 7/8 to 1-1/8 in. in width and almost invariably 1/8 in. in thickness. Eleven still have copper or brass rivets attached and two still bear iron buckles, one a bar buckle and the other a roller buckle. Sixteen specimens, or 57 percent of the sample, were recovered from rooms 3, 4, and 5 at the corral, Building 18.

Two pieces recovered are believed to be halter throat straps patterned after the regulation issue item, although neither fits the specifications as delineated in *Ordnance Memoranda No. 29* (USWD 1891: 11). One of the two, recovered from Building 18, room 4, is constructed of three thicknesses of leather, which have been both sewn and riveted together as the specifications prescribe. At one end of this fragment is a portion of a hole believed to have held the throat strap bolt. The second specimen, recovered from the surface, is nearly complete (Fig. 64 *d*). This strap is 4½ in. long and ¾ in. wide and is made of three thicknesses of 1/8 in. leather, held together with three copper or brass rivets. The specification calls for a length of 6 in. and a width of 7/8 in. There can be little doubt as to the function of this item, however, as it still holds a throat strap bolt and an iron ring 2¼ in. in diameter at one end, while a loop for the throat band is present at the other end.

MISCELLANEOUS ITEMS

The four artifacts described here cannot be assigned to any of the previous categories, although the possibility exists that the first item may have been a harness part. It is an end of a strap, 5¼ in. long and 3/16 in. thick, with a bulging or swelled shape (Fig. 64 *e*) that does not occur in any of the illustrations of government issue saddle or harness gear. The strap was apparently reinforced at the tip with another thickness of leather, as holes from machine stitching are present along the edges and down the center for a distance of 3¼ in. from the tip. Although the shape of this strap end is by no means a definite identification, it is somewhat similar to that of straps seen on early 20th century valises and grips.

Along with the above strap fragment, two other leather items were recovered from Building 18. One, perhaps a button, a decorative concho, or a hat chin strap slide, is 1-1/8 in. in diameter and 1/8 in. thick; two holes, 3/16 in. in diameter, have been cut or punched through it, and its perimeter is cut in a decorative serrated edge (Fig. 64 *f*). The other, thought to be a round button, is 1¼ in. in diameter and 3/16 in. thick and has a hole, approximately 1/8 in. wide, in its center (Fig. 64 *g*).

A round leather object recovered from the trash dump is probably a washer. This piece is 3/16 in. thick, has an outside diameter of 13/16 in., and has had a 5/16-in. hole punched through its center.

SCRAP

Ninety-six percent of the scrap is material that was discarded in the process of making or repairing leather articles. More than two-thirds of the sample was recovered from only two buildings – the corral and the post trader's store. Rooms 1, 3, and 4 of Building 18 yielded 28 pieces, while rooms 4 and 10 and the inner court of Building 35 accounted for 20 pieces. Other proveniences that yielded scrap leather were Buildings 26, 30, 33, and 39 and the trash dump.

Almost all of the scraps recovered are rectilinear shaped pieces ranging from 1/8 to 3/16 in. in thickness. A piece of particular interest is 1/8 in. thick and roughly rectangular in shape. It shows two round holes, 1 in. and 1-1/8 in. in diameter, that are very even and regular in shape, indicating that discs were punched or stamped and removed from it. Although the use to which these discs were put is unknown, the leather washer and buttons described above suggest distinct possibilities.

6. MISCELLANEOUS MATERIALS

BONE

In addition to the faunal material, which is discussed in Chapter 7, 44 artifacts made from bone were recovered at Fort Bowie. These items are buttons, an assaying cupel, game pieces, utensil handles, poker chips, and toothbrushes. Most of these artifacts were probably made from cattle bone, as buttons generally were (Luscomb 1967: 25), but the process of manufacture has destroyed any detail that would make identification possible.

Eight bone buttons were recovered at the fort, half of them from Building 26. These buttons range in size from 21 to 27 lignes (see p. 37 for definition of *ligne*) and are all four-hole sew-throughs. Seven of the specimens are of the style with a recessed central area through which the holes were drilled (Fig. 68 *a*). The one exception is a concave, or dish-shaped, button (Fig. 68 *b*). These buttons are unornamented and were probably used on trousers or underwear (Luscomb 1967: 25).

One bone cupel, an object used in assaying, was recovered from Building 10, one of the cavalry barracks. It is a small, saucer-shaped vessel made from pulverized calcined bone or bone ash, which has been moistened with water and molded into the required shape (Mine and Smelter Supply Company 1912: 548). The specimen recovered (Fig. 68 *c*) is 1½ in. in diameter, one of seven sizes that were sold by the Mine and Smelter Supply Company (1912: 170) and by other mining supply firms.

Nine bone objects believed to have been parts of a game were recovered. Six came from Building 35, room 7, listed as the billiard room at the post trader's store (Montgomery 1966). Seven are discs that were probably produced on a lathe; they range from 1-1/16 to 1-3/8 in. in diameter and have a maximum thickness of .2 in. (Fig. 68 *d*). All seven have serrated edges and a ¼-in. threaded hole in the center. The other two objects are lathe-produced shafts or pedestals. One of these has at one end a ¼-in. threaded shaft that can be screwed into a disc, with the latter forming a base (Fig. 68 *e*); the other end is broken off. Although no such objects have been found in any catalog, it is possible that they are pieces from a chess set that could be disassembled and stored in a small portable container.

Three bone handles were collected from the trash dump and one from Building 1. One is 4 in. long and has a hole 1/8 in. in diameter in one end that may have served to haft a

fork or spoon. A second handle, rectangular in cross-section, probably had a similar function. A fragment measuring 1-7/8 by 1-1/8 in., and only 1/16 in. thick, may have been part of a knife handle. The fourth specimen is a small cylindrical object (Fig. 68 *f*) that is only 1-1/16 in. long. In one end is a hole 5/8 in. deep and 5/32 in. in diameter, for the shank of what must have been a very small implement – perhaps a tool from a manicure set or a small buttonhook.

A total of 15 bone poker chips (Fig. 68 *g*) was recovered from Buildings 10, 18, 26, and 35, as well as from the trash dump. They range in thickness from .05 to .117 in. and in diameter from 1-3/16 to 1-5/16 in. Nine of these specimens, all 1-3/16 in. in diameter, were recovered from Building 10. Two others, both 1-5/16 in. in diameter, came from Building 26. One of the latter two has an arrow crudely scratched onto each side.

The incomplete remains of eight bone toothbrushes were recovered from Buildings 1, 26, and 106, the surface, and the trash dump of the new fort. Five of the eight pieces are handles that range up to 4¼ in. in length and are generally oval-shaped in cross-section. Bristles, none of which were preserved, had been set into holes drilled in the head of the brush; they were held in place with a wire that fitted into lengthwise grooves in the back of the head. The bristle holes are arranged in either three or six rows in the specimens recovered; one complete head contains 148 holes in an area measuring 2 by 9/16 in. (Fig. 68 *h*). One nearly complete specimen (Fig. 68 *i*) has the following legend lightly stamped into the handle: 'M.L. Rhein/Prophylactic Tooth Brush/Florence/Patented Oct. 21 1884.' On that date, patent #306,776 was granted to Meyer L. Rhein of New York, New York, for a toothbrush "having a handle curved one way throughout [and] a projecting tuft of bristles on the extreme end of the brush" (USPO 1885b: 197). This brush was listed in the 1892-3 Marshall Field catalog (p. 287) at $2.50 per dozen.

SHELL

A total of 43 pieces of shell and shell artifacts was recovered at the fort. Three partial oysters, *Crassostrea* sp., were found, two of them in Building 35. Also found in Building 35 was a portion of a cowry; this *Cypraea* sp. shell is unidentifiable as to species because of its incomplete nature, but it is not of Pacific coast origin. A fifth unmodified but broken

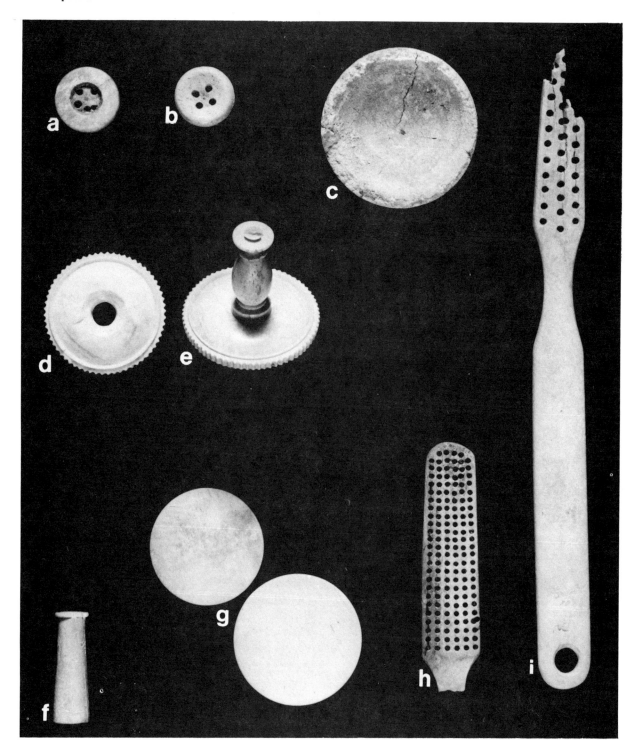

Fig. 68. Bone Artifacts   Length of *f:* 1-1/16 in.
        a. Button   *f.* Handle
        b. Button   *g.* Poker chips
        c. Cupel   *h.* Toothbrush
        d. Disc (game piece?)   *i.* Toothbrush (M. L. Rhein)
        e. Disc with pedestal (game piece?)

shell is a cockle; the major diagnostic key, the umbo, is missing, and therefore the genus and geographical distribution could not be ascertained.

A total of 36 shell buttons of several types was recovered at Fort Bowie. Twenty-three are two-hole sew-throughs ranging in size from 12 to 36 lignes (see p. 37 for definition of *ligne*). Two of the largest of these buttons are very thin, one measuring only .14 in. in the vicinity of the two holes. These buttons are mostly white, but several are grey or brown. The eight four-hole sew-throughs range from 16 to 28 lignes in size. Two white buttons recovered, both 27 lignes in diameter, were attached by means of a metal post or shank set into a recess cut into the back of the button; one is missing the entire shank, while the second contains a portion of a brass shank. The specimen with the brass shank has a monogram with the initials 'AJ' scratched into its front surface. Two other buttons lacking any means of attachment were probably crimped or clamped into a metal backplate. One of these is quite small, measuring 10 lignes, and may possibly have been a collar button; the other measures 30 lignes. One other button, measuring approximately 30 lignes, is made of mother-of-pearl. This one-piece button is of the style used as non-permanently attached collar buttons and shirt studs.

Two shell Indian-made artifacts were collected. One is a fragment, approximately .15 in. wide, from a small bracelet made from a *Glycymeris* sp. shell. The second item is a bead fashioned from an *Olivella* sp. shell; the bead was made simply by grinding away the spire of the shell. These artifacts are types commonly associated with the prehistoric Indian cultures in the Southwest.

FABRIC

Approximately 52 pieces of fabric, representing some 14 separate items, were recovered from the trash dump and from Buildings 6, 10, 18, and 35. While most of the items could be identified by type of fiber, generally cotton or wool, specific functional identification could be made for only seven.

Five military uniform shoulder straps, or rank insignia, were recovered from Building 6, and foundation material from one other came from Building 35, room 10. The five specimens from Building 6 are all captains' insignia, while the sixth example is too incomplete to allow a determination. The Army regulations pertaining to uniforms from 1851 through 1888 show that the shoulder strap could be worn in place of the shoulder knot on unspecified occasions, presumably those requiring less than full dress uniform. For that entire period the shoulder strap dimensions remained constant at 4 in. in length by 1-3/8 in. in width, with an embroidered gold border ¼ in. wide. The only change specified in captains' shoulder straps occurred in 1872, when the color of the double bar insignia was switched from gold to silver (Jacobsen 1972b). Since the original color of the embroidering no longer remained on the embroidered borders or bars, this chronological marker could not be applied to these items. Because of deterioration and discoloration of the material it was not possible to determine the branch of service these specimens represented.

Three pieces of light blue wool were found embedded in an adobe brick high in the south wall of Building 10; one of these had a piece of white cotton sewn to it. Two other samples of wool fabric came from two locations in the trash dump; both are burnt portions of a thick, loosely woven fabric having only seven threads to the inch.

Twenty-nine pieces of blue cotton fabric were recovered from Building 18; these fragments, probably a cotton canvas, appear to be parts of a single unidentified object. Three pieces of brown cotton were found in Building 35, room 10. Another cotton specimen is a fragment from a canvas shoe upper or a legging. It is constructed of four thicknesses of white cotton and has four brass eyelets with a 1/8-in. inside diameter. Portions of a cotton two-ply shoelace are present in two of the eyelets.

One piece of recovered cloth is of an unidentified fiber. It is light brown in color, is very finely woven, and has a slight sheen to it, suggesting the possibility that it is silk.

The remains of a spool of burnt thread were recovered from Building 35, room 10. The thread is probably cotton and is constructed of two twisted strands, each composed of several plies. The diameter of the thread measures approximately .01 in., but the oxidation may have caused some degree of constriction.

An enigmatic article (Fig. 69 *a*), recovered from the west privy of Building 35, is composed of both metal and fabric. It consists of a cotton belt 1-3/8 in. wide, to which 3/8-in. wide cotton loops have been sewn. These loops served to hold a separate band made of thin iron wire looped around two strands of 1/8-in. diameter rope (Fig. 69 *b*); the iron wire has itself been wound with cotton thread, the latter perhaps serving as insulation. The use of this article is not understood, although the presence of the wire suggests some

Fig. 69. Unidentified article of fabric and metal. Wire wrapped with thread and wound around two strands of rope (*b*) is attached to cotton belt 1-3/8 in. wide (*a*).

sort of electrical function. One possibility, which could not be verified, is that this "belt" represents part of a pseudo-medical electrical curative device. Perusal of newspapers and catalogs of the period reveals many types of electrical "therapeutic" instruments and devices that were marketed during the late 19th century.

RUBBER

Only 12 of the 73 items in this category were of soft or flexible rubber, the majority being of the hard rubber made by the vulcanization process developed by Charles Goodyear, Jr., and patented in 1851.

A portion of a hollow rubber ball recovered from Building 26 is decorated with the figures of at least two weight lifters. Wearing clothing painted in red, yellow, and blue, the figures are holding weights marked '100' and '150.' The mark of the manufacturer, 'NYR Co,' is present in a small shield on the outer surface of the specimen and most likely refers to the New York Rubber Company, a firm incorporated in New York in 1851 (Moodys 1920: 1224).

One nearly complete bulb recovered from the trash dump (Fig. 70 *a*) is approximately 3½ in. long and 1¾ in. in diameter. This type of bulb could have been used on several objects, including atomizers and nasal and ear syringes (Pyne Press 1971: 57; 60). According to an 1880 catalog, the syringes were frequently sold in sets that included from two to five pipes or tubes of various sizes and shapes. One complete syringe pipe and a fragment of a second were recovered. The whole specimen (Fig. 70 *b*) is 4-1/8 in. long, with four holes in the distal end and a threaded hole 9/32 in. in diameter in the proximal end. Tubes of this size were used for enemas and for vaginal douches.

Three rubber nipples or bulbs from medicine droppers, or "French Pipettes" (Pyne Press 1971: 56), were recovered, two from the privy of Building 33, the 1887 hospital. The one complete specimen (Fig. 70 *l*), from Building 35, is 1¼ in. long. A hard rubber syringe (Fig. 70 *m*) found in the trash dump is nearly complete. It is composed of three rubber parts, and only the end of the handle and the piston packing are missing. 'THE HANOVER RUBBER CO.,' the name of the manufacturer, is present on the top of the screw cap, but location and dates for this firm were not found. The 1880 Whitall Tatum and Company catalog identifies items of this type as urethral, ear, and nasal syringes (Pyne Press 1971).

The 19 rubber buttons recovered range in size from 22 to 40 lignes. Most are four-hole sew-throughs, but one specimen has a molded box shank and another has an iron ring and cloth on the back. Five buttons can be attributed to two manufacturers. Three were produced by the Novelty Rubber Company, a firm located in New Brunswick, New Jersey, and organized in 1855 (Albert and Kent 1949: 406). One backstamp of this company is interesting in that the '12' at the end of 'Rubber' is reversed and upside down. A second backstamp of the same company, which occurs on one of the few two-hole sew-throughs (Fig. 70 *c*), reads 'N.R.C. Goodyear's P=T. 1851.' Two buttons that are products of the India Rubber Comb Company are identical specimens. This firm produced combs and buttons in New York City in the 1880s and 1890s (Albert and Kent 1949: 405).

Other noteworthy rubber buttons include one measuring 29 lignes, with a woven fabric design impressed on its face (Fig. 70 *d*). This specimen has a box shank with a single hole running through it at its base. One of the buttons was attached by a technique not entirely understood. A ring of iron has been implanted into the back of the button, apparently to hold the circle or disc of fabric in place (Fig. 70 *e*). A hole through the rubber portion provided either a place to sew through or a hole for a metal loop shank.

Hard rubber combs were widely used during the period of Fort Bowie's occupation. Portions of 11 combs were recovered from buildings in the old and new forts, as well as from the trash dump at the new fort. Most of these are single-edged combs with teeth of one size per comb; the teeth range from 3/8 to 1 in. in length (Fig. 70 *f*, *h*). Only one specimen has both fine and coarse teeth and only two specimens are of the fine-toothed, double-edged variety (Fig. 70 *g*). Three combs, including both of the double-edged variety, have a stamped reference to Goodyear's 1851 patent. Two of these, plus one other specimen, were the product of the India Rubber Comb Company, New York. Albert and Kent (1949: 405) date this firm to the 1880s and 1890s, but precise dates for the firm were not ascertained. Also found was a fragment of an unmarked and undecorated hair pin.

Three objects of rubberized fabric were recovered from Buildings 23 and 39. Two are discs, 1-1/8 in. and 1¾ in. in diameter, composed of two layers. The other, an oval measuring 3½ by 2½ in., is composed of four layers. The specific function of these items is not understood, although their shape and material suggest the possibility that they were used as gaskets. One other object, recovered from Building 8, room 5, appears to be a fragment of a hose or tube (Fig. 70 *i*). It is tubular in form, with a corrugated surface and a wall thickness of only 1/32 in. The piece is now rigid, but appears to have been flexible originally.

Two rubber handles were recovered at the new fort. One, broken at both ends, was obviously a toothbrush made of black hard rubber (Fig. 70 *j*). The other was possibly the handle from a fork or spoon; it is 3-5/8 in. long, is made of brown rubber, and contains a portion of a broken iron tang from the object to which it was attached.

One complete hard rubber pen holder and fragments of two others were recovered. The complete item is 6-15/16 in. long and still holds a small rusted fragment of a steel point (see Fig. 19). This specimen and one of the fragments is made of a red and brown "marbleized" rubber, while the third piece is plain brown.

Nineteen complete and fragmentary hard rubber pipe stems, generally used on briar pipes, were recovered from a variety of buildings, the surface, and the dump at the new

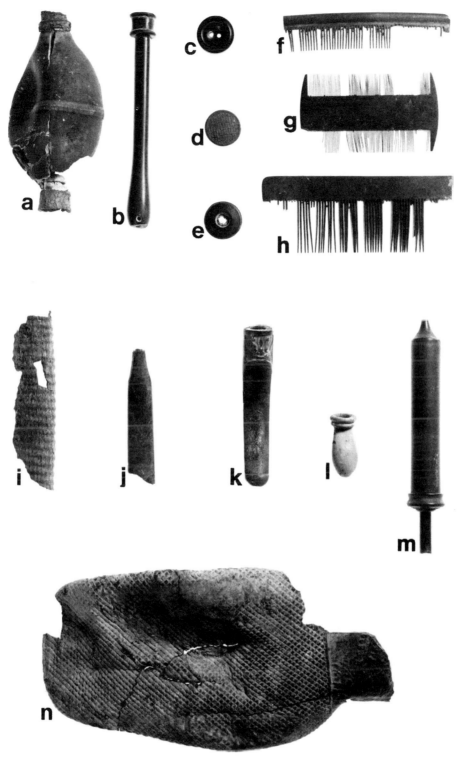

Fig. 70. Rubber Artifacts   Length of *b:* 4-1/8 in.
    a. Bulb   *h.* Comb
    b. Syringe pipe   *i.* Hose or tubing
    c. Two-hole sew-through button   *j.* Toothbrush handle
    d. Button (face with impressed fabric design) *k.* Pipe stem
    e. Button with fabric inset   *l.* Bulb
    f. Comb   *m.* Syringe
    g. Fine-toothed comb   *n.* Shoe sole

fort. Ten are curved, five are straight, and four are fragments too incomplete for shape to be determined. Six stems have manufacturers' marks of some sort and some could be linked to a specific firm. One specimen has the initials 'WDC' enclosed within a triangle and three others have 'WD' impressed near the distal end of the stem. The initials 'W.D.' occur on a variety of ceramic pipe stems (R. Wilson 1971), as they do on rubber stems. As in the case of the various ceramic 'TD' pipes (see Chapter 4), the designation may be more generic than specific to a particular firm. Other markings noted include an 'A' on one specimen and 'A,1' on another. Only one rubber pipe stem is decorated (Fig. 70 *k*). On both the upper and lower side of this stem, near the distal end, a fleur-de-lis style design is present in a panel with a stippled background. This stem, like many of the others, had a threaded fitting by which it was attached to the bowl of the pipe.

Two pieces from the sole and heel of a rubber boot or shoe (Fig. 70 *n*) were recovered from the trash dump. When glued together, the two pieces measure 7 in. long and 3-3/8 in. across the ball of the foot. A portion of a company logotype remains on the uncheckered instep: 'Crack Proo[f]' above an incomplete circle enclosing '−nion in−.' The *Annual Report of the Secretary of War* (USWD 1884b: plate 35) illustrates an Arctic Overshoe with a vulcanized rubber sole and heel; although the Fort Bowie fragment is similar in appearance, it is by no means certain that it is from one of these government issue shoes.

Other rubber artifacts, all found at the dump, include a section of rubber tubing, ¼ in. in diameter, perhaps used with a bulb type syringe as described above. Two unidentified fragments of hard rubber may also be portions of the various types of syringes made and used during the period.

Fig. 71. Wooden chess pieces.
Height: 2¼ in.

PAPER

The only paper recovered at Fort Bowie was the remains of two paper packages that originally held French cigarette papers. Measuring 2-7/8 by 1½ in., both originally contained the product of Leonide La Croix, Fils, of Angoulême, France. This firm registered its trademark, "the words RIZ LA and the symbol of a cross following the words," on December 27, 1881 (USPO 1882a: 1822). This patent date appears on one of the packages, along with the trademark and the claim that the paper is the predecessor of numerous imitations. The other wrapper does not bear the patent date, but notes several expositions – in 1880, 1883, 1885, and 1888 – at which silver and gold medals were won. While these two packages were produced no earlier than 1882 and 1888 respectively, it is not known how late they might have been made, for 'RIZLA✚.' brand papers are still being sold in the United States in the late 1970s.

WOOD AND OTHER VEGETAL MATERIALS

Only 14 pieces of wood were recovered during stabilization of the fort. These included construction lumber, a wooden utensil handle, and two chess pieces.

Eleven pieces of wood used in construction were recovered. This small number is evidence of the reported "cannibalization" of Fort Bowie for scarce building materials after its abandonment in 1894. A portion of a *Juniperus* sp. post from Building 2 was recovered, as was part of a window sill, possibly of *Sequoia* sp., from Building 35, room 1. Seven of the specimens were classified as possible *Sequoia* sp. by the Laboratory of Tree-Ring Research, University of Arizona. Other genera represented are *Pinus* sp., *Populus* sp., *Acacia* sp., *Prosopis* sp., and *Abies* sp. Unfortunately, this material was no longer available for inspection when the artifact analysis was undertaken.

Two identical chess pieces, both thoroughly burned (Fig. 71), were recovered from Building 35, room 7. These are bishops, 2¼ in. high, with a diameter of 1-1/8 in. at the base. They were fashioned on a lathe, and the grooves at the top were then cut by hand.

One wooden handle, recovered from the surface, measures 3-1/8 by 3/4 by 7/16 in. A brass pin, .07 in. in diameter, is still in place through the handle. It is unclear how the tang of the tool or utensil, which was presumably of metal, was removed from the handle without withdrawing the pin, which appears to be firmly in place.

All 28 pieces of cork recovered are cylindrical stoppers for bottles or jars. The smallest piece collected is 7/16 in. in diameter and the largest 1-7/8 in., with lengths ranging from 3/8 to 1½ in. The majority were most likely used in champagne, wine, or beer bottles, which had stoppers ranging approximately from ¾ to 7/8 in. in diameter and from 1-5/16 to 1¼ in. in length. Six of the stoppers of this size have the number '20' stamped on the top and one has an '8' or possibly an incomplete '18.' The proveniences, which were not completely recorded, include Buildings 6, 25, and 35 and the trash dump.

Seven other specimens of vegetal material were recovered. One peach pit was found in Building 6. Also collected was a small piece of bluing, or indigo, which is a dye made from various plants of the genus *Indigofera*.

The five remaining artifacts in this category are amber pipe stems recovered from Buildings 6, 26, and 35, and the surface of the new fort. Amber is a fossil resin of vegetable origin that ranges from yellow to reddish brown in color. This variation in color is represented in the five specimens found. The stems were all made to be attached to the pipe by a threaded wood shaft, and at least a portion of that shaft remained in all of them; in two cases a fragment of the pipe remained as well. One translucent reddish-brown straight stem is attached to a meerschaum pipe shank. Another specimen has a brass washer between it and a small fragment of a wood pipe shank. A third specimen is attached to a brass ferrule, which is 15/16 in. long and has an inside diameter of 3/8 in.; it is possible that this item was a cigarette holder. None of these items could be dated or identified as to manufacturer. Three of the amber stems were apparently produced in a two-piece mold, for they display a crack or seam along the entire length of both lateral edges. The other two show no seam, indicating that they were produced from a single solid piece of amber. It was not determined whether this difference was a function of the date or place of manufacture or, perhaps, of the quality and cost of the pipe on which the stem was used.

PAINT

Five specimens of paint were collected from Buildings 18, 26, and 35, and two other specimens have no recorded provenience. Four of the samples of paint collected from the buildings are of a light blue that is similar, if not identical, to the color used on Army wagons during the period that the fort was occupied. The three other specimens are a heavy dense orange paint believed to be "red lead," an anti-rust coating frequently applied to iron.

MINERALS AND COMPOSITE SUBSTANCES

Minerals collected at Fort Bowie include manufactured artifacts, as well as several pieces of raw material apparently collected by the fort's inhabitants. Three pieces of chrysocolla and one of malachite were recovered from Building 35, as was one of the three pieces of stalactite or stalagmite found. A piece of native sulphur was found in room 2 of Building 18, and two pieces of worked turquoise were recovered from Building 1, one of the officers' quarters.

Eleven of the 13 pieces of graphite recovered are pencil leads. Two of these, found at Building 45, are rectangular in cross-section and measure .1 by .22 in. The remaining nine pencil lead fragments have round cross-sections, with diameters ranging from .07 to .22 in. Two pieces of graphite, both 1.8 in. thick, were taken from the privy of Building 33. One is a disc 1½ in. in diameter, while the other has had a disc cut from it. The function of the graphite discs is unknown.

One well-used but complete billiard cue chalk was recovered from Building 35, room 7, listed in 1890 as the billiard room at the post trader's store (Montgomery 1966). This chalk is white, whereas modern cue chalks are frequently blue. A remnant of what appears to have been a red marking or lumber crayon was recovered from Building 18. This item is 1¼ in. long and ½ in. square in cross-section, and has remnants of black japanning on two surfaces. Listed in the 1897 Sears, Roebuck catalog (Israel 1968: 352) is a red marking crayon, ½ in. in diameter, but with a hexagonal rather than square cross-section; it was covered with paper that had a black japanned finish.

One piece of asbestos from Building 35 is 1/8 in. thick. It most likely was used as fire-proofing material. Four fragments of plaster were collected from Buildings 18 and 26, and two small fragments of concrete were recovered from Building 35.

STONE

All but 20 of the 48 pieces of stone collected have been modified to some degree. Eight pieces are artifacts of the Anglo occupants of the fort, while 20 others are Indian ground or chipped stone artifacts, apparently collected by the soldiers.

Six pieces of slate recovered from two proveniences probably belonged to the same billiard table. One fragment recovered from the trash dump and five fragments recovered from Building 35, room 3, fit together to form a piece measuring 62 by 11-7/8 by 1 in. (Fig. 72). Cutting marks on the edge of one of the long sides are cruder than those on the other edges. The indication is that this large fragment is a piece cut from one end of the table. Round holes 3/8 in. in diameter, with countersunk tops, originally held bolts or screws that fastened the slate to the table base. Rectangular slots, measuring 1½ by 3/8 in., originally contained nuts held in place with lead. A bolt was inserted through the edge of the slate and threaded into the nut, the combination serving to fasten the cushions, or rails, to the slate. This object has been described as part of a billiard table because the remaining corner of the fragment lacks any provision for a pocket, as would be the case if the table had been built for snooker or pocket pool.

One white quartzite sphere, possibly a marble, was found in Building 35, room 7. Although not absolutely round, it measures approximately .95 in. in diameter. A small protrusion, 1/5 in. in diameter, is undoubtedly a remnant of the manufacturing process.

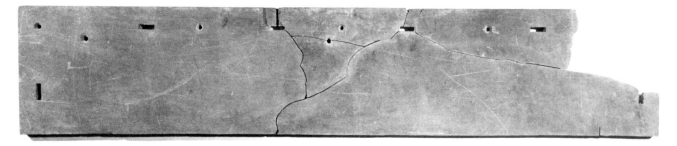

Fig. 72. Slate from billiard table.
Length: 62 in.

A whetstone or fine sharpening stone was recovered from Building 8, room 3, one of the cavalry barracks. This object is well worn, tapering from 7/8 to 1/8 in. in thickness from one end of its 4-in. length to the other. This stone is broken at its thick end, but three deep grooves on that end indicate its reuse after being broken.

Twenty lithic artifacts recovered at and around Fort Bowie are chipped and ground stone items of Indian manufacture. The ground stone specimens consist of three manos, two of porphyritic rhyolite and one of quartzite, a rhyolite pestle, and a fragment of a fully grooved quartzite axe. The three manos came from Building 18, the pestle from Building 30, and the axe from the trash dump. In addition, six pieces of chert, jasper, and obsidian chipped stone debitage, a rhyolite scraper, and a biface were found, the latter two in the vicinity of Building 45. A jasper projectile point recovered from Building 13 is possibly of Apache manufacture. One other complete projectile point, made of porphyritic rhyolite, is thought to date to the San Pedro stage (2000 B.C.– A.D. 1) of the Cochise culture (Willey 1966: 183).

Twenty other pieces of stone collected variously from Buildings 18, 28, 35, and 43, as well as from the trash dump, are samples of slate, basalt, and quartz.

UNIDENTIFIED MATERIALS

Two poker chips recovered from the trash dump are made of a material that could not be identified. These specimens are both 1½ in. in diameter and are distorted because they have been burned. Beneath the surface these items are slightly vesicular in appearance, but they are not identical to either the bone or the ceramic poker chips recovered. One of the specimens has the outlined letters 'CH' incised on both sides. Another object, recovered from Building 35, room 10, appears to be a heat-fused conglomeration of earth and discs or poker chips that are similar to those just described. These discs display no lettering but are the same size and shape and were apparently made of the same unidentified material as the poker chips. This mass or conglomerate measures 7 by 4 by 1¼ in.; it may have assumed its uniform shape when a box or container holding the material burned.

A washer or gasket, 3 in. in diameter and ¼ in. thick, was recovered from Building 30. The material from which it is made has defied identification. It smells of sulphur when burnt, and is possibly a fine organic clay with small white clastic particles.

7. FAUNAL REMAINS

Faunal remains can contribute important cultural, economic, ecological, and chronological information about the human occupation of an archaeological site. Faunal remains that have been butchered in patterned ways can often amplify and refine the inferences drawn from other sources.

The vertebrate material excavated at Fort Bowie includes 4,758 pieces of bone and four samples of hair. The bone is summarized in Table 16. The 933 specimens listed as "scrap" are pieces of bone that are incomplete and unidentifiable. When the scrap category was discounted, the 3,162 specimens of beef bone represented 82.75 percent of the remaining sample. Only 45 specimens were readily identifiable as representing either pig or sheep. The balance of the *Artiodactyla* sp., although listed as "Artiodactyla Unknown," is most likely either pig or sheep. On the basis of this preliminary finding, it was decided that a butchering analysis would be the most productive and informative approach to the faunal material. This analysis and much of the following discussion was provided by John B. Clonts. An analysis of the bird bone was prepared by Alan Ferg.

BUTCHERED BONE

Cultural and ethnic differences in diet are a widely recognized and accepted fact. There are definite distinctions in ingredients and in methods of preparation between, for example, Mexican, Chinese, and Italian dishes. Perhaps more relevant in the case of the material excavated at Fort Bowie may be dietary reflections of socioeconomic or class differences. For instance, the data presented below seem to indicate the purchase of more expensive cuts of meat for the Army officers and less expensive cuts for the enlisted men.

The cost differential between various cuts of meat is not a recent phenomenon, but existed in the past as well. It is influenced by two major factors, one culturally derived and the other physiologically controlled. Social groups prescribe, in part, what is desirable (tasty) to eat and what is undesirable. Generally, parts of an animal that are in high demand command a higher price. While any bone can be used as a soup bone and any meaty part can be ground, only a small part of the animal yields choice steaks – hence the higher cost of the latter cuts.

Chronological data are somewhat more difficult to obtain from faunal remains. Knowledge of butchering techniques and tools is required. One major indicator that can

be useful in studying remains of the recent past is the distinction between hand-sawn and power machine-sawn bone. The nature, direction, and patterns of the striations left by sawing on the bone recovered at Fort Bowie indicates hand rather than machine work. This is to be expected, since the era of Fort Bowie was well before electricity and power equipment came to the butcher shop. Other chronological markers may include the occurrence of wild versus domesticated species of certain animals, particularly in areas where the extinction of wild species is known.

The bone analysis indicates that the meat consumed at Fort Bowie consisted very largely of beef. Among bones identifiable by cut, those from front quarter cuts clearly predominate. The front quarter was generally further broken into the chuck and the rib. The chuck was frequently found divided into very large sections. The evidence seems to indicate that the meat was carved off the bone after cooking, and it seems likely that these large sections represent a division for distribution – to a military company, for example. Many soupbones were lengthy enough to have required an extremely large cooking pot. They could have been combined with the regulation seven-pound cakes of desiccated vegetables that would make 42 gallons of soup. These large cuts of beef were not found in the old fort area. The explanation for this may be that the old fort served as married men's housing, where family meals would have been served.

In Building 6, the bachelor officers' quarters, and Building 25, the commanding officer's home, there were abundant proportions of hind quarter cuts. This finding may reflect the higher socioeconomic position of these individuals, in terms of both the preference they may have been given in allotments and their financial ability to supplement their basic rations.

As for butchering techniques, almost all the vertebrae have been sawn longitudinally. This manner of splitting the spine is an operation generally performed at a slaughterhouse. There is also a disproportion between the numbers of front quarters and hind quarters of beef, front quarter cuts being much more abundant in the total collection. Herds were maintained at the post at various times, and they are mentioned in various historical accounts (see Mulligan 1965; Murray 1951); however, if the herds had been the sole source of meat, a more equal representation of remains of the entire animal should be expected. This finding, together with the professionalism of the butchering and the longitudinal splitting of

TABLE 16

Faunal Material

Provenience	Artiodactyla				Bird	Fish	Scrap	Unknown	Total
	Beef	Pork	Sheep	Unknown					
New Fort Building									
1	14	–	–	2	–	–	–	–	16
5	10	–	2	2	–	–	–	1	15
6	58	–	2	3	16	–	–	–	79
8	–	–	–	4	1	–	–	–	5
10	4	–	–	1	1	–	–	–	6
18	51	1	–	5	1	–	15	–	73
19a	2	–	–	–	–	–	–	5	7
25	83	9	–	6	–	–	–	1	99
26	12	–	–	1	–	–	5	–	18
27	2	–	–	3	–	–	–	–	5
28	3	–	–	–	–	–	–	1	4
30	18	–	–	7	–	–	35	10	70
33	24	–	–	5	–	–	35	10	74
35	255	–	–	55	6	–	42	16	374
39	1	–	–	–	–	–	–	–	1
43	14	–	–	–	–	–	2	–	16
Old Fort Building									
101	23	2	–	–	–	–	6	–	31
104	1	–	–	–	–	–	–	–	1
107	5	–	–	4	–	–	–	–	9
108	1	–	–	–	–	–	–	–	1
110	2	–	–	3	–	–	4	–	9
116	24	–	–	1	–	–	17	–	42
Trench									
1	–	–	–	–	4	–	–	–	4
2	143	–	–	14	12	–	91	2	262
3	1733	29	–	270	33	1	407	18	2491
4	679	–	–	82	10	1	274	–	1046
Total	3162	41	4	468	84	2	933	64	4758

the spine, suggests that the fort was purchasing beef from a slaughterhouse. By so doing, the fort could obtain professional butchering and purchase beef cuts in any combination desired – mostly the cheaper front quarter for the enlisted men, as the data seem to indicate, and a few hind quarters for the officers. Indeed, Murray (1951: 163-4) states that "few food difficulties arose in the 1880's . . . although in 1886 complaints were made against one contractor for supplying the post with poor beef."

Two bones, one in Building 18 and the other in Building 30, were butchered but not in the usual manner. They are not *Bos taurus* and may represent wild game animals obtained

in hunting. Hunting was an activity restricted to periods of peace, when it was safe to venture away from the fort (Murray 1951).

BIRD BONE

All of the bird specimens are fairly well preserved, and many bones are complete. Several exhibit dark red-brown spots where they had evidently been in contact with rusting metal, and one has a bright green patch, doubtless from resting next to a piece of copper or brass. Only two of the bones, both from buildings, have been gnawed by rodents, which suggests perhaps that trash dumps at the fort were kept covered. Two bones are lightly burned. Examples of almost all major elements were recovered, including sternum, coracoid, furcula, humerus, radius, ulna, pelvis, femur, tibiotarsus, fibula, and tarsometatarsus.

Following is a summary list of the bird bone recovered at Fort Bowie. The minimum number of individuals (MNI) was calculated using the "maximum distinction method" suggested by Grayson (1973), and used by Hewitt (1975) in analyzing the faunal material from Tubac Presidio.

Anas platyrhynchos, wild mallard (4 specimens, MNI 1).

Anas platyrhynchos, domestic mallard (2 specimens, MNI 2).

Anas acuta, pintail (4 specimens, MNI 1). Pintail would be a winter visitor to southeastern Arizona.

Anas cf. *americana,* American widgeon (1 specimen). Also a winter visitor.

Gallus gallus, domestic chicken (66 specimens, MNI 23). By far the most numerous species represented at Fort Bowie; both mature and immature, male and female birds present. Some of the bone shows evidence of butchering.

Meleagris gallopavo, domestic turkey (6 specimens, MNI 5). Both mature and immature, male and female birds present. (Charmion McKusick identified these specimens as domestic rather than wild turkey on the basis of size, using a comparative collection.)

Galliformes, chicken or turkey (1 specimen).

Chicken is believed to have been the most common domestic bird at Fort Bowie, and this is indeed borne out by the recovered remains. One soldier writing from the fort stated: "The Lieutenant and I own some goats and chickens, and so with milk, fresh eggs, fresh meat and commissary stores are quite comfortable" (Widney 1965: 88).

Unmentioned in the historical records is the presence of domestic mallard and domestic turkey at some time during the occupation of Fort Bowie. The domestic turkeys recovered were not the very heavy meat producers that are common today, but they were progressing in that direction.

Domestic mallards are generally distinguished from their wild relatives by their much greater size. The measurements of the two Fort Bowie specimens indicate that they, like the turkeys, had not yet become the large bird known today, but they were heavier than any wild mallard examined.

Conspicuous by its absence is wild turkey. Murray (1951: 158, 171) states that in the 1870s and 1880s both the officers and enlisted men of Fort Bowie engaged in hunting as a form of recreation as well as for the purpose of procuring fresh meat. He specifically notes that they brought in "a great amount of game, particularly deer, antelope, and turkeys." Phillips, Marshall, and Monson (1964: 30) state that in the 1880s the wild turkey populations of southern Arizona were markedly decreased, and that the last record of wild turkey in the Chiricahua Mountains was in 1906. Only further investigation might settle the question whether the soldiers of Fort Bowie really shot large numbers of wild turkey and thus may have contributed to their disappearance from the Chiricahuas. The evidence was not observed in the archaeological record.

Hunting also presumably accounts for the presence of wild mallard, the pintail individual, and what appears to be an American widgeon. All these are large dabbling ducks, meaty and quite suitable for eating.

HAIR

Four samples of hair collected from Buildings 5 and 6 and from the west privy of Building 35 were analyzed by Walter H. Birkby of the Department of Anthropology, University of Arizona. All four specimens are nonhuman in origin, but more specific identification could not be made. One sample consists of a quantity of dense, coarse hairs, all approximately 9/16 in. long; these may represent the bristles from some sort of brush. The object recovered from the privy at Building 35 appears to be a felt gasket or piece of packing. The sample recovered from Building 5 was found embedded in the plaster of one of the walls; it is known that hair was frequently used as a binding material in plaster.

8. DISCUSSION

INTERPRETATION OF THE ARTIFACT COLLECTION

As explained in the Introduction, the sampling techniques and the manner in which provenience data were recorded for the material have significantly influenced the types of analyses that could be undertaken. Comprehensive and refined spatial analyses were precluded mainly by an inability to control possible skewing of the statistical significance of the presence of artifacts from one provenience as compared to another. The developmental sequence of buildings, for example, may be reconstructed more competently through use of documentary sources, rather than by relying on the artifactual material of the present collection.

Intrasite variation is an aspect that can be discussed only in general or gross terms. Scrap metal, for example, was most often recovered from the shops of Building 18, where the blacksmith was located, and from the trash dump. Some came from Building 35, which was apparently used as a blacksmith's shop some time between 1890 and 1894 (Sheire 1968: 77). Similarly, datable material collected from buildings at the old fort correctly indicate their utilization well past 1868, when the second fort was occupied. Detailed and specific chronologies, however, are not ascertainable from the artifacts recovered.

Another interpretive limitation results from an absence of certain material. If Fort Bowie had been excavated without benefit of the documentary sources that were used in this study, it would have been quite clear that it had been a military post occupied during the late 19th century. On the basis of the material culture alone, however, it would not have been possible to discern the specific and distinctive role that the post played in the conquest of the Apache, for there is little that reflects the direct relationship between the site's inhabitants and the Apache. In the absence of historic documents, there would have been no way of discovering the existence of the important heliograph station that was located on Helen's Dome, overlooking the fort. These examples show how deficiencies in the archaeological record can sometimes be offset by the use of documentary sources – a tool available to historical but not prehistoric archaeology.

In spite of the problems with the assemblage of material culture collected at Fort Bowie, several patterns of phenomena are discernible. The common picture painted is of the garrison soldier fed monotonously on salt pork or beef that was invariably boiled in a stew, generally with desiccated vegetables. Hardtack, bread, rice, and potatoes formed the balance of the basic diet, which was prepared by untrained personnel assigned to the task as a detail. These uninterested and perhaps unwilling cooks are almost universally reputed to have made the worst of what was at best marginal fare. Although this picture is accurate as far as it goes, it is not the complete story. Frequently overlooked is the presence of the sutler or post trader, who supplied a variety of foods that broke the monotony and upgraded the diet, although at prices that were a financial hardship to poorly paid enlisted men.

While contemporary accounts such as these of Bourke (1891), Britton Davis (1929), and Summerhayes (1939) depict many aspects of the life of the frontier military, some details are of course omitted or glossed over. The frontier military and those people associated with them definitely led a difficult and hard life, but there were moderating elements. The artifacts collected at the fort, for example, document the presence of perfume, fine ceramics, decorative glassware, and parts of dolls and other children's toys. As for the table fare, numerous indications of a variety of delicacies, both imported and domestic, were found – bottles and cans reflecting the presence of imported French plums, champagne, wine, and mustard, as well as British ale, jams or jellies, and Worcestershire sauce. Also available were soda pop, olives, olive oil, cranberries, pickles, horseradish, peppersauce, and even ice cream, to judge from the part from a patented ice cream freezer that was found. Several oyster shells were recovered and may well have come from the Gulf of California. It can be shown, however, that even this is a misleadingly incomplete sample. A list of canned goods shipped to Fort Bowie from San Francisco and received in February 1869 details an order of 3,093 cans of food, most of which weighed 2 or 2½ pounds apiece (Letter Box 1, Record Group 98, U. S. National Archives). Included in this shipment, which was to be sold to the officers and enlisted men, were tomatoes, corn, peas, lima beans, string beans, asparagus, peaches, apples, pears, plums, assorted jams and jellies, oysters, lobsters, salmon, sardines, mixed pickles, and pickled onions. While this array is not representative of the daily menu, of course, it certainly does not conform to the usual description of the diet available to the 19th-century frontier military.

Another aspect of the site reflected by the material culture is the variety of roles and occupations of the inhabitants. It is possible to discern the presence of civilians as well as military personnel, but not all the components of either group are represented by the artifacts. The presence of officers and enlisted men is amply indicated by numerous articles of uniforms and equipment, including buttons, metal hat and helmet insignia of unit and branch, and officers' cloth insignia of rank. The variety of government-issue horse equipment clearly points to the presence of the cavalry, while uniform buttons and helmet insignia illustrate the existence of the infantry at the post. The presence of the medical corps is indicated by hallmarked cups and saucers of the medical department and by bottles with the embossed names of both the medical and hospital departments. Evidence of several of the numerically less prominent components of the military at Fort Bowie is lacking, however. Although all ranks of officers from second lieutenant to general were at the post at one time or another, only captains' insignia were recovered. Neither the Signal Corps nor the Indian Scouts are represented in the collection of artifacts.

The presence of nonmilitary personnel is reflected in the collection, but somewhat less comprehensively than that of the military. Numerous sources mention the presence of women and children; indeed, the wife of Second Lieutenant Wilder gave birth to a boy at the fort in 1884 (Corbusier 1969: 202). Artifacts documenting the presence of children include marbles, doll parts, toy ceramic cups and saucers, and other toys, as well as a few children's shoes. Several women's shoes were recovered, as were several dress stays, garter parts, and buttons that are obviously from feminine garments. The quantity of decorated porcelain tableware and the perfume bottles also indicate the presence of women.

Montgomery (1966) mentions the presence of another distinct group of nonmilitary personnel — the proprietors of a Chinese laundry. A number of artifacts recovered appear to attest to the presence of Chinese people at Fort Bowie. In addition to opium tins, a small amount of Chinese porcelain tableware and several ceramic containers believed to have held "Tiger Whiskey" and soy sauce were found. Also recovered were two glass Chinese medicine bottles that are identical to bottles recovered by the Tucson Urban Renewal Archaeological Project from known Chinese-occupied sites.

The picture of civilians at the post is not complete, however, for several categories of people known to have been present are not indicated by the material culture. Civilian construction workers were hired on several occasions. Without historical records it would not be known, for example, that masons, plasterers, and roofers were brought in to work on the fort in 1879 (Murray 1951: 167). Also present at various times were civilian packers and teamsters who worked the mule trains. Maps of the post indicate that laundresses resided at Fort Bowie, but no artifactual material recovered specifically documents this fact.

Another pattern noted in the collection of material is the greater abundance of chronologically late artifacts. This general trend is apparent in several types of material. Free-blown bottles are absent, and only one bottle has a pontil scar, indicating pre-mechanized manufacture. All bottles had been produced in a mold, and one even displays a crown finish, an innovation dating to 1892. Although metallic cartridges did not replace combustible cartridges until several years after the establishment of the fort, only 13 of the earlier type were identified among some 2,000 bullets and cartridges recovered. The dates of patented items also reflect this trend to some extent. Of the patents that were located for artifacts recovered at the fort, only nine date prior to 1870, while 37 date to the 1870s and 26 to the 1880s.

Basically there are three possible explanations for this pattern of preponderantly late artifacts: (1) there were fewer people at the fort during the earlier period of its history, and a concomitantly smaller accumulation of trash; (2) the abundance of later trash may be due not only to a larger resident population, but also to a change in the transportation and supply situation; and (3) the pattern may be more apparent than real, since, as was noted above, the archaeological method applied to the site may have produced a skewed sample. These explanations are not mutually exclusive, of course.

The fact that the methods of transportation improved during the existence of Fort Bowie as a functioning military post is known and documented. The construction of the railroad in southern Arizona, completed in 1881, included a stop at Bowie Station, 13 miles from the fort. The railroad had definite consequences in easing the supply situation at the post and the possibility that this is reflected in the trash deposits is very real. Clonts, in his preliminary report on the Fort Bowie material culture, notes the association of a large percentage of the horse and mule shoes with butchered cow bone, which he dates to the 1880s and 1890s on the basis of the butchering technique (1971: 94-5). He postulates that the presence of the railroad increased the availability of metal to the extent that worn horse and mule shoes became common articles of trash instead of valued sources of reusable metal. Unfortunately, the present study could neither refute nor substantiate this possibility, since the many articles and pieces of reutilized metal remain essentially undated.

Among the collection of artifacts from Fort Bowie there is a relative scarcity of whiskey bottles, a circumstance apparently not unique to Fort Bowie. In his discussion of the bottles from Fort Union, New Mexico, Woodward (1958: 129) also observed that whiskey bottles were in the minority. At Fort Bowie, the ratio of beer to whiskey bottles is striking. More than 1,600 beer bottles were recovered, but only 31 bottles are identifiable as having contained hard liquor.

There are several plausible explanations for this ratio, such as the use of casks and kegs for whiskey, instead of bottles, and the relatively high cost of hard liquor as compared to that of beer. However, these factors are most likely secondary causes. In 1881, the Adjutant General of the U.S. Army, R. C. Drum, reported: "Fully recognizing the baneful effects of intemperance on the morale and efficiency of the Army . . . the sale of intoxicating liquors was, early this year, by order of the President, prohibited at all military posts and stations" (USWD 1881: 45). This prohibition was interpreted as exempting beer, champagne, and wine, and undoubtedly accounts for the predominance of beer bottles over whiskey bottles in the Fort Bowie remains.

An important aspect of the collection of material from Fort Bowie is that it traces part of the developmental sequence for several articles of military uniform and equipment, and also demonstrates that changes appearing in the published government documents were actually put into effect on the southwestern frontier. A number of items could be cited in this connection, but the buttons recovered probably provide the clearest illustration.

Although the earlier pattern, or pre-1884, general service buttons outnumber the later style by a ratio of four to one, the later style buttons were indeed worn at Fort Bowie within the 10-year period between their adoption in 1884 and the abandonment of the post in 1894. Other late buttons present are metal suspender and fly buttons. The pattern identified became regulation issue in 1885, and therefore the 44 specimens recovered could only have been deposited during the final nine years of the occupation of the post. The 19 military issue suspender buckles were also a relatively late item. Officially adopted on September 4, 1883, they were supplied with suspenders to enlisted men at the rate of one pair per year (USWD 1884b: 614, 671).

Other artifacts that were recovered document changes in the dress helmet: side buttons, ventilators, insignia, plume socket bases, and attachment devices, which are common to both the pattern 1872 and pattern 1881 helmets, changed in size or style. The various parts found that belonged to saber belts document the presence of pre-1874, pattern 1874, and pattern 1885 belts.

Along with such specific changes in military equipment, the artifacts reflect much more fundamental developments in a wide range of technologies of the late 19th century. The presence of certain artifacts and the absence of others provides some evidence of the nature and magnitude of the changes that were in progress at the time, in both military and civilian life. The evidence provided by the Fort Bowie collection is perhaps most graphic in the following four classes of industrial manufactures of the period: ammunition, glass bottles, nails, and shoes.

In 1862, when the fort was founded by the California Volunteers, the standard ammunition was the combustible cartridge. This muzzle-loaded cartridge had a number of serious liabilities that led to the development of metallic cartridges. In 1866 the military adopted .50 caliber as the standard size round for shoulder arms, and in 1873 the size was reduced to .45 caliber. During this period the military also adopted the internally primed metallic cartridge as the standard type of round. Its major disadvantage was that it could

not be reloaded, but this drawback was in turn overcome with the introduction of externally primed centerfire metallic cartridges in 1882. Although these dates apply to U.S. military cartridges, the chronology for civilian ammunition is approximately the same. Apart from the earlier era of transition from flintlock to percussion cap weapons, the sequence outlined above probably represents the most important period in the development of modern ammunition, and the Fort Bowie specimens include bullets, cartridges, and primers that illustrate this major transition from combustible to reloadable, self-contained rounds.

The Fort Bowie artifacts also reflect a change in the technology of manufacture of glass bottles. All the bottles recovered were manufactured at least partially in molds, and technological advances are observable in the various types of molds employed. These reflect a decrease in the amount of hand work involved and a trend toward mechanization. The largest amount of hand work was required by the bottles produced in a one-piece dip mold, which then required the shoulder, neck, and finish to be hand-produced. Next in the sequence were those bottles that were made in a mold except for the finish, which was hand-applied. Later, bottles were produced in molds that included the finish.

The nails collected reflect another technological change that occurred during the 19th century. The general sequence in the development of nails was from hand-wrought nails to cut nails and then to wire nails. As Nelson (1968) has pointed out, differences within as well as between these major types can be of value in dating and establishing building additions, alterations, and maintenance. While a detailed analysis of the types of nails recovered was not undertaken, the technological advances of the period are easily discerned. Most of the hand-wrought nails found came from the supposed Butterfield Stage Station, a structure in use from 1858 to 1861. The majority of the nails recovered, however, were cut nails. Wire nails did not become the dominant type until the 1890s (Nelson 1968), and, as would be expected, relatively few nails of this type were recovered at Fort Bowie.

A fourth industry that experienced an important developmental period while the fort was occupied was the shoe industry. While early wooden-pegged shoes are not present in the collection, virtually every other method of manufacture of 19th-century footwear is represented. The late 19th century was a period of great experimentation in shoe construction, and this situation is reflected by the wide variety of techniques displayed in the relatively small sample of footwear from Fort Bowie. Hand-nailed boots and shoes were found with both iron and brass nails, while machine-nailed specimens utilized iron nails. Shoes with the soles screwed to the upper were constructed with either brass or iron screws. Examples of sewn footwear display both the earlier McKay stitching and the later Goodyear Welt. One stitched specimen, dating from the late 1880s, was sewn with a thread that had a wire core, a product patented under the name "metalin."

These examples illustrate some of the kinds of information yielded by the material culture collected at Fort Bowie. The collection does create some understanding of what it meant to live and work at a frontier military post during the last half of the 19th century. It is possible, in some cases, to trace the development of specific items or of a class of items, and it is also possible to visualize some of the broad and sweeping advances that occurred then, altering lives and lifestyles.

SUGGESTIONS FOR FUTURE RESEARCH

A conscious effort not to overextend the data limited interpretation and conclusions in several areas. Developmental sequences and specific functions of buildings could not be determined, except in broad terms, on the basis of the material recovered. More important, however, was an inability to draw definitive conclusions about behavioral patterns. The inference that the presence of the railroad significantly affected the reutilization of metal, for example, could not be tested. Limitations such as these point up the need for research designs for future work. It is believed that this report illustrates the wide range of material present at sites of this type, and thus provides a basis for the development of hy-

potheses and test implications for future research.

There are obviously a great many questions that could be asked and explanatory hypotheses that could be developed. The use and reuse of buildings at Fort Bowie needs to be examined in some detail. The effect of the construction of the railroad upon the supply of equipment and materials should be explored. What specific types of behavior were modified and to what degree when the railroad began running near the fort in 1881? The entire aspect of diet requires more detailed work. What, for example, were the differences in diet between officers and enlisted men? How did the diet of soldiers with families living at the post differ from that of the rest of the population? The identification of soda pop originating in Deming, New Mexico, leads to a question about the role of local and regional businesses in the lives of people at Fort Bowie. The presence and role of the various types of individuals at the fort, particularly the civilians, is another question requring additional study. These are but a few of many questions that can be asked about Fort Bowie, answers to which require more definitive research. A carefully constructed research design for future excavations at Fort Bowie might answer these and other questions about military life on the western frontier.

Courtesy of the Arizona Historical Society

Fig. 73. Troopers leaving Fort Bowie. The buttressed wall in the background is the west wall of the corral, and behind it is the post trader's store. The presence of the telegraph pole (center) indicates that the photograph was taken sometime after 1877.

REFERENCES

NOTE: Original editions of catalogs are listed by company name; reprint editions are listed by editor or publisher.

Adams, Samuel Hopkins
  1906   *The Great American Fraud.* P. F. Collier and Son, New York.

Albert, Alphaeus H.
  1976   *Record of American Uniform and Historical Buttons.* Boyertown Publishing Co., Boyertown, Pa.

Albert, Lillian S., and Katheryn Kent
  1949   *The Complete Button Book.* Doubleday, Garden City, New York.

Alfano, Louis S.
  1974   U.S. Customs opium stamps. *American Revenuer,* June, pp. 180-6.

American Druggist
  1884   Advertisement for No. 4 genuine Eau-de-Cologne. *American Druggist* 13(2): 14.

Anderson, Adrienne
  1968   The archaeology of mass-produced footwear. *Historical Archaeology 1968* 2: 56-65.

Arey, Leslie Brainerd, William Burrows, J. P. Greenhill, and Richard M. Hewitt (Editors)
  1957   *Dorland's Illustrated Medical Dictionary.* 23rd ed. W. B. Saunders Co., Philadelphia.

Baker and Hamilton
  1889   *Baker and Hamilton Catalogue.* San Francisco and Sacramento.

Bannerman Sons, Francis
  1936   *Military Goods Catalogue.* Francis Bannerman Sons, New York.

Barber, Edwin Atlee
  1893   *The Pottery and Porcelain of the United States.* G. P. Putnam Sons, New York.

  n.d.   *Marks of American Potters.* Cracker Barrel Press, Southhampton, New York. (Originally published 1904.)

Barlow Hardware Company
  1907   *The Barlow Hardware Co. Catalogue.* Corry, Pennsylvania.

Barnes, Frank C.
  1965   *Cartridges of the World.* Gun Digest Co., Chicago.

Baron, Stanley W.
  1962   *Brewed in America: A History of Beer and Ale in the United States.* Little, Brown and Co., Boston.

Barret, Richard C.
  1958   *Bennington Pottery and Porcelain.* Bonanza Books, New York.

Bearse, Ray
  1966   *Centerfire American Rifle Cartridges 1892-1963.* A. S. Barnes and Co., South Brunswick, New Jersey.

Bedford, John
  1965   *Old English Lustre Ware.* Walker and Co., New York.

Berge, Dale L.
  1966   Camp Grant Horseshoes. MS on file, Arizona State Museum, Tucson.

Bishop, J. Leander
  1967   *A History of American Manufactures from 1608 to 1860,* Vol. 3, Johnson Reprint Co., New York.

Blair, C. Dean
  1965   *The Potters and Potteries of Summit County 1828-1915.* Summit County Historical Society, Akron, Ohio.

Blumenstein, Lynn
  1965   *Redigging the West for Old Time Bottles.* Old Time Bottle Publishing Co., Salem, Oregon.

  1966   *Bottle Rush U.S.A.* Old Time Bottle Publishing Co., Salem, Oregon.

  1968   *Wishbook 1865 Treasure Hunters Relic Identification.* Old Time Bottle Publishing Co., Salem, Oregon.

Bourke, John G.
  1891   *On the Border with Crook.* Charles Scribner's Sons, New York.

Boyd
  1889   *Boyd's Directory of the District of Columbia 1889.*

  1894   *Boyd's Directory of the District of Columbia 1894.*

Brinckerhoff, Sidney B.
1967 Military Headgear in the Southwest 1846-1890. *Museum Monograph* 1. Arizona Pioneers' Historical Society, Tucson.

1972 Metal Uniform Insignia of the Frontier U.S. Army 1846-1902. *Museum Monograph* 3, 2d ed. Arizona Historical Society, Tucson.

1976 Boots and Shoes of the Frontier Soldier. *Museum Monograph* 7. Arizona Historical Society, Tucson.

Brittan, Holbrook and Company
1871 *Catalogue of Stamped and Japanned Ware.* Brittan, Holbrook and Co., San Francisco.

Brose, David S.
1967 The Custer Road dump site: An exercise in Victorian archaeology. *Michigan Archaeologist* 13(2).

Busiest House in America
1889 *13th Annual Illustrated Catalogue of the Busiest House in America.*

Butler Brothers
1915 *Our Drummer 1915.* Chicago.

Cayuga Chief Manufacturing Company
1869 *Cayuga Chief Manufacturing Co. Catalog.* Auburn, New York.

Century House
1965 *Illinois Glass Co. Illustrated Catalogue and Price List 1903.* Century House, Watkins Glen, New York.

Chappell, Gordon
1966 Brass Spikes and Horsehair Plumes. *Museum Monograph* 4. Arizona Pioneers' Historical Society, Tucson.

1972 The Search for the Well-Dressed Soldier 1865-1890. *Museum Monograph* 5. Arizona Historical Society, Tucson.

Clonts, John B.
1971 Fort Bowie, Arizona Territory, As Seen in the Material Culture. Preliminary Report. MS on file, Arizona State Museum, Tucson.

Coburn, Frederick W.
1920 *The History of Lowell and Its People.* Lewis Historical Publishing Co., New York.

Cochran, T. C.
1948 *The Pabst Brewing Company: The History of an American Brewer.* New York University Press, New York.

Coggins, Jack
1962 *Arms and Equipment of the Civil War.* Doubleday and Co., Garden City, New York.

Cohen, S.E.
1860 *Cohen's Philadelphia City Directory, City Guide, and Business Register for 1860.* Hamelin and Co., Philadelphia.

Colcleaser, Donald E.
1967 *Bottles: Yesterday's Trash, Today's Treasures.* Betty's Letter Shop, Vallejo, California.

Collard, Elizabeth
1967 *Nineteenth Century Pottery and Porcelain in Canada.* McGill University Press, Montreal.

Corbin, P. and F.
1885 *Illustrated and Descriptive Catalogue and Price List of Hardware, Manufactured by P. & F. Corbin.* New Britain, Connecticut.

Corbusier, William T.
1969 *Verde to San Carlos.* Dale Stuart King, Six Shooter Gulch, Tucson, Arizona.

Cramp, Arthur J. (Editor)
1912 *Nostrums and Quackery,* Vol. 1. Press of American Medical Association, Chicago.

1921 *Nostrums and Quackery,* Vol. 2. Press of American Medical Association, Chicago.

1936 *Nostrums and Quackery and Pseudo-Medicine.* Press of American Medical Association, Chicago.

Crown Publishers
1969 *The 1902 Edition of the Sears, Roebuck Catalogue.* Crown Publishers, New York.

Cummings, Ellen
1971 Ceramic Ink Bottles of Fort Bowie. MS on file, Arizona State Museum, Tucson.

Curran, W. H. L.
1888 *Los Angeles City Directory.* W. H. L. Curran, Los Angeles.

Davis, Alec
1967 *Package and Print.* Clarkson N. Potter, New York.

Davis, Britton
1929 *The Truth About Geronimo.* Yale University Press, New Haven.

Davis, W., and Sons
n.d. *Catalogue No. 24. W. Davis & Sons... Wholesale Saddlery.* San Francisco. (Published ca. 1900.)

Deming Headlight
1918 Death claims John Corbett. *Deming* (New Mexico) *Headlight*, May 24, p. 1.

Dennis, Dolores
1973 The reign of Rumford. *The Federation of Historical Bottle Clubs Journal* 1 (1): 24-7.

Devner, Kay
1964 *Backward Through a Bottle.* Kay Devner, Tucson, Arizona.

1968 *Patent Medicine Picture.* Tombstone Epitaph, Tombstone, Arizona.

1970 *At the Sign of the Mortar.* Tombstone Epitaph, Tombstone, Arizona.

Dover Publications
1969 *Montgomery Ward & Co. Catalogue and Buyers Guide No. 57, Spring and Summer 1895.* Dover Publications, New York.

Drew, Allis and Company
1891 *The Worcester Directory.* Drew, Allis and Co., Worcester, Mass.

Edwards, William B.
1953   *The Story of Colt's Revolver.* Stackpole Co., Harrisburg, Pennsylvania.

Eggenhoffer, Nick
1961   *Wagons, Mules and Men.* Hastings House Publishers, New York.

Emilio, Luis Fenollosa
1911   *The Emilio Collection of Military Buttons.* Essex Institute, Salem, Mass.

Fairbanks Company
1906   *Illustrated Catalogue and Price List of Supplies.* Catalogue number 416. Fairbanks Company, Albany, New York.

Fellows, Paul E.
1969   Preliminary Analysis of Cartridges and Related Items from Tucson Urban Renewal Area Excavations. MS on file, Arizona State Museum, Tucson.

Ferguson, Dewey P.
1972   *Romance of Collecting Case Knives.* Dewey P. Ferguson, Fairborn, Ohio.

Ferraro, Pat, and Bob Ferraro
1964   *The Past in Glass.* Western Printing and Publishing Co., Sparks, Nevada.

1966   *A Bottle Collector's Book.* Western Printing and Publishing Co., Sparks, Nevada.

Fike, Richard E.
1965   *Handbook for the Bottle-ologist.* Richard Fike, Ogden, Utah.

1966   *Guide to Old Bottles, Contents and Prices.* Richard Fike, Ogden, Utah.

Fontana, Bernard L., and J. Cameron Greenleaf
1962   Johnny Ward's ranch: A study in historic archaeology. *Kiva* 28(1-2).

Fontana, Bernard L., William J. Robinson, Charles W. Comack, and Ernest E. Leavitt, Jr.
1962   *Papago Indian Pottery.* University of Washington Press, Seattle.

Fortune
1940   McKesson and Robbins: Its fall and rise. *Fortune* 21(3): 72-5, 120, 123-6, 128, 130-1.

Freeman, Larry
1964   *Grand Old American Bottles.* Century House, Watkins Glen, New York.

Gardner, Robert E.
1963   *Small Arms Makers.* Bonanza Books, New York.

Godden, Geoffrey A.
1963   *British Pottery and Porcelain 1780-1850.* Arthur Barker, London.

1964   *Encyclopedia of British Pottery and Porcelain Marks.* Crown Publishers, New York.

1966   *An Illustrated Encyclopedia of British Pottery and Porcelain.* Crown Publishers, New York.

1968   *The Handbook of British Pottery and Porcelain Marks.* Frederick A. Praeger, New York.

1971   *The Illustrated Guide to Mason's Patent Ironstone China and Related Wares — Stone China, New Stone, Granite China and their Manufacturers.* Praeger Publishers, New York.

Gopsill
1878   *Gopsill's Philadelphia City Directory for 1878.*

Gould, David B.
1870   *Gould's St. Louis City Directory for 1870.* David B. Gould Publisher, St. Louis.

1871   *Gould's St. Louis City Directory of 1871.* David B. Gould Publisher, St. Louis.

1873   *Gould's St. Louis City Directory for 1873.* David B. Gould Publisher, St. Louis.

1883   *Gould's St. Louis Directory for 1883.* David B. Gould, St. Louis.

Grayson, Donald K.
1973   On the methodology of faunal analysis. *American Antiquity* 38(4): 432-9.

Greer, Georgeanna H.
1971   Preliminary information on the use of the alkaline glaze for stoneware in the south 1800-1970. In *The Conference on Historic Site Archaeology Papers 1970* (vol. 5), pp. 155-70.

Hackley, F. W., W. H. Woodin, and E. L. Scranton
1967   *History of Modern U.S. Military Small Arms Ammunition.* Macmillan Co., New York.

Hammer, Kenneth M.
1970   *The Springfield Carbine on the Western Frontier.* Old Army Press, Bellevue, Nebraska.

Hanson, Charles E., and Archer L. Jackson
1965   The 1881 Springfield shotgun. *American Rifleman* 113(6): 52-4.

Haven, Charles T., and Frank A. Belden
1940   *The History of the Colt Revolver.* Bonanza Books, New York.

Hayes, M. Horace
1960   *Veterinary Notes for Horse Owners: A Manual of Horse Medicine and Surgery.* Revised by J. F. Donald Tutt. Arco Publishing Co., New York.

Hermann, Robert K.
1960   *Tobacco and Americans.* McGraw-Hill Book Co., New York.

Hewitt, James M.
1975   The faunal archaeology of the Tubac Presidio. In *Excavations at the Tubac Presidio*, by Lynette O. Shenk and George A. Teague. *Arizona State Museum Archaeological Series* 85, pp. 195-232.

Hibbard, Spencer, Bartlett and Company
1891   *Hibbard, Spencer, Bartlett & Co. Catalogue.* Chicago.

Hicks, James E.
1940   *Notes on United States Ordnance*, Vol. I. *Small Arms, 1776 to 1940*. James E. Hicks, Mt. Vernon, New York.

Hill, Frank P.
1884   *Lowell Illustrated*. Lowell, Mass.

Hill Directory Company
1925   *Richmond Virginia City Directory*. Hill Directory Co., Richmond, Virginia.

Hillcrest Shop
n.d.   *Net Price List of the East Liverpool Pottery Co.* Hillcrest Shop, Spring City, Tennessee. (Originally published ca. 1900.)

Hillier, Mary
1968   *Dolls and Doll Makers*. G. P. Putnam's Sons, New York.

Holbrook, Merrill, and Stetson
1911   *General Catalogue No. 138*. San Francisco and Los Angeles.

Holbrook, Steward H.
1959   *The Golden Age of Quackery*. Macmillan Co., New York.

Hotchkiss and Sons
1861   *Hotchkiss & Sons Price List*. Sharon Valley, Connecticut.

Hughes, G. Bernard
n.d.   *English and Scottish Earthenware 1660-1860*. Abbey Fine Arts, London.

Humphrey, Richard V.
1969   Clay pipes from old Sacramento. *Historical Archaeology 1969* 3: 12-33. Bethlehem, Pennsylvania.

Huntington Hopkins Company
1890   *Illustrated Catalogue and Price List of Hardware, Iron, Steel, Coal, Pipe, Pipe Fittings, Machinists' and Builders' Supplies*. San Francisco and Sacramento.

Hutchins, James S. (Editor)
1970   *Ordnance Memoranda No. 29. Horse Equipments and Cavalry Accoutrements*. Socio-Technical Publications, Pasadena, California.

Israel, Fred L. (Editor)
1968   *1897 Sears, Roebuck Catalogue*. Chelsea House Publishers, New York.

Jacobsen, Jacques Noel, Jr. (Editor)
1968   *Accoutrements of the Army of the United States as Described in the Ordnance Manuals 1839, 1841, 1850 & 1861*. Manor Publishing Co., Staten Island, New York.

1972a   *Regulations and Notes for the Uniform of the Army of the United States 1851*. Manor Publishing Co., Staten Island, New York.

1972b   *Regulations and Notes for the Uniform of the Army of the United States 1872*. Manor Publishing Co., Staten Island, New York.

1972c   *Horstmann Bros. and Co. Catalogue of Military Goods for 1877*. Manor Publishing Co., Staten Island, New York.

1973   *The M. C. Lilley & Co., Manufacturers of Military Clothing and Equipments, Columbus, Ohio. 1882*. Manor Publishing Co., Staten Island, New York.

Jensen, Al, and Margaret Jensen
1967   *Old Owl Drug Bottles and Others*. Al and Margaret Jensen, Mountain View, California.

Jeweler's Circular Publishing Company
1915   *Trade Marks of the Jewelry and Kindred Trades*. Jeweler's Circular Publishing Co., New York.

Jewitt, Llewellynn
1970   *The Ceramic Art of Great Britain*. Ward Lock Reprints, London.

Jones, May
1963a   *Bottle Trail*, Vol. 2. Southwest Offset, Hereford, Texas.

1963b   *Bottle Trail*, Vol. 3. Southwest Offset, Hereford, Texas.

1964   *Bottle Trail*, Vol. 4. Southwest Offset, Hereford, Texas.

1968   *Bottle Trail*, Vol. 9. May Jones, Nara Vista, New Mexico.

Kalbach, Joan
1971   Bottle Companies. MS on file, Arizona State Museum, Tucson.

Ketchum, William C., Jr.
1970   *Early Potters and Potteries of New York State*. Funk and Wagnalls, New York.

1971   *The Pottery and Porcelain Collector's Handbook*. Funk and Wagnalls, New York.

Kidd, Kenneth E., and Martha Ann Kidd
1970   A Classification System for Glass Beads for the Use of Field Archaeologists. *Canadian Historic Sites: Occasional Papers in Archaeology and History* 1. Department of Indian Affairs and Northern Development, Ottawa, Canada.

Knight, Edward H.
1881   *Knight's American Mechanical Dictionary*, Vol. 2. Houghton, Mifflin and Co., Boston.

Krebs, Roland
1953   *Making Friends is Our Business*. Cuneo Press, St. Louis.

Langley
1880   *Langley's San Francisco City Directory*. J. B. Painter Co., San Francisco.

1881   *Langley's San Francisco City Directory*. J. B. Painter Co., San Francisco.

Lantz, Louise K.
1970   *Old American Kitchenware 1725-1925*. Thomas Nelson, Camden, New Jersey.

Lathrop, William G.
1909   *The Brass Industry in Connecticut.* Price, Lee and Adkins Co., New Haven.

Lewis, Berkeley R.
1956   *Small Arms and Ammunition in the United States Service 1776-1865.* Smithsonian Institution Press, Washington, D.C.

Lief, Alfred
n.d.   *A Close-up of Closures: History and Progress.* Glass Container Manufacturers Institute, New York.

Liesenbein, William
1973   The Pre-1891 Use of "ENGLAND" on Ceramics. MS on file, Arizona State Museum, Tucson.

Lipscomb, H. G., and Company
1913   *Wholesale Hardware and Associated Lines.* Nashville, Tennessee.

Little, W. L.
1969   *Staffordshire Blue.* Crown Publishers, New York.

Logan, Herschel C.
1959   *Cartridges.* Bonanza Books, New York.

Lorrain, Dessamae
1968   An archaeologist's guide to nineteenth century American glass. *Historical Archaeology 1968* 2: 35-44.

Ludington, M. I. (Compiler)
1889   *Uniform of the Army of the United States from 1774 to 1889.* Quartermaster General, U.S. War Department, Washington, D.C.

Luscomb, Sally C.
1967   *The Collector's Encyclopedia of Buttons.* Bonanza Books, New York.

McCallum, Henry D., and Francis T. McCallum
1965   *The Wire that Fenced the West.* University of Oklahoma Press, Norman.

McElroy
1850   *McElroy's Philadelphia Directory for 1850.* Edward C. and John Biddle, Publishers, Philadelphia.

McKearin, George S., and Helen McKearin
1941   *American Glass.* Crown Publishers, New York.

McLean, Donald B. (Editor)
1969   *The 1873 Trapdoor Springfield Rifle and Carbine and 45 Revolvers: Colt's M 1873, S & W Schofield.* Normount Armament Co., Forest Grove, Oregon.

Madis, George
1971   *The Winchester Book.* Art and Reference House, Lancaster, Texas.

Marshall Field and Company
1892-3 *Marshall Field & Co. Catalogue.* Chicago.

Mathews, J. Howard
1962   *Firearms Identification,* Vol. II. University of Wisconsin Press, Madison.

Maxwell
1895   *Maxwell's Los Angeles City Directory and Gazetteer of Southern California.* Los Angeles Directory Co., Los Angeles.

Mazzanovich, Anton
1931   *Trailing Geronimo.* Anton Mazzanovich, Hollywood, California.

Milholland, Marion, and Evelyn Milholland
1971   *Milhollands Complete Glass Insulator Reference Book.* Mr. & Mrs. Marion C. Milholland, Sequim, Washington.

Miller, J. Jefferson, and Lyle M. Stone
1970   Eighteenth-century ceramics from Fort Michilimackinac. *Smithsonian Studies in History and Technology* 4. Smithsonian Institution Press, Washington, D.C.

Mine and Smelter Supply Company
1912   *Catalog No. 24.* [New York.]

Missouri Historical Society
1960   St. Louis business and industry, 1877. *Missouri Historical Society Bulletin,* January, pp. 168-9. St. Louis.

Montgomery, Jon B.
1966   Historic Structures Report, Part 1: Fort Bowie, Arizona, MS on file, Western Archeological Center, National Park Service, Tucson, Arizona.

Moodys
1920   *Moodys Manual of Railroads and Corporation Securities. 1920 Industrial Section.* Poor's Publishing Co., New York.

Moos, Harry
1968   U.M.C. shotshells. *Shooting Times Magazine* 9(7): 38-41. Peoria, Illinois.

Morris, Don P.
1967   Stabilization Report 1967. Fort Bowie National Historic Site. 3 vols. MS on file, Western Archeological Center, National Park Service, Tucson, Arizona.

1968   Stabilization Report 1968. Fort Bowie National Historic Site. MS on file, Western Archeological Center, National Park Service, Tucson, Arizona.

Mudge, Jean M.
1962   *Chinese Export Porcelain for the American Trade 1785-1835.* University of Delaware Press, Newark.

Mulligan, Richard A.
1965   Apache Pass and Old Fort Bowie. *Smoke Signal,* No. 11. Tucson Corral of Westerners, Tucson.

Munsell
1965   *Munsell Book of Color.* Munsell Color Division, Kollmorgen Corp., Baltimore.

Munsey, Cecil
1970   *The Illustrated Guide to Collecting Bottles.* Hawthorn Books, New York.

Murray, Richard Y.
1951   *The History of Fort Bowie*. M.A. Thesis, University of Arizona, Tucson.

Nelson, Lavinia, and Martha Hurley
1967   *Old Inks*. Cole Printing Co., Nashua, New Hampshire.

Nelson, Lee H.
1968   Nail chronology as an aid to dating old buildings. *Technical Leaflet* 48. American Association for State and Local History, Nashville, Tennessee.

Newhall, Ruth Waldo
n.d.   *The Folger Way, Coffee Pioneering Since 1850*. J. A. Folger and Co., San Francisco.

Noël Hume, Ivor
1969   Pearlware: Forgotten milestone of English ceramic history. *Antiques* XCV(3): 390-97.

1970   *A Guide to Artifacts of Colonial America*. Alfred A. Knopf, New York.

Olsen, Stanley J.
1955   The development of the U.S. Army saddle. *Military Collector and Historian* 7(1): 1-7. Washington, D.C.

Pacific Hardware and Steel Company
1902   *Hardware Sporting Goods. Iron and Steel*. San Francisco, California.

Parsons, John E.
1950   *The Peacemaker and Its Rivals*. William Morrow and Co., New York.

Phillips, Allan, Joe Marshall, and Gale Monson
1964   *The Birds of Arizona*. University of Arizona Press, Tucson.

Plume and Atwood Manufacturing Company
1965   *The Plume and Atwood Manufacturing Company Illustrated Catalogue of Kerosene Oil Burners, Gas and Oil Lamp Trimmings, Lamps, Oil Heaters, Etc. Catalogue No. 9B*. Reprint of 1909 catalog. Dorset Division, Thomaston, Connecticut.

Porter, John S. (Editor)
1925   *Moody's Analysis of Investments*. Moody's Investors Service, New York.

1931   *Moody's Manual of Investments*. Moody's Investors Service, New York.

Putnam, H. E.
1965   *Bottle Identification*. H. E. Putnam, Jamestown, California.

Pyne Press
1971   *Whitall, Tatum & Co. 1880*. American Historical Catalog Collection. Pyne Press, Princeton.

1972a   *Lamps and Other Lighting Devices 1850-1906*. Pyne Press, Princeton.

1972b   *Pennsylvania Glassware 1870-1904*. Pyne Press, Princeton.

Quellmalz, Carl Robert
1972   Chinese porcelain excavated from North American Pacific Coast sites. *Oriental Art* 18(2): 148-54.

Rainwater, Dorothy T.
1966   *American Silver Manufacturers*. Everybody's Press, Hanover, Pennsylvania.

Ramsay, John
1939   *American Potters and Pottery*. Hale, Cushman and Flint, Boston.

Randall, Mark E.
1971   Early marbles. *Historical Archaeology 1971* 5: 102-5.

Rice and Miller Company
1919   *General Catalog of Rice and Miller Company*. Bangor, Maine.

Rickey, Don, Jr.
1963   *Forty Miles a Day on Beans and Hay*. University of Oklahoma Press, Norman.

Ripley, Warren
1970   *Artillery and Ammunition of the Civil War*. Van Nostrand Reinhold Co., New York.

Ritter, T. J.
n.d.   *The Peoples Home Medicine Book*. R. C. Barnum, Cleveland.

Robacker, Earl F.
1971   Stick-spatter ware. *Antiques* IC(2): 245-51.

Romaine, Lawrence B.
1960   *A Guide to American Trade Catalogs 1744-1900*. R. R. Bowker Co., New York.

Sackett, Richard R.
1934   Historical clay pipes of the Minnesota area. *Minnesota Archaeologist* 9: 68-82.

Sampson, Davenport and Company
1868   *The Boston Directory*. Sampson, Davenport & Co., Boston.

Sargent and Company
1866   *Sargent & Co. Catalogue*. New York.

1910   *Sargent Hardware*. New Haven.

Schroeder, Joseph J., Jr. (Editor)
1970   *1896 Illustrated Catalogue of Jewelry & European Fashions, Marshall Field & Co.* Gun Digest Publishing Co., Northfield, Illinois.

Seger, Hermann A.
1902   *The Collected Writings of Hermann August Seger*, Vol. II, edited by Albert V. Bleininger. Chemical Publishing Company, Easton, Pennsylvania.

Sheire, James W.
1968   *Historic Structures Report, Part II: Fort Bowie National Historic Site*. National Park Service, Division of History, Office of Archeology and Historic Preservation, Washington, D.C.

Silva, Bev, and Joe Silva
1967   *Research on San Francisco Whiskey Bottles.*
Hansen Enterprises, Niles, California.

Smith, G. Hubert
1960   Archaeological investigations at the site of Fort
Stevenson (32HL1), Garrison Reservoir, North
Dakota. *River Basin Surveys Papers* 19. Bureau
of American Ethnology, Smithsonian Institution,
Washington, D.C.

1972   Like-A-Fishhook Village and Fort Berthold Garrison Reservoir, North Dakota. *Anthropological
Papers* 2. National Park Service, Washington, D.C.

Smith, H. R. Bradley
1966   *Blacksmiths' and Farriers' Tools at Shelburne Museum.* Shelburne Museum, Shelburne, Vermont.

Smithsonian Institution
1961   *Uniform Regulations for the Army of the United
States 1861.* Smithsonian Institution, Washington, D.C.

Stout, Wilbur
1923   History of the clay industry in Ohio. *Bulletin of
the Geological Survey of Ohio,* 4th series, No. 26.
Columbus, Ohio.

Summerhayes, Martha
1939   *Vanished Arizona: Recollections of My Army
Life.* Lakeside Press, Chicago.

Switzer, Ronald R.
1974   The Bertrand Bottles. *Publications in Archeology*
12. National Park Service, Washington, D.C.

Taylor, Arnold H.
1969   *American Diplomacy and the Narcotics Traffic
1900-1939.* Duke University Press, Durham, North
Carolina.

Taylor, Louis
1966   *Bits: Their History, Use and Misuse.* Harper and
Row, New York.

Thompson, James H.
1947   *Bitters Bottles.* Century House, Watkins Glen,
New York.

Tibbits, John C.
1964   *Chips from the Pontil.* John Tibbits, Sacramento,
California.

Toulouse, Julian Harrison
1969a   A primer on mold seams. *Western Collector* 7(11):
526-35; 7(12): 578-87.

1969b   *Fruit Jars.* Thomas Nelson, Camden, New Jersey.

1971   *Bottle Makers & Their Marks.* Thomas Nelson,
Camden, New Jersey.

Trow
1862   *Trow's New York City Directory.* Trow City Directory Co., New York.

1884   *Trow's New York City Directory.* Trow City Directory Co., New York.

1887   *Trow's New York City Directory.* Trow Publishing Co., New York.

1890   *Trow's New York City Directory.* Trow Publishing Co., New York.

1892   *Trow's New York City Directory.* Trow Publishing Co., New York.

Underhill, Ruth M.
1939   Social Organization of the Papago Indians. *Columbia University Contributions to Anthropology* 30.

U.S. Patent Office (USPO)
1864   *Report of the Commissioner of Patents for the
Year 1862,* Vol. 1.

1865   *Annual Report of the Commissioner of Patents
for the Year 1864.*

1868   *Annual Report of the Commissioner of Patents
for the Year 1867,* Vol. 2.

1869a   *Annual Report of the Commissioner of Patents
for the Year 1868,* Vol. 1.

1869b   *Annual Report of the Commissioner of Patents
for the Year 1868,* Vol. 4.

1870   *Annual Report of the Commissioner of Patents
for the Year 1868,* Vol. 2.

1871   *Annual Report of the Commissioner of Patents
for the Year 1869,* Vol. 2.

1872a   *Annual Report of the Commissioner of Patents
for the Year 1870,* Vol. 2.

1872b   *Annual Report of the Commissioner of Patents
for the Year 1871,* Vol. 2.

1873   *Official Gazette of the United States Patent Office,* Vol. 3.

1874a   *Official Gazette of the United States Patent Office,* Vol. 4.

1874b   *Official Gazette of the United States Patent Office,* Vol. 5.

1875   *Official Gazette of the United States Patent Office,* Vol. 7.

1876a   *Official Gazette of the United States Patent Office,* Vol. 8.

1876b   *Official Gazette of the United States Patent Office,* Vol. 9.

1877a   *Official Gazette of the United States Patent Office,* Vol. 10.

1877b   *Official Gazette of the United States Patent Office,* Vol. 11.

1878a   *Official Gazette of the United States Patent Office,* Vol. 12.

1878b   *Official Gazette of the United States Patent Office,* Vol. 13.

1879a   *Official Gazette of the United States Patent Office,* Vol. 14.

1879b   *Official Gazette of the United States Patent Office,* Vol. 15.

1880a   *Official Gazette of the United States Patent Office,* Vol. 16.

1880b   *Official Gazette of the United States Patent Office,* Vol. 17.

1881   *Official Gazette of the United States Patent Office*, Vol. 18.

1882a   *Official Gazette of the United States Patent Office*, Vol. 20.

1882b   *Official Gazette of the United States Patent Office*, Vol. 21.

1883a   *Official Gazette of the United States Patent Office*, Vol. 22.

1883b   *Official Gazette of the United States Patent Office*, Vol. 23.

1884   *Official Gazette of the United States Patent Office*, Vol. 24.

1885a   *Official Gazette of the United States Patent Office*, Vol. 28.

1885b   *Official Gazette of the United States Patent Office*, Vol. 29.

1885c   *Official Gazette of the United States Patent Office*, Vol. 30.

1886   *Official Gazette of the United States Patent Office*, Vol. 35.

1887   *Official Gazette of the United States Patent Office*, Vol. 37.

1888a   *Official Gazette of the United States Patent Office*, Vol. 40.

1888b   *Official Gazette of the United States Patent Office*, Vol. 42.

1890a   *Official Gazette of the United States Patent Office*, Vol. 47.

1890b   *Official Gazette of the United States Patent Office*, Vol. 49.

1891   *Official Gazette of the United States Patent Office*, Vol. 55.

U.S. War Department (USWD)

1861   *The Ordnance Manual for the Use of the Officers of the United States Army*, 3rd. ed. J. B. Lippincott and Co., Philadelphia.

1862   Office of the Quartermaster General, Letters Sent (Clothing and Equipage), Vol. 20, p. 271. National Archives, Washington, D.C.

1871   *Report of the Secretary of War; Being Part of the Message and Documents Communicated to the Two Houses of Congress at the Beginning of Second Session of the Forty-second Congress*, Vol. 1.

1872a   *Report of the Secretary of War; Being Part of the Message and Documents Communicated to the Two Houses of Congress at the Beginning of the Third Session of the Forty-second Congress*, Vol. 1.

1872b   *Ordnance Memoranda No. 13. Infantry Equipments. Cavalry Equipments. Knapsacks, Haversacks, Canteens, & C. Horse Equipments. Tools and Materials for Cavalry.*

1874a   *Description and Rules for the Management of the Springfield Rifle, Carbine, and Army Revolvers. Caliber 45.*

1874b   *Ordnance Memoranda No. 18. Proceedings of the Board of Officers Convened under Special Orders Nos. 238 and 253, A.G.O., 1873, on Horse-Equipments, Cavalry Equipments and Accoutrements, Saddlers' and Smiths' Tools and Materials, and Standard Supply-Table of Ordnance Stores for the Cavalry Science.*

1875   *Ordnance Memoranda No. 19. Proceedings of the Board of Officers Convened under Special Orders No. 120, A.G.O., 1874, on Infantry Equipments, and Materials and Supplies Necessary for Efficient Outfit of Infantry Troops in Field and Garrison.*

1876   *Report of the Secretary of War; Being Part of the Message and Documents Communicated to the Two Houses of Congress at the Beginning of the Second Session of the Forty-fourth Congress*, Vol. 1.

1877a   *U.S. Army Wagon Harness (Horse and Mule).* Quartermaster's Department.

1877b   *Report of the Secretary of War; Being Part of the Message and Documents Communicated to the Two Houses of Congress at the Beginning of the Second Session of the Forty-fifth Congress*, Vol. 1.

1879   *Report of the Secretary of War; Being Part of the Message and Documents Communicated to the Two Houses of Congress at the Beginning of the Second Session of the Forty-Sixth Congress*, Vol. 1.

1880   *Annual Report of the Secretary of War for the Year 1880.*

1881   *Report of the Secretary of War; Being Part of the Message and Documents Communicated to the Two Houses of Congress at the Beginning of the First Session of the Forty-Seventh Congress*, Vol. 1.

1882a   *Report of the Secretary of War; Being Part of the Message and Documents Communicated to the Two Houses of Congress at the Beginning of the First Session of the Forty-Seventh Congress*, Vol. 3.

1882b   *Specifications for Means of Transportation, Paulins, Stoves, and Ranges and Lamps and Fixtures for Use in the United States Army.*

1883   *Report of the Secretary of War; Being Part of the Message and Documents Communicated to the Two Houses of Congress at the Beginning of the First Session of the Forty-eighth Congress*, Vol. 1.

1884a   *Report of the Secretary of War; Being Part of the Message and Documents Communicated to the Two Houses of Congress at the Beginning of the First Session of the Forty-Eighth Congress*, Vol. 3.

1884b   *Report of the Secretary of War; Being Part of the Message and Documents Communicated to the Two Houses of Congress at the Beginning of the Second Session of the Forty-Eighth Congress*, Vol. 1.

1885   *Report of the Secretary of War; Being Part of the Message and Documents Communicated to the Two Houses of Congress at the Beginning of the First Session of the Forty-Ninth Congress,* Vol. 1.

1887   *Report of the Secretary of War; Being Part of the Message and Documents Communicated to the Two Houses of Congress at the Beginning of the First Session of the Fiftieth Congress,* Vol. 1.

1889   *Report of the Secretary of War; Being Part of the Message and Documents Communicated to the Two Houses of Congress at the Beginning of the First Session of the Fifty-first Congress,* Vol. 1.

1891   *Ordnance Memoranda No. 29. Horse Equipments and Cavalry Accoutrements, as Prescribed by G.O. 73, A.G.O., 1885.*

1899   *Annual Reports of the War Department for the Fiscal Year Ended June 30, 1898. Report of the Chief of Ordnance.*

Utley, Robert M.
1962   *Historical Report on Fort Bowie, Arizona,* 2nd ed. U.S. Department of the Interior, National Park Service, Region Three, Santa Fe, New Mexico.

Van Schaack, Stevenson and Reid
1874   *1874. Annual Prices Current . . . Drugs, Chemicals, Medicines. . . .* Chicago.

Vinson, Carlos
1968   Collecting shotshells. In *Gun Digest,* 22nd ed., pp. 91-97. Follett Publishing Co., Chicago.

Walker, Iain C.
1974   Binford, science, and history: The probabilistic variability of explicated epistemology and nomothetic paradigms in historical archaeology. In *The Conference on Historic Site Archaeology Papers 1972* (vol. 7), pp. 159-201.

Watkins, Lura Woodside
1950   *Early New England Potters and Their Wares.* Harvard University Press, Cambridge.

Waverly Heating Supply Company
1932   *1932-33 Complete Waverly Catalog: Stoves, Ranges, Repairs, Furnaces, Boilers, Stove Dealer's Supplies.* Waverly Heating Supply Co., Boston.

Webster, Donald B.
1971   *Decorated Stoneware Pottery of North America.* Charles E. Tuttle Co., Rutland, Vermont.

1973   The beaver-and-maple-leaf motif on Canadian ceramics. *Connoisseur* 182(732): 117-23.

White, Gwen
1966   *European and American Dolls.* Putnam's Sons, New York.

White, Henry P., and Burton D. Munhall
1967   *Pistol and Revolver Cartridges.* S. A. Barnes and Co., South Brunswick, New Jersey.

Widney, J. P.
1965   Letter from Ft. Bowie, 1867. *Kiva* 30(3): 87-9.

Wildung, Frank H.
1957   *Woodworking Tools at Shelburne Museum.* Lane Press, Burlington, Vermont.

Willey, Gordon R.
1966   *An Introduction to American Archaeology,* Vol. 1: *North and Middle America.* Prentice-Hall, Englewood Cliffs, New Jersey.

Wilson, Bill, and Betty Wilson
1968   *Spirits Bottles of the Old West.* Antique and Hobby Publishing Co., Amador City, California.

1969   *Western Bitters.* Northwestern Printing Co., Santa Rosa, California.

1971   *19th Century Medicine in Glass.* Antique and Hobby Publishing Co., Amador City, California.

Wilson, Rex
1971   *Clay Tobacco Pipes from Fort Laramie National Historic Site and Related Locations.* Office of Archeology and Historic Preservation, National Park Service, Washington, D. C.

In Press   *Bottles on the Western Frontier.* University of Arizona Press, Tucson.

Woodward, Arthur
1958   Appendices to Report on Fort Union 1851-1891. MS on file, Arizona State Museum, Tucson.

Yale and Towne Manufacturing Company
1884   The Yale & Towne Manufacturing Co., Stamford, Connecticut.

Young, James Harvey
1961   *The Toadstool Millionaires.* Princeton University Press, Princeton.

1967   *The Medical Messiahs.* Princeton University Press, Princeton.

INDEX